Reading Between the Lines

Reading Between the Lines

A Memoir

Janis Paige

All rights reserved. No part of this book may be reproduced or utilized in any form or by any means, electronic or mechanical, including photocopying, recording, or by any information storage or retrieval system without permission of the copyright holder.

Copyright © 2020 Janis Paige Gilbert, Trustee of the Sixth Amendment and Restatement of the Janis Paige Gilbert Living Trust – May 23, 2018

ISBN: 978-1-7344447-1-1

All photos are from the collection of Janis Paige.

Cover Design: Andrew Neighbour

Interior Design: Mary Neighbour

*Don't say the old lady screamed.
Bring her on and let her scream!*

-Mark Twain

CONTENTS

The Beginning 1

Section I – The 1920s
September 16, 1922 5
My Mother or My Life 15

Section II – The 1930s
The Great Depression 23
Hard Times Party 33
The Roxy 37
The Brown Castle 41
Emmett Kelly 45

Section III – The 1940s
Home to High School to Hollywood 49
Red Skelton 59
Howard Hughes 61
Joan Crawford 69
Clark Gable 75
Frank Sinatra 79
A First Marriage 87
Bette Davis 93
Rome 99
La Strada Buia 103
Dinner with a Mussolini 109
Aunt Julia 113

Ingrid Bergman 117

In the Palm of My Hand 123

Field Marshal General Bernard Montgomery 125

Orson Welles 129

Section IV – The 1950s

Vaudeville, Nightclubs & Whatever 141

Surviving a Prophesy 153

Dr. Arnold A. Hutschnecker 165

Bert Lahr 169

Sammy Davis Jr. and Ciro's 173

"Remains to Be Seen" 181

Ruth Anderson 185

Helen Hayes 191

Marlene Dietrich 193

The Raincoat 199

Marlon Brando 203

President Richard Milhous Nixon 207

George Abbott and "The Pajama Game" 213

Rosalind Russell, a Beautiful Soul 221

"The Pajama Game" Meets the Queen Mother 227

James Michener 229

Lucille Ball and Desilu 237

Fred Astaire 241

Section V – The 1960s

Robert Mitchum 263

Meeting Ray Gilbert 267

David Niven	273
Bob Hope and the U.S.O.	283
Christmas with Castro	291
Writers, Writers, Writers	293
Michel-Marie Poulain	295
Two for the Road	301
Lana Turner—Korea 1962	315
"Here's Love"	321
Vietnam	329
Judy Garland	337
Dinner at the White House	343
Henry Fonda	349
My Moveable Feast	353
Denmark	356
Munich	357
Dachau	359
Salzburg	360
Vienna	361
Venice	363
Israel	364
London	368
"Mame"	371

Section VI – The 1970s

South Africa	385
The Cape of Good Hope and the Wild Coast	411
The Christmas Tree	419
Ray Gilbert, You Died Tonight	425

After Ray/Life 101 433

My Sociopath 439

Japan 447

Section VII – The 1980s

Reveille 455

Therapy and Dr. Jack Rosenberg 461

The False Self 467

Victory over Myself 471

The Gray Area 473

Australia 477

Soaps 481

Section VIII – The 1990s & 2000s

Losing My Voice: A Lesson Finally Learned 493

A New Millennium 497

Boundaries 499

Loyalty 501

What Pisses Me Off 505

The Murder of the American Soul 511

I Have Found Another Day 513

The Beginning

To love is to risk not being loved in return. To hope is to risk pain. To try is to risk failure, but risk must be taken because the greatest hazard in life is to risk nothing.

—Anonymous

As I write this beginning to my book, I am 97 and still a work in progress. This all began when I entered therapy and was taught to journal. It was first used as a tool against collected stress, tension and the countless emotions unraveling in me through the therapeutic process.

"Put your feelings on paper, Jan," Dr. Jack Rosenberg said. "It will be a help to you."

One day, instead of a page about me, I found myself writing about my grandfather, the memories of a father I never knew, growing up a child of the Great Depression and how we made it through. As I wrote, the memory doors came flying open and I was in therapy again, albeit differently. This time, I was both therapist and client, doing and re-doing my life, much of what I hadn't yet touched.

Because my days dwindle down to a precious few, most of my life is behind me now. I've been blessed with an incredibly intact memory, but I've also inherited severe glaucoma on both my mother's and my father's sides.

As my eyesight began to fail, I turned to the Jules Stein Eye Clinic at UCLA. There isn't an operation to save my sight that I haven't had, including an artificial corneal graft. There are no absolutes and the glaucoma continues to limit my sight. I don't want to leave my book or its history of a time long gone unfinished or untold. I'm deeply grateful to the doctors and those who help me to continue while I can.

This book is my journey. It is deeply personal, filled with people, places, events and times that are only history now. To still be a living, breathing and excited woman about life fills me with gratitude and wonder.

I've lived a quietly spectacular life and have done it without drugs and rock 'n roll. I left out sex, but in case you think I was deprived, rest assured, I wasn't. I just choose not to fall into today's version of sexuality as it's played out on the internet.

I never had a kid without the benefit of marriage. I never went to jail while giving the proverbial finger to the law. I was taught to respect rules and the rights of others. I was also taught never to shame myself by indulging in shameful behavior.

I often wonder if that amazingly teachable word (shame) is even a part of our vocabulary anymore. Shame simply gets in the way of the out-of-control and often disgusting and degrading behavior we witness today. Whatever happened to our much-needed self-control over our self-indulgence?

Madonna, liberally sprinkling her f-bombs while contemplating blowing up the White House, comes to mind. If I'm still allowed a personal opinion, she's just another aging and out of date female screaming for her long-lost adoration. Stick a sock in it, Madonna. Sorry, I forgot to say please.

Even with my strict upbringing, I made some very bad choices and careless decisions. I screwed up more than a few times. Coming from the zipped-up generation of my family did not help to prepare me for life's realities.

At the virginal age of twenty, I was thrust into motion pictures. I didn't ask for it, seek it or expect it when I was discovered by MGM. However, my five years at Warner Bros. built my early career and was the launching pad for the amazing life I've known.

Most of the time, I flew by the seat of my pants. I was blessed with an insatiable curiosity about life, but I also learned, painfully, to take responsibility for my own emotional junk, admit my mistakes, apologize, and keep on keeping on.

If I made any of this sound easy, believe me, it wasn't. Nothing happens "overnight" except stardom, and even that comes with the price of the hard work it takes to stay in any exalted places. Self-censorship and the invaluable friends that often risk the relationship to speak the truth, anyway, are a gift.

Someone once said, "We listen but we don't always hear." When I finally heard, I could read between the lines for the truth that I have too often been unwilling to accept.

Don't waste time saving face. Say "thank you," give and receive hugs, mend some fences if you can, and get on with life and what's next.

As I spanned the generations, I discovered and re-discovered my own life. The resentments, the hurts, the losses and the goofs fade, their importance at the time ultimately growing inconsequential. What came shining through were the hard-won victories, the amazing people, the romances, the rejections, the fear-filled sleepless nights, the loving friends, my courage, failures and—when I hit bottom—my suck-it-up guts.

My life is unendingly richer because of daring to jump without a net into life's obstacle course.

From the beginning to the end, every thought, word and deed were my own. No dictating, no taping, and no talking worked for me. I tried it all, but due to my limited eyesight, the only way I could write was to do it myself. The emotions of memories were too personal to share. Reliving every page became at once tearful, joyful, painful, and exhausting but always kept me moving forward.

When I was in Hawaii many years ago, I picked up one of those slick, well-produced "What's Happening in Honolulu" magazines one finds in hotel rooms. As I leafed through it, I began to read an article concerning some quotes from famous people.

There was Professor Albert Einstein, Victor Borge and a short remembrance by the comic genius Red Skelton.

Red was a young boy, surrounded by his grieving family. His grandmother was very ill and close to death. Everyone was whispering out of respect when suddenly from the bed came his grandmother's voice, strong, loud and clear.

"Stop whispering!" she admonished. "I know I'm dying, but I'm still learning." That was a forever mantra for me. I want to live that way, too.

If I can change or alter someone's thinking at a time of stress or fragmentation when confusion reigns, and if my words—born of my own shaky decisions—have helped someone, my observations will not have been in vain.

To me, the most important gain in life is wisdom. I finally have some, so I'm tossing it to the winds of chance.

Trust your gut; it's your second brain. And *bon courage*! In case you're confused, that's French for "Good luck!"

Section I
The 1920s

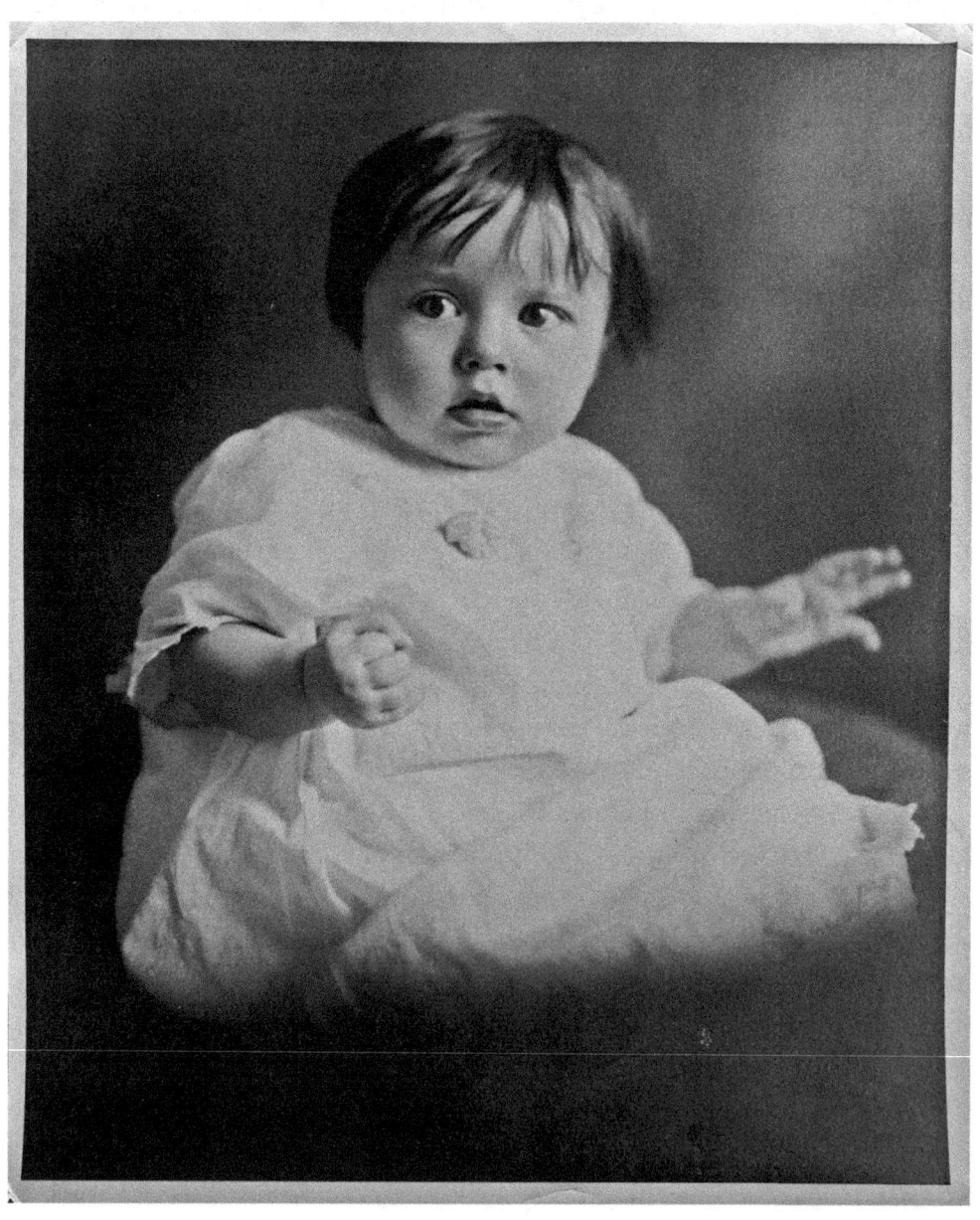

September 16, 1922

Courage is the first of human qualities because it is the quality that guarantees the others.

—Confucius

I HAD DONE NOTHING to deserve it, but the doctor whacked me. I cried, and a healthy little girl—though probably pissed at the treatment she received—joined the world.

I was born Donna Mae Tjaden to Hazel Leah Paige and George Tjaden, twenty-three and twenty-two, respectively. I opened my eyes in a big old red brick building called St. Joseph's Hospital in my hometown of Tacoma, Washington. My sister, Betty Jane, was born in 1925 in the same facility.

I can't introduce you to my father. I never knew him, save for two small but vivid memories that I still carry in that mass of others, stored somewhere just below remembering.

So, let's start there.

In my still developing brain, I remember something about having "only an hour with the plane, let's go!" Sitting in the back seat of the car, I heard my mother warn, "It's not safe," while my father answered, "Oh yes it is."

We drove under a sign that read "Tacoma Airport," resembling absolutely nothing of what we call an airport today. There stood a small building and a few airplanes, all of them alike. We parked and my mother took my hand as we found our way to one of those strange-looking machines. I was four years old and about to make a memory I can still recall today.

My father put a cap on my head that covered my ears and strapped closed beneath my chin.

"What is this, Daddy?" I asked.

"it's called a helmet, sweetheart," he replied. "Pilots wear them to keep out the wind and cold."

He put me in a jacket that was way too big, tied a scarf around my neck, adjusted the fit of something he called "goggles" and hoisted me into the first seat. He strapped me in and made me promise that I would not touch anything.

My father then put on his own helmet, jacket, scarf and goggles like mine and climbed into the seat behind me. The last thing I heard before the roar of the engine left my "Let's go, Daddy!" to the wind was my mother yelling, "Please don't take chances, George. Please be careful!"

I will never forget that day with my father. I left the world I knew below as my mother grew smaller and smaller, then disappeared entirely.

We were flying in what was called a World War I "Jenny." It was a biplane, which meant that it had two wings and a single propeller. The noise was fierce. No wonder they wore helmets.

My father yelled something that I could not hear and suddenly we were flying upside-down, rolling over a few times and coming right side up with me screaming, "More, Daddy, more!" He did all the flying tricks he knew, including figure eights and something he called Immelmann turns.

My pleas for "more" finally ended and we came back down to earth. Sitting in the front seat, I really had a rare view as the ground rose up to meet us. I remember feeling happy and sad at the same time. Meanwhile, my mother had not moved, frozen in fear for my safety.

Driving home, I was chattering away with my usual questions. The one I remember the most was, "When can we go again, Daddy?"

"Anytime, sweetheart," he replied, "anytime you want."

Anytime never came, however, and all of my questions went unanswered.

"Were you a fighter pilot in the war, Daddy?"

"Where did you learn to fly?"

"Why did they call the airplane 'Jenny,' Daddy?"

"Where did you go, Daddy, and why didn't you come back?"

The other memory of my father recalled the time when angry voices disturbed my sleep.

"Don't you dare wake her up, I just got her down for a nap."

My mother's demand was met by my father saying, "She loves these, and I'm going to give her one."

With that, I felt my mouth gently pried open and a giant licorice gumdrop placed inside. I fell back asleep chewing on my favorite candy. Every time I see those puny, tasteless little blobs of nothingness they dare to call gumdrops today, I still recall and savor that massive and seriously delicious licorice treat.

The next time I saw my father, I was thirty-five. My overriding curiosity forced me to look for and find him. I never shared my secret search with my mother. Even at thirty-five, I did not dare risk the explosion that would surely have followed my confession.

He lived in a small but very neat little house in Alhambra, a small community about ten miles northeast of downtown Los Angeles. He had been married to the same woman for twenty-nine years, so he couldn't be all bad. This was my thought as I settled into a chair across from them.

Hard as we tried to move past it, you could cut the tension with a knife—and no wonder. My hoped-for clarity about my parents' relationship and divorce began and ended with my first question.

"What happened between you and my mother, Dad?"

I heard his wife softly say, "George." Her tone was a warning.

"Your mother loved you very much, Donna Mae," my father replied.

"I didn't ask that, Dad. Betty and I have no history. Your name was never mentioned or allowed throughout our lives."

"How is Betty?" he asked.

"Please answer me, Dad. I've waited such a long time."

With that came a second warning: "George."

He said, "I couldn't handle your mother and your grandfather. They were tough."

"But we were your kids, Dad."

There was an uncomfortable silence.

"Do you know who I am, Dad?" I inquired.

My father assured me that he did and had followed my career for years.

"Why didn't you try to reach me?" I asked.

"I didn't want to bother you," he said.

At that moment, I felt something in me let go. It was as if I had turned off the flame under a burner. No further words seemed necessary.

I stood, and with a quiet realization that I'd never had a father, I thanked him and his wife for seeing me. I wished them both well and said "Goodnight" as they wordlessly let me go.

Driving home, my unsatisfied curiosity took its place with everything else I'd never know. If I was finally free of that whore called hope, then why did I feel so lonely? It would not be the last time I felt loneliness at letting go.

I never saw my father again, nor did he make any attempt to contact me or my forgotten little sister. After all, he owed a great deal of child support. Maybe that omnipresent fact is what kept him mute about what happened to my parents' marriage.

Margaret Mitchell described my feelings best when she wrote *Gone with the Wind*. At the end when Rhett Butler finally leaves her, Scarlett cries out, "Where will I go, Rhett? What will I do?" He simply turns to her and quietly says, "Frankly, my dear, I don't give a damn."

Neither did I.

With no one left now to unearth the mystery of my parents, I continue to add to the bits and pieces of what I don't know and make my own history. I never looked back. My father gave me life, a big licorice gumdrop and an unforgettable airplane ride. It's now quite enough.

In spite of the unending unknowns, I'm more than grateful to them both. But other memories endure.

Around the age of three, I started to sing. My mother loved music, so I grew up listening to the latest hits, along with some opera. My grandfather, who was a carpenter among his many other skills, made me a little rocking chair. I loved that chair, and it soon became my very own space. My sister was still a baby, so I spent most of my young life alone.

There was a small room in our old house. When my parents' arguments would begin, I'd run to my chair. I'd rock and sing to the record on our wind-up Victrola, and when the Victrola's speed ran down, I'd wind it up again, jump back in my chair and continue my familiar routine.

Sometimes I'd feel my mother standing quietly, listening to me. She never physically abused me, but I was always afraid of her presence, so I pretended not to see her. There was always something threatening I'd feel, and to a much lesser degree, it continued throughout my life.

We all have those old, elusive, nameless "leftovers." Speaking for myself, I no longer run to a rocking chair, but observing anger or feeling betrayal always creates that old fight-or-flight syndrome. I've simply learned to live with it, reminding myself that "it" is something that happened to me; it's not who I am. It doesn't define me.

It also doesn't always work.

By the way, when Gene Austin, the Frank Sinatra of his day, introduced the tune *My Blue Heaven*, it was the first song I ever learned. I can still sing the lyrics today. I can't remember a time when I didn't sing. It introduced me to my life.

Not long after the airplane ride and the last time I saw my father, my grandparents took us to their house. Of course, there was no explanation. Just a lot of tears and silence, resulting in a lifetime of secrets. Any "Where's Daddy?" was met with a look, a closed door and, as usual, no answer. Ever.

We soon learned not to ask. I was always frightened of my mother's reaction, so my father took his place alongside all the rest of our unspoken and secret history that would never belong to my sister and me.

"Little pitchers have big ears" was one of the phrases used for not including children in whatever discussion the grownups felt should be hidden.

This kind of behavior succeeded only in forcing us to find our own answers. Without even basic information, we began to form the kind of conduct that would please those around us. If we "pleased" enough, perhaps we could "fix" whatever was wrong. No wonder Betty and I both grew up neurotic, with a part of us screwed up and omnipresent.

Our house at 4303 North 24th Street in Tacoma was very small, maybe a thousand square feet. There was one tiny bedroom, one tiny bathroom and a tiny kitchen with a tiny living room/dining room combination.

There was also an attic that my grandfather fixed up for us, and we slept there for years, with my mother and sister in a double bed and me on an army cot. The ceiling slanted, and I always felt claustrophobic. It followed me into adulthood, although now I know how to take care of it. To this day, I don't know how we managed. When you have nothing and no choices, I guess you manage somehow.

My grandparents' sacrifices for us are unforgettable. The two of us came first, and there was no question about our care. Selfless is the word that comes to mind. I loved them both dearly.

My grandfather was the epitome of integrity. He was the most honest, trustworthy and responsible person I've ever known. He did not tolerate lies, people who did not fly the flag on holidays, and disloyalty. He loved and respected this country with a passion. Very early on, he told my sister and me, "This country and what it stands for is bigger than you or me or anyone." I grew up with that same philosophy. You couldn't help it. He lived every minute of his words.

Grandpa was a dyed-in-the-wool "New Dealer," which meant he believed in our President Franklin Roosevelt. But as a strict Constitutionalist, he would not tolerate his hero running for a third term in 1940. One day when I was getting ready for school, he announced to my grandmother that he was going to vote. He was dressed in his old shiny black suit, his scuffed-but-shined shoes, a shirt, tie and his ever-present old black fedora.

"Are you going to vote for Roosevelt, Frank?" my grandmother asked.

"No, I'm going to hold my nose and vote for Alf Landon," he replied. "I never voted Republican in my life, but that *sonofabitch* Roosevelt is running for a third term. it's going against the Constitution, and God knows where this stuff will stop if we don't stop it now!"

Oh, Grandpa, you would be sick to see how divided our country is today.

I was almost six when one day our excited grandfather took my sister's and my hands and led us outside.

"I want you to see something you may never see again," he announced.

It was twilight, starting to get dark, when the sky suddenly lit up like it was on fire, with rainbow-colored flashes of light streaking across the sky. We gasped in awe and wonder at this phenomenal example of nature's artwork.

"What is it, Grandpa, what is it?" I asked excitedly.

"They're called the Northern Lights," he replied. "You can't see them all of the time. If we lived in Alaska, we would see them often. I didn't want you to miss them."

We stood there for a long time watching this magic until we began to get cold and it was bedtime. If it hadn't been for Grandpa, we would have missed this miracle. I never did see them again.

At Christmas in 1928, Grandpa gifted us with a lighted globe of the world. We had never seen anything like it and immediately became fascinated with this new view of where we lived. We turned it on its axis as our grandfather patiently answered our endless questions.

I don't remember where Betty wanted to go, but there was only one place that captivated my curiosity. My finger found South Africa and the Cape of Good Hope.

"Why don't people fall off if they live down there?" I asked.

Grandpa clearly offered his rendering of the gravity concept.

"Oh Grandpa," I said, "I'm going there."

"It's very far away. You might not make it."

"You watch, Grandpa," I insisted, "I'm going there someday."

"We'll see," he said, nodding. "We'll see."

Sadly, he didn't live long enough to know that I did see the Cape of Good Hope after all, many decades later. I walked that long, steep road to my destination and my first thought was of him.

"I made it, Grandpa!" I proudly announced. "I made it! It took me forty years, but I'm here."

When I was six, I started school. There was no adult to salve the fears of that day. Everyone had to work. If there were tears with those fears, I hid them and off I went in my new Buster Brown shoes, my lunch in a brown paper bag and my courage screwed tightly against what this day might bring.

When I reached the corner of our street, I looked back, hoping with all of my heart that someone would see how scared I was and help me to face this terrifying day.

There I stood, holding every ounce of fear that a little six-year-old girl could know. But my silent prayers reached no one.

It was then that I heard something that sounded like my name. When I turned to look, I saw a miniature little girl sitting on my shoulder. Her legs were crossed, her feet clad in black patent Mary Janes. She wore a cute little plaid dress covered with a tiny white sweater. Her hair was cut in the "Twenties" style, called a "bob"—short with bangs a lot like mine.

The next thing I remember was hearing her voice.

"Don't be afraid. I'm your Guardian Angel. I'm here to protect you. I'll always be here, and I'll never leave you. Now let's go, we can't be late."

I never looked back as the two of us started school together. I'll never know where she came from. I only know that she helped me begin that "one small step on my journey of a thousand miles."

Something moved my paralyzed legs toward school that day. Something bigger than being alone with no parent to walk me into my new and unknown future. My Guardian Angel marked me with the most important addition to my budding character that morning, and it was courage.

I somehow stepped over my fears and moved forward. I only know that she has appeared countless times in my life—sometimes as a woman, sometimes a man, sometimes a beloved pet. Something came along to help me through those powerful doubts about my ability to survive and to succeed.

Now you will think what you will, but today as I live my 97th year and increasingly finite life, I can still recall with great clarity my Guardian Angel and the moment we met.

As I approached Washington Grade School that first morning, I realized she was gone. I was on my own again and wondering where to go first. The school was made of red bricks and, to a scared little girl, it was big and intimidating.

There were kids and parents everywhere, so I simply followed them into the building where I stood in one spot until a woman asked me who and how old I was. I barely spoke above a whisper when she took me to a classroom with the words, "You belong here."

I found my way to a desk and waited. The door opened and in walked a tall, thin, gray-haired woman.

"Good morning, class," she said, "I'm Miss Hopkins and this is the first grade."

There was no smile. I would never see her smile.

"I'm passing out enrollment cards," Miss Hopkins continued. "Please fill them out and bring them to me." I printed my name, address, age and mother's information. I only knew my father's name. His age, place of birth and occupation were left blank. I simply had no idea.

As she went through the pile of cards, the teacher asked each student to stand and say his or her name. When she got to me, I stood to hear, "Why didn't you fill out the part about your father?"

All of the little heads turned toward me, but I had no answer.

"Where is your father?" she persisted.

"I don't know," I admitted, barely above a whisper.

"You don't know where your father is?" she taunted.

By now, there were little titters and whispers as I wished I could die.

"Answer me, Donna Mae!" the woman demanded. "Where is your father?"

The words would scarcely come as I muttered, "My mother and father are divorced."

More sounds from the class. The embarrassment continued to build.

"Divorced," she repeated, her voice rising. "Your mother and father are divorced?"

From that moment on, I became this woman's verbal football. She never missed an opportunity to embarrass me or make me feel inadequate.

Divorce was rare and frowned-upon in those days. Was it my fault that my mother and father were divorced? Of course not. I was so unfairly judged by people who were far more screwed up than I at my innocent six years of age. I just didn't know it.

I can still see you today, Miss Hopkins. Blue skirt, white blouse with a bow, a burgundy-colored sweater, lisle stockings and ugly, brown, "sensible" shoes. There was never any makeup or even an attempt to improve that first impression of "Be afraid, be very afraid."

I hated you for such a long time, Miss Hopkins, and it took me years of therapy to understand that you, too, were a product of your time. Your bitterness toward me was constant and hurt me deeply. It wasn't until I was blessed with a lovely second grade teacher, who began to turn my learned self-loathing toward the light, that I not only began to accept school but to love it.

Education was everything when it came to us. I've wondered so many times about the missed opportunities in my grandfather's life. I owe him more than I could ever repay. The greatest gift of all was the moral compass he furnished me that got me through some very rough times.

The difference between right and wrong was clear to our generation, both male and female, along with the strict rules of behavior. I did not go to college, but the instruction I received in grades one through twelve was better than any higher education I could receive today.

Not a single teacher tried to influence me politically. Until I graduated, I was never asked the political affiliation of my family nor did I know their choices. Their job was to prepare us for adulthood and a better future.

Little did I know that my days of picking blackberries, playing with the polliwogs in the creek across the street, bringing home a sack of loganberries for one of Grandma's pies, climbing trees, picking apples and cherries and feeling safe and free were coming to an end.

How could we know that all too soon, we would be shocked into a reality that was at once terrifying and unpredictable?

The year was 1929. Something happened that would test our survival skills beyond anything we could ever imagine.

My Mother or My Life

*IF WE DON'T CHANGE, WE DON'T GROW. IF WE
DON'T GROW, WE AREN'T REALLY LIVING.*

—GAIL SHEEHY

MANY YEARS AGO, when I read Gail Sheehy's book, *Mothers and Daughters*, I—like millions of others—ran searching for those all-elusive answers hopefully contained within.

Speaking for myself, I desperately wanted to be free of that feeling of impending doom that always seemed to hover around the presence of my mother. An emotional pattern had already formed, but I was completely clueless as to its meaning. It would leave and then at the oddest times reappear. I didn't have to see it. Its presence was all-powerful, often leaving me feeling helpless and adrift just as I'd felt as a child.

When I finally struck out on my own in those very early career days, perhaps escape would have been a more descriptive word. I simply could not put some order to the ever-gathering storm that pursued me through my successes and struggles. It never stopped me, but I often felt punished with guilt for using what my mother assured me was "her talent," while trying to find my inalienable right to my own space.

It was only after I entered therapy much later in my life that I begin to understand my complicated and often miserable mother/daughter relationship. With enlightenment has come a far deeper understanding of myself on my way to the grace of acceptance. I finally realized that the only one I can fix is me, and that job is never finished.

Therapy, therapist, neurotic, bipolar, PTSD, depression, rehab and the countless definitive terms used to describe emotional imbalance were not a part of our tiny world when I was born and growing up. Education about the somatic part of ourselves was archaic compared to what we know today.

Consequently, back then, too many sad and helpless souls often became the victims of brutish experiments when they would have benefited from some of the trained verbal treatments of the present. This could not only have saved their sanity but their very lives as well.

We did not have psychiatric hospitals or treatment centers then as we have today. What we *did* have was a mysterious and frightening place called the Fort Steilacoom Insane Asylum.

As a child, I have vivid memories of passing that dark, intimidating place on our way to a day spent at Lake Steilacoom. It looked like what it was. Old with turrets, silent and forbidding outside and bars on the windows, with hundreds of patients inside enduring God knows what. It was a time of very limited knowledge of mental or emotional illness, let alone how to cure it.

When I was about ten, my Aunt Evelyn's sister-in-law was found wandering naked in the street. I remember that she was sent to Steilacoom, and any talk of "Nettie" was buried in the secrets of the family. Betty and I never knew what happened to her or if she spent her life in that horrible place. As usual, that was a subject not discussed in our presence.

My sister and I were raised in the era of phrases—short, whispered and always incomplete. When it came to family history or those well-hidden skeletons in their deep, dark and musty closets, our natural curiosity was constantly stifled. All too often, we'd hear the all-too-familiar refrain, "Be quiet, the children will hear."

Did it not occur to them that we "heard" everything, anyway? Evidently not. This secretiveness succeeded only in sending our imaginations running rampant, with very little foundation for the too-often-skewed results.

We grew up in a house of secrets, and as we grew into young adulthood, we too began to keep secrets. It's what we knew. We never learned to trust sharing our thoughts, so we hid them away, creating more secrets.

Too many of those growing-up secrets provoked immeasurable pain and mistrust, resulting in hostility, rage and often family separations. Trust became iffy.

Young children require little information, but it is frightening to them when nothing is supplied to respond to their natural curiosity or ease their fears. It is mystifying to me that no one read our faces, our body language or even saw us as human beings.

Unlike in today's world, children did not demand anything back in those days. We were fed, clothed and educated. We did not ask for or expect more.

My mother was a beautiful woman, with masses of dark red hair, large hazel green eyes and long shapely legs in a stunning five-foot-seven-inch figure. She adored clothes and shoes and was very much the fashion plate of her day.

She was also attractive to men and there were many, but they never seemed to hang around very long. Maybe having two little kids to care for was part of the commitment problem. She was also talented, from singing to playing piano to writing lyrics. She even had a song published, and I cherish my lone copy of the sheet music.

With all her beauty, style and talent, however, my mother was the most difficult and erratic person I have ever known.

This behavior was further complicated by her unpredictability, untruthfulness and a fiercely explosive temper. Her acting-out was always followed by slammed doors, silence and often tears. These incidents could last for a full day or even two, causing everyone to walk on eggshells.

During the holidays, when my mother found a way to destroy the joy, anticipation and celebratory atmosphere, her familiar questions would cut through our silent sadness: "Why all the long faces?" or "What's everybody so quiet about?"

Did we ever really matter to you, Mom? Until you felt better, there would be no joy in Mudville.

Growing up under the rule of my erratic mother set in motion a mass confusion as to our value. I never seemed to be good enough. Along with my learned-fixer role, I became an ambivalent pleaser, with an ever-growing hostility at someone I should love but didn't know. My ability to sing often prompted sudden recitals for my mother's friends, and I was summoned to perform whether I felt like it or not. Consideration of my feelings was non-existent.

My sister and I never enjoyed the comfort of maternal sharing, understanding or the empathy we so needed as children.

I was thirteen when I woke up one particular morning and got ready for school. I turned on the light and felt myself being shoved in the back, something thrown on the floor beside me and the door slammed shut. It was then that I saw my blood-stained pajama bottom. I picked up the elastic thing and a Kotex. I hadn't a clue as to how to use this thing in my hand. But calling my mother to help me was impossible.

I stood in that tiny bathroom until someone yelled that I'd be late for school. I was forced to ask my mother for help. All I can remember were her shaking hands, but no words of comfort or support.

I went to school that day still unprepared until one of my teachers sent me to the nurse. My need for female information began there.

My poor little sister was an early participant in what should have been a normal process. She began her period at eleven and thought she was dying. I guess my mother helped her because no mention was ever made of it again, until we were adults and could finally discuss it between ourselves.

Unhappiness, anger, depression and thoughtless behavior were so extreme at times that fear and silence were all that followed as we both tried to find ourselves following one of our mother's outbursts. Her reasons for inflicting such pain were never clear, buried in her own secrets.

I don't really know when understanding became acceptance, but it did, and it took a long time. It was only through the dedication of two courageous and caring therapists that I finally lifted that emotional curtain and exposed the skeletons in my own long-neglected closet.

I wish with all of my heart that my mother could have had the same help I received. Would she have listened and accepted it? From what I witnessed throughout my life, my guess is probably not. Apologizing for her behavior was not available to her, and she remained forever right in her own mind.

Dr. Phil McGraw, TV's "Dr. Phil," calls these people "Right Fighters." My mother needed something that we could not give her, and no one was capable of exerting damage control. Her behavior often left us bewildered, cautious and afraid.

At a very early age, I somehow adopted feelings of guilt at my lack of success in trying to fix her. Instead, of course, I fixed nothing. I remained a constant and disappointed failure until my eyes and ears were opened to the possibility of change. I not only listened to the therapeutic help I finally received, but I actually heard it, too.

If I could speak to my mother now, I would tell her, "The most difficult pill to swallow about your behavior, Mom, was the complete absence of an apology. We all knew you were destructively wrong, but why did this glaring fact elude you? Good therapy answered so many of my childhood questions, but the rest of the story is buried and lost forever in your dark and moldy emotional pile of bones, with the family history gone forever. Your refusal to ever say so much as 'I'm sorry' was wielded like a deadly weapon.

"I never thought that I was special, and that stemmed from being the persistent target of your wrath. 'Don't forget,' you'd often remind me, 'your talent comes from me. I gave you your talent.'

"As I write and remember my own theatrical road, I found out that it takes a lot more than just talent to be successful. You never understood or supported my struggles just to pay the bills. I starred in vaudeville all over the country and yet to you, it was me 'hitting bottom.' When you came to see my show at the Adams Theatre in Newark, your first words were not about the performance I'd given but how 'disgusting' the bathroom was and 'how far' I'd fallen. I so desperately wanted your praise, but that was too much for you.

"I'm truly sorry you never had the opportunity to express your talent as I did. I don't know why it was me and not you, Mom. The peaks and valleys of my career journey were amazing and their residual gifts often stunning. It was also terrifying, depressing, discouraging and lonely. But it was worth it, Mom. I'm sorry you never understood that."

When our storybook drama and hyperbole come crashing to earth—and they do—then the hard work and self-exploration must inevitably begin. We must bare our soul to find the truth—*our* truth. Truth begins with oneself. An apology often opens that first door to one's humanity along with self-respect. Until I entered therapy, I never understood that.

My family raised us the only way they knew how. Teaching discipline, good manners, honesty and a moral foundation was considered good parenting. Shame was the operative word. One did nothing to shame one's family by shaming oneself. I realize now that discipline often kept us from making stupid mistakes and, all too often, irreparably bad choices.

The sadly limited part of my life's education was the emotional imbalance of that time. People simply "sucked it up" and kept on keeping on no matter how isolated and devalued they may have felt. If children were only seen and not heard, how could they find their own life voice?

We found them anyway—more slowly, by today's standards, but highly effectively in spite of our old-fashioned and disciplined lifestyle.

A few years after my husband, Ray Gilbert, and I were married (this would be many years later), we picked my mother up at the airport, en route to a visit with my sister and her grandchildren. Ray was wonderful with her, but my mother and I maintained the polite but protective barrier that separated us.

Even as an adult, in the presence of my mother, I would revert back to becoming a cautious child, feeling her seeming inability to show love or affection. I remember at that moment asking myself why I couldn't just reach across that ever-widening gap and hug her, forgive myself and be the much bigger person.

My deepest regret is that nothing was ever resolved. I asked Ray how he could handle her, while I couldn't.

"She's not my mother, honey," he said simply.

No matter how broken the fences or how deep the hurts, disillusionments and disappointments in any relationship, always clean up your part and don't wait for the other person. You may be rejected and forced to listen to accusatory words of anger, but listen anyway.

Anger and hurt are back-to-back emotions, and without some clarity on one's true feelings, you continue down the same old road. My unresolved relationship with my mother taught me to never let it happen again. If I were to have another chance, I would do my part and a little bit more. Sometimes, it's the "little bit more" that finally eases the pain.

Do I have regrets? I have deep and lasting regrets. My mother and I were like those proverbial ships that pass in the night. Neither one of us could ever open that door leading to a cleaner and safer place where we could begin to know one another.

I played the hand I was dealt, sometimes with one step forward, two steps back and one hand tied behind my back. But quitting was never an option. There is much work still to be done in my life, but I welcome it every day. It means that I'm still alive and still have time to grow. After all, the biggest surprise is the one that's yet to come.

Hazel Leah Paige
August 26, 1898 - January 15, 1972

If this chapter can help someone rowing the same leaky boat as I, it has a raison d'etre.

-Janis Paige

Section II
The 1930s

The Great Depression

Hard times do not create heroes. It is during the hard times when the hero within us is created.

—Bob Riley

The Great Depression started in October of 1929. As young as I was, I remember the feeling of fear that permeated our tiny house in the Thirties. I had just turned seven when our world changed forever.

My sister and I had never heard words like suicide. *The Tacoma News Tribune* was filled with the tragic stories of people losing everything. Some jumped from the tops of buildings while others chose to simply end their lives in a less dramatic way. The shocking reality of what had happened hit like an earthquake. Everyone got hurt, but if you didn't have much to begin with, you *really* got hit.

Unlike today, we had no soft place to land. There was no welfare, no food stamps, no unemployment insurance, no disability checks, no Medicare and no Medicaid. There were none of the social safety net programs we have today, and suddenly the newspaper began to run pictures of what would come to be known as breadlines. It was sad beyond words to see hundreds of people patiently standing in long lines waiting for a bowl of soup or stew and a piece of bread. With no jobs, no money and families to feed, there was very little choice. Hunger hurts.

My mother was a telephone operator at the Bank of Tacoma when the "runs" of money on the banks began. Depositors, terrified at losing everything, "ran" to the bank demanding their money at once. There was a kind of mob mentality caused by the intense fear, and the bank was forced to shutter its doors.

This was not unique to Tacoma. The entire country was in the same sinking boat.

A survival mode started and ended each day. We began to save everything. The oldest clothes were washed, darned and ironed to be worn again. We were always counting pennies until the time came when we had no pennies to count. The bills just piled up in the center of the dining room table.

I was doing homework one night when I heard my grandmother sobbing.

"Oh, Frank, what are we going to do?" she cried.

"Well, Julia, I know what we're not gonna do. We're not gonna take a damned dime from this government. The day we know how it feels to stand in a breadline will be over my dead body! We'll make it on our own."

And we did. No wonder the Great Depression formed us, shaped us and taught us. In his book *The Greatest Generation*, Tom Brokaw wrote glowingly of us, the Depression children who went to war, countless of them still in their teens.

My new Buster Brown shoes would have to last me for almost two years. I walked a mile and a half to school and back and holes began to form in their soles. There was no money for new soles, let alone new shoes.

I have an everlasting picture in my mind as I'm getting ready for school. As usual during the winter months, it was still dark as I got dressed, all except for my shoes. Then I ate my "stick to the ribs" oatmeal, whether I wanted it or not, and cleaned my dish.

While I was having my breakfast, my grandfather was sitting at the little postage stamp of a table in our postage stamp of a kitchen, painstakingly cutting out cardboard to fit inside my leaky Buster Browns. Each day, he would carefully measure and fit and cut and fit until my tired little shoes were once again ready to get me to school. If he hadn't, I'd be walking on the pavement.

Washington state was famous for its rainfall, so cardboard or not, my feet were wet five minutes after I left home. I got used to the wet feet, but never the holes in my shoes. I was always trying to hide them.

A longtime mantra of mine comes to mind: "When there's a crisis, always look for the opportunity." Nothing is all bad. My shoe deprivation left me with a love of shoes. I guess you'd say I developed a shoe fetish. Needless to say, I now have plenty of shoes and a distant but still living and loving memory of my worn-out Buster Browns.

The soles may have been gone, but they survived.

So did we.

Our entertainment was restricted to a tabletop Philco radio and a wind-up Victrola turntable. Five nights a week, as seven p.m. approached, we would gather around to listen to the likes of Amos 'n' Andy, Jack Benny and Fibber McGee and Molly and their famous closet. We would forget the myriad problems and laugh until we hurt at people we couldn't even see but had come to love.

Our imaginations ran wild as each of us saw something different in those radio stories. Even today, the radio is still my favorite form of entertainment. I can't imagine my life without it.

The Great Depression also bred a generation of rootless, jobless and homeless men called hobos. They traveled by boxcar, looking for work from one coast to the other. They became a threadbare community in themselves.

My grandmother's baby brother was one of these lost souls. She never knew where he was until he would show up out of the blue. He always looked terrible, but she lavished hugs and tears of joy on him. He was fed, cleaned up and given new clothes. The old ones were washed, repaired and ironed, to be used, hopefully, by the next needy, hungry hobo to grace our back door. I never saw her turn anyone away. It wasn't in her nature.

The contrast with today's generation is stunning. There was no television, computers, internet, cell phones, tablets, Facebook, Twitter, etc., etc. Deprivation today can mean not having the latest smartphone or the most expensive Nike running shoes.

What happened to the set of values so necessary to becoming a responsible, self-reliant human being, let alone citizen? Don't tell me that times are different now. I am saddened and often embarrassed at the differences.

What happened to the moral compass so necessary for our self-guidance and genuine feeling of self-worth? I'm not speaking about ego. God knows there's far too much inflated egotism today. When I watch this bloated, arrogant and unyielding government tell us how to live, work, spend, feel and, yes, think, it leaves me incensed. It is obvious to me that integrity has been replaced by a blinding sense of entitlement, undeserved and self-corrupting.

But I digress.

I never saw my grandmother without her darning basket. She took in mending and ironing, too, so she always had a pile of socks with holes in them. But nothing was ever thrown away. She would place the hole over her darning egg, and slowly she would weave and mend the holes. Those socks lived to be worn another day. And another.

We sorely needed heroes, and from the ashes of what we once had came men like Will Rogers. He became the philosopher of the time. With his razor-sharp wit, his political honesty and his down-home persona, he was adored. When he died in a plane crash in Alaska in 1935, the country's heart collectively broke.

Another hero, unlikely perhaps, but one nevertheless, was a horse named Seabiscuit. He was a rather small, giant-hearted, courageous and remarkable horse. He became famous for never letting another horse get ahead of him. The newsreels would show hordes of people in old, worn clothes, crowding the rail as he thundered down the stretch.

Seabiscuit never let them down, becoming a symbol of who we were at that time. He was a fighter and so were we. He was the only horse to be named Thoroughbred Champion of The Great Depression. They even made a movie about him.

Hard work was a way of life for us—like a cup of coffee in the morning. Each day around 5 a.m., my grandfather would get up, light a fire in the old wood stove in the kitchen, put the coffee pot on to boil, bring extra wood in from the back yard and begin to wake everybody. Each of us knew what we had to do and—like the good soldiers of the Depression—we did it without complaint.

We had no washing machine, no electric dryer, no refrigerator, no freezer, no dishwasher, none of the time-savers of today. Clothes were washed in a big, oval-shaped copper tub. It was made that way so that it could fit over two of the burners on the stove. It was filled with water and when it boiled, in went the washing. Soap was added, and my miraculous grandmother would stir it with a broomstick until the clothes were clean.

Grandma was small, feminine and soft-spoken, but she could work like five men. The wet, dripping clothes were transferred to a tub with a hand wringer. When I got old enough to help her, the wringer was my job.

Monday was wash day, and my grandmother would don her apron with the big pocket in front filled with wooden clothespins. There were several clotheslines in the backyard, and she would hang the sheets, etc., over the lines, held on with the pins.

My sister and I can still remember playing Hide and Seek as we wrapped the laundry around ourselves. There is no perfume to equal the scent of a wind-whipped day of Monday's washing flapping on the clothesline, making its own special music. The memory of the two of us playing among the freshly washed clothes stays with me, even today.

Our refrigerator was a literal icebox. Twice a week, the big, burly iceman with his black leather vest would bring a giant block of ice. He would lift it from his shoulder, put it in the icebox and leave with, "See you on Thursday, Julia."

Tuesday was ironing day. Grandma would get out the ironing board and put the iron on the stove to heat. When it was hot, she would iron until it cooled down and she would have to heat it again. There were no electric irons. There was always a bowl of water nearby for sprinkling.

Today, we have steamers or steam irons. She had to make her own steam to wipe out the wrinkles. In between waiting for the iron to heat, she would shell peas and boil whatever was ripe or ready in our vegetable garden for canning and putting into Mason jars.

My mother went to work very early and did not get home until around six in the evening, so it was up to Grandma to save the day. No wonder my grandparents died at sixty-four and sixty-three, respectively. They worked themselves to death.

When Prohibition began in 1920 and booze was against the law, my grandfather would spend days in our little dirt and spidery cellar. I never went down there because I was terrified of spiders, A few weeks later, we would hear explosions from the cellar that would wake us up.

"What was that?" we'd yell.

"It's nothing, go back to sleep," Grandpa would assure us.

What we didn't know was that he was making and selling bootleg beer to both pay something on the bills and to barter for what we needed. He always made sure that we had his homemade root beer, too.

The day before Thanksgiving that year, Grandpa came home with a huge turkey he had won in a raffle. I can still hear the screams of delight as he plopped that big bird on the table and said, "C'mon kids, you have to help me pick out all of the pin feathers so that Grandma can get the turkey ready."

We pulled pin feathers for hours until this bird was totally clean.

Thanksgiving Day came, and we invited Aunt Mandy and Uncle Mac and their two kids who lived next door. When the turkey was done, Grandma set it aside on our little screened-in back porch to cool while she got everything else ready to go on the table.

The excitement was palpable, when suddenly we heard a loud crash and a scream. We looked on in helpless horror as a poor, thin and mangy dog carried off our turkey across the yard and disappeared.

"He just broke through the screen," Grandma cried.

There stood our shattered old screen door in pieces.

After a very long silence, Grandpa said, "Julia, let's get everything else on the table. We may not have turkey, but I smell your dinner so let's eat."

We all had vegetables, biscuits, gravy, cranberry sauce and apple pie made from our apple tree. Grandma's memorable stuffing, however, left along with the turkey.

"We may not have turkey, but we still have a lot to be grateful for," Grandpa assured us, "and so has that dog."

With the Depression in full swing in 1935, a man named Major Bowes and his Amateur Hour began a radio phenomenon. Its excitement spread throughout the country in the form of amateur shows. There was no age limit to perform, so people flocked to be seen, heard and perhaps even become a star.

Of course, my mother entered me in the competitions, and I began a small round of shows. Most of the time, the famous gong was heard and that meant, "Thank you, now get off the stage." Maybe it was luck, talent or a combination of both, but I never got gonged, so I just kept singing.

My career probably began there when I first faced an audience and heard that addictive thing called applause.

As we endured the Great Depression, we were buoyed by the election of Franklin Delano Roosevelt in 1933. He called himself a "New Dealer," and there was no doubt about his plans for America. He ran for four terms and died shortly after being sworn in for his fourth.

Roosevelt instituted program after program, all designed to put people back to work. The results of his famous CCC (Civilian Conservation Corps) program can still be viewed throughout the country. CCC camps were established to build parks, forestry projects and more.

The Timberline Lodge at Mt. Hood in Oregon is a living example of the talent and artistry of the men who built this famous edifice of the Great Depression. In 1977, it was declared a national monument and is still enjoying great popularity today. It was and always has been a spectacular ski lodge. I've been there and it took my breath away.

From thousands of unemployed men, incredibly beautiful artistry was discovered and nurtured. Timberline Lodge is filled with the talent of these nearly forgotten "hobos" who had no place to stand but left their legacy for all to touch, admire and appreciate.

You don't find this human and magical struggle in the small confines of the newest tablet, software or smartwatch. Unlike the internet, which is devoid of a heart, these men shared theirs in the gifts they left behind.

My seventieth birthday was spent with my best friend and her family in Portland, Oregon. We decided to visit Timberline Lodge. I had never seen it so off we went, driving through a warm, sunlit and simply beautiful Indian Summer day. We parked, took a few steps, opened a door and time-traveled back to a part of my history. The initial view was stunning.

Everything was aged wood that was worn, touched and caressed by the thousands who visit and ski at the Lodge. Once inside, there is a gigantic window from floor to ceiling, while just outside sits the majestic Mt. Hood—seeming close enough to touch.

"Let's order some coffee, Nina, I just want to take in this beauty," I said.

As we sipped our coffee, the sun began to fade, the sky got dark and as if on cue, huge, fluffy snowflakes began to fall, and Mt Hood disappeared behind the snowstorm until it passed a half-hour later.

I don't know where it came from, but Mother Nature pulled out all the stops and gave me a glorious birthday present. When we finally had to leave, we drove through the snow to the road below where the sun was waiting to see us home. Magic waits everywhere.

Sometime in early 1934, my grandfather left early in the morning, only to return that evening with a wonderful new job. He managed several buildings owned by the Rhodes Investment Company, having been hired by Mr. Rhodes himself. When it came time to sign the contract, Grandpa stuck out his hand and uttered the words, "This is my contract, Mr. Rhodes. This is all you need."

Things were finally looking up. No more holes in my shoes and no more hand-me-downs for my sister.

One day, we came home from school to find boxes being packed and the little house in a mess. Like everything else, moving was also a secret and everything changed in one school day. All of the mysterious papers, pictures, toys and memorabilia were tossed out without a thought for Betty and me and the history we would one day cherish and miss.

What were they hiding? To this day, I hate secrets. I loathe the pain they cause, the gossip and the unwarranted power in the wrong hands. Witness the cruel secrets and lies of today's internet.

Suddenly, we lived in an apartment near to my grandfather's work and my mother's job at the bank. It was small, one bedroom with a single bathroom, living room and kitchen. It was on a corner, so it was bright for the most part. It was also on a hill, as was most of Tacoma, and still cobblestoned.

Each winter when it would snow, Betty and I would stand at the window and watch the cars try to make it up the hill to Market Street. It was only one block, but hardly anyone accomplished it. The tires would spin as they simply slid back down to Broadway. It was our entertainment until the powers that be decided to pave it. There went our fun.

As a child, I remember meeting a real Indian chief. My grandfather had taken me with him when we saw the chief walking toward us. He wore a black suit, white shirt, black bolo tie and his full feathered chief's headdress. He was chief of the Puyallup Indian Tribe. He was awe-inspiring, to say the least, and I was simply speechless when my grandfather introduced me.

I couldn't have grown up in a better place than Tacoma. It's changed now, but the house in which I was raised still stands. The last time I was there, the neighborhood looked much the same. The tiny Proctor Theater become a national monument. To me, it always was.

I saw my first Fred Astaire movie there, and during the Depression, on a Saturday at The Popeye Club, I was voted "Miss Olive Oyl." That same day, I won a five-pound box of candy bars. I was all of ten years old when I proudly presented it to the family.

This was my first taste of stardom. Being a kid, it didn't last long—and neither did the candy bars.

Hard Times Party

Tough times never last, but tough people do.
—Robert H. Schuller

The Hard Times Party was a perfect example of needing and finding laughter. My grandfather had an infectious sense of humor, and he loved hosting one of these neighborhood soirees. The rules were that everyone would bring something to eat, no matter how small the offering, and always arrive in costume. There was no money, but their imaginations more than made up for it.

My sister and I were still very small, and we will never forget my grandfather's creation. He came out of his tiny bedroom dressed for the evening, wearing one of my grandmother's hats with a tiny veil over one eye. Around his neck was a string of green beads that I'd never seen before. He had donned a collar-frayed white shirt with tie to match, over which he had placed his suspenders holding up his old shiny pants with both of its legs rolled up to his knees. All of this revealed his black garters and mismatched socks.

Our old upright piano held the only really good thing we still owned. It was called a piano scarf and was one of the stars of the Roaring Twenties. Most homes owned one, and ours was hand-embroidered in massive silk roses of brilliant yellows, pinks and oranges. Its beauty set off on a large pale green silk square with its borders adorned in long silk variegated fringe to match its floral display.

It was definitely not going to remain on the piano, as we watched Grandpa pilfer it for the completion of his costume. He folded the scarf into a triangle, draped it over one shoulder and knotted it on his other side. To this day, I'll never understand how he kept the fringe out of his homemade beer, the tub of popcorn or anything else that got in its way.

The old adage "Less is more" would never have described our grandfather that night. He was a picture for his grandchildren's memories. Unforgettable!

My grandmother's sister, Lillian, and her husband, Jimmie, were professional Adagio dancers. The Adagio and piano scarves were very Roaring Twenties, and we had both. Betty and I had a hiding place under the stairway leading to the attic where we could see without being seen.

At one point in the evening, we saw Uncle Jimmie tie a bandana around his head and grab Aunt Lillian, and their Adagio began. It was like a Tango, except there was a lot of throwing poor Aunt Lillian to the floor, picking her up with a few dance steps and then throwing her down once again, often slamming into the walls as she slid from his seemingly angry behavior.

Our little house that wasn't even a thousand square feet was definitely not made for Adagio dancing. Betty and I were horrified that Aunt Lillian would be hurt, but she waved our worries away with, "It's all a bag of tricks and I know how to fall." My sister and I never did figure that one out.

Grandpa would make a huge tub of popcorn on our old wood stove. When it came time to eat, he would bring out the *pièce de résistance* of the evening, bottles of homemade Prohibition beer for the men. It was against the law, of course, but my grandfather loved their reaction and they loved him. They filled our little house that night with laughter and fun, while my sister and I hid, watching them all be silly and, for a short time, worry-free.

From the popcorn to the illegal homemade brew, to building the chicken coop so we'd have eggs, Grandpa's tasks were done with a quiet expertise and commitment. He was a leader whether he knew it or not and lived his mantra throughout his life. "We're all dealt a hand," he used to say, "and we must play it the best way we can and never stop."

"We the People" could surely use you today, Grandpa, but they'd never appreciate or deserve you. We used to sing *My Country 'Tis of Thee*, but now we sing, *My Country 'Tis of* Me.

THE ROXY

*TELEVISION WILL MAKE YOU RICH, MOVIES WILL MAKE
YOU FAMOUS, BUT THE THEATRE WILL MAKE YOU GREAT.*
—TERRENCE MANN

WHEN I TURNED eleven, I discovered the stage. Little did I know at that somewhat insignificant age that I would spend my life to one degree or another in that place that makes magic. Of course, it can also break your heart, your spirit, your hopes, your dreams and confidence, not to mention your bank account.

The magic always waits, however, until you find it again.

Imagine my surprise when I awoke that September 16 to find that one of my birthday presents was a shiny ten-cent piece for a movie. The Roxy was only a block and a half away from our new home on Ninth and Market, so off I went, alone, safe and feeling very grown-up.

When the movie was over and "The End" announced itself, everything changed, including me.

The house went dark, with the sounds of instruments coming from the orchestra pit. Suddenly the music began, and the footlights flooded the stage with light so bright it made me blink. The spotlight moved to the proscenium arch, and from the side of the stage came actual people—one after another after another—until I moved to the first row so that I could be closer to them.

The motion picture was black, white and gray, but the people were all in brilliant color. Even their shoes were in color. "Where did they ever find shoes like that?" I wondered.

It never occurred to me then that I'd been bitten by the showbiz bug. I was simply hypnotized and enjoying my fourth vaudeville show of the day when the person next to me tapped me on the arm. He pointed to a policeman, who motioned for me to come with him.

My pure and perfectly behaved little eleven-year-old heart sank. "What did I do?" I thought, as I dutifully followed him. Then I saw my mother standing at the top of the aisle. By the look on her face, I knew I was in trouble. I, who never did anything wrong.

I was always too scared not to be a good girl. But it simply never occurred to me that I had been in that theatre for about six hours, watching the vaudeville show over and over again.

It was nearing six in the evening and my mother was frantic enough to call the police. I was embarrassed and absolutely terrified. I'd never seen her so angry.

"But Mom, you knew where I was. You didn't have to call the police," I reasoned.

"You be quiet!" she yelled. "And don't you ever do this to me again! We've been worried sick!"

"But Mom . . ."

"You shut up and I mean it!"

That block and a half from The Roxy was the longest walk I ever took, as she angrily dragged me home. I never said a word as my grandparents met me at the door with a stony silence.

I was definitely in the doghouse and I knew I was wrong. I didn't mean to scare everybody, but I was so busy watching those amazing and beautiful people on stage that I simply forgot to remember how late it was. I had never done anything like that before.

The worst punishment my family could impose was absolute silence, so nobody spoke to me at dinner except for my sister's sing-song taunt.

"You made us *laaaate*, shame on *yoooou*!" she teased.

"Be quiet!" my mother said.

The silence was deafening as we all got punished for what I'd done. I felt completely alone, too terrified to ever share my unforgettable day at

The Roxy. *Alone* was a word I would come to know well. it would become a source of my strength as I faced my own unknown and uncertain future.

The Roxy and the cute boy in the vaudeville act had stolen my heart. The die was cast; I was going into vaudeville. The "how" part would be left to fate and a series of extraordinary events.

Little did that eleven-year-old girl know that she would have the tensile strength and fortitude one has to have to accomplish anything, let alone be good at it.

Vaudeville began in the early 1800s. It supposedly died in the early 1930s. Not true! The only addition to a vaudeville show was a motion picture, so the vaudevillians simply took a deep breath, accepted change and kept on keeping on.

The genre actually took its last sweet breath in the Fifties, but it prepared me for the life I've had and my ability to survive its inevitable ups and downs.

I was a movie star when vaudeville taught me how to be an entertainer and a professional. I'm eternally grateful to my generous vaudevillian teachers and our "life upon the wicked stage." Rest assured, it was anything but wicked with four and five shows a day.

The Roxy looks the same today, but now it bears the well-deserved title of historical national monument. It still plays films and stays very much alive, but the vaudeville is long gone. The human contact that occurred between the audience and those unforgettable performers is also gone, but the experience left an indelible mark on every aspect of my life.

You bet I arrived overnight. Over a few hundred
nights, in the Catskills, vaudeville,
clubs and Broadway.

–Danny Kaye

The Brown Castle

Even in high school, I was very interested in history, why people do the things they do. As a kid, I spent a lot of time trying to relate the past to the present.

—George Lucas

At the age of one hundred and thirteen, it stands today. A huge, stunningly beautiful edifice called Stadium High School. Its alumni still lovingly call it "The Brown Castle." It's an invaluable part of my history that brought me into the present.

As the Northern Pacific Railroad continued to enlarge the Northwest, the need for a hotel arose and the famous American architect Stanford White was commissioned to build one in Tacoma, Washington. He chose a site high on a hill with breathtaking views of Puget Sound, its busy port and beyond, to many of the countless islands we inhabit and enjoy today.

Speaking for myself, it was often difficult to keep my mind on the books when everywhere you looked was a hypnotic daydream. It was often in the form of a ship entering or leaving the harbor, wishing I was digging clams at Dash Point or watching a dark and rainy day with its gathering thunderstorms.

With all of that, we graduated with the best education one could wish for. We were ready to pick up where our parents' generation left off, including going to war.

During its near completion around the turn of the century, there was a fire and part of the hotel burned. It was then that the decision was made to finish it as a much-needed high school. It opened in 1906 and never stopped its educational aims.

The Brown Castle offered everything from science to sports, music, history, languages, shorthand and typing. Proper grammar, as well as spelling and punctuation, started in the first grade. There were shop skills for boys, home economics for girls. Civics on how the government works, the Constitution, the Bill of Rights and how to protect and cherish the laws under which we were governed.

I've lived and worked all over the world and saw firsthand what it means not to be protected by our First Amendment of free speech. Freedom is never free. It comes with the price of defending it.

I had mentors. Clayton Johnson, head of the music department, was nothing but encouraging. Thanks to him and his leadership, my musicality blossomed and grew. I starred in two musicals presented by the school.

My yearbook voted me Most Talented and Prettiest, but it was countered by the title of Class Vamp. Could I help it if I liked boys?

Unlike today, we had crushes, and the feelings were often reciprocated—but that's where it stopped. Sex, potentially leading to an early pregnancy, was completely off limits. We were to find those experiences with love, marriage and kids. We were expected to use self-control, self-responsibility and respect for one another.

The boys and girls worked together to accomplish what was, at times, very difficult. But rules were rules and we didn't break them. The punishment for misbehavior was severe and could last a lifetime, depending on the consequences. Remember that I write of *then*, not of now.

I entered the Brown Castle in 1938. The structure remained the same even with its half-steps stairway, which accommodated the long skirts and wardrobe of the turn-of-the-century female students. A regular-sized stair was too difficult to maneuver; hence, the little half-steps. They were still in use when I entered high school.

Those stairs were worn in the middle from the thousands of footsteps through the years. There was always the smell of oil on the wood and bits of sawdust left in the corners, missed when they were swept every morning before school started. The beautiful old newel posts were also caressed and worn with the years.

My sister and I were both sent to the principal's office when we—in our bobby socks, saddle shoes and much shorter skirts—impatiently took three stairs at a time and got caught.

"It's not ladylike," we were warned. "Please don't do that again."

It was an embarrassing no-no. The temptation for "three at a time" remained, but we dutifully took them as promised, one by one.

Many years later when I returned for a class reunion, our tiny half-stairs had been replaced with standard-sized steps. I don't know when they disappeared, but they were the first thing I noticed and missed when I toured our school once more. It's funny what our memories choose to remember.

We were such unsophisticated and naïve children at that time. It was over all too soon with the bombing of Pearl Harbor and our entry into World War II. My graduating Class of 1941, like so many others, was scattered to the winds of war, many never to return.

Thank you for your service.

Emmett Kelly

> *I REMEMBER IN THE CIRCUS, LEARNING THAT THE CLOWN WAS THE PRINCE, THE HIGH PRINCE. I ALWAYS THOUGHT THAT THE HIGH PRINCE WAS THE LION OR THE MAGICIAN, BUT THE CLOWN IS THE MOST IMPORTANT.*
>
> —Roberto Benigni

I WAS BORN IN another century, with one grateful foot planted firmly in my memories of the clowns who touched my heart. At a very young age, I was introduced to and fell in love with the artistry of the clowns. Each one was unique, each one a story in my imagination.

From the circus to vaudeville to films to television, clowns bridged the span of time and all too soon were gone forever.

How sad it is to hear that in today's world, clowns breed fear, suspicion and even terror. It breaks my heart to listen to the twists and turns toward the negativity that today's minds can so readily accept as fact.

Clowns were once admired, revered and sought as a brief panacea for the pain in the world. Now they are the opposite of their original purpose. No longer can children dream of being a clown someday, as we once did.

Our ever-growing suspicion breeds lies, hatred and, worse, the refusal to find the truth. The clown makeup, costumes, masks and their personally inventive attire is now lost in a sea of dishonesty. Are they really clowns or predators hiding to strike the innocent?

My first experience with a clown was in the middle of the Great Depression, around 1934-35. My grandfather had finally gotten his first good, well-deserved job in that era. The circus had come to town, and he wanted to treat my sister and me to our first.

As we headed for the circus grounds, the calliope could be heard for miles. Excitement reigned as we parked and suddenly stepped into the circus life. It was a beautiful day with the smell of sawdust, animals and the fresh salt air from Puget Sound magically comingling.

My twelve-year-old eyes stared in awe and wonder at the sparkling costumes, the bespangled horses and their riders glinting in the sunlight.

It was the clowns, however, that initially fascinated me.

In a patchwork of crazy costumes, they sat on the steps of their wagons, chatting and smoking, their painted faces animated and otherworldly.

"Are they real?" I wondered.

We entered a huge tent with banners flying from its top. There was a very large ring and rows of bleachers surrounding it on various levels. We found our seats and I entered first. I sat at the end of the row where all of the acts made their entrances and exits. I was in heaven, and it was endlessly exciting to see the aerialists and the beautifully decorated horses, with women in beautiful costumes standing on their backs doing tricks like handstands, backbends and other death-defying stunts.

It was all magic, with clowns interspersed, making us laugh with their crazy antics.

When the tent went dark once more, not four feet from me appeared a man with a big broom in his hand. He stood in the dark until a spotlight inside the ring was lit and then moved to its edge, where he was visible. He never moved until the audience quieted down and one could hear a pin drop.

He wore an old black fedora hat and a baggy, much-too-large jacket over an old shirt and tie. His pants were also too big, as were his funny, floppy shoes. Everything he wore looked like it had once belonged to someone else.

When he turned to the light, we saw his face with its big, white, oversized and oh-so-sad mouth. His eyes, too, were sad, matching his mouth and never cracking a smile or change of expression. All of this heavy-laden sadness was topped off by a bulbous red nose and a jawline painted black as if he were badly in need of a shave.

He was irresistible.

His body language told us that he was very tired as he began to slowly sweep around the ring. Suddenly, a man yelled, "Oh, good lord, he's sweeping up the spotlight!"

The laughter began to grow, and every once in a while, the spotlight would misbehave or move away from his assigned task. He would stop. give it a sad, "Why me?" look, and patiently begin again.

By now, the audience was completely mesmerized by this plaintive figure before us. After more games and jousting with the spot, he finally swept what was left of his elusive partner to the same place where he had entered.

He stood for a moment in the dark, bathed only in a small ring of white light—all that was left of his spot. With one more look up and a tiny sweep of his broom, he and his playful but tormenting spotlight disappeared.

In the dark, I watched him walk past me and lift a corner of the tent flap. The sun lit his face for a moment, still sad.

Then as suddenly as he had appeared, he was gone.

How could I know then that I had just seen someone who would come to be known as the greatest clown in the world? I had witnessed the act of the wondrous Emmett Kelly and his unforgettable Weary Willie.

He invented and dedicated Weary Willie to the hobos, that lost generation of men who could not find their place of belonging during the Great Depression. He studied to be a cartoonist, but all of that changed with his invention of this character.

Emmett Kelly died at eighty in Sarasota, Florida, on the opening day of the circus. Thank you for the joy.

Emmett Kelly
December 8, 1898 – March 3, 1979

Section III
The 1940s

Home to High School to Hollywood

I HAVE A STAR ON HOLLYWOOD BOULEVARD
WHERE PEOPLE WALK ALL OVER ME.
AT THE END OF THE DAY, THOUGH,
I'M STILL SHINING, STILL THERE.

—JANIS PAIGE

IN 1941, I somehow graduated from high school. But if the algebra teacher Mr. Kennedy had his way, I'd still be there.

Math was always difficult for me. But when the mandatory semester of algebra began, suicide seemed the only way out of my misery. Miss Hopkins, my first-day-of-school torturer, had simply traded her old blue skirt for Mr. Kennedy's old gray suit—and I was in the soup again.

I worked very hard in school, and it didn't help my learning process to hear my mother constantly reminding me that she couldn't understand why I was "so terrible" in math when she was "so good" at it.

I was not aware that math was genetic, Mom, I thought.

My mother had a vocabulary of zingers. With my life hanging on my answering a simple algebra problem, I had to accept my "death" sentence. I was the only one in my class that Mr. Kennedy failed.

Nonetheless, I loved school, especially when I found my voice in more ways than getting through math. I'd been singing since I was three. It was something I did as I walked to school and home again. I sang as I played and I sang during church services every Sunday until around age eleven, when I was asked to begin singing solos.

My voice was advanced far beyond my years, but to me it was just something I had always done, like breathing. I was not a good student by the rules of the day, but singing seemed to set me apart from the pack of straight-A kids, whom I constantly strived to live up to but could never reach.

I got A's in history because of my interest and my razor-sharp memory, but anything to do with math would tear me apart. I'd be back in that deep, dark hole again where nothing mattered except my embarrassment at not being good enough.

I was good at anything artistic, but the Three R's were number one on our academic agenda. And no matter how admired my talent may have been, it would not get me graduated. I needed the whole package. Readin' and ritin' were a cinch, but "'rithmetic" was an eternal monkey on my back. Our teachers' commitment to their students was written in stone, and none of them ever gave up on me except for Mr. Kennedy.

Singing, dancing, writing, painting, etc., were things we did in our spare time. Homework came first. When I found that I could make up the math credit, I worked my tail off. The very thought of not graduating with my class was abhorrent to me.

Between starring in *The Merry Widow* and *The Desert Song* in high school and my solos in church, I was gaining a little sense of myself. However, each day that I crossed the threshold of Mr. Kennedy's algebra class, I shrank to my true size and, once again, my hoped-for invisibility.

Around my high school years, my mother decided to get me singing lessons. Once a week, we would drive thirty-five miles to Seattle. My teacher was an elderly, *bel canto*-trained Italian, and I learned to sing properly. He was the first person to encourage me to study opera. I had been singing along with the opera stars on the radio, but I otherwise had no idea what they were saying because everything was in Italian, French or German.

On the way home, we'd stop at the only restaurant en route, The Halfway House. We'd eat, fill up the car with gas and continue on. It's long gone now, and if you don't look at your mileage to see if you're halfway home or not, there are no signposts.

That thirty-five-mile drive used to be dressed in the beauty of the everlasting forests where we lived in that gorgeous part of America. There is very little of that left now. The airport, Sea-Tac, is now halfway, and there are even towns with their neighborhoods, shopping centers and the generic sameness of our country today.

I am fully aware of the changes that progress brings, but old Interstate 5 is now six or eight lanes wide. Civilization is on either side, with the constantly increasing angry snarl of congestion and traffic.

Around 1932, my mother met her second husband, Fred. Between fights, separations, bigger fights and a few calms before the next storm, they were married. It took them seven and a half years (before they married) to finally discover that they were a really bad match.

Fred lived and worked in Seattle, so they bought a house in the Green Lake district. Believe it or not, there really was a lake. I was in high school, so I stayed in Tacoma and lived with my grandparents. My poor little sister, however, was moved to Seattle with our new parental setup. I visited on the weekends, and when I graduated in 1941, I, too, had to move.

It was a lovely home, but it was filled with the same yelling, hitting, fights, standoffs, tensions and depressions as before. Nothing changed except the geography.

I got a job with the Botting Plumbing store, waiting on customers until the owner Bill Botting began to teach me how to solder drain pipes in his spider-filled basement storeroom. I, obedient and trusting, did as I was told until my voice began to be affected by the soldering fumes, so I stopped. I finally got fired because it just wasn't worth the fifteen dollars a week that he was paying me.

December 7, 1941, brought us into World War II, and everything and everyone shifted gears. My mother was no different.

My singing teacher suggested to my mother that we go to Hollywood. It was the last place in the world that we knew anything about. But several weeks later, her secret plan was in place.

Were we consulted? Of course not. The same hidden world of my mother was still in place, and outside of the ever-widening gulf in their marriage, life continued in the same erratic pattern as before. Oh, there were hints of change, but we'd heard it before—so life went on.

After Fred had left for work one day, Mom announced our future. Betty would finish high school in Tacoma and live with my grandparents, and she and I would go to Hollywood for my career.

The only thing I knew about Hollywood was from the various movie magazines and a short visit with my chum's family when we finished high school. Of course, I talked about it, but never expected something so drastic or so final.

We left our new home, our dog, our family in Tacoma, everything—including Fred—and drove to California. Everything was as secret as it always was. My sister happily went back to Tacoma, our blessed grandparents and high school, where she successfully graduated with her class.

We never learned if there was a divorce from Fred. We also never asked. Forgiving myself for not getting answers to the countless questions that always waited in the wings of my mind never leaves me.

Could I have altered the road we traveled? Perhaps, if I'd been someone else, but I wasn't, and I did the best that I could at the time. I had no options. Not until the full impact of my mother's influence over my life became clear did I make some drastic changes of my own.

Life is the toughest teacher we'll ever have, and bad decisions or wrong choices are not mistakes as long as we learn from them. It just takes time to find that out.

If it hadn't been for my mother and her often brutal decisions, life would have been quite different for me. I owe her a great deal of gratitude for, first, giving me life and helping me get to where I am today. Unfortunately, however, I never knew her or the deeply buried reasons for her deep and abiding unhappiness.

To this day, she remains a sad and lasting mystery.

Our first Southern California home was in Pasadena, but my mother soon discovered that it was too far from her intended goal and we shortly found a tiny apartment on Leland Way in Hollywood.

There was a Thrifty Drugstore on the corner of Hollywood Boulevard, and it was a rare treat on Sundays when we could eat at the counter. I remember having Thanksgiving dinner there once or twice. I can't imagine a drugstore having a counter where you could eat real food today. But it was very affordable and a big help in 1942.

My mother got a job at the Guarantee Trust Bank, and I got one behind the ribbon counter at the Kress dime store on Hollywood Boulevard. I could count the change despite my limited math skills, but not if I had to include the new tax on the sale.

How did I solve the problem? By not charging the tax. After all, it was only a penny or two.

I also had an excruciating time trying to figure out what a third of a yard of ribbon cost. I was soon found out because they were short at the end of the day. I was too pretty to fire, however, so they put me behind the makeup counter, where I ran into that nasty few pennies tax again.

They tried to help me, but all I heard was Mr. Kennedy and my mother asking, "Why can't you get it?" My job at Kress lasted all of two weeks before they fired me for good.

The only thing I knew really well was how to sing.

My mother soon found the Hollywood Canteen that was just two blocks from the bank. She began helping the USO serve the thousands of wartime armed forces coming through on their way to wherever. It was unique in that stars would show up and also serve these lonely, homesick kids going to war.

One night, Mom announced to me, "You're singing at the Hollywood Canteen tomorrow night." Naturally, I was not consulted, and I protested.

"I only know opera, Mom, and they don't want to hear opera," I reasoned.

"Well," she replied, "they're expecting you and you have to show up."

I showed up and sang "Un bel di" from *Madame Butterfly* in English. As always, these soldiers were the best audience a performer could ever ask for.

When I left the stage, there was a woman waiting, asking if she could speak with me.

"My name is Ida Koverman," she said. "I'm the assistant to Louis B. Mayer, and we would like to see you at the studio tomorrow."

I stood there, not knowing who she was talking about when she said, "Perhaps you know him as the Mayer in Metro Goldwyn Mayer or MGM."

The light finally went on.

"You want to see me?" I asked, still not completely comprehending.

"How about one o'clock tomorrow?" she asked. "Come to the big building on your left, tell them why you're there and ask for me. I'll be waiting."

Mrs. Koverman gave me her card and left with the words, "See you tomorrow."

My thinking in those far-off days did not go much beyond being in a state of excited disbelief.

I dressed that next day, wearing almost everything I owned. The words "simple" and "chic" had not yet penetrated my fashion vocabulary.

I took a Red streetcar on Highland Avenue, then transferred to the Red Car on Washington Boulevard that would let me off in front of the MGM Executive Building on my left. I entered, and as I stood for a few moments, I heard Mrs. Koverman say, "Here I am, Donna Mae. I'll meet you at the top of the stairs."

I did as I was told, and she took me to meet Louis B. Mayer.

I entered what was to me a gigantic office. A man was sitting behind a big oval desk atop wall-to-wall white carpeting. He stood up and asked me to have a seat across the desk from him. He asked a few questions and then told me, "Mrs. Koverman has spoken very highly of you."

I murmured my thanks, and heard him say, "I think she'll do fine, Ida. Sign her up, get her to wardrobe, makeup and hair and have her meet Bob Alton. She has to learn that dance number."

Mr. Mayer ended our conversation by turning to me and saying, "Welcome to MGM," and that was that.

I came to Hollywood, I saw Hollywood and I conquered Hollywood. Oh, Donna Mae, what a naive little baby you are. You ain't seen nothin' yet.

The wardrobe department was a kid's fairy tale. My eyes were like saucers as I saw the famous figure forms of the MGM stars. There was Judy Garland, June Allyson, Ava Gardner and Greer Garson, among others. There they stood, headless, in various stages of being fitted until they could fit the real person.

I, too, joined this headless bevy of dummy figures. They measured and poured a strange concoction onto my body, and when it set, there I was, ready for those first fittings while we continued to rehearse. This amazing system of fittings was a part of every studio. God help you if you gained weight.

There wasn't a single thing that was not available when needed. The *pièce de résistance* was the salary I received at the start of my contract. They paid me $150 per week. That was more than my mother earned in a month in Tacoma. The contract was the usual sliding scale. At the end of the first six months, they could choose to pick up your option or let you go.

In 1944, they put me in a picture called *Bathing Beauty*, starring Esther Williams and co-starring Red Skelton, with Ethel Smith and Carlos Ramirez. Metro cast me in a musical number with Red and gave me one line of dialogue.

I played a schoolgirl who runs into a room excitedly chattering, "They're here, they're here!" The Music Box Theatre in Tacoma showed the movie and the marquee read, "Janis Paige in *Bathing Beauty* with Esther Williams and Red Skelton."

Only my hometown would give me billing like that. When the cast credits rolled, I was last on the list.

They changed my name, of course. There had been a famous WWI performer named Elsie Janis. Because I'd been discovered at the Hollywood Canteen, I was ripe for the publicity they could generate. They gave me her last name, and I fought to keep my grandfather's name of Paige.

Of course, the publicity faded as it always does, but I was stuck with the name of Janis. To this day, I've never felt like a Janis. At $150 per week, however, who was I to argue over a name?

That was all I did during my six months at Metro. Mrs. Koverman had found me an agent and one day, he called to say that he would meet me in her office the following day.

We were ushered in, sat down and told that they were not picking up my option. In plain words, I was out. Mrs. Koverman kindly explained that they had Garland, Allyson, Gloria DeHaven, Lucille Bremer, etc., etc.

"You're too offbeat," she said. "We don't know what to do with you."

There it was again. I can't do math, I can't make change and now I'm too offbeat and they don't know what to do with me.

"Well, if they don't, who does?" I cried as I left the studio.

At that moment, I thought that my life was over. That I was a failure. My agent quickly told me that we had an appointment with Solly Biano, head of casting at Warner Bros.

"When?" I blubbered.

"In about an hour," he said. "Now stop crying, forget Metro and start smiling."

So I left Metro heartbroken, pulled myself together on the ride to Warner Bros. and walked in to meet a smiling, energetic and warm Solly Biano.

I'll never forget his first words.

"Oh, my gosh, has Delmer seen her?" he expressed to my agent.

"No, we just got here," my agent replied.

Mr. Biano picked up the phone and asked to speak to Delmer Daves.

"Delmer, it's Solly," he said into the phone. "Listen, I have a young lady in my office, and I think you should see her." Then, after a pause, "Great, I'll bring her to the set now."

Not only had I never heard of Delmer Daves, but everything was happening so fast that I hadn't had a chance to say anything besides, "It's very nice to meet you, Mr. Biano."

Suddenly, we were being ushered onto the sound stage. It was filled with people milling about in various costumes.

"They've already started to shoot the picture," Mr. Biano said, adding, "Delmer, we're over here."

A warm and smiling gentleman was introduced to me. He shook my hand as Solly Biano said, "Well, what do you think?"

"Solly, I think she's perfect! Get her to wardrobe, hair and makeup. She works tomorrow." Then to me, "Welcome, Janis, I'll see you soon."

In the span of a few hours, I had lost my job, only to find a new one. I was speechless, scared, excited and feeling like I was the luckiest person in the world. I hadn't even thought to ask what I do "tomorrow." I only knew I didn't have to tell my mother, "I've been fired. Where do we go from here?"

The name of the film was *Hollywood Canteen*. The leading roles were played by Joan Leslie, Robert Hutton, Dane Clark and me. The storyline was ours, and the stars had the small roles, just as it was in the real Canteen.

My first day was spent with Dane, a wonderful actor. With Delmer Daves as the director, I could not have had anyone better to guide me through this all-important time in my young life and budding career.

Each day on the set, the movie magazines I'd read sprang to life. I was meeting and working with the real thing!

In those days, Warner Bros. had messenger girls and boys. That's what they were called then. Political correctness had not yet found its way into our much less confusing and simpler life.

We were dressed in uniforms the color of Warner Bros. Everything was a lovely soft shade of celadon green, and so were we. Because I played a messenger girl in the film, their uniform was part of my wardrobe.

As I walked back to the set one day, I heard someone rapping on the window and gesturing for me to come inside. I had no intention of being late, so I ignored him and kept on walking. Suddenly, I heard a man's voice ask, "Please, may I talk to you?"

"I'm sorry, sir," I said, "but If I stop to talk, I'll be late, and I can't do that."

"My name is Edmund Goulding," he explained, "and I'm a director here. I'll make a call and I promise you, you won't be in any trouble."

He took my arm and steered me into his office, where he picked up the phone and asked, "Who do I call for you?"

I told him that I was working on *Hollywood Canteen* and that he should let them know where I am and why.

"Oh my God, I'm so sorry!" he apologized. "I thought you were one of our messengers."

"I play one in the movie," I replied.

Mr. Goulding immediately called the stage, introduced himself and proceeded to tell them that he had a movie for me.

"I only need fifteen minutes," he added.

With that, he turned to me and said that he was directing *Of Human Bondage* and he wanted me for one of the important roles in the film.

"Now, you relax, don't worry, go back to work and I'll call Jack and tell him that I found who I was looking for," Mr. Goulding said.

When will I touch down again? I wondered.

I kept working, and Warner Bros. kept picking up my option. It was one movie after another. In between, there were publicity junkets and grooming me for stardom, until the world knew who I was.

There was a very important group of men known as the Motion Picture Exhibitors. They owned the theaters throughout the country. Each year, they ran a poll for the public to choose the stars and newcomers they most wanted to see. Believe it or not, around 1946-47, I was voted in fourth place, and Elizabeth Taylor was fifth.

After five years at Warner Bros. earning $500 a week and sitting on top of the world, life and the studio handed me a very large lemon. Never mind me making lemonade, I was too devastated to do anything but wonder about the next minute, let alone the next year.

Jack Warner's exact words to me were, "I'm sorry, Janis, but we're letting you go."

"But why, Mr. Warner?" I pleaded, tears gathering. "Did I do something wrong?"

"No Janis, you're just too offbeat. We don't know what to do with you when we have Ann Sheridan, Virginia Mayo, Jane Wyman, Joan Crawford and Bette Davis."

There it was again, I thought. *That horrible word. "Offbeat." I wasn't too offbeat for five years*, I thought. *What happened?*

Maybe I was born offbeat, never to be *on* beat.

*Failure is the condiment that gives
success its flavor.
-Truman Capote*

*When speaking of fate, destiny and coincidence, I
cannot ignore the countless components that lead
us to our fate, destiny or coincidence.*

-Janis Paige

Red Skelton

Live by this credo: Have a little laugh at life and look around you for happiness instead of sadness. Laughter has always brought me out of unhappy situations.

—Red Skelton

In 1943, Louis B. Mayer of the famous MGM Studios signed me to a contract and the next day I was learning a song-and-dance number for a picture called *Bathing Beauty* starring Esther Williams and Red Skelton. I wasn't yet 21.

I was a naïve, virginal young woman completely inexperienced in the ways of adulthood, let alone the highly charged atmosphere of Hollywood and the inflated world of motion pictures. I was a rank amateur in everything having to do with sophistication, and I was so naïve that I didn't even know what I didn't know.

I expected the best from everyone. Tacoma taught me that. But like Dorothy when she first viewed Oz and said, "Toto, I've a feeling we're not in Kansas anymore," I was surely not in Tacoma anymore.

Red Skelton and his oftentimes crazy behavior left me terrified. I was also clueless as to why people laughed when I often became the brunt of his remarks. I was taught not to hurt people's feelings but frequently felt embarrassed and hurt myself.

I would learn during my years of working with comics in my nightclub days that they would do almost anything for a laugh, no matter who it hurt. However, as the headliner, I learned that my quick, firm "Knock it off!" made them find another victim.

When Red got into television, I did several of his shows. I was just a comedic foil in his hands, and making people laugh was mother's milk to him. He soon discovered that I could not stop laughing once that laugh bubble burst in me.

From his natural talent at the age of ten, through burlesque, vaudeville, minstrel shows, a few early films and on to TV, Red just became more and more developed. He was ruthless in the laugh department when I came on the show.

When we had a sketch together, I'd take him aside and very seriously ask him not to make me laugh.

"Please, Red," I'd beg, "please just stick to the script. It'll be funny and I'll be able to get my lines out without breaking up. Please, Red."

He'd screw up that clown face of his, assure me that he'd stick to the script, and then all comedy hell would break loose and I'd be gone again.

After the show, Red would always apologize with, "I can't help it, Janis. You're such a great audience, I can't resist."

One of the Skelton shows I did was for Thanksgiving, and Red was going to stuff the turkey. If you can find it somewhere in cyber heaven where the old TV shows go, watch it and discover not only a clown but a comic genius as well.

Richard "Red" Skelton
July 18, 1913 - September 17, 1997

Howard Hughes

*I'm not a paranoid, deranged millionaire.
Goddammit, I'm a billionaire!*

—Howard Hughes

Around 1944, I was summoned to the office of a producer at Warner Bros. The secretary ushered me in and there stood a tall, thin man, dressed in a rather worn beige sport coat, wrinkled jeans and a well-worn shirt with a tie to match.

"Janis, I'd like you to meet Howard Hughes."

In a strange, twangy kind of voice, Mr. Hughes said, "I'm happy to meet you, Janis."

I murmured something in the same genre, wondering all the while, "What am I doing here?"

A bit more small talk followed, and then I was excused, and I left, still wondering.

The next day, the phone rang. My mother answered it, and as she fainted, she breathlessly whispered the words, "Howard Hughes wants to speak with you."

By way of explanation, my mother was enamored of anyone bathed in fame, which did not make her the best judge of one's character. I gave her the *Shhhhhhh!* sign and said into the receiver, "Hello, Mr. Hughes."

"Do you remember me?" he asked. "We met yesterday."

"Of course I remember you," I chuckled.

Howard Hughes then proceeded to ask me to dinner.

I wasn't called to that office for a potential job; I was called there for a potential date. Feminine street smarts had not yet entered my life as I stood there, calmly terrified.

What would happen if I refused?

"Well, what do you say?" he twanged.

Unlike my mother, who would have sold me then and there to the famous Mr. Hughes—believing that I would be set for life and so would she—I hesitated. I did not want to be alone with him, so in my own way, I balked.

I still can't believe I said this, but out of my mouth came the words, "Mr. Hughes--"

"Call me Howard," he corrected.

I started again, "Howard, I don't know you at all. Could I bring my sister?"

Without a moment's hesitation, he said, "Of course, bring her along!"

Greatly relieved, I accepted his invitation.

We lived in a tiny apartment on Rockledge Road off Camrose Drive, near Highland Avenue in Hollywood. It was an old house that was turned into a duplex. We lived upstairs. It was crowded, but cute.

As my sister Betty and I waited all dressed up for dinner, a car drove up. Howard Hughes got out and came to the door. My mother let him in, and I was relieved to see that she didn't curtsy. Meeting the world-famous Mr. Hughes was astoundingly moving for my mother. I was simply nervous.

The evening began for me in quiet disbelief. Mr. Hughes was dressed in the same tacky, unpressed jacket he had worn the day before. The blue pants were clean, but other than that, they looked like they had been slept in.

I don't remember the color of his shirt or tie because all of this elegantly dressed splendor was topped off by a pair of well-worn, rather soiled tennis shoes.

Meanwhile, Betty was decked out in her best dress, high-heeled shoes and a cute little hat. I was similarly dressed. My sister didn't know where to put her look of horror, so she wore it until a strong nudge from me erased it.

Here stood a billionaire, the first one either one of us had ever met, looking like he didn't have two nickels to rub together. I didn't dare look at my mother's face. It was surely a combination of awe and disillusionment.

"We're having dinner in San Francisco," he said, "so we'd better get going."

"Isn't it a little late for dinner in San Francisco?" I answered.

"I guess I should have told you, I'm flying us there. We'll have a nice dinner and then fly home."

Betty and I were on Cloud Nine. No standing in ticket lines for us. Mr. Hughes drove onto the tarmac, parked and, as we walked toward the plane, I wished that all of Tacoma could see us now.

My sister and I were so excited we could hardly breathe. He seated us, fastened our seat belts and moved to the pilot's area. He began to turn things on. Little lights began to flash, and we waited to take off into the wild blue yonder.

Mr. Hughes was obviously having trouble with something, and after about twenty minutes I heard that familiar twang.

"Goddammit!" He turned around and said, "There's something wrong with the radio and we don't fly without a radio. Sorry!"

Our flight and dinner in San Francisco disappeared in a puff of smoke. Our deflation was palpable.

"C'mon, we'll have dinner at the Ambassador Hotel," Mr. Hughes announced. So off we went to the elegant area of the Wilshire District—truly a world unto itself.

On the south side of Wilshire was the gated community of Fremont Place. You needed a passport to enter that little kingdom. Even today, when I need to go back to a comfortable time and place, I buy a few freshly baked doughnuts from Bob's in the Farmer's Market on Third Street and a carton of black coffee. Along with my Jack Russell, Lulu, and my ever-present imagination, I walk, admire and remember.

Here sits the history of the turn of the Twentieth Century. You can still see porticos where the horse-and-buggy-drawn passengers would alight. There are still a few with carriage houses, built to match the main house. So much of our history is lost to the bulldozers and wrecking balls with a deep nod to progress.

What if one day there is nothing left but the ravages of progress? Who will we be then? The people who love and cherish this part of our city remain the caretakers for someone like me.

Gone now are the Brown Derby Restaurant, the Ambassador Hotel, the legendary Cocoanut Grove nightclub, the famed Perino's, and the department stores Bullock's Wilshire and I. Magnin. Gone, too, are the immaculately dressed and well-trained salesladies in Bullock's and I. Magnin.

Instead of turning a page in history forward, I turned it back so that you could better view this three-way dinner date unfolding before us.

As we entered the Ambassador, I could see that Mr. Hughes was no stranger to the place. He was greeted warmly but politely. Everyone around us was dressed in a fashion befitting the locale.

As we approached the Gold Room, Mr. Hughes opened the door to find it completely empty. As we stood there, we must have been a picture for the archives. Two little young ladies, dressed in their best, and a gentleman wearing his wrinkled costume and soiled tennis shoes.

An employee rushed up and assured, "Oh, Mr. Hughes, we're closed today but not to worry, we'll be happy to serve you. I have your usual table ready, right this way."

Without even a tiny glance at Mr. Hughes' attire, we were shown to the table. By the squeeze of our hands, my sister and I knew that we were in Never-Never Land.

When we were seated, the captain gave us huge menus, and of course all we could see were the prices. Mr. Hughes asked if we liked steak. Without a breath, we both agreed. Good lord, who wouldn't want steak from the Ambassador Hotel dining room—free?

There wasn't another person in that huge place except a few waiters scurrying about at the maître d's orders. We only had a sea of white-clothed tables around us, but Betty and I knew that we were dressed befitting that elegant place.

On the other hand, there sat the world-famous Howard Hughes, completely comfortable in his scruffy and unkempt formality. "I guess a billionaire can wear a barrel," I thought.

As the maître d' hovered about, the waiter arranged our plates. Then began what could only be called a kind of ritual. It fascinated me to the point that I don't remember what I ate.

First of all, there was complete silence during dinner. Mr. Hughes began by carefully separating what he always ordered: peas, mashed potatoes and steak. The peas were pushed into their own little room on the china, while the mashed potatoes met the same fate.

He then proceeded to cut his steak into little pieces, separated from the lonely little veggies. Nothing touched anything else. My sister and I were transfixed by this drama unfolding in front of us. He ate silently, first the peas, then the potatoes, and then the steak, completely engrossed until there was not a morsel left of anything.

Like a good little boy, Howard had cleaned his plate.

Today, I believe his behavior is called OCD (short for Obsessive Compulsive Disorder). Back then, the descriptive term was "eccentric." He was all of that but so much more.

Mr. Hughes ordered dessert. Of course, it was something exotic, gorgeous, delicious and unfamiliar to us. That was the beginning of my lifelong love affair with chocolate soufflé. It arrived with a flourish, hot and with the soufflé bathed in chocolate that was definitely not Hershey's.

He patiently waited while we finished our dessert, and finish we did. He asked us if we were ready to leave. I answered that we were, thanked him profusely for a lovely evening, and he drove us home. He was not a man for small talk. He thanked us for joining him, said goodnight and was gone.

My mother breathlessly met us at the door.

"Did he ask you out again?" were the first words out of her mouth.

"Gosh, he's strange," my sister observed, as she related the eating routine.

"What did you talk about?" my mother asked.

"Nothing much," I replied. "He's kind of quiet."

"Are you going to see him again?"

"Mom, I don't know. I don't even know if I want to."

"Don't be silly," she said.

"I'm not, Mom. He's a nice man but kind of creepy."

A few days later, I answered the phone to hear a strange crackly noise and Howard's voice over it.

"I'm in Mexico City, on my way to L.A. I'll be there in about three hours. Will you have dinner with me?"

"Tonight?" I asked.

"Yeah, is that all right?"

I mumbled out an "I guess so" and waited once again for the mysterious Mr. Hughes. When he arrived, he was still wrinkled and wearing those same worn tennis shoes. He was picking me up directly from the flight, and we had dinner in some rather obscure, quiet little place not far from where I lived.

When we were seated, he said, "Tell me about yourself." He seemed interested and not so remote. I hardly had much history, so there wasn't much to tell. I told him where I was born, about Tacoma, about how much I loved my hometown and my grandparents. He asked about my childhood, how I got to Hollywood, etc.

He was much more talkative this time and asked a lot of questions. He told me that he was building an exploratory airplane made of wood and was very animated about the project.

"I'll have to take you flying one of these days."

I told him about my father being a pilot and that I had my first plane ride at the age of four. He asked me what kind of airplane it was.

"I remember my dad calling it 'an old World War I Jenny'," I replied. "It was a two-seater bi-plane. He strapped me in and did figure eights, Immelmann turns, flew upside down, and all I did was scream for more."

"Where's your dad now?" he asked.

"I only remember him one more time and then he was gone," I said. "I don't know where he is. He never came back."

As Mr. Hughes drove me home, I asked him if he had ever married or had children. He said no.

"I had one love in my life," he said, "and between her family and the studio, we parted. Did you ever hear of Billie Dove? She was the most beautiful woman I ever saw, and I'll love her all of my life."

We were silent the rest of the way. He had closed up again.

Mr. Hughes called a few more times, including once from South America. Something about a movie. Then he'd not show up for hours. "Bad weather" or something.

I was too young and inexperienced to know or to understand a relationship with the complicated Howard Hughes. Besides, at twenty-two, I was falling in love every five minutes. I finally wasn't home to receive his calls, and they ended.

When my grandfather was dying, I could not get a seat on a plane because of the priority for our servicemen and women. I called Howard, who owned TWA at the time. I nervously gave my name to the secretary and suddenly I heard him say, "Hello, Janis, how are you?"

I explained the situation, and without hesitation he said, "I'm so sorry. Of course I'll get you home and back. Not to worry."

When I got to the airport, there was my round-trip ticket waiting for me with a note: "If there is anything else that I can do, let me know. Howard."

I was with my grandfather when he died. I would not have made it without the kindness of one Howard Hughes.

If you want to know about sex, you'll have to get it from someone who can speak from experience. An affair with Howard Hughes never crossed my mind. He was, however, brilliant, powerful, courageous, unpredictable and unafraid. Those qualities intrigued me. I also thought he was very decent and very lonely. One often hears that word ("lonely") when describing a genius.

He was a quiet mover and shaker who simply heard the sound of a different drummer. I hope that sound also brought him some happiness and well-earned gratitude.

Howard Hughes
December 24, 1905 – April 5, 1976

Joan Crawford

I never go outside without looking like Joan Crawford, the movie star. If you want to see the girl next door, go next door.

—Joan Crawford

When I became a part of the Warner Bros. roster, there were the leading ladies, the box office stars who could be counted on to sell tickets. No one was bigger than Joan Crawford and Bette Davis.

World War II was on, and certain items were rationed for the war effort, including chrome. This shiny metal was, in essence, a car's jewelry and was always used liberally. The car bumpers were huge and designed to fit their particular model.

It was impressive, to say the least. From the bumper to the radiator to the hood ornament, everything was covered in chrome. In addition to all of this automotive finery, there were the door trims, locks and side strips to protect another car door from marring its beauty.

The cars were simply gorgeous in their chromium splendor. Until the war ended, however, car makers had turned to using a kind of two-by-four plank of wood in place of the bumper. It was painted the color of the car. Ugly but practical.

I had bought a house in the hills above Barham Boulevard, the street that passed by Warner Bros. We had only one car, and needless to say I did not drive it, nor did I know how. My sister and my mother drove, but I wasn't considered reliable enough to drive. So I was dependent on my mother to get me to work and home again.

Walking to work on that busy, winding sidewalk-free thoroughfare was out of the question, so her power and my dependence remained until my revolution of independence came.

My sister had begun to quietly teach me how to drive. Of course, I'd never done it solo. But once on a quiet little street in the Valley, Betty changed seats with me and let me drive. I was jerky and erratic at first, not to mention terribly nervous that we would somehow be found out.

We repeated our driving lesson one more time before my revolt came.

I don't recall what the argument with my mother was about, but it turned into a fight. All I could think about was to get out of the house. The car keys were on the table next to the door. I grabbed them, started the car and began to slowly and carefully drive down the hill to the stoplight below at Barham.

I was shaking as I turned toward the studio gates. The guard at the gate said "Hello," and I headed for my dressing room, driving about two miles an hour.

I saw a parking place and carefully pulled in. I had to straighten the car but hadn't parked before. I'd come this far, however. and if I were careful, I could do this too, I thought. I got it lined up, put it in reverse gear and it shot back like a bullet before it was stopped by the bumper of another car. *Smash.*

"Oh, please God, take me now, what have I done?" I thought, in a panic. I sat in the car waiting for someone to say something, but no one came. I finally got out and dared to look at what damage I had wrought.

It turned out that absolutely nothing had happened to that two-by-four green bumper, but I was not so lucky. We had a pre-war car with chrome, and there was no hiding the mess I'd made. I got back in the car to gently move it away when I saw the name on the dressing room door. It read "Joan Crawford."

I'd hit Joan Crawford's car!

Now what do I do? I was frantic, absolutely terrified and trying to figure out if this was a good time to finally run away from home.

I carefully checked out the impenetrable green bumper and it had not even a hint of a scratch. I knew I had to go home and thanked my lucky stars that I had not damaged Miss Crawford's car. But most of all, I was grateful beyond words that no one saw me, because I didn't have a driver's license.

Imagine the trouble I would have been in. Imagine the headline, *"Warner Bros.' New Young Star Busted For Driving Without a License After Smashing Into Joan Crawford's Car."*

As I made my way oh-so-carefully back up the hill, I readied myself for what I knew would come when mother saw the car. I parked outside the house and went inside to face the music.

"Where have you been?" she demanded. "We've been worried sick. You can't drive. You don't even have a driver's license. Are you crazy?"

"Don't yell at me, Mom!" I shot back. "If someone in this house doesn't teach me how to drive my car, the one I bought, I'll find somebody who will. The back bumper is a little caved in because I hit something when I tried to put it in reverse and didn't know how. I have a right to drive that car. It belongs to me, too."

I never told her I hit Joan Crawford's car. I didn't dare.

The bumper was fixed, and the only price I paid was a cold silent stare. I learned to drive the car because my boyfriend at the time taught me. I don't know which was worse, an impatient and angry mother or an impatient and angry boyfriend.

However, my newfound freedom was worth it all.

Joan Crawford and I became friends, but I always remained a little awestruck. She aged without the facelifts of today while always claiming her fame. I never told her about hitting her car. If she were alive today, I would have admitted it and she'd have had a great laugh about it. Or would she?

Joan had a beautiful home on Bristol Circle in Brentwood, and I'd been invited to a dinner party there. Everyone knew of her fetish for perfection, and it showed.

I wore a gorgeous black dress as befitting the evening and the hostess. I'd also donned a little black hat with a perfectly placed small ostrich feather to the side and slightly over one eye. It made me look very sophisticated and very sexy. Black, closed toe, high-heeled suede pumps completed my outfit.

"You look beautiful," my date said, and off we went.

I did not feel beautiful for long. When we entered Joan's large, rotund foyer, paved in shiny black and white marble, I was asked to remove my shoes so that the floors would not get scratched by my heels. No one had ever asked me to do something so ridiculous.

When my shoes came off, I felt like Margaret Hamilton as she "melted" in *The Wizard of Oz*. "I'm melting, I'm melting," she cried.

My sophistication left me. My sexiness left me. I would have felt much better if my hat had come off, too. Suddenly, I was off balance, feeling humiliated and vulnerable.

Sometime in the Crawford era, I was told that if the help did not care for those floors as per her instructions, she would get down on her hands and knees and shine them herself. Today, we call that OCD. It must have been torturous for Joan to have to live with that, not to mention her children and servants.

There was much more that I never knew, but in those days of ultra-powerful one-man control of the studios, they were also powerful enough to kill any slander about their stars—and did.

Joan was always kind and gracious to me, and I had no reason to doubt her. If her private life was erratic, painful and unacceptable to those around her, the woman she presented to the world was the opposite. She knew how to be the ultimate movie star and never disappointed her fans.

Her contracts with Warner Bros. and Metro had reached their limitations. Hitting forty was the beginning of the age downslide at that time. Thank God that stupid, wasteful mindset has changed greatly. Today, as we grow older and our talent ripens, many of us are given the opportunity to enrich our craft at any age. Finally, the work is being recognized and often honored by our peers, among whom are writers, directors and producers.

In Joan's day, there was a different rule and it was rigid. Only a very few of the so-called leading ladies continued to work beyond the superficial cutoff date.

In 1962, Joan and I worked together in the film *The Caretakers*. While I played a resident in a mental ward, she played a hospital administrator. When I dropped by the set to say hello, she looked every inch the star she always was. She had even worn some of her own gorgeous jewelry.

Joan had met and married a very successful businessman named Alfred Steele, the head of the Pepsi Corporation. She seemed very much in love and genuinely happy.

When my husband Ray and I were married in Nice, France, in 1962, we drove through the lake districts of Italy. When we checked into our hotel in Lugano, there was a huge basket of goodies, a bottle of cold champagne and a sweet note from Joan.

It read: "Darling Janis and Ray: Wishing you the same happiness that I found with Al. My love to you both. Joan."

I never found out how she knew where we were, but she remembered, and I was deeply touched.

Joan lived in New York and we in California, traveling a great deal to Brazil and Europe. When Al died, I began to hear rumors of her taking over Al Steele's corporation and making a lot of unnecessary trouble for everyone. I chose not to comment on my friend. I never saw her much-rumored and discussed behavior, and if I had been victimized by it, I'd have been long gone.

If one takes the time to read her history, they will know how self-made she was. Her fierce determination, courage and guts to become Joan Crawford leaps off the page. There is much to be admired, but in my opinion the price paid for stardom was far too high.

Joan never forgot a Christmas note on her familiar blue stationery. Her final message to me read, "Janis darling. This will be my last Christmas note to you. As ever, love to you, Joan."

She died five months later with so much left unsaid and uncovered.

Joan Crawford
March 23, 1904 - May 10, 1977

Clark Gable

The only reason they come to see me is that I know life is great, and they know I know it.

—Clark Gable

In 1942, after the death of his wife Carole Lombard, Clark Gable enlisted in the Air Force. Lombard died in a plane crash while on a War Bond tour. They were both highly patriotic and began very early on to work for the war effort. He was forty-one, well past the draft age, and heartbroken.

At Officer Training School, Gable finished in thirteen weeks and asked to fly combat missions. They made him an aerial gunner, and because of his experience with a camera, he also became a combat photographer. He flew several missions over Germany and nearly lost his life on one of these bombing raids. He was respected as a soldier and well-liked by his company.

"He wasn't Clark Gable, he was just the same as the rest of us," said one of his fellow flyers.

Because of his age, he decided to retire from his Air Force duties and, at forty-three, with his release papers signed by Captain Ronald Reagan, The King came home.

MGM wanted to welcome him back as only they could. They took over a soundstage and set up long tables bathed in white linen, lovingly set with flowers and individual place settings at intervals along the way. The food was, of course, spectacular.

Everything was exactly as it should have been. After all, it had to be fit for The King. His Metro crew members, camera men, directors, producers, agents, friends and the countless stars with whom he had worked all joined together to say, "We're glad you're back, Clark. Welcome home!"

Metro had mailed out printed invitations, and I got one, too. They also had gone to great lengths to set up place cards so that we all knew where to sit. When I found my way in and sat down, I was welcomed by Greer Garson and Jack Oakie sitting across the table from me. Walter Pidgeon was next to me.

Imagine having lunch with Mr. and Mrs. Miniver!

The room was filled with talk and laughter and the anticipation of seeing Clark Gable again. Suddenly, the talk and laughter began to fade while heads turned toward the door. Oh my God, there he stood in our stunned silence. Then an explosive roar rose up and everyone stood and gave him their hearts.

As long as I live, I will never forget how he looked. He wasn't wearing his brass-filled officer's uniform. Instead, he was dressed in one of those beautiful khaki-colored shirts and trousers that the officers wore. He had his cap in his hand and the biggest grin I ever saw, topped off of course by his famous dimples.

I could understand why people described him as bigger-than-life and how he filled a room. No wonder men and women alike adored him. He possessed a rare masculine sex appeal that seemed to reach out and touch you—and only *you*. He was tall, strongly built, with the broadest shoulders I had ever seen. No padding in that shirt. He had a beautifully shaped head that sat comfortably on his muscular body.

I was a very young, unsophisticated, unworldly twenty-two-year-old, and I was gone, bonkers, mesmerized and over the moon for him. My heart turned over, righted itself after a few tries, and I was his.

Don't get too excited, I told myself. He had a reputation for bedding his co-stars and I never got any closer than seeing him that memorable and historic day when he came home to MGM.

His cast always praised him for being on time, knowing his lines and being a professional to his bones. He was such a good actor that he was not always lauded for his acting ability. He must have had something extraordinary, though. He won three Oscars. He was eternally exciting and never let us down. There was always only one Clark Gable, never duplicated.

I remember that I wore a new Mr. John hat that day. It was small with flowers, and it tied under my chin with a green satin ribbon. Perhaps, if he had seen my beautiful little hat and the look of love on my face, I would have had the chance to know him better.

He left a lasting impression on me that is still alive and well, with my thoughts still concentrated on the impossible possibilities of the what-ifs. The closest I ever got to him was when he paid his respects to every single person there.

When he reached Greer Garson, she got a hug. I got a dimpled "Hello there." My momentary mental fling with The King always stayed with me, tucked away in my twenty-two-year-old memory. As I write of him, there is no chance of it ever fading away.

No wonder he was chosen to play Rhett Butler. Clark Gable *was* Rhett Butler!

Whenever *Gone with the Wind* is showing, I'm compelled to stop whatever I'm doing, sit down and wait for that first shot of him. As Scarlett ascends the elegant and graceful stairway in Twelve Oaks, she glances back and says to a young woman beside her, "That man is looking at me as if I have no clothes on."

No words are necessary, just *that look* and *those dimples*.

Clark Gable
February 1, 1901 – November 16, 1960

Every picture I make, every experience of my
private life, every lesson I learn, these are the keys
to my future. And I have faith in it.

Frank Sinatra

You gotta love livin', baby,
'cause dyin' is a pain in the ass.
—Frank Sinatra

Unforgettable was one Frank Sinatra. He left our world too many years ago, but we still have him through his remarkable voice. He was bigger than life, always to be remembered, never forgotten. Hearing a Sinatra song today always invokes memories of an old love, a lost love, life's ennui and his always amazing ability to make us yearn for another time.

In 1946, Warner Bros. sent me to New York City. At that time, these trips were called publicity tours. They had steadily been building me as one of their young stars, and now I was ready to represent the Brothers Warner. No matter how they "built" me, though, I was still a kid from Tacoma, unsophisticated, naïve, excited and totally unaware of what was ahead.

If the studios invested in you, it was first class all the way. They began to outfit me for my trip in that fantasy world of the wardrobe department. There, I was loaned my clothes, jewelry and gown for my appearance at the Strand Theatre in Times Square.

Along with all of this borrowed finery went a rented mink coat. I looked absolutely gorgeous, and had I not been tethered by gravity, I would have flown on my imaginary wings into the wild blue yonder. Excitement wasn't a big enough word for the joy flooding through me.

Next came my borrowed luggage, because I had none of my own. The final step was my visit to the publicity department and the itinerary for the journey. I had been wrapped in tissue paper, tied with a ribbon and protected as a Warner Bros. star. In my secret heart, the cherry on the cake was that I would be on my own, so to speak, for the first time in my life. Oh, it was heady stuff!

We had two trains, The Chief and The Super Chief. I was to travel by Super Chief. This mode of transport was luxurious beyond your imagination. Even today, I can recall my exhilaration and disbelief at the size of the compartment I had all to myself.

I was headed to Chicago, where I would be met by a lovely woman named Lucia Perrigo, the Warner Bros. publicity representative in Chicago. She would board the train and accompany me to New York City for my week there.

All of this attention and care made me feel like a person I had never known.

My giddy excitement was understandable. I had never been on a train. I had never seen New York City. And I had never been by myself anywhere. There was nothing I wanted that I didn't have. Maybe I was dressed in borrowed finery, but for now, everything was mine—and my beautiful coach had not turned into a pumpkin yet.

As we sped through the country, I remembered the Great Depression and the holes in the soles of my Buster Browns. I had come an awfully long way from those humbling days.

The soft-voiced, uniformed porter announced that the dining car was open and ready to serve lunch. I was hungry, as usual, and made my way to a sight I can still see in my mind today. For those of you who travel Amtrak, I will now make you mourn for the trains of long ago.

The first things I saw were the white-clothed tables, with china, glassware, real hotel silver and tiny vases of flowers on each table. Everyone was warmly greeted by white-jacketed waiters who helped with the menu, making suggestions and finally declaring, "You made a very good choice, Miss Paige."

I still wonder if I made the choice or he did. I simply didn't care.

The Super Chief served gourmet food, cooked in a narrow, train-sized kitchen and presented looking like the cover picture on *Bon Appetit*. In the Forties, there was still time for civility and any other behavior was unthinkable, let alone acceptable. I was in heaven!

Lucia met me in Chicago as planned. The Super Chief took on its load of the famous and delectable Lake Michigan whitefish, and we were on our way for the overnight trip to New York City.

We detrained the following day and dodged our way through crowds of people seemingly always in a hurry. Suddenly, I stopped. I was standing in Grand Central Station, its size dwarfing me while I stood staring at the beautiful ceiling and the wonder of this place that helped trains and people come and go.

I grew up with the radio, and my imagination was all that I had to help me see those places I could only dream about. We had a radio drama called *Grand Central Station*, and I recalled the opening words of that show. The porter would always announce in a loud voice, "Grand Central Station!" and the drama would begin.

There were so many firsts in my young life, I could hardly breathe, much less keep track.

Lucia led me to our vehicle waiting outside. It wasn't like any car I knew. First of all, it was about a mile long, shiny black and with a uniformed man in the driver's seat.

"Good morning, Miss Perrigo," the driver said to Lucia. "Good morning, Miss Paige," he said to me, "welcome to New York City."

He opened the door for us as Lucia said, "We're going to The Gotham." Off we went, driving through the biggest city I had ever seen, with the tallest buildings and people who all seemed to know exactly where they were going.

If I hadn't been so excited, I would have had time to be intimidated.

After seemingly no time had passed, the driver announced, "Here we are, Miss Perrigo."

The first thing I saw was the red carpet and the mirrored, shiny brass railings. There were four or five steps to the lobby of The Gotham.

"Here I go again," I thought. "This is my first hotel."

All of the bellhops wore uniforms. The Gotham's were burgundy colored with lots of brass buttons. Lucia signed us in and then we were in the elevator, going up to my room.

Did I say "my room"? When they opened the door, I was standing in a marble-floored foyer, with a table holding a huge vase of flowers. Next was a giant living room, a guest room, two bathrooms and my master suite. I grew up with five people using one tiny bathroom for years, and believe me, I could have lived in the one that belonged to me in The Gotham.

Oh, did I mention that the guest room had a bathroom, too? I swear that my suite was bigger than the entire house in which I grew up.

While I was unpacking, Graham arrived. He was New York City's counterpart to Lucia in Chicago for Warner Bros. Now I would have two professionals to help me through the haze of the maze I was in at this new and unfamiliar life I was experiencing.

Both Lucia and Graham became my friends for a long time, enriching my very new and untried steps into what could have been a shaky future.

Because I could sing and entertain, the studio sent me to be part of a new movie opening during my five-day stint at The Strand Theatre. It was my first time on a stage in New York City, and all went very well. The days flew by, filled as they were with countless interviews, along with the theatre appearances and those amazing audiences. It was all so new and thrilling that my feet never seemed to touch the ground.

One morning a few days after I finished my stint at The Strand, and as I began to awaken, I listened for the music of hustle and bustle that defines New York City. But that familiar hum was strangely absent.

As high as my suite was, I could still always hear the New York traffic as it started its day. I lay there for a while, reliving my hectic but electrifying time in the city, when I really began to wonder why it remained so quiet outside.

I went to the window and saw a rather empty Fifth Avenue. Very few cars, and very few people. Very strange.

"What day is this?" I wondered. I had completely lost track of what day it was or even what year. I was having the experience of my life, so who cared? As I looked out the window, the doorbell rang. When I opened it, there stood my favorite bellhop.

"Good Morning, Miss Paige," he greeted me. "Before I leave for the day, do you need anything?"

"Yes," I said. "Please tell me, what day is this?"

He gave me a funny look and then replied, "Why, it's Thanksgiving, Miss Paige. Aren't you going anywhere to celebrate?"

I could hardly answer him. I covered as best I could by saying that this is a "family" day and my family is in California.

"I guess everyone thought I had somewhere to go," I said. "Well, I'm in luck, I haven't had a single moment to see New York City, and that is exactly what I'm going to do today. I can't wait!"

"Well, in case you don't get turkey, I'm going to bring you a turkey sandwich." And he did.

I quickly dressed and readied for my big Thanksgiving Day adventure. I went back to the window and started to plan my day. I know this will come as a shock, but this happened more than seventy years ago, and we had no toys to constantly remind us of the time, place, date or where we would be in the next minute or two.

No, there was just me and the realization that this was another first. I had never been away from home on a holiday, and I guess I missed my grandmother's stuffing and watching my grandfather carve the bird. Remembering him now, and the praise that followed his expertise, was probably his own fifteen minutes of fame. The man asked for so little.

I looked up and down Fifth Avenue, not knowing uptown from down or east from west.

"What if I get lost?" I wondered, not remembering that this was America and we spoke English, even in New York City. I could always ask for directions. Then I remembered my mother's warning before I left, that there were "white slavers" in New York.

"You have to be very careful," she cautioned.

Oh, Mom, you wouldn't know a "white slaver" if he came up and bit you and neither would I, I thought. When will you ever knock off the drama? Why do you always have to scare me instead of telling me to just have a good time?

These were the thoughts racing through my mind when the phone suddenly rang, jarring me from my daydream.

"Who can that be?" I said to no one.

"Hello?" I answered.

"Is this Janis Paige?" a male voice inquired.

"Yes, I'm Janis," I answered.

"Well, Janis, this is Frank Sinatra."

"Who?" I asked, not believing my ears.

"Frank Sinatra," he repeated.

After I caught my breath, I said, "Oh c'mon, you're not Frank Sinatra. I don't even know Frank Sinatra. I've never even *met* Frank Sinatra. Who is this? Stop teasing me!"

A soft laugh and then, "Well Janis, this *is* Frank Sinatra. I heard you were alone today."

"How did he know that?" I mouthed.

"I'm at the Latin Quarter doing my show and I thought it would be nice if you could join us," the man claiming to be Frank Sinatra continued. "You could see the show, have dinner and not be alone on Thanksgiving. Whadda ya say?"

When I picked myself up off of the floor, the voice on the phone became more and more familiar and I began to believe that he really *was* Frank Sinatra. My reverie was interrupted by, "Now, it's cold outside. Grab your coat and go to the lobby. A man called Jilly will pick you up and bring you back to the apartment. You'll meet my wife, Nancy, and a small group of friends. I'll see you soon."

Is this real? I pondered as I put on my rented mink coat. *I'll either disappear forever, or I'll be able to tell everyone about a very special Thanksgiving Day,* I figured. When I reached the lobby, it wasn't but a few minutes before a man came through the swinging doors and promptly announced, "Hi, Janis, I'm Jilly. Let's go see Frank."

As we walked out the door, there waited my second limo of the trip and off we went. I could be wrong about this, but I think Frank lived at the Sherry-Netherland, another beautiful New York City hotel.

Jilly and I got in the elevator, he pushed a button and when we got out, I could hear voices through an open door. Jilly guided me in, and there he was. True to his word, it was Frank Sinatra. His wife Nancy said, "There's Janis" and my entrance was followed by a warm hug from Frank.

"Come meet my wife," he said. Nancy welcomed me, saying, "We're glad you can join us, Janis." Frank introduced me to the rest of his friends and very soon, I began to relax. Awestruck as I was and still pinching myself, Frank, Nancy and his friends made me feel as if they'd known me for years. Everything seemed so incredibly easy.

Our table at The Latin Quarter was big and right smack in front of where Frank performed. There he was, doing what he did best. His famous Sinatra charisma, charm and talent spread throughout the packed room.

We had a beautiful dinner and then stayed for the second show. When it was over and we were waiting for Frank, I realized that I had been gone for hours. I felt that I should excuse myself and not wear out my welcome, so to speak. When Frank joined us, I told him how grateful I was for his generosity and thoughtfulness, but it was getting late and I should end this spectacular day and evening.

"Not yet," he said. "It's still early and we're all going back to the apartment to have a bite and relax. Don't worry, we'll get you home."

The next time I looked at my watch, it was two-thirty in the morning and well past my bedtime. Again, I made my way to Frank, always rather tongue-tied when trying to express my feelings. He thanked me for joining them and sharing their Thanksgiving. If he'd only known that if not for him, my Thanksgiving dinner would have been a turkey sandwich, eaten alone.

As I said my goodbyes to everyone, and just before Jilly and I left, I heard Nancy quietly say, "Please, honey, get some sleep. It's late."

"I'm not tired yet," Frank said. "Leave me alone."

Why do we always seem to know better than those who love and care for us? I've never been able to figure out that one.

Unlike some members of the press, the people who wrote unwarranted books about him and the gossip lovers, I never met anyone who didn't love and respect Frank Sinatra.

He quietly took care of sick and out-of-work actors and entertainers, and when Sammy Davis Jr. got a chance to play Las Vegas with Frank, he had a problem. Being black, Sammy could work the club, but he had to live in the area of Las Vegas that allowed blacks. Until Frank heard about Sammy, it was an unwritten rule. But it all changed with Frank. He didn't have to say much. He simply went to the bosses, and after a short conversation, he declared, "No Sammy, no Frankie!" The "rule" was changed forever.

Through the years, I would run into Frank from time to time—at a dinner party, or a musical event where he would be appearing. If I was alone, he was always the one to seat me for dinner, announcing the wine for the evening and his recommendation.

"You choose," I'd always answer.

The next thing I knew, there was a glass of wine beside my plate, the one that Frank liked.

The last time I saw Frank perform, his son, Frank Jr., was conducting for him. As I watched them work together, I saw and felt such a mutual admiration for each other. Frank Jr. conducted with the sensitivity that comes from knowing someone deeply. He musically "breathed" with his father.

It was a beautiful evening and it warmed my heart, as did any and all memories of one irreplaceable Frank Sinatra.

Frank Sinatra
December 12, 1918 - May 14, 1998

Nothing anybody's said or written about me
ever bothers me, except when it does.

A First Marriage

> *Men marry women with the hope they will never change. Women marry men with the hope they will change. Invariably, they are both disappointed.*
>
> —Albert Einstein

In 1947, the studio sent me to San Francisco on a promotional tour for one of their films. When I came off the stage one night at the beautiful old Golden Gate Theatre, I was introduced to Frank Martinelli Jr. He was tall, blond, handsome and charming, with the sophistication that came from living in that extraordinary city and the trappings that went with it all.

"I'm a big fan," he said, "and I'm about to ask you out after your last show." He added with a laugh, "I come with references. My friend here can vouch for me."

He was very charming, and I said, "Yes."

Over a glass of champagne and some utterly delicious little things filled with cheese, we got to know one another. I learned about the Martinelli family, the famous Bal Tabarin nightclub that the family owned, his love of San Francisco and his crush on me. There was an immediate attraction not only to him but to San Francisco as well. They were both seductive.

I met his mother, father, sister and their beautiful, old home at the top of Greenwich Street in Russian Hill. It was three stories high, with a breathtaking view of the Bay, the bridges and Alcatraz with its infamous guests. At the bottom of the hill was North Beach and the Bal Tabarin club, with its stellar list of the world's great entertainers. It was there that I met Sophie Tucker, Joe E. Lewis, Tony Martin (who was discovered there) and the unforgettable Ted Lewis, the "Me and My Shadow" man.

The Martinelli family came from Northern Italy, around Lucca. Frank's father, Frank Sr., was handsome, sophisticated, blue-eyed and dark-haired. He spoke fluent Italian and English and didn't seem to like me. It was like he was saying, "She's an actress, what does she want from us?"

The food at the club was spectacular, managed by Frank's father. His partner, Tom Gerun, was responsible for the talent and show end of the operation.

I still can't figure out if I fell in love with Frank or with his mother. Her name was Irene, and I'll never forget her as long as I live. She had suffered a stroke and her right side was fairly useless. She had been a gourmet cook and—right arm or not—she still was. It was in Irene's kitchen that I had my first cup of real coffee, freshly ground, its irresistible aroma permeating the morning. My family drank Hills Bros. that came in a can.

Every day found Irene up with the dawn, squeezing fresh grapefruit juice, her heavenly coffee ready and waiting with some kind of delicious bread from North Beach. If you've never had fresh San Francisco sourdough, lightly toasted with homemade marmalade, you haven't begun to live.

Everyone sat down in the dining room to eat. Irene was formal in that respect, and her table was always set with china, silver and crystal ready for her feasts. These were always accompanied by Frank Sr.'s choice of his latest discovery in support of California's burgeoning wine industry. Until I met the Martinelli family, I had never had a glass of wine. Beer was Tacoma's drink, and there wasn't much of that.

Oh, how we dined! Through my Martinelli family education, I learned to appreciate these additions to my palate. I was surrounded by gourmands, always urging me to taste everything, even things I'd never before heard of. We chatted, laughed and solved the woes of the world over Irene's spectacular food. She always ended dinner with her split of sweet wine or champagne.

Along with her guts and grit, kindness and generosity, she was blessed with a sensational sense of humor. She dearly loved to laugh, which she did often. How Irene managed to accomplish so much was inspiring. Shall we talk about overcoming? She could have given lessons. And oh, did Irene love her kids. They got anything they wanted and could do no wrong.

It wasn't long before I was regularly visiting Frank and his family. Long distance romances can be difficult, but not so, ours. On the contrary, it was romantic and exciting, and everything seemed just as it should be.

I had never known anything like the Martinelli style of living, and we soon began talking marriage plans. We were both youthful idiots, and like so many other youthful idiots, common sense was adrift in our void.

Irene lavished a great deal of love on me and was demonstrative in her feelings, always letting me know how loved I was. I came from the opposite extreme. Everything was so new, and I was a sponge, soaking up all she had to give me. She was definitely the hub of the family, and she made everything work.

She had two children. Besides Frank Jr., there was her daughter Tosca, who was leaving for college the day we met, so I never got to know her. There was, however, no question that Frankie was the apple of her eye. I saw this very early on and wondered at why she so seemed to spoil him.

Perhaps it was because Frank and his father didn't get along. Frank Sr.'s family was first generation Italian in San Francisco. There was love there but I also felt an underlying friction, too. Frank's father did not trust me, and my mother hated Frank. What a perfect way to begin a marriage.

Of course, we ignored the obvious obstacles and married on December 27, 1947, in The Little Church in the Valley.

Unlike today, when everyone lets everything hang out, it was the last thing we would do. No matter how unhappy, unsure, disappointed, disillusioned or hurt we were, we kept quiet. At least I did. So many times, I wondered if I had made a mistake. Well, if I had, it was mine.

What to do about it now? I was between a rock and a hard place, but I grew up that way. I was in familiar territory, but as usual, I was shaky and insecure.

I kept working at Warner Bros. and he was always looking for that big break. To me, it seemed like pie in the sky stuff, while Frank's mother kept quietly sending him cash. It bothered me, but it didn't seem to bother him. Nothing, in fact, seemed to bother him.

"Don't you ever worry about anything?" I'd ask.

"Like what?" he'd ask back.

There was no therapist to help me answer why I was losing respect, not only for Frank but for myself as well. When I look back on that time, I know that a big part of marrying was to get away from home. Naturally, I never knew that. But let's face it, the truth remained the truth.

I kept all of these feelings from Irene. I couldn't bear hurting her. We were all mixed up in the same problem, but for different reasons—none of which we wanted to admit.

Instead of those famous words, "I love you, will you marry me?" a better question would be, "Will you fix me?"

The truth, however, is that my job was not to fix him, and his job was not to fix me. Whatever problems, neuroses, insecurities, etc., there are cannot be fixed by getting married. Often, in fact, it's just the opposite. A marriage merely exacerbates the individual problems both parties bring into the union, and we were uneducated, unaware and oblivious to a solution.

I wasn't his problem, and he wasn't mine. Until we understood where the real trouble lay, the one seeming to cause the pain will continue to do so until the real truth comes out.

If marriage could talk, it would surely say the following: *"What the hell do you want from me? I'm doing my best to handle your individual needs, wants, demands, passive-aggressive behavior, moods, demands, anger and that old, often abused dumpster called sex. When you find the answers to my questions, try it again. Until then, knock it off, I have a headache."*

With all of the turmoil, doubts, disappointments, anger, hurts and self-destructive behavior on both sides, I owe a debt of gratitude to Frank. He made me go to Rome, where I began to discover a new life and the beginning knowledge and the courage to eventually live it. He forced me to think about the personal quagmire my life had become and to find that small but glimmering light that began to expose new roads toward the future.

After returning from Rome and leaving 1949 to history, I found myself in vaudeville and nightclubs, on my own again. I was booked for a week in Miami, and along with my usual travel sticker-covered baggage, I also packed my marital problems and what to do about them.

In other words, everything was status quo.

On the bill was a newly successful singer who was funny, warm, attentive and all-around attractive. I was accustomed to fending off inappropriate advances, and so far, I'd had no trouble with him.

I was getting ready for one of our four shows a day when he passed by and said, "Hi Janis, you're here early."

"I'm always early," I replied. "I love to be here before the theatre wakes up, so to speak. I guess I love all of the ghosts."

I turned back to finish putting my hair in curlers when I heard the door close, the lock click and, before I could ask, "What are you doing?," I was involved in a long, deep and knee-shaking kiss. I did not resist him, nor did I understand what was happening to me. The result was something he called an "orgasm."

"It's about time," he said, and quietly left. I'd never even heard the word before, let alone experienced one.

My behavior that morning was so unlike the woman I thought I knew that I became a mass of guilt, shame and embarrassment. These emotions were made even more unbearable when they were accompanied by a sense of curiosity about this newfound and undiscovered part of myself.

My "sin" was demanding a lot of me, and I didn't have a clue as to how to solve anything. Except for the shows, I finished my week behind closed and locked dressing room doors. Again, there was no place to run, and now another problem to add to my growing list of lies in my life.

A growing distance between Frank and me became the unspoken norm as I continued to work and to wonder and worry about the time when I'd find the guts to face the truth about everything.

As it happens, 1950 consisted of life piling on me even as I cried "Uncle!" over and over again. My work was always a kind of panacea between life's challenges and onslaughts, many of them caused by my hiding the truth that percolated within me.

Ultimately, my way didn't work, and near the end of the year, I asked Frank for a divorce. It was countered with a plea for a separation, but no divorce.

There was no moving him, so I relented. He lived in California and I in New York. I insisted that we sell the house no matter what transpired. It's not my home anyway, I said, and it's one less rent to pay.

"I'll take care of that, Jan, and thanks," Frank finally said.

"For what?" I asked.

"For getting a separation and not a divorce."

When I hung up the phone that day. I knew that I had taken on another lie.

In 2010, I was performing at the Razz Room in San Francisco. All I could think about was to see that house on Greenwich Street one more time. We drove by, and as I looked down Russian Hill, I knew the house was gone. The cement lions guarding the door were no longer there. Nothing was there, in fact, except for a new, almost invisible house, set back from the street behind an iron fence and locked gate. There were trees and a garden where our house had stood.

Thomas Wolfe was right. You can't go home again. Life doesn't stop for yesterdays.

Frank L. Martinelli Jr.
June 9, 1922 - July 1, 2000

Bette Davis

To fulfill a dream, to be allowed to sweat over lonely labor, to be able to create, these are the meat and potatoes of life. The money is the gravy.

—Bette Davis

"Janis dear, I miss you."

There it was in 1960, sounding the same as the first time I heard it. Here was the irreplaceable, unforgettable and often mimicked voice of my friend Bette Davis: "I've rented a house in Holmby Hills. Come to lunch."

My excitement at the prospect of seeing her again was much the same as the first day we met.

That year was 1948, and the film was *Winter Meeting*. She didn't like the script, did not want the new and very untried leading man and did not want to do the picture. All of this joined her fight with Jack L. Warner about her work rights.

Miss Davis was the reigning female star on the Warner lot, but she was still a contract player and was expected to fulfill her contractual obligations. She was tired of not having choices over her material, loan-outs and the same salary made by her male counterparts.

Her battle for more control over her career was well known on and off the soundstage. Playing ditzy-but-likable came easily to me, so here I was, playing a rather ditzy secretary in a Bette Davis movie.

Stage 18 was known as The Bette Davis Soundstage. Everything I'd ever heard about her fueled my admiration for her work ethic, and the mystery always surrounding someone with her fame was about to become a part of my life. I just didn't know it then.

I was always letter-perfect with my lines, but I rehearsed what I'd say to her and how I'd act while at the same time being scared to death.

"Ready, Janis?" the assistant asked.

As I followed him to the set, I heard that one-and-only voice first. She was being lit for her close-up and talking to the cameraman. There she sat in a perfect replica of the world-famous Broadway restaurant Sardi's. I had been there once and was awestruck at what the studios could build.

The assistant's voice prodded me into reality when he said, "Let's meet Miss Davis."

All of my rehearsing went out the window when she stuck out her hand and said, "Good morning, Janis. Welcome."

I said something that sounded like, "I'm so pleased to meet you, Miss Davis."

"Oh, call me Bette, Janis. Our next scene is here. Why don't you sit down?"

I slid into that familiar Sardi's booth and simply loved one Bette Davis on sight. There I was, acting with this Oscar winner and feeling almost comfortable with her.

When we finished, Miss Davis patted my hand and said, "You're very good, you know." I said a quiet "Thank you" and left, completely stunned.

No matter her contractual problems, her seeming disappointments with the script, leading man and even the director, I never saw Miss Davis as anything other than professional.

Even female stars like Bette Davis, Olivia de Havilland and Joan Crawford lived and worked in a male-dominated profession. I don't remember one titled female executive in the Forties except for Ida Koverman. She was the assistant to Louis B. Mayer, the head of Metro-Goldwyn-Mayer.

She was powerful, influential, respected and smart, but the operative word was still "assistant."

Every studio had its glass ceiling, and these quiet, pioneering movers-and-shakers helped to crack it for those who followed.

I remember when Ida Lupino wanted to direct and the word was, "But she's a woman. What does she know about directing?" She did it anyway, and to hell with what "they" said. They soon found out that she was very good and became the first female director on the Warner lot.

So, here's a deep bow of gratitude to the brave beginners whose courage to jump without a net paved the road for those of us who benefited from their dedication to a cause whose time had come.

For me and others, the process of grooming for stardom involved a variety of talented and caring women. They were the acting teachers, singing coaches and wardrobe designers like Leah Rhodes, Helen Rose and Edith Head. They had to be better than best on the screen. They engineered a way to hide any figure faults that one might have, and we all looked perfect because of them.

Fast forward to 1960. My heart was beating out of my chest as I pulled into the driveway of a lovely two-storied home. I rang the bell and Bette opened the door, greeting me with a big hug and a bigger smile.

Bette was in reality a lot smaller than she looked on the screen. It was strange, because she filled each part so completely that she always looked tall.

"C'mon, Janis," she began, "lunch is ready, and we have a lot to talk about."

She was very upbeat and looked great, wearing a skirt, a silk blouse that outlined her famous chest and high heels that clicked on the wooden floor as I followed that walk belonging only to her.

"I thought we'd eat in our cute little breakfast room," Bette suggested. "The dining room is so big."

I met Bette's daughter and her housekeeper and sat down. I couldn't take my eyes off her. She had a fierce energy that fascinated me. As I watched her fussing over our food, I thought, *Bette Davis and I are having lunch together. What a memory this will be.* And it was.

Bette asked me what I was doing. I told her that I was filming *Please Don't Eat the Daisies* with Doris Day and David Niven, and loving it.

"I don't have a scene with Doris," I told her, "but I love working with David. He's funny, generous and an all-around nice man."

"Just don't fall in love with him," she warned with a laugh. "He's still an actor."

I asked her about her plans and—with that Bette Davis determination—she informed me that she had "turned this place into a health spa. By the time Gary Merrill and I were divorced, I felt untalented, unattractive, incapable and completely worthless. I will never allow another man to make me feel that way again. I don't think I'm very good at choosing a mate."

Bette continued, "I thank God for my kids, I can't imagine my life without them, but I couldn't make this last marriage work, either. Maybe I'm just no good at it."

There wasn't a moment of self-pity in her words. I reminded her that there were two people involved in what can be an incredibly complicated relationship.

"Well, from now on," she replied, "I'm concentrating on us. I'm going back to work and raising my kids, and I'm ready!"

We spoke of many subjects, including me. I brought her up to date with me both personally and with my career. She was always interested, interesting and very literate.

I never knew the Bette Davis of her daughter's book about life with her mother. I didn't want to. The Bette I knew was open, educated, opinionated and very articulate. I'll leave it that way.

As the years passed, Bette continued to work and performed some absolutely marvelous roles. She defied age like no female star I've ever known. During the Golden Age of Motion Pictures, forty was usually the cutoff to continue to play leading ladies. It was brutal and unnecessary, but it was the unspoken and unwritten rule of its time. Only a very few managed to allow their public to see them age as they committed the sin of getting older. Bette was one.

I'm so grateful that I never quit. Now, I've been around long enough to realize and experience the fact that age has a place in our profession. It's finally being respected and nurtured with many of what used to be called over-the-hill actresses now winning Oscars and Emmys. Bette Davis was my first introduction to one of these remarkable creatures.

My career took me all over the world, and except for those times when we would be together at one of those star-filled benefits, I'd lose track of Bette. Each time we reconnected, she'd give me one of those hugs of hers, look me straight in the eyes and say, "Well, Janis darling, it's a whole new world, isn't it?"

She was older each time, but there was no artifice, no surgery, nothing to hide that force living inside.

The last time I saw her, breast cancer had taken a terrible toll physically. But when we sat together and spoke, her voice was strong, and out came those words that I knew so well.

"Well, Janis darling, it's a whole new world, isn't it?"

I assured her that I longed for just part of the past, but progress wouldn't allow it.

She seemed restless, looking around the room.

"Are you all right, honey?" I asked.

Bette took my hand and said, "Do you mind, Janis, dear? I see many old friends here tonight, and I want to say hello."

"They'll love seeing you, Bette, as I do."

I kissed her on the cheek and watched her walk to another table. Sadness filled my heart.

It was the last time I saw her. She died shortly after that evening. But she died as she had lived, uncompromisingly, brave and dedicated to her craft. She was a wonderful friend to me. I couldn't have asked for more.

If there were one word to describe Bette, it would be powerful.

Bette Davis
April 8, 1908 – October 6, 1989

There are new words that exclude everybody. Give me the good old days of heroes and villains, people you can bravo or hiss. There was a truth to them that all of the slick credulity of today can't touch.

Rome

*The Creator made Italy from designs
by Michelangelo.*

—Mark Twain

After Warner Bros. let me go in 1949, I was waiting for the phone to ring—when it did.

It was producer Mike Frankovich, offering me a movie to be filmed in Rome, Italy. He had taken over the Scalera Studios, and he and his wife, actress Binnie Barnes, had moved there.

Mike might as well have asked me to go to the moon. The moon and Rome were the same to me. They were both far, far away. I had never been out of the United States during my twenty-seven years of life. Any travel sophistication had not yet discovered me.

The most valuable thing my husband, Frank, ever did was to make me say "Yes" to the job. Mike told me that I would only be there for six weeks and not to worry about anything. He and Binnie would take care of it all.

As I readied for our journey, all the usual self-doubts reared up before me again, and I constantly had to push them aside. Contracts were signed, bags were packed and before I could overthink it, we were on our way. "So far, far away," I whispered to myself.

On the flight over, the pilot's voice was loud and clear.

"There are storms ahead, and we're forced to land in Nova Scotia. Please fasten your seat belts."

Nova Scotia, I thought. *That's up by Newfoundland. What are we doing up there?*

Twenty hours later, we took off, but not before we had met and eaten with hundreds of other world-weary travelers in the same bad weather spot as we were.

The poor Nova Scotians who had to serve and feed us were not happy Nova Scotians. Especially when they ran out of food. It was the first of June and freezing cold up there.

Twenty-three hours later, a warm, flower-filled Italian-speaking Rome said, "*Buongiorno!*," put his arms around me, and I was a smitten fool. What had happened to me? I didn't much care. I was in love, deeply and abidingly. No schoolgirl's first love crush. Not even first-marriage love. No, Rome had found me, and I had found Rome. It was a different love at first sight. The real thing.

Mike and Binnie had leased a beautiful apartment at 37 Via Basento, in the lovely Parioli district of Rome. It belonged to the mistress of Signore Scalera, who owned the studio where we would film the movie.

Mistress and wife, lover and husband were part of the Italian lexicon, and one became accustomed to hearing it. It was so unlike America in those days. We weren't much different, I guess; we just hid everything.

Never had I seen anything like our new home. There were hand-painted tiles in the large and lavish bathroom. The tub was extravagantly large. and besides the loo there was a strange-looking piece of plumbing called a bidet. I pretended that I knew what it was and ignored my own curiosity. There was something about the darned thing that I just found embarrassing.

Antiques were everywhere you looked. and whoever decorated the woman's home spared no expense. They had immaculate taste and obviously the money to match.

As we walked down the hall, a sweet-faced Italian woman appeared and nervously greeted us. In her best Italian, she told us that she was Anna and that she went with the apartment. She lived in a little room off the kitchen with her six-year-old son. Compared to the apartment above, the kitchen was almost archaic, but she managed without a word of complaint.

When my Italian got better, I asked Anna about her husband.

"*È morto in guerra,*" came the simple words, meaning, "He died in the war."

"I'm so sorry, Anna," I said.

"*Grazie tanto, Signora, grazie, grazie!*"

And so, we started our Italian life, and I was right. It was on the moon. It couldn't have been farther from my tiny childhood home or Ninth and Market in Tacoma, across from the First Baptist Church.

One day, I screwed up my courage and asked Anna about the bidet. She giggled, blushed profusely and then proceeded to show me, in detail, how it was used. Not only were the Italians romantic, but pragmatic as well.

I could not get enough of our apartment, and I would often wander through in disbelief at some undiscovered treasure. When I saw the bedroom, I was speechless. The walls were covered in a soft, almost indescribable green silk.

When I visited Venice some years later, I found almost the same color with its mysterious patina on the walls of the famous Ca' Rezzonico on the Grand Canal. It was a color I would see often in Italy, but for some reason it was still unknown to me. I was never able to duplicate it in my own bedroom.

The place at 37 Via Basento that was leased for us during my stay for work was a far cry from the house in which I grew up. I was a child of the Great Depression, with holes in my shoes, often limited food and a sparse school wardrobe. Needless to say, the Army cot I slept on was light years removed from the exquisite and luxurious boudoir of the Italian actress who had leased her apartment to us.

Rome was a poem, pressed into service as a city.

-Anatole Broyard

La Strada Buia
(The Dark Road)

> *Roma è la più bella città del mondo.*
> *(Rome is the most beautiful city in the world.)*
>
> *This was the first phrase the Italian people taught me.*
> —Janis Paige

In order to save this historic jewel during World War II, the Italians surrendered to the Nazis and declared Rome an open city.

Most of Rome was left without running water, because the Nazis had bombed some of the reservoirs. In the classy Via Parioli district where we lived, there was no running water. If you wanted water, you filled buckets from the fountains and the piazzas and carried them home. I simply learned to do without. I could always shower at the studio, and did. They had the benefit of a generator. Besides, there was so much else to fill my new Italian life.

There was very little English spoken. This was a new culture, the pages of my school geography and history books reminding me at every turn that I was no longer in America. The ages of the ages were all around me. There was the Colosseum, the Roman Baths, the monuments, the piazzas, the fountains and the Spanish Steps with all of the flowers surrounding that beautiful place.

I could not turn a faucet on for water, but it didn't really matter. Each day, the bucket parade would begin. Baths were out of the question, but water for the toilet, that was a necessity, so there was a constantly refilled bucket beside the loo.

As poor as we were during The Great Depression, we always had a faucet that worked and a toilet that flushed without assistance. So, in that sense, I had regressed.

There was very little meat, and everything seemed to be rationed in Italy. I learned to love spaghetti sandwiches with that great, always fresh Italian bread. I loved the strong black coffee. I loved the food, the wine and the new challenges that presented themselves every day. I loved the fountains surrounded by their always unique piazzas.

I loved everything about Rome, but what I especially loved were its warm, friendly, welcoming, emotional, hot-blooded people.

Did I mention Italian men? Nothing or no one could raise your self-esteem like these men. Of course, all the attention and adoration can't last, and like the proverbial Chinese food, they're hungry again an hour later. I know that I'm exaggerating, but come to think of it, I'm not. They were seductive, charming and, like peanuts, addictive.

I even became somewhat accustomed to having my tush pinched. When I questioned this intrusive activity, I was assured that it was the Italian male's sign of approval.

This was a country waiting for me, and it spared nothing.

Frank was with me in Rome, but he loved to sleep and sleep he did. I wanted to see everything, and I did on my days off. Because the studio had a generator, we had water and electricity and would shoot a lot at night.

On my free days, I would walk, ask where I was, get directions and go again. Sometimes, I would catch a horse-drawn carriage so that I could go farther. I was frantically studying Italian and getting better each day. The drivers would speak to me in Italian and I would speak back, haltingly, falteringly, but trying.

One day on the set of the film, I was getting made up when the makeup man remarked in Italian, "You have no American accent, Janis."

"Oh, my gosh, do you mean that? Is it really true?"

"Ask the crew," he replied. "We are very proud of you."

The crew always helped me, and now I was finally speaking Italian—and without an American accent!

We shot the film all over Rome, taking advantage of the historical places and the beauty and drama of this ancient city. One day, we were set to shoot a morgue scene. I walked into a very old building and down a wide hallway where I saw two men standing, smoking and quietly chatting outside a closed door.

As I drew closer, I could see blood on their white aprons and on their shoes. In disbelief, as I stared at them, I could hear sobbing and wailing and then, across the hall from the bloody men, I saw a gurney and a bloody sheet covering what could only have been a body.

I stood there in shock. We were shooting here today and, obviously, this was not a set but the real thing!

"How can I do this?" I asked in a whisper.

The scene found me identifying my husband's body. *Good lord*, I wondered, *was I going to have to stand among actual dead bodies while I performed?*

I turned around, found the assistant director and asked the same question.

"Can't you find a room in this big old place without real blood and dead bodies and do the scene there?" I asked in a panic.

"Don't worry, Janis," he answered, laughing. "The only corpse in the room will be that of your murdered husband. The real ones will be off in the corner."

"Are you kidding? I never thought you meant the real morgue."

My protests continued.

"How can we do this scene with those poor grieving people out there? It's disrespectful!" I proclaimed. "I feel terrible."

This being Italy, when they were ready to shoot, I acted, corpses in the corner be damned.

We also used the elegant and stunning palazzos, which were now available for rent to the studios. The wealthy and the royalty had also known the ravages of war, and they were forced to lease their homes.

We filmed where there were Bellinis and Titians on the ceilings and walls. I could almost reach out and touch them. I had only been as close as an art book, and here they were. The greatest painters in Italian history were their decorators, in a way. What I saw made me gasp in awe and reverence.

I remember filming in a mirrored hall in a famous old palazzo. The beauty was breathtaking, and as I looked around, I saw that one of the mirrors had been broken and there were scratches on the gilded frames. The marble floors were scratched now as well, and as careful as the crew tried to be, the actions of cameras, equipment, lights and people earning a living began to take its toll. It was inevitable, but it made me sick.

From Tacoma, Washington, to Rome, Italy. From 4303 N. 24th Street to 37 Via Basento was a life-changing journey for me. I did not grow up with the master painters. I had not been near a war, except to collect tin foil and experience rationing during World War II.

Here in Rome, I wanted to save everything. Nothing should be lost or broken. Outside of Rome, there was so much devastation, yet here I was living and working in what to me was a magnificent, living museum. I touched and often caressed these gifts before me.

I wondered many times as I traveled the streets of Rome, *How can I go home again after this?* My imagination would take flight as I tried to rationalize not returning to the problems and responsibilities, to my unhappy and unfulfilled mother, to my very shaky pretense of a marriage and to the decisions that awaited.

It finally hit me. I could come back, maybe, but I had to go home first.

One day while walking on the Via Condotti, I spotted a tiny shop named Gucci. There was room inside for about two people, and everything there was spectacular. Signore Gucci made women's bags, and what bags they were! The workmanship was perfection and I immediately bought two.

When America found his talent and Gucci stores began to flourish, he never repeated the two bags I had purchased that day in Rome. I often asked, but to no avail.

The bag was a kind of satchel. One was covered in a beautiful navy-blue leather. The bag was also lined in a soft, cushy leather and was made with Italy's usual expertise. What set this apart from his women's bags was the companion piece that accompanied it. It was a double-sided cover made to fit over the original bag. This was accomplished with the use of hidden snaps on the bag.

In other words, you purchased one bag, but you really got three. Mine was equipped with a plaid on one side and red on the other. When I returned to America, I was constantly stopped by women wanting to buy one just like it. When I mentioned that I had purchased it in Rome, they wouldn't believe me.

"You just don't want to tell us where you got it."

Women!

I used those precious bags until they were pretty well worn out. They were as unique as the Italian who made them and, like Gucci, one of a kind. I'm so sorry that I didn't keep them, for history's sake and Gucci's.

Although I didn't realize it at the time, the lasting life lessons I learned came from the difficult challenges of living and working in a country struggling to find its way back to what would never be the same again.

My six weeks turned into six months, and I found an exciting new life in its aged mysteries, its ravages of war and the countless inconveniences, along with the ever-present, water-filled bucket beside the loo. If the bucket was empty, you'd better not use that water closet under penalty of death!

None of the difficulties seemed to matter to me. There was always something more important around the corner during my time in Roma.

Ernest Hemingway called Paris a moveable feast. Rome was the same, the only difference being the food. Mine was Italian and so, finally, was I.

Dinner with a Mussolini

> *It is humiliating to remain with our hands folded while others write history. It matters little who wins. To make a people great, it is necessary to send them to battle even if you have to kick them in the pants. That is what I shall do.*
>
> –Benito Mussolini, "Il Duce"

Mike Frankovich, the producer of our movie, and his wife Binnie Barnes had invited us to dinner.

"It'll be a very unusual experience," they said, "and we don't want you to miss it."

We found our way through Rome's winding and often narrow cobblestoned streets to a strange and unknown Roman neighborhood where Mike and Binnie were waiting. There was no sign saying "ristorante," no lights, just a very old door at street level.

Once inside, we had to quickly descend an ancient stairway carved out of sheer rock. A smiling maître d' met us and escorted us to our table. The ever-romantic candles lit the room, and as my eyes became accustomed to the light, my first look took my breath away.

We were in a cave of some kind, carved out of a time somewhere in Roman history. As usual, it was preserved, used and remembered by anyone fortunate enough to share it. The ceiling and the walls were like the stairs, rough-hewn and with sharp-edged shapes that permitted the light to create its constant changes.

What prompted such a difficult task? Human beings and human hands built this magical place using archaic tools. How I wished I knew its life story.

Binnie startled me from my reverie.

"I don't have to ask you what you think. I can see it on your face," she observed. "I felt the same way when I first saw it."

"Oh, Binnie," I said, "thanks to you and Mike, I have another Roman memory to live on."

White linen tablecloths, candles in wine bottles, a small vase of flowers, china, wine goblets and silver completed this odd and mysterious Roman wonder.

The room was filled with men and women who looked to me as if they had never seen a war. Everyone was beautifully dressed, with the women's tastefully bejeweled hands animating the various conversations—in Italian, of course.

Mike and the maître d' were busily discussing the wine as we were handed the menus. Good lord, I thought, one would never have even known it was here. From the appearance of the diners, men in their perfectly tailored suits and couturier clothing on the women, this was not a place where you worried about the price of the dinner or the size of the bill.

Mike ordered wine, and we settled into choosing the food for the evening. After the war, there was enormous rationing in Italy, but you'd never know it from looking at the list of feasts before us. I had not seen such food since I'd been in Rome. As much as I had learned to love spaghetti sandwiches, this was a rare treat, as was The Cave.

While we were enjoying our wine and that addictive freshly baked Italian bread, we became aware that the table talk, the rattling of dishes and the clinking of wine glasses had begun to wane from somewhere near the back. This quiet soon enveloped the room and we wondered what had happened.

Suddenly, I heard Mike say, "Oh my God, there's Mussolini's daughter at the top of the stairs."

I looked up to see a blonde woman just standing there at the top of the stairs glaring at the room full of people below. She did not move, and the silence felt as if people weren't breathing.

After what seemed an eternity, she began to slowly and defiantly descend the stairs one at a time, still wearing her hate-filled, intimidating expression.

There was no sound anywhere as she was shown to her table. With one more withering glance, she sat down. For several minutes, the room didn't breathe as we continued to sit in silence.

She had brought her pain to dinner.

Finally, we began to turn our thoughts away from Edda Mussolini Ciano and the intense drama we had just witnessed. Slowly, we tried to make our way back from the sullen and penetratingly angry woman sitting in our presence. It didn't work.

Ever so tentatively, the conversations began again. The waiter brought our gorgeous and delicious food. The wine glasses clinked once more. But things had not returned to normal.

I, for one, would never be the same.

As we ate, I questioned Mike about Mussolini's daughter. Her father and his mistress, Clara Petacci, had been executed and hung, upside-down, in a gas station in Milano. Both corpses became the focus of ridicule and abuse. They were stoned by the Italian people. It was a terrible time in Italy.

While we dined in 1949, their deaths were still very much alive, and Mussolini's name would evoke all sorts of opinions, from intense anger to remorse, guilt and shame. He, the war, the destruction, his betrayal of the Italian people, the economy, Hitler and everything else was aimed at Mussolini.

Edda had been a close and trusted confidante for her father during his political career and rise to power. It didn't matter. "Il Duce" and Hitler had condemned her husband, Count Ciano, to death by firing squad. When, on her knees, she begged for her husband's life, her father turned his back and let him die.

Even today, I can still recall that room. I see the shadows bouncing off the candlelight. I feel the breathless tension and see that woman at the top of the stairs. We all felt the depth of her hatred and grief. No one escaped it.

Whether it was five years or five minutes, Edda Mussolini Ciano kept it all painfully alive. I felt like I was walking through a history book, turning the pages as I grew into my own life.

Edda Mussolini Ciano
September 1, 1910 – April 4, 1995

Aunt Julia

One is not born a woman, one becomes one.
—Simone de Beauvoir

In 1949, if you went just a little of the way into the Italian countryside, you could still see the ravages of the war. Rome had been declared an open city, but not so the countryside of Italy. The signs of battles were always visible. It was rare not to see a bullet-riddled wall in an abandoned house.

Italy was left poor, and most of her citizens in poverty. Even the wealthy were renting their exquisitely beautiful villas to motion picture companies to be used as sets.

My husband Frank's Uncle Albert and Aunt Julia lived outside of Perugia. They owned tenant farms and lived in a big old villa covered with grapevines. It was summertime, and the fields were bearing their best for our simple but delicious meals. All of this splendor was topped off with those unforgettable Italian flowers everywhere.

Frank's father and uncles all came from Lucca in Northern Italy. Aunt Julia did, too. She had long, shiny dark hair pulled back with a fat knot at the nape of her neck and piercingly brilliant blue eyes. She was elegant and beautiful, resembling the famous Italian actress Anna Magnani.

Aunt Julia was simply hypnotic to me with her no-nonsense presence that filled the space she occupied. I was crazy about her. She spoke perfect

English and, of course, perfect Italian. She was forever worried about their farmers and the children, constantly bringing whatever she could find to meet their needs.

What you saw was what you got with her. There was no time for foolish façades. She was a fighter who had seen her country devastated, and there was work to be done.

"*Andiamo*" ("Let's go") was her mantra.

One morning, she asked, "I'm going to see the gypsies, Janis. Would you like to come along?"

"Gypsies!" I exclaimed. "You have gypsies? Are they real gypsies?"

"Painted wagons and all," she replied.

"Oh, Aunt Julia, I'd love to go with you."

She loaded me up with three bags of her supplies, picked up another three big sacks, and off we went, walking down an old cart-rutted road for about a half mile.

Suddenly, there in the center of a clearing were the brightly colored wagons, the fire and the clothes that matched the wagons and their life. My heart was pounding, and I felt as though I had stepped into a page of my history book in school.

Here I stood, an American woman from a far-off land, experiencing the ravages of a war-torn country in the middle of a gypsy campground. Go figure life. The more you try, the further behind it leaves you.

I was transfixed at the sight before me when Aunt Julia propelled me, my gigantic sacks and herself toward the center of the camp. A brightly costumed man stepped up to greet her and to thank her for coming.

She wasted no time, speaking forcefully and fearlessly about the children being ill and never clean enough.

"Good lord, they're your children," she charged. "You can do better than this."

Aunt Julia meant business, and they all knew it. She also knew that she was fighting an interminable problem.

As I helped her to unload the various items she'd brought, she patiently explained how the medicine was to be used until she was sure that the man understood her directions. Then we shared the toys and clothing that she'd gathered with the children and their mothers.

I'll never forget those kids in their mysterious gypsy garb. *When and where did this gypsy life begin?* I wondered. Secretive and strange to the outside world, they lived by their own rules and traditions.

The children waited shyly and quietly as each was given some castoff toy from a strange someone, somewhere.

"*Grazie, grazie,*" they whispered as each child began to treasure his or her gift. Aunt Julia explained that they were from children who lived very far away in America. Their big dark eyes just continued to stare in silence.

A gypsy child, a Catholic child or really any child was desperately in need of everything. One could easily become overwhelmed and hopeless at this unending desperation, but not Aunt Julia.

Goodbyes were traditionally formal.

"*Ciao, ciao,*" they called as we began our journey to another small group of families. I could see that wherever she went, she was loved, respected, but most of all, needed.

I've met royalty, known and worked with show business stars, met Presidents and attended an illustrious State Dinner at The White House. But no one ever left me as awestruck as did Aunt Julia. She had a massively charitable heart, housed in one beautiful and powerful Italian woman I will never forget.

Sometimes she had very little for her families, sometimes more. Whatever she could find went to them. She was unbelievably courageous in the face of so many obstacles. Frank's family had collected and sent huge packages of used clothing and anything else she needed. I finally got a chance to see the recipients of her benevolent efforts.

When we finished and headed home, a priest stopped to greet her. They spoke in Italian, and after my introduction and the usual pleasantries were exchanged, she let him have it,

"You keep these people poor, with too many children. Some don't live past the age of seven and you do nothing to help them."

"It's God's will," he countered. "You can't interfere with God's will."

"What kind of God lets children go hungry, get sick and die with no medicine while you take what little money they have? The church is rich, you do not need it. Shame on you!"

The look of horror on the priest's face said, "I've got to get out of here." With that, he bid her a hasty but polite farewell and hurried on his way.

"You've just seen my ongoing fight," she said. "It's me against the priest, and the people listen to him. Sometimes I want to throw up my hands and give up, but I can't, and I won't! How can I ignore the constant need I see every day? I do what I can and it's never enough."

There was fire in those beautiful blue eyes, and when I look back, I realize that I had met my first women's libber, so to speak. A selfless and ferocious mover-and-shaker who changed me and helped me to walk my new path.

Aunt Julia, in the country outside of Perugia, fought for rights, for truth, for education and the greater good. She allowed me to share a part of life that I would never have seen had it not been for her dedication, bravery and honesty.

Julia Martinelli
Age unknown and I never asked. She was beyond time.

Ingrid Bergman

I've gone from saint to whore in one lifetime. I have no regrets. I wouldn't have lived my life the way I did if I had to worry about what people would say.

—Ingrid Bergman

Rome always woke me very early. I would lay there in that night-shaded dawn, watching the day begin. It would slowly lighten the lovely silk fabric on the walls of our bedroom. The shadow patterns replaced by another day closer to never seeing my Roman home again.

Obviously, no expense had been spared providing the home's owner the kind of luxury I had never known. I took great care to be a good tenant. How I wished it were mine.

I dressed quietly, so as not to wake my sleeping husband who was doing what he did best, sleep. How could he throw half the day away when there was still so much to see?

I'll never figure you out, Frank, I thought, *and you'll never know me. Love is not enough, not when avoiding the truth about us has become a way of life. I'm scared Frank, and you're not. Why not?*

I shivered in the cold and I felt as dark and overcast as the day ahead. Soon it was leavin' time, and what seemed to be my unending sadness matched the onset of a Roman winter. Here in this war-torn, impoverished country, I had found a freedom that was completely unnatural to my young and inexperienced life.

I fantasized about finding a way to stay, knowing all the while that I had problems to solve. What do I do about my marriage, the bills, my mother, my marriage, a job, my marriage? Rome couldn't hide me from me, and I eventually had to go home.

I held my fear in check, but the anger lived just below the surface. My ever-happy, self-accepting husband was still sleeping when I left. I'd rather spend the day alone, anyway. At least I can talk to myself.

I had promised my sister Betty that I would bring her some fabric for the recovering of her couches. Someone had told me where I could find what I was looking for, and I set off, walking those ancient streets I had come to love. I walked every chance I got, making memories I would keep forever.

Roma and its people had changed me. I would never be the same. But what was I to do with this new and unfamiliar person I had become?

As I walked toward my destination, I stopped to watch a funeral slowly making its way down the street. Everyone was naturally dressed in black, accompanied by the sad, black funereal music. I recalled the words of a carriage driver one day, as we waited for a funeral to pass.

"The Italian people are in debt all of their lives," he said. "First they owe for the marriage, then they owe for the funeral. It never ends."

In 1949, I could still witness a people steeped in pageantry, tradition and the strict rules of its historical behavior. Each day, I soaked up everything Roman surrounding me. Rome seemed written in stone, saved by the ages for the ages to come.

By contrast, my family threw everything away. If there were a painful memory, it was tossed, until our rightful heritage was gone forever. They never thought about us, the children who should be "seen and not heard." I still resent their thoughtlessness, but a lot of good it does me.

Our family history doesn't go very far, so it's left for us to make our own. What is missing in me is treasured by the Italian people, and I feel it deeply and gratefully.

I finally found the address I was looking for. It was a tiny, cobblestoned street off Via Condotti. Walking on cobblestones was hell in heels, but it always made its own special music as one's steps echoed against the aged walls.

As I turned the corner, the first thing I saw was an ancient Della Robbia wreath over the door. It clearly had been there for a very long time, perhaps forgotten under its layers of dust. How many had come and gone under the watchful presence of Della Robbia? I had only seen them at Christmas time, when we could order a fresh pine bough facsimile of the real thing. Now I knew what the real thing looked like. Thank you, Roma.

When I opened the door, I almost immediately stepped onto a very narrow, rather steep stairway leading to the room above. I could see a light and hear voices as I started my climb. There were two rickety closet poles for railings, so I hung on and, as I got about halfway, I saw a figure starting down from the opening above.

"*Mille grazie, buona sera*," ("Thank you very much, good evening") came a voice vaguely familiar.

Where have I heard that voice before? I wondered.

The woman attached to the voice began to carefully make her way down the stairs when I saw that she was very pregnant. As she got closer, I greeted her, in my almost perfect Italian, with, "*Scuzi, Signora*, please wait and I'll go back down. It will be easier for you to manage the stairs."

"*Mille grazie, Signora*, but we'll be fine," came her reply.

As she spoke, the proverbial bolt from the blue shattered my senses and I was frozen to the spot. Suddenly, I found myself looking into the radiantly beautiful face of the wondrous Ingrid Bergman,

She giggled as she said, "You squeeze one way, and I'll squeeze the other. We'll be fine."

A million words crossed my mind. *Oh my God, how am I going to crowd everything into a few precious moments? How do I tell her how wonderful she is? That her work is perfect? Could she send me a picture? Should I congratulate her?*

Instead, I said nothing.

You see, Ingrid Bergman was not only radiant and wondrous, but notorious and scandalous, too. She was carrying another man's child while still married with a child of her own. Unlike the world of today, she was a product of the time and had become a pariah to America.

Standing there, the memory of her scandal with Roberto Rossellini, the famous Italian director, was still fresh. We in Rome had known for some time that she was pregnant with his child, but the Italians saw things differently and welcomed her.

Whatever her reasons for the choices she made belonged to her and her alone. She paid dearly in countless ways for many years as she was denied work, losing the respect of millions of adoring fans along with her marriage and daughter.

The woman had fallen about as far as she could when the *coup de grace* was dealt. In a Joint Session of Congress, Bergman was officially vilified, shamed and finally ostracized from her adopted country.

There I was, the recipient of her dazzling smile and hypnotic presence. There stood the Ingrid Bergman of my fantasies, the Ingrid Bergman of *Casablanca* and *Gaslight*. Each film illustrated her stunning beauty and extraordinary talent.

I took a deep breath and—with my inner, quiet and respectful "No, Jan" filter in place, left her to her privacy, grateful for the brief moment belonging only to me.

When she reached the bottom of the stairs, she pulled her coat closely against the cold, opened the door and left me with one last *"Ciao!"*

"Ciao to you, too, *Signora,"* I called, and my moment was gone forever.

I stood in that same spot where we had "squeezed" past one another, trying to take in this event in my life. Finally, I turned toward the room upstairs and my intended errand. I wasn't ready for what I saw. My Italian friend was right. I was, after all, in Rome.

From the dimly lit staircase, this vista of dazzling color was astounding. It made me think of my sister.

"Oh, Betty, I wish you were here to see this incredible place. *If I can't find what you want here, I won't find it anywhere."*

I wandered from table to table, feeling the tactile and beautiful silks, laces and woolens, when a huge bolt of red plaid linen caught my eye.

Perfect, I said to myself. *Like the day, this is just perfect.*

As I paid my bill, I took one more look around. I wanted everything set in my now overflowing memory bank. It was a gallery of vivid and unforgettable fabric art. This was 1949, and there was still time to stop and smell the roses. If one wanted to be constantly surprised, Rome never disappointed.

I picked up my package, thanked everyone, wished them a good evening and made my way back down the stairs into reality. As I reached the door,

I looked back, recalling everything that had just transpired. If I came this way again, it would never be the same.

I grew up a little more today, I said to myself as a gust of cold air woke me to the long walk home. I could not stop ruminating about my unbelievable encounter with Miss Bergman.

I remembered that she had seen an Italian film called *Open City*, by director Roberto Rossellini. She was so impressed with his work that she wrote him a letter offering the services of "a Swedish actress" who spoke "very little Italian."

Rossellini immediately responded to this world-famous woman, and she flew to Rome for meetings on his film called *Stromboli*. Of course, the script was still just an idea, but she agreed to do it and off they went to their destiny and a very rocky future.

When I arrived in June, all of Italy seemed to know about the affair. Being Italians and romantic, they were thrilled, unlike in the United States. Americans saw things very differently in the Forties. We greatly valued and expected too much of women of stature like Ingrid Bergman.

We only knew her from her films. When we discovered that she, too, had feet of clay like the rest of us, we punished her severely. I did not envy her position, no matter how romantic the situation seemed.

A very wise man once said to me, "Better to be the one who hurts than to be the one who does the hurting. The price is too high!"

On February 2, 1950, Bergman gave birth to their son, Roberto Jr. She and Rossellini were married on May 24, 1950, and on June 18, 1952, she gave birth to twin daughters, Isabella and Isotta.

Of course, Ingrid Bergman was too gifted, too worldly-wise and too courageous not to revive her career. She went on to receive countless awards throughout the world, including her Oscars from America.

It would be more than two decades later before an apology was given Bergman by the United States Government for its arrogant and pompous hypocrisy.

Ingrid Bergman
August 29, 1915 - August 29, 1982

In the Palm of My Hand

*Life is ten percent how you make it and
ninety percent how you take it.*
—Irving Berlin

Shortly before we left Rome for home, I was asked by an Italian reporter to give an interview. We met at the famous Excelsior Bar, and little did I know that Rome had another epiphany waiting for me. The writer's name was Vittorio Foschini. He was unusual, to say the least, but so was Rome and the Italian people.

We ordered wine and began to talk. He spoke perfect English, and by then my Italian was very good, so we chatted back and forth—some in English, some in Italian. It was fun, and so was he.

At one point in the conversation, he asked to see my palm. I put out my hand and a look came over his face that made me uncomfortable.

"What do you see?"

"You are going to be very ill next year."

"Ill?" I asked. "Any more good news for me?"

He told me that this was no joke. I would not die, but my life would be changed forever.

"I'm sorry to tell you that your marriage will not survive," he added.

As usual, Frank laughed and Vittorio said, "Let me see *your* hand."

Frank laughed again when Vittorio told him, "Oh, *Signore* Martinelli, no one can be as happy as you are and live in this world."

Frank didn't get it, but I did. I knew exactly what Vittorio was saying. I just never heard it put so succinctly.

I asked him when his gift of palm reading began.

"Around the age of five," he said. "As I began to grow into my teen years and then early adulthood, I knew when I would score with a girl. This gift of reading the future kept me alive when I was a prisoner of war under the Nazis.

"I told the guards that I could read the end of the war and the end of them. They didn't believe me but kept me alive to find out. I was right by one day. Thank God, the Americans freed us. I had the extreme pleasure of seeing those bastard Nazis change places with me."

"I don't know what to think or to say," I replied. "It seems that 1950 doesn't seem so promising for me after our conversation."

"I'm sorry, Janis, but I see what I see," he said. "You'll survive and grow. Please let me know how you are."

With that he gave me his card, thanked me and we bid one another "*Arrivederci, Ciao!*"

"You didn't believe him, did you?" Frank asked as we started home.

"I don't know what to believe right now," I replied, "but I found him fascinating. I'd love to know more."

"He's a creep," Frank concluded. "How can anyone be *too* happy? That's what we're supposed to be, isn't it?"

"He wasn't talking about that, Frank."

What is the use if I get it and you don't? I thought, so I kept quiet. I had a lot to think about while walking home and into 1950.

Field Marshal
General Bernard Montgomery

Every soldier must know, before he goes into battle, how the little battle he is to fight fits into the larger picture, and how the success of his fighting can influence the battle into the larger and how the success of his fighting can influence the battle as a whole.

–Field Marshall General Bernard Montgomery,
November 1949 aboard the *Queen Elizabeth*

In November 1949, I was about to embark on my first voyage aboard an ocean liner, let alone the famous H.M.S. Queen Elizabeth.

The day we left Southampton was reminiscent of all of those old movies with the *bon voyage* parties: The champagne flowing from glass to glass, confetti and the excitement of five and a half days of sheer unadulterated pleasure at sea. It took about a day to discover that I was getting seasick. No, I take that back: I *was* seasick.

Misery knew no bounds.

There was no Dramamine or anything else to aid those of us who weren't good sailors in '49. The only thing I heard from those around me was, "You'll get your sea legs and you'll be fine."

All of those smug, seaworthy passengers found my predicament amusing. Everyone was whooping it up, dressed to the nines, dining on mounds of caviar, glorious food, fine wines and dancing and gambling the night away.

Needless to say, I was not there.

Bundled against the cold, I walked the decks, breathing deeply and getting soaked from the spray of the North Atlantic as we pitched, tossed and rolled our way to America. The nausea never left me, and my situation wasn't helped by visits from my always-happy husband describing what I was missing.

"Have you tried throwing up?" he'd ask.

"Oh, good lord, Frank, I would brave that deep, dark, stormy and terrifying sea if I could just lean over that railing and let everything go. I've stuck a finger down my throat, had visions of how wonderful it would feel to throw up and I just can't. Why don't you understand that?"

"Well, you're not much fun to be around and you don't have to yell at me," my husband said.

"Yes, I do have to yell at you. Who else am I going to yell at? The captain for not controlling the damned Atlantic?"

I'm miserable, jealous, exhausted, cold and alone. The only sleep I get is in a wet deck chair, and the only thing I'm missing is the weight I've lost and my sense of humor.

By now, I was really feeling sorry for myself. A warm shoulder would have helped, but Frank and his shoulder left without an offer.

Not long into my marriage, I discovered that Frank liked life with no pain—not his and certainly not mine. He fled back to his fun and friends where everyone was happy, leaving his bitchy wife on that wet deck.

On the afternoon of our fourth day at sea, I began to notice that the nausea was diminishing. Is this real? Oh my God, I was actually feeling hungry! *Careful*, I warned myself. *Don't go crazy.*

As the day wore on, it was true. I definitely felt better. I had my first dinner that night in the ship's gorgeous dining room. There is nothing in the world like food when you're starving, and I ate my share of Queen Elizabeth's heavenly feast accompanied by the finest of French champagne.

Then, I waited. What a relief! I didn't feel sick! I thought, *I think I'm going to live!*

As we sailed into New York Harbor the following day, the bags were packed and so was I. The day had finally arrived when I could set my shaky self on terra firma and never get on water again.

I was in our stateroom waiting to leave when there was a knock on the door. A uniformed man stood before me and said, "Good morning, Miss Paige. The captain would like to see you. I'll take you there."

Now that I'm leaving, the captain wants to see me? I thought. *What's going on?*

"Of course, I'd love to meet the captain," I replied. After all, I thought, maybe I could ask him why he seemed to lose control of The Queen through that vicious North Atlantic Ocean. I didn't, however, because I had found my charming self again.

As we approached the upper deck, I began to see photographers and people milling about and lots of excitement in the air.

"Is there someone important on board?" I asked.

He didn't have time to answer because I was suddenly in front of, and being introduced to, the all-important someone who had also sailed aboard the ship to New York City.

There, in his famous beret. beautifully tailored general's overcoat and his magnificent military bearing stood one of the greatest heroes of World War II. It was Field Marshal General Bernard Montgomery.

I was standing in front of Monty and struggling to find my voice, when he said, "I'm pleased to meet you, Miss Paige."

"Oh, General Montgomery," I blurted, "I'm so thrilled to meet you. May I thank you from one grateful American?"

That was all I could find to say. I was then introduced to the woman standing at his other side. She, too, had crossed while I was trying to find my sea legs. Bonita "Bunnie" Granville stuck out her hand and said, "Hi, Janis," and shook mine.

The cameras began to flash, one after another after another, until everyone was satisfied that they'd gotten their pictures.

As quickly as all of this history took place, it was gone and so was Field Marshal General Montgomery. The pictures that were taken that eventful day reached the front page of every newspaper in the world, including *The New York Times*.

Frank and I finally joined the passengers crowding the decks, trying to pick out familiar faces in the equally excited welcome-homers on the docks below. The angry North Atlantic was now far behind us as the clear, cold November sunlight filled the day.

I stood, impatiently waiting to set my feet on something, anything that wasn't moving, when Frank and I spotted his excited mother. Her Frankie was home, and so was Janis. No matter what might happen with our marriage, I would love Irene Martinelli forever.

As we prepared to dock, we were all talking at once. And like everyone else, we were catching up and filling in, finding our luggage, laughing and hugging and finally grabbing a cab.

We scattered as if we'd never spent five and a half days together. As we headed for our hotel, my mother-in-law said, "I got us wonderful tickets to see Lee J. Cobb in *Death of a Salesman* tonight. It's a huge hit show."

"What a great homecoming!" I said excitedly.

Luckily, I was sitting on the aisle at the show, because halfway through the first act something hit me.

"Oh my God, I'm getting sick!" I blurted. "What am I going to do? Can I make the ladies room?"

I jumped out of my seat and began to run up the aisle. All the while, I'm thinking, *Not now! Not now! Please God, not now! Just let me make it to the john!*

As I reached the stall, the North Sea finally extracted her punishment for my being such a lousy sailor.

I never saw the rest of the show. For the next three days, I was in bed with the aftereffects of seasickness.

"You just didn't get your sea legs, Miss Paige," observed the cheerful, informative doctor.

"No shit!" I whispered. When I got my land legs, we went home.

General Bernard Law (Monty) Montgomery
November 17, 1887 - March 24, 1975

From service in World War I through World War II until he died at age 88, Field Marshal General Montgomery served his country and the world. I am so proud to have met him. I'll bet he had his sea legs.

-Janis Paige

Orson Welles

Good Evening, ladies and gentlemen. I am an actor. I am a writer. I am a producer. I am a director. I am a magician. I appear on stage and the radio. Why are there so many of me and so few of you?

—Orson Welles

Sometime in September of 1949, we were shooting on a soundstage at Scalera Studios in Rome, Italy. When we finished the scene, we heard the door open and a sonorous voice call out, "Mike? Where's Mike?"

Onto the set strode a man dressed in a flowing black cape, a soft black felt hat pulled rakishly to one side. Except for a white shirt, he was all in black, including a droopy silk tie. In one hand he held a cane and in the other a young girl he introduced as his daughter, Rebecca.

The man embraced our producer, Mike Frankovich, and in turn Mike introduced him to the cast and crew. Someone brought chairs as he seated himself, still in character, his silent and shy Rebecca beside him.

The soundstage was big, but he was bigger. He walked in and the air disappeared. Everyone else seemed to disappear, too, in his commanding presence while he held court.

I just stared in awe at what seemed to me to be Orson Welles imitating Orson Welles imitating John Barrymore. There was an aura of unreality to it, and why not? Here sat the man who had terrified parts of the world as he related the purported Martian Invasion on the radio.

In 1938, Welles was all of twenty-three years of age when, for a short time, he left us paralyzed with fear with his *War of the Worlds* broadcast.

His visit to our set was brief but compelling. He stood, took his invisible little daughter by the hand and left the same way he had entered. Even his goodbyes were done with a flourish.

Like everything one experiences that seems to be bigger than life, there is a silence while the air is allowed to take its rightful place once more.

When did the genuine flamboyance of an Orson Welles die? As the decades passed, in my opinion, it simply morphed into a huge club whose insignia is a $ sign, branded into the word Power.

The dues are simple. You'll need at least a million or two to get your foot in the door. Then you erase your sense of humor if you ever had one, adopt groupthink, learn the script and don't deviate a single word from it. Don't hurt anyone's feelings even if you don't know what feelings they were feeling at the time they think they got hurt. Use your bullhorn to scream your epithets at only those who disagree with you.

Oh, please. Stop the world, I want to get off!

I'm going to give myself a break and express my eternal gratitude for the flamboyant, amusing and at times downright unforgettable people I've known. They enriched my life. The great Orson Welles was certainly one of them.

Orson Welles
May 6, 1915 - October 10, 1985

The absence of limitations is the enemy of art.

Right:
My baby picture, 1923.

Bottom left:
Me at age 3 in our old neighborhood in Tacoma, WA, doing the watering.

Bottom right:
Grandpa Frank and Grandma Julia in the 1930s, after the Depression. This is the way they always looked, every morning of their lives – dapper and elegant. That's just who they were.

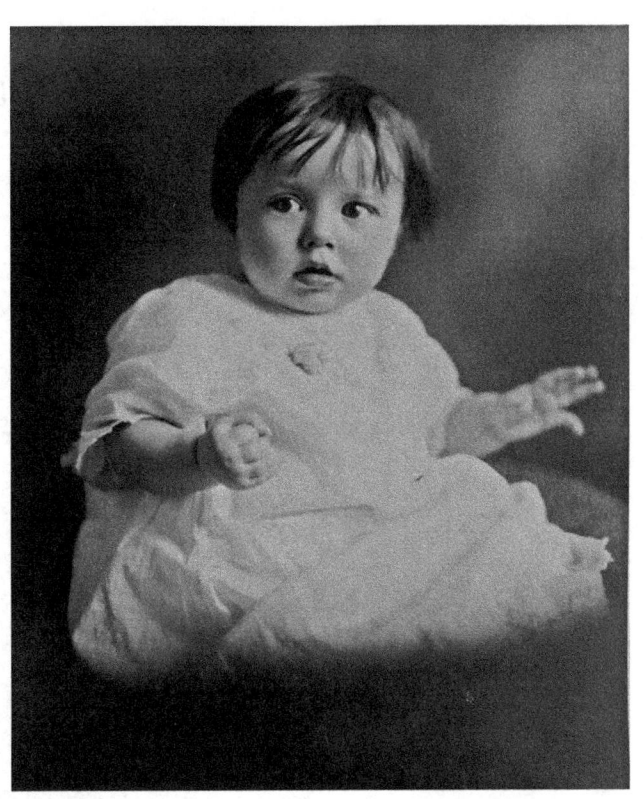

Right:
My mother, Hazel Leah Paige. She was a beautiful woman.

Bottom left:
My mother, posing dramatically.

Bottom right:
The Packard. My grandfather's pride and joy. The car cost $6,000, which was a fortune. We didn't have a car at all during the Depression.

Right:
My grandfather Frank in his later years, during a camping trip in Camas, WA. Even out on a drive or camping, he had a suit and tie on. I never saw him dressed casually, ever. And his shoes were always shined.

Bottom left:
Me on the right with an unidentified girlfriend from high school, with our schoolbooks.

Bottom right:
My high school senior picture.

Above:
Early in my career while under contract to Warner Bros., probably 1944.

Opposite page, top left:
Posing inside with a Navy airplane during the war, at the Naval Air Station in Los Alamitos, CA.

Opposite page, top right:
Anchors Aweigh – and woof-woof!

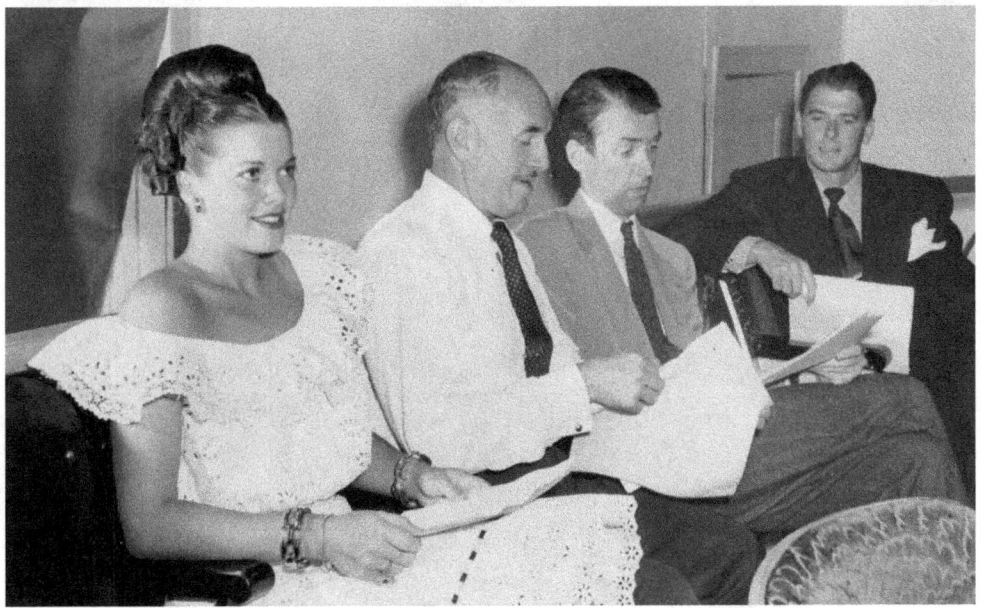

Above:

What an exciting moment this was for me. I remember being completely tongue-tied, participating in Mutual Network Air Force Day in 1944. (L to R) Me, Jack L. Warner (the driving force behind the Warner Bros. Studios), Jimmy Stewart and future President Ronald Reagan. Just wow.

Left:
During the publicity tour for the feature The Time, the Place and the Girl *(1946).*

Below:
The publicity tour for the 1947 feature Cheyenne. *I'd been in high heels all day and it was hot outside. My feet were killing me! Finally, I had a chance to relax. I'm with two of my costars, Dennis Morgan and Bruce Bennett.*

Above:
Marrying Frank Martinelli Jr. on December 27, 1947. A big mistake.
My sister Betty is at left.

Right:
A Warner Bros. holiday publicity photo. I was Miss Christmas in 1948 while shooting the film One Sunday Afternoon.

Above left:
A nightclub appearance in New York in 1948, while I was still with Warner Bros.

Above right:
On the marquis at the Oriental Theatre (now the James M. Nederlander Theatre) in Chicago during the dawn of my time in vaudeville, around 1949.

Bottom left:
I was voted Miss Atomic Energy 1948 in advance of appearing at the First Annual Atomic Frontier Days in Richland, WA.

Above:
Starring in the 1950 Italian film La Strada Buia *(The Dark Road), here in a scene with Eduardo Cianelli. Shooting the movie in Rome changed my life.*

Right:
Dr. Arnold A. Hutschnecker, a wonderful man and a brilliant doctor. He was there for me in my hour of need in 1950 – and beyond.

Section IV
The 1950s

Vaudeville, Nightclubs & Whatever

> *Success is not final, failure is not fatal. It is the courage to continue that counts.*
> —Winston Churchill

For the better part of five years after my Warner Bros. contract wasn't renewed, I was thrust into the role of entertainment vagabond working in vaudeville and nightclubs. It lasted from the end of 1948 through 1953, not straight through but during large swaths of that time.

In 1950 when I returned from Rome, home was a lovely house on a hill in Longridge Estates. I spent all of eight weeks there, mostly moving in. I don't remember moving out because I was always working somewhere.

Along with my marriage, mother and the eternal bills, there was now a new house. Everyone was waiting for me to do something, but as usual, work came first. The omnipresent voice of obligations was all I could hear.

My Warner Bros. home and family were gone. I no longer knew the security of my next film or the paycheck each week. I had two houses to pay for, bills and no job. It was up to me to plan my own future.

Talk about the blind leading the blind. I was clueless as to my next move, including my first step on my own.

I had a world-renowned name thanks to the Brothers Warner, more than a dozen movies under my belt, and I knew how to sing with the best. My next step seemed destined for me.

Jack Carson and Robert Alda were taking their show into the big old vaudeville houses for about six weeks or so and asked me to join them. We were all ex-Warner Bros. stars, and Jack and I had done several films together. We would begin the tour in Chicago. The city was always a wonderful place to work, and business was great. From there, it was Detroit, Philadelphia, New York City, Newark and anything else our agents could find.

Both Jack and Bob had come from early burlesque, and when I was in school, they were just beginning their careers as vaudevillians and perfecting their craft. While Hollywood was making its movie magic, its former stars were making their own magic in front of audiences who were, perhaps, unaware that they were seeing the last of something wonderful.

When Jack, Robert and I were in front of those footlights, perhaps feeling that we may never do this again, each and every show brought us closer to the end of an era.

We would go on, but those of us still left playing vaudeville owed it a big, special lavender spot as we held its hand, heard it drawing its last breath.

But first, there would be the tour.

The sticker shock came when I had to provide and pay for everything myself. Gone was the Warner Bros. publicity department and their assistants to arrange travel, hotels and interviews. Gone were the makeup, hair and wardrobe departments. Gone too was the studio orchestra with its gorgeous arrangements. The star's entourages of today weren't born yet, so I became my own.

After five years at Warner's, I was earning $500 a week. With two mortgages to pay, I couldn't go very far without a job. So, I had to learn this new world on the go.

Even so, I was often paralyzed with fear for the future. I had it very tough. But this was a time when you toughed it out and didn't complain—at least, not much.

I may have been up a creek without a paddle financially, but I was the breadwinner and bills are bills—so I called my agent. I also quietly seethed at the condition of my marriage and at my mother for quitting work when she was still young and vital enough to help. Whatever I did never seemed to be enough.

This all contributed to my state of mind. So did the fact that I felt so alone. For a week, the vaudevillians and I would unpack, grab friendships and then—like ships that pass in the night—we would move on to a new theater in a new town.

My operative word, however, remained "alone." I traveled alone. I worked alone. I met hotel rooms alone. I encountered dressing rooms, airports, train stations and everything else, always alone.

My vaudeville days found me flying by the seat of my pants. Thanks to Warner Bros., my films and the following they attracted, I was an instant headliner. I could put fannies in the seats, as they say. But I was nonetheless a novice when it came to the stage. From my entrance to my exit, the vaudevillians themselves were my teachers.

Actually, my vaudeville career began back in 1948, at the Oriental Theatre in Chicago, when I got a chance to work with the well-known Joey Adams. The experienced pros all seemed to sense that I needed help here and there, and Joey was one of them. He was a storyteller and a comic, so his timing was impeccable.

"Why did you get a laugh on that line?" I'd ask, and he would explain as best he could.

"You have to have a natural feeling for comedy," he'd say, "and you have it. Don't worry about it, just do it. Do sketches, watch the comics and watch the acts."

I ended up doing a bit with Joey. Finally, I was on my way.

However, outside of always loving the fact that I could entertain, make people laugh, wear beautiful gowns and sing my heart out, I very quickly learned to know what I didn't know. I didn't know how to take a good bow, let alone learn how to milk it. I began to stand in the wings, trying to figure out the mystery of the bow by studying the experts, just as they were taught by the experts who preceded them.

The opening act would send its energy through the theater, and the show would begin to work its magic. "It's showtime!" were the famous words I'd always hear in the wings, as their music played them on. To this day, as I stand waiting for my entrance, "It's showtime!" is the last thing I say as I make my way to the audience. It's our mantra, so to speak. It means,

"Get up, take a deep breath, smile and fall in love with the moment. The audience is waiting."

As a matter of fact, it's not a bad mantra for life, even when it hands you lemons. When I think about it, "It's showtime!" also translates to "Make lemonade." No matter how you felt in the wings, everything changed when the spotlight hit you and you were on.

I learned to pack and unpack, silently praying that I hadn't forgotten something at the last theater I played. I passed out my precious and expensive arrangements to the band du jour and collected them when we moved on. I took care of my costumes, did my own makeup and hair and dressed myself ready for the show.

What we now call multi-tasking became my new talent. Often, I'd ask for and receive advice from the vaudevillians, always eager to help. I was growing up, albeit the hard way. Alone, on my own and sometimes quietly terrified, I began the most valuable facet of my professional career.

When I worked with Bob Hope, I was ready. He, too, was from vaudeville, although it was called "music hall" when Bob trod the boards in his native England.

The accent may have been different, but the comedy was the same. No matter what it was called, funny was funny. True comedy is in one's DNA.

One day, I was rehearsing a sketch with Mr. Hope. I was doing a couple of double-takes, and he was doing a couple of his double-takes, when he stopped and said, "Where did you learn to do double-takes? They're good!"

I gave Bob some of my background, only to hear him say, "From now on, you're my bladder baby."

"Your what?" I asked.

"My bladder baby," he repeated.

The term "bladder baby" comes from burlesque. The straight man would have a bladder ready, and at the right moment, after the comic's line, the straight man would hit the comic over the head. I realize this loses something in the translation because I can't begin to tell you why it worked or why it was funny, but it never failed to get the audiences rolling in the aisle.

Believe me, it took more than a double-take or two. It took talent, work and fine tuning until it was perfect and deserved those laughs.

Today's laughs, by contrast, are usually generated at the expense of someone, or actually finding laughs while people are being physically hurt.

I'll take the harmless bladder hit any day. We didn't hurt people, or their feelings. Our only job was to entertain and be funny.

From the Oriental in Chicago, to the Earle in Philadelphia, to the Fox in Detroit, to the Golden Gate in San Francisco, to Milwaukee, my years in vaudeville wound through Minneapolis, Harrisburg, Kansas City, Omaha, Wheeling, Boston, New York City, Pittsburgh, Montreal, Buffalo, Newark, Miami, Baltimore, Denver, New Haven, Hershey, Dallas, Ft. Worth, Cincinnati, Dayton, Cleveland, Columbus, Warren, Evansville, Youngstown, St. Louis, Indianapolis, Atlanta, Akron, Springfield, Birmingham and a few I know I've missed.

Each theater I played was a part of my education and experience, with the good and the bad all mixed in. You can't have one without the other.

"I never heard of anything so awful," a friend once said. "What a terrible way to earn a living."

"What a shame you haven't lived," I replied. "You don't know what you missed. I missed nothing."

I conquered blizzards, the tail-end of a tornado, stifling heat, twenty-six degrees below zero in cities like Milwaukee and Minneapolis, trains, buses, cabs, hunger, weariness, bad hotel rooms, puddle-jumping planes, storms, discomfort, dirty bathrooms and dusty dressing rooms. Mother Nature could and did throw everything my way, but somehow, I never missed a show.

It wasn't for the timid or the weak. It built a strong underbelly, and all of it was under the banner of show business. I wouldn't give away a minute of it.

I was earning my living alone, doing it all myself. The countless personal decisions remained unsolved, however, reminding me that they were still impatiently waiting.

I wouldn't give up a second of that often sad, scary and lonely period in my life. With all of the emotional bumps and bruises, it was also the most exhilarating and instructive.

I had no musical conductor. I couldn't afford one, so I got used to rehearsing with whatever band they had. How I survived the eight a.m. band rehearsals in the bottom of some old vaudeville house is still a mystery.

One day, after hearing some of my music played incorrectly, I gently suggested to the genius making the mistake that he was playing the wrong chord. He immediately pulled his musical rank on me and told me to show him what chord I wanted. I wish I'd had the guts to say, "Try playing the one that's written," but of course I kept quiet and let him win.

My beautiful arrangements were often pared down to a musical skeleton. Not only was I growing up, I was becoming a diplomat as well. When I refrained from punching the pianist in his untalented nose, I was taught to own my mistakes, but all too often, I did not receive the same treatment in return.

When I walked into my dressing room in Wheeling, West Virginia, a big rat ran across my path and disappeared into some hidden home known only to him. Through my scream, I heard the manager say, "I'm sure sorry about that, Miss Paige. I guess we missed him when we cleaned up the place. The last show that played here was six months ago."

Through everything, that old adage "The show must go on" was the order of the day. After all, this was vaudeville. People bought their tickets to see the real thing. There were no retakes, cut the tape or let's start again. When you were on, you were on, and you had one shot at it.

My agents were MCA, then the largest talent agency in the world, and seemingly they knew it. Except for taking their 10% cut of my paycheck and sending over my new itinerary, I was invisible to them.

My next date turned out to be in McKeesport, PA. My heart sank along with my frail ego when I found out they had booked me into a bar! I was once a movie star, but at that point I didn't know who I was.

The place reeked of stale beer from a bar made of glass bricks, lit from below. It made everybody look like death warmed over, including me and the female bartender.

I would squeeze my way through a narrow opening and make my entrance past the people at the bar, laughing, talking and drinking. A few steps ahead was a three-piece band whose trumpeter's lip was shot. He played notes that were definitely not on my charts or even in the universe.

I entertained to the best of my ability as I endured a week of feeling degraded and finished. As I write about it, I can still feel the sickening shock. I didn't even have a conductor to save me from some of the embarrassment at trying to reach musicians who couldn't have cared less.

A year before, I had been a stellar part of the great Warner Bros. roster and known the world over. Now, I was lost in a bar in McKeesport.

I'll never forget it as long as I live. As I write about it, I can still feel the gut-wrenching shock as I viewed my latest job.

For five eventful years, every decision had been made for me by Warner Bros. Now, I was often paralyzed with fear. No offers came my way except the next theater, nightclub or, if I were lucky, one of the lovely rooms in the hotel chains.

I may have been forgotten to Hollywood in this new career I had forged for myself, but I was paying the bills and seeing parts of America that had only been little dots on a map. I knew no one, so I spent my days discovering parts of our history I never knew existed.

There was always some generous citizen with hometown pride there to help me find the little-known places of interest. I was increasing my education along with my ability on a stage.

What I still didn't know was how to clean up, clear out and face the reality of my personal life. To touch that battleground made me feel like an instant failure. The same childhood fear about speaking up for myself was alive and well and festering. You can run, but you can't hide from yourself.

I traveled with two huge, black Masonite telescoping cases. One held my music and all of my arrangements in case I got lucky and got a full band; the second held my stage wardrobe, makeup, jewelry, props, hair stuff and the ever-present candy bars in case I hadn't eaten. Believe me, they were often all I had between me and the familiar hunger pangs.

Sometimes, trains didn't pull into a station until four in the morning. The only thing open was a White Castle with those tiny, delicious hamburgers swimming in their special sauce. My vaudevillian teachers were always there to help, and one of them instructed me to "buy a sack, you'll finish them"—and I did! Much as I love caviar, nothing could ever compare with those White Castle burgers when you're starving.

Today, performers are seldom alone. Beginning with the manager and agents, we have the road manager, wardrobe and makeup people, publicists, personal assistants and a few gofers. I realize that times have changed, but looking back, I believe that my aloneness taught me to survive and to experience events in my life that I would not have experienced had I not been alone.

I just put one foot in front of the other, did what I had to do and, by a kind of osmosis, learned to wear my stage face, to be brave, to fight for myself and—if need be—a few others along the way.

Of course, there were times when I was simply panicked. I remember going to the airport in Terre Haute, Indiana, after playing the theater in Evansville. My agents had told me that I could catch a plane for Chicago at five a.m. and make my eight a.m. music rehearsal at the theater. I'd had no sleep, but I got me and my little dog, Jody, to the airport, only to find that they weren't open that early.

Damn MCA and their precious ten percent that they take out of my tired hide. I was frantic. Dawn was breaking when I found a night watchman. I related my sad, scary story and he said, "Well, you could get a cab to drive you there."

"A cab!" I cried. "What's that going to cost me?"

Approximately a half hour later, Jody and I, my wardrobe, my music and two sacks of White Castle burgers—one for us and the other for the cabbie—were headed to Chicago. The drive cost me $100, plus a tip. I made the rehearsal, dumped my stuff and Jody in the dressing room and began to prepare for an 11:30 show.

When I look back on my journey of a thousand miles, even Lao Tsu would have had to ask, "Why did she ever take that first step?" Once in a while, the train pipes would freeze with icy water covering the floor. The flooded compartment never mattered as long as your wardrobe and orchestrations were safe and dry.

If I could get to the theater early, I always made a visit to the empty house with only a work light on the stage. What I saw each time was beautiful. I looked beyond the first few rows into the boxes, the ceilings and the proscenium arches.

Each theater was different, carved, painted and gilded by some artisan, now long forgotten. I listened for the voices of those preceding me and I never doubted that vaudeville waited so that I could know it, even if it was breathing its last sweet breath.

Besides making my own way through countless travel hazards and personal challenges, I became a vaudevillian. I learned my craft through each and every show. Never less than four and sometimes five and even six shows a day on weekends. I learned to "smell the house" and develop the third ear for the audience that Carol Channing spoke about.

I saw the quiet insides of every theater I ever played. I wrapped my hands around every proscenium arch, watching in my mind's eye as they milked their bows. The voices are long silent, but if you listen you can hear them, too.

If any of you can find an old theater, I challenge you to sit quietly and lose yourself in meditation and you'll feel them, all around. They, as I, live in the old gilded wood, the seats, the stage, the loges, the balconies, and never, ever forget the ceilings. A world of art lived up there, always different, and never to be repeated, or duplicated.

When I enter an old theater, I always find something to touch, knowing that some artisan of the day built the beauty and imagination that decorates the ancients. Sadly, too many of those old white elephants have fallen to the wrecking ball, along with a history buried in the rubble.

We somehow need to make way for this new world of superstars, super sound and super screens, ear-splitting volumes, hi-fi and all of the other hi's and fi's being discovered constantly.

I miss the Judy Garlands, Peter Allens, Fred Astaires and Gene Kellys. I miss those performers who could stand onstage like Ethel Merman or Mary Martin without anything but themselves. They were always bigger than what surrounded them. They had to be. The tools and tricks of the trade today weren't available. They had only themselves, their awesome talent, their voices and their unstoppable guts.

Time and progress, like everything else, steps over us, does not look back and keeps on keeping on.

Maybe there is a tiny part in your heart of hearts that will be stirred with my memories. In vaudeville, we enjoyed a lasting and special place in the hearts of our audience, and they in ours. There are a few performers today who can reach beyond the rim of the stage and deliver their own kind of vaudeville. But in my opinion, they are few.

In today's show world, sound is the star. I have to stick my fingers in my ears whenever I hear the Dolby sound system begin to play. My very good hearing is assaulted, and I simply wait it out.

I come from a time of lyric writers who wrote of our pain, love affairs, rejections, patriotism, blissful, sun-filled days and romantic, star-filled nights. We fell in love, broke up, went to war and came home. Everything lived through the words of the song.

I am constantly finding myself an utter failure in trying to understand how these new lyricists are interpreted by today's singers. Like Dolby, sound and tone are oblivious to what the words mean. Come to think of it, maybe it's better that way. The art of rhyme and inter-rhyme, except for those precious exceptions, seems to be lost in some dark and scary place called the extended teen years.

When vaudevillians didn't have microphones, they made their own sound with a big dose of heart spanning the footlights into the last balcony. Professional, and with that born-in-a-trunk security, you could feel it in your bones.

No wonder. Their acts were perfected through a generational theme passed from family to children to family again and again. Progress, age and the winds of change moved right over us without looking back, and they are working somewhere else now.

There are not enough "Thank yous" in me for my vaudeville years. What would I have done without them? Maybe I wouldn't have made it at all.

When the old Metropolitan Opera House in New York City was torn down in 1967, its fans and friends loudly protested this travesty. I, along with everyone else who had ever heard the operas in that hallowed place, was stunned.

"The voices! You're killing the voices!" we cried.

Those voices died with that magnificent old place, where they would drink, toast, be merry and sing their hearts out. After the opera, we always went to a little old hole in the wall in Little Italy called La Luna, where the grandpas would gather in a room at the back.

There was homemade wine, fresh pasta, a sauce to die for and the memory of the opera. We would toast the evening, the Met, New York and ourselves, and drink and dine like they did in *La Traviata*. Whatever the opera, we always left thirsty and hungry, and we always relived it at La Luna.

The trouble with memories is that we can't pass them on like jewelry or money or a keepsake. They only come around once, and they live with us until we go. I guess that's the price we pay for having them, enjoying them and remembering them.

Whatever the price, it's worth the memories I have as I write and leave this small part of them and my history.

Growth, courage, choices and getting in and out of trouble do not come with instructions. Life and living produce the choices we make. How we choose is the difference between happiness and hell, success and living lives of quiet desperation.

I've experienced it all at one time or another, and for me, the rewards far outweigh the losses.

Jack Carson
October 27, 1910 - January 2, 1963

Robert Alda
February 26, 1914 - May 3, 1986

Janis Paige
September 16, 1922 - Still truckin'

Warner Brothers made me a star.
Vaudeville made me an entertainer.

-Janis Paige

Surviving a Prophesy

> *Our survival depends on our courage and tenacity to challenge not only the forces without, but the forces contained within as well.*
>
> –Janis Paige

Survival is a complicated word. We survive to grow, to learn, to be healthy, to gain success, to lead, to help others and to make our lives matter. In 1950, however, the word survival meant only one thing to me and that was to keep on keeping on through what I could only call life's piling on.

I did not yet know the physical toll that my inability to face the dishonesty in my life would take. Work took me away from the constant trauma caused by family, but it still lurked just under my thin emotional skin.

Neither did I have the deep, sharing friendships so invaluable in times of need. I hid everything that could be used as gossip. As I recall that alone and relentlessly frightening time in my life, I simply survived. After all, this being 1950, we did not have the luxury of therapy nor could we safely admit that we needed it. I was completely clueless on the subject of anything somatic.

Italy was over and pushed aside for the next job. Between my dead-end marriage and not facing the truth about it or us, I was trapped in a kind of sickening stagnation.

Frank was never good about the need to face facts, anyway, so I was on my own and scared that I was right. Wrong was easier to face, it just verified that I wasn't good enough—so stay stuck.

Lying to myself and to Frank was making me sick. *Why won't he help me? Why won't he see there are two of us living in Hotel Futility?* I thought.

I felt my newfound Roman freedom slipping away. I had almost six months of finding my own way in a new country, a new language, a new culture and the constant discovery of the wonders of Rome, its history and its beauty beyond description.

The time I spent alone in Rome would prove to be a place of great strength for what was to come.

Home meant going back to what would never be changed, never be different, never be fixed. With no answers forthcoming, I felt trapped in a kind of angry hopelessness that never left me.

After six months in Italy, our new house was a stranger. Unlike Rome, we had running water, no rationing, no bucket brigade for the toilets and of course, no bidet. America didn't seem ready for that yet. If I worried about my next job, I didn't have to wait long. I lived there all of eight weeks. It was never my home.

Jack Carson and Robert Alda were taking their show into the big old vaudeville houses for about six weeks or so and asked me to join them. We were all ex-Warner Bros. stars and Jack and I had done several films together. We would begin the tour in Chicago at the old but still beautiful Chicago Theatre.

As we neared our vaudeville tour date in New York, my mother had been complaining about never seeing my shows, so I sent her a plane ticket.

"I've never been to New York and I have nothing to wear," she said.

"Take my mink stole, Mom."

I got her a seat for the biggest hit show on Broadway, *Born Yesterday* starring Judy Holliday, When my husband heard, he asked, "What about me?"

"I'm doing five shows a day, Frank," I reasoned. "You'll have to decide for yourself."

Frank flew in and all hell broke loose.

I had just finished my fourth show of the night and headed back to my dressing room. We only had about an hour and a half between shows.

I changed my clothes and was preparing to get a quick bite to eat when someone said, "Telephone, Miss Paige."

The voice on the other end announced himself as the manager of the hotel where we were staying.

"I'm sorry to disturb you, Miss Paige, but we have a problem with your mother and your husband," the hotel manager warned. I wanted to throw up.

"They had a fight in the hallway, and your mother called the police. We can't have this kind of behavior in our hotel."

"I'm so deeply sorry, I'll be right there."

To hell with my bite to eat. I grabbed a cab and headed for my loving family. I was too livid and embarrassed to hear their so-called sides. Their hatred for one another was palpable.

"I only have a half hour before I get ready for the last show," I angrily told them. "Both of you shut up and listen to me! Mom, I want you packed tonight, ready to leave on the first plane in the morning. The same for you, Frank!"

"Your mother started it!" Frank argued.

"But you couldn't end it, could you? Not even for my sake. I don't give a damn who started it. I'm at the end of my rope with this crap. I don't want to hear another word about your disgraceful behavior. I'll have to try to mend fences and pray to God that the press doesn't get hold of this mess."

Back in 1950, we in my profession kept everything from the press. Any personal stench could ruin a life, let alone a career.

I remember what we did to Ingrid Bergman and Robert Mitchum. He was arrested and jailed for smoking a bit of marijuana. Today, the country can't wait to legalize and allow unending supplies of pot without a thought to the addictive qualities of this drug. Smut of every kind feeds the internet, and we even make multimillionaires from the exposure of their videoed, sexual exploits.

The only difference between the millionaires and basic porn is that they don't require a plain brown wrapper to obscure it anymore. In 1950, scandal could mean the destruction of one's very life. Either way, the hypocrisy is stunning.

"Neither one of you has an ounce of shame at what you've done!" I fumed. "Go home! Apologies are in order but, as usual, I hear nothing."

I was shaking as I got dressed for the show. *Get hold of yourself, Janis*, I said to myself. *How much longer are you going to lie to yourself? You can't live like this. You're going to get sick and then where will you be?*

I left the rage and fears in the wings and forgot for an hour or so that anything was wrong. I took my bows, picked up the ever-growing pile of problems I'd left inside the proscenium arch and wondered about my next step. I was clueless to the fact that I was an emotionally battered, twenty-seven-year-old woman without a clue as to her next step.

But I didn't have to wait long.

The thought of going home was repugnant to me, so I decided to stay in New York. I took an apartment where I had stayed before. Back then, it was called the Park Central Hotel on 56th and Seventh Avenue. I felt at home there, away from the hell and failure I felt every time I went back to LA.

Perhaps some time to myself would yield an answer to the as-yet-unanswerable mess in which I found myself.

A short time after I moved in, I began to feel sickish. I thought it was the stress of the past weeks, but wrong again, Jan. I woke one morning at four a.m. vomiting like I'd never stop.

My God, now what? I asked as I crawled back to bed. Now I have food poisoning?

I was still sick a few days later, so I phoned a friend for the name of a doctor. I called for an appointment and he asked, "Can you come now? You might have to wait a little, but it won't be too long."

I thanked him and made my way to his office on 54th Street, not far from the hotel. A short time after I arrived, a nurse ushered me into his sunny office. I was soon examined, tests were taken, questions were asked and answered, and then, "I'll call you in a couple of days with the results of your visit. Get some rest and try not to worry."

As I walked back to the hotel, worry was all I did; it had become my middle name.

A few days later, the doctor called to say he wanted to see me. I walked to his office and waited. *What's wrong with me? What is he not saying? What am I going to hear? What will I do?*

Finally, the nurse said, "You can go in, Miss Paige."

The doctor looked up, asked me to sit down and began to speak.

"You're pregnant, Miss Paige," he said.

"Oh my God, no!" I cried. I tried to hold back the tears, but they poured out in despairing sobs. He was quiet and let me cry this horror out.

"What's wrong, Miss Paige? Tell me."

Oh, I wish I could, I thought. My basic job in my eyes was to hide anything about my mother's unpredictable behavior and the constant fear that her compulsiveness and knee-jerk reactions would jeopardize the very thing that she said she wanted and had sacrificed for, namely my career.

My other job, as I saw it, was to protect my reputation and that of my husband's happy, acceptable life. What a lousy, thankless job it was. I don't remember when it wasn't my job to fix my unhappy, scary and sad mother. *Where is the anybody who will help fix me?*

I stopped my mental and emotional punishment and got control of myself. The tears finally stopped flowing.

"What do I do now?" I asked the doctor.

"I want you to understand the problem you will likely have with any pregnancy," he told me. "You have a very rare blood type. You are AB Negative with an RH factor."

He could have been speaking Greek for all I knew.

"Please help me understand what you're saying."

"What I'm saying, in a nutshell, is that RH babies do not stay long in the uterus. Miscarriages occur usually in the first five weeks to two months. It varies. The body does not want an RH baby. We don't always know why. There have been experiments with completely changing the blood of the baby if we can bring it to term. You would have to go to bed for the entire nine months so as not to risk a miscarriage."

I sat there paralyzed.

"If anything happens or you need me," the doctor tried to reassure me, "call anytime."

As I walked back to the hotel, everybody seemed so carefree and content, but those feelings had become foreign to me—except when I was in costume, with footlights, a mike, a band and an audience. I felt safe there. It may have been safe, but it was also deeply sad.

Back in my apartment, I sat, dreading the call to Frank. What was he going to do? Be happy? *How were you going to help, Frank?* I wondered. Then I thought, *My mother, oh my God. I can't tell my mother, at least not now.*

I knew I had to at least call Frank.

"It's Jan, Frank. We have to talk. I'm pregnant, and there are problems."

I reiterated the talk with the doctor and the iffy prognosis. He was as confused as I but thrilled at the news. I didn't have the strength to pursue a conversation.

"Please do not tell my mother—*please!*" I begged.

"I won't, don't worry about that," Frank said.

I thanked him and said goodnight. There was no offer to come to New York and I didn't ask. Another sleepless night, wondering about the unknown and vomiting. When does it stop? I finally gave up trying to sleep and got up.

I made coffee and realized the cupboard was bare. Maybe a trip to Gristedes grocery store would clear my head—although food was the last thing on my mind. With my list in hand I headed for the elevator.

Hey, Gristedes, how about selling a little advice, a little help, a hug, anything that would rid me of this constant, never-ending nausea. I heard a door shut and felt someone standing beside me.

"Good morning, Ms. Paige, how are you?" I turned to the voice and found myself looking into the smiling and sweet face of Mrs. Eleanor Roosevelt, the former First Lady.

Before I could respond, she told me how happy she was to meet me and how much she admired my work. I tried not to be speechless, so I thanked her for her recognition of me.

"Meeting you is a thrill, Mrs. Roosevelt. I only wish that my grandfather could be here. I grew up in the house of a New Dealer. He had great faith in the President. My grandfather loved this country and was a patriotic and respectful citizen. My sister and I grew up with those same values."

The elevator door opened, and Mrs. Roosevelt pushed the button for the lobby. She was one of the warmest, most available people I ever met, and as we made small talk on the way down, I wished with all of my heart that she would ask me, "What's wrong, Miss Paige? You can talk to me."

I had, after all, just received word from my doctor that I was pregnant with a baby who likely wouldn't make it to full term, and I was feeling devastated. I knew that if I mentioned this to Mrs. Roosevelt, I'd get a hug, reassurance and a "How can I help you?" but I could never do anything like that.

The former First Lady asked me if she could drop me somewhere.

"I'm going in the opposite direction, Mrs. Roosevelt, but thank you. I'll never forget meeting you. You are very important to us, so take care of yourself."

With that, I got my hug. The former First Lady gave me a hug!

Visiting Gristedes proved the mental relief I needed. I put everything away in the kitchen and tried to nap when the phone rang. No "Hello, how are you"? Just the sweet voice of my mother demanding, "What do you think you're doing, getting pregnant? You're ruining your career. Are you crazy?"

I could scarcely breathe.

"Hello, Mom. How did you know?"

"Walter Winchell announced it on his radio show. Everybody knows!"

So much for my precious privacy. What I didn't know was that the famous Mr. Winchell had his offices in the Park Central Hotel, and he paid the operators to listen to the phone calls of those who could provide him with a scoop.

I don't remember falling asleep, but I'll never forget what woke me up. I was hemorrhaging and terrified. I called the doctor while I grabbed a towel from the bathroom. How long had it been since I'd seen him? He'd called a few times to ask how I felt, but aside from that, I felt too lousy to do anything but stay quiet.

"This is your doctor, Miss Paige. What's happened?"

No tears or panic now, just strangely calm.

"I'm bleeding, doctor, and it won't stop," I explained. "What should I do?"

"I'm calling Doctor's Hospital right now." he said, "Grab a cab and get there as fast as you can. They'll be expecting you."

I stuffed a few more towels in me, had the presence of mind to put on a big coat and grabbed the elevator for the lobby. I jumped into a cab and said, "Get me to Doctor's Hospital fast, please."

"Do you want to go through the park or take Fifth Avenue?" the cabbie asked. "The park is longer, but it's faster."

Oh my God, this is no time for choices! I thought. "Please, just go fast," I said.

"Okay," he replied, "I'll take the park."

And with that, I leaned my head back on the seat. Something about the park, Fifth Avenue, the honesty of the cabbie or the insanity of this unreal situation provoked a giggle that traveled up and out until it was a full-blown laugh that I couldn't stop or control.

Here I was, hopefully not bleeding all over his back seat, and laughing.

"Did I say something funny, Miss?" the cabbie asked.

"Oh, thank you so much, you did," I answered.

The look on his face in the rearview mirror was loud and clear: "This lady is kinda crazy."

At that particular moment, he may have been right.

"We're here, lady. Good luck."

I shoved some money into his hand and got through the hospital door as quickly as I could. *God, please don't let me bleed on the floor or through my coat.* I ran to the desk and told the receptionist my name.

"Yes, Miss Paige, your doctor called. I'll get you to a room."

Soon, I was in a bed, legs raised, and someone gave me a shot to stop the hemorrhage. I don't know how long I was asleep, but I awoke while it was still dark. I lay there trying not to support all of the questions that traveled in and out of my tired brain.

No one knows where I am, so I thought I'd better call Frank and asked the operator to get me a number.

"This is Jan, Frank. I'm in Doctor's Hospital. I had a bad hemorrhage. I haven't seen a doctor yet, so I can't tell you anything."

"I'll leave in about an hour," he said. "I'll be there in three days or a little less."

"You're driving?" My voice and my blood pressure rose in tandem.

"I have to, Jan. I have some business to take care of in New York and need my car. I should be there the day after tomorrow."

Why am I not surprised, Frank? I thought. We were so wrong for each other, and for ourselves.

I was finally visited by a doctor and his assistant. He poked and prodded me, met by my cries of pain. The discomfort of his examination was easier to tolerate than his passive-aggressive hostility toward me.

I was scared to death by the whole situation, and now I was scared of him. "What's wrong with me?" I asked. "Can you do something to help me?" His answer sickened me.

"We don't do that sort of thing here, Miss Paige. Don't ask again."

Oh my God, that's not what I meant! Before I could protest, he was gone. This was 1950, and he left me devastated and feeling dirty.

Somewhere between falling asleep and waking up, a blurred but definite decision had formed. I had to get out of that hospital room. I came in with nothing but the clothes on my back and I was leaving the same way.

I was putting on my shoes when the nurse came in. They all treated me very well, but she said, "Miss Paige, what are you doing? You can't leave. I have to call the doctor."

"The only permission you need is mine," I said, "and if you try to stop me, I'll kill you. I'm sorry, but please get out of my way."

I'll never forget the look on that poor nurse's face as she said, "Oh, Miss Paige, Miss Paige," as she moved away from me. I guess I finally knew how it felt to have my back against that proverbial wall. No matter what happened, I was coming out swinging!

I finished dressing, put on my coat, grabbed my bag and headed for the elevator. The only thought in my mind was to get out to a place where I could breathe.

I heard the elevator doors open and out walked Frank. He had a two-day growth of beard and looked exhausted.

"Frank, get me out of here!" I said in a panic.

"What are you doing, Jan?" he asked, confused. "Where are you going?"

"Please get me out of here, Frank. They'll try to stop me, and I can't stay here another minute." With that, we grabbed the elevator, walked swiftly toward the lobby doors and out to the car.

"What do you want me to do, Jan? What happened? What's going on?"

"I need to call the doctor, Frank, so please, let's go back to the hotel. Besides, you need a shower and a shave."

When I called the doctor, I said to the nurse on the phone, "I've left the hospital, and I need to see the doctor. It's important."

"Let me tell him, Miss Paige."

He came on the phone and asked if I could be in his office around one o'clock. "I'll work you in, Janis."

We were on time, and so was he. I introduced him to Frank and asked him to explain what was wrong with me. When he finished, he looked at both of us and said, "It will be a miracle if you have this baby. It's just a matter of time before something happens that could be worse."

He looked at us for what seemed a very long time and then said, "I don't do the kind of operation you need, but I'm giving you the name of someone I trust very much. I'll call him for you. He's a very fine doctor and he's just around the corner. You'll be safe with him. I'll do this for you, but we must never speak of this again, or him. Let's see when he can see you."

Every instinct, every thought I'd ever had about one day having a happy marriage, a child, that normal life that's out there somewhere was gone. It was now just a part of the terror, guilt and any other damnation I could hang on myself.

I was about to do something that I swore I'd never do, that happens to someone else but not to me. I had started to bleed again, and I was scared to death.

At seven o'clock that same night, I entered a lovely office on 54th Street near Fifth Avenue. A uniformed and very kind nurse ushered me in and helped me to get ready.

When the doctor came in, he took my hand and told me not to worry.

"You're safe here," he assured me. "Your doctor filled me in completely and you're doing the right thing."

I went to sleep. When I awoke, there was more kindness and empathy from both the doctor and nurse. When we sat down with him in his office, he asked me about the "butchers" in the hospital.

"They had no right to examine you as they did. It must have been painful," he said. Still groggy, I just nodded. We left with instructions for my recovery and a follow-up appointment. I remember sleeping for almost two days, and when I finally woke up, I physically felt fine, but I never got over thinking about that little life I would never know.

When I finally married the right man years later, I wanted to have our child. I was almost thirty-nine. No tests were necessary to tell me I was pregnant. I just knew. I could get pregnant but could not carry past five or six weeks.

I saw many experts in the baby department, but nothing worked. The last time I was pregnant, I was forty-five, with the same old result. I was oftentimes depressed and sad.

One day, my patient husband simply said, "No more, honey, no more."

When I finished *Mame* in 1969, my birthday present was a beautiful mare called Joy. We were in the middle of horse country in Maryland, having just bought her. Excitement, disbelief and the sheer wonder of what my husband had done prompted me to say, "How do I say thank you, sweetheart? What can I do for you, honey?"

"Let's look for a place to eat," he said. "We're out in the middle of corn fields and you know how much I love corn on the cob."

An epiphany hit me.

There was a big hardware store about five miles back near our motel.

"Stop at the next corn stand and get what you want and don't ask questions," I instructed.

He got the corn, I bought a pot, a hot plate, butter, salt and pepper, paper plates and a huge package of paper napkins.

"I'm going to fix you corn on the cob, honey, as many ears as you can eat," I said.

"But how?" he asked.

"Oh, for gosh sakes, I'm from vaudeville. You have no idea of what I can do without a kitchen."

The room held twin beds. I set up the hot plate on the floor between them, filled the pot with water and waited for it to boil. One bed became the table, set with plates, napkins, butter, salt and pepper and the fresh corn waiting to be quickly boiled. Plastic utensils joined the party.

I watched my loving and generous husband enjoy himself in a kind of Maryland white corn orgy. Between bites, he managed to murmur, "I don't believe this, I don't believe this."

"Told ya," I laughed.

When we bred Joy and her delivery time grew near, I slept in the stall next to her. At three-thirty on a freezing March morning, her foal was born, and I helped bring him into the world. His foreleg got stuck and I had to reach inside my mare and gently straighten it out. When I did, he shot out onto my lap, soaking wet and me crying all over him.

When I'd freed him, Joy lifted her head and uttered a soft little nicker to her newborn foal. It was the most endearing sound I'd ever heard. I couldn't stop crying as I tended to her precious newborn baby, cleaning his eyes and nose, giving him an enema and finally getting him on his feet so that he could have his first meal from his momma.

I never had kids myself, but I had the blessing of an up-close and deeply moving experience with birth. It was the most precious gift I ever received.

Great minds discuss ideas. Average minds discuss events. Small minds discuss people.

-Mrs. Eleanor Roosevelt

Dr. Arnold A. Hutschnecker

Depression is a partial surrender to death.
—Dr. Arnold A. Hutschnecker

A FEW WEEKS AFTER I had physically recuperated from the trauma of an unsuccessful pregnancy in 1950, I was offered a film called *Mr. Universe*, to be shot in New York City. I would co-star with Jack Carson and Robert Alda, the great Bert Lahr and a new young man named Vince Edwards. He would go on to television fame as Dr. Ben Casey. Working again with old friends from Warner Bros. days was a joy, as was the cast.

We were getting ready to shoot a scene when suddenly I felt myself hemorrhaging again. The floor beneath me was puddling in blood, and the sheer terror, embarrassment, fear and panic drove me in a breakneck run anywhere but where I was at that horrifying moment.

I raced until I ran into the far wall of the soundstage, where I simply sank to the floor. All I remember were hands and arms trying to help me, but I was only concerned with not being there or being seen in that condition. I was hoisted onto a work table, my legs were elevated and I was told that my doctor was on his way.

I looked down to see bloody towels and blurry, scared faces around me. I stared up and away, pleading with God to let me die.

Sometime early that same year, I did a television special with the wondrous Art Carney and produced by the talented and innovative David

Susskind. I did not have a manager, and David said, "You need one, Janis, your business is changing."

Her name was Ruth Aarons, and she and her brother would guide me for many years. When she found out that I didn't have a doctor in New York, she introduced me to Dr. Arnold A. Hutschnecker. My guardian angel was watching over me again.

Dr. Hutschnecker was a slight man, with a kind and caring aura. This would be my first time to see him as a patient. He quickly thanked everyone and quietly asked them to leave so that he could examine me. He gave me a shot to stop the bleeding and held my hand, calmly assuring me that I would be all right while silent tears rolled down my cheeks.

The next day, I went to his office. I sat across the desk from someone who would not only alter the way I looked at life, but how I approached relationships, starting with the one I had with my mother.

He had escaped the horror of the Nazi experiments and landed in New York City with $35 to his name. He began to practice, like so many of our finest doctors who got out of the same fate. They simply refused to obey the demands of Hitler and barely escaped with their lives.

Dr. Hutschnecker was in the early stages of writing a book. It was to be the first book ever written for the layman on psychosomatic medicine and its effects on the human condition. I now know that my traumatic encounter with Arnold was instead actually an epiphany, a life-changing event, and there would be many more epiphanies on this long road I was traveling.

He and his wife, Florita, took me into their hearts, and I spent countless weekends in their sculptor-built house in Sherman, Connecticut. It reminded me of Hansel and Gretel's house in *Grimm's Fairy Tales*.

While Florita worked her magic in the kitchen, Arnold and I would sit at their big, old, age-scarred table that looked like it had come from some castle on the Rhine. My imagination allowed me to hear the knights with their goblets raised, praising some battle they were about to wage.

Little did I know that my own battle toward a more integrated and useful life was just beginning.

Arnold was writing *The Will to Live*. He would read a chapter to me and then ask me if I understood what he had written. I was encouraged to ask questions and discuss the subject until I was clear, or at least clearer.

One day, Arnold said, "You're my guinea pig, Jan. After all, I'm writing this book for people like you."

I began to see myself in the pages, and that's how I started my journey to elementary enlightenment and beyond.

We would sit around that beautiful old table, a fire in the huge baronial fireplace and a jar of fresh caviar in front of us. I had never before tasted caviar, and I wasn't particularly interested in doing so until I heard Arnold say, "Just try it."

Oh, what famous last words! I was hooked for all time. Every Christmas, my present to myself is still a two-ounce jar of fresh caviar, toast points, finely chopped onion, crumbled egg yolks and a squeeze of lemon. I invite no one. I make no excuses for my selfish behavior and I'm in heaven until every little bit of egg is gone.

Oh, I almost forgot the champagne. "Never eat caviar without champagne," he would remind me with a laugh. "Good champagne."

Those two utterly amazing people are gone now. Florita died in 1966, Arnold in 2001. He was 102. How we could use his wisdom, vision and truth now. Anyone who knew him got his very best, always.

"You'll meet your mother all through your life," Arnold would assure me. "There will be familiar and disturbing signs in some personal relationships, and your job is to recognize the similarities from your childhood."

He would continue, "Be careful of rigid and closed-up people. They'll pretend they're not, but don't get fooled."

The only thing he didn't tell me was that it would take a lifetime of constant work and recognition to know and avoid the old familiar junk. Sometimes I succeeded, and sometimes not so much.

Why do we expect to shortcut to a rainbow in the middle of the storm instead of riding out the waves, learning how to stay afloat to see a rainbow rising over calmer waters? Why do we all too often feel deserving of the prize without knowing the pride we could feel in the struggle to win it?

You were the beginning for me, Arnold. Self-discovery still intrigues and fascinates me. I can't imagine my life without the constant growth it brings.

Dr. Arnold A. Hutschnecker
May 13, 1898 - December 28, 2000

Bert Lahr

That was my one big Hollywood hit, but in a way it hurt my picture career. After that, I was typecast as a lion, and there just weren't many parts for lions.

—Bert Lahr

Certain performers are blessed or doomed, depending on how we look at their uniqueness. There are particularly delicious, rare and perfectly cast roles that only come to life when the chosen actor shines his or her light on the character.

Bert Lahr did just that when he delivered a never-to-be-forgotten performance as a lion. He set the standard for playing lions, and we all identified with him. He was, after all, the Cowardly Lion who dared to find "C-c-c-c-c-ourage."

In 1939, I, along with millions of others, was forever enchanted by a film called *The Wizard of Oz*. Magic was created, not only in its perfect cast, its perfect score and its everlasting, Technicolored beauty, but also in its message that *we are enough*.

Each delectable character in the film was searching for what they already possessed. But like so many of us, they just didn't know it yet. The day that I saw it, I left the theater forever adoring everyone but, in particular, one Bert Lahr.

It wasn't until 1951 that we finally met on the set of *Mr. Universe*. The day we all sat around a big table to read the script, I couldn't take my eyes off Bert. Whether in repose, reading his role or just interacting with the cast, he was funny. He didn't mean to be but "We had faces then," to quote Gloria Swanson in her famous film *Sunset Boulevard*.

Men like Bert, Red Skelton and Gene Sheldon wore their marvelous faces easily and without artifice. They had long before mastered the art of a subtle change in expression befitting the material, or the reaction of an audience.

Emmett Kelly, on the other hand, had a face that was a blank canvas when he began to "paint" the most famous clown of all, Weary Willie, with his broom and often playfully elusive spotlight.

Each day on the set, I'd think of a way to ask Bert to do his Cowardly Lion roar. And each time, I'd back off not wanting to bother or embarrass him.

Then one day, out of the blue, I got my wish.

We were sitting around waiting to work when Bert suddenly roared. At first, I didn't think I'd heard it, but then, there it was again, and I was on The Yellow Brick Road once more.

Between my unstoppable laughter was my gratitude for the gift he'd given me forever, Bert was a quiet, soft-spoken giant in our profession who left an indelible mark on anyone who was fortunate enough to know him, even a little.

In 1960, Bert and I along with Boris Karloff and a stellar group of actors were cast in a David Susskind television special called *The Secret World of Eddie Higgins*. Bert and I played clowns. On my way to my dressing room one morning, I passed by Bert's. His door was open, and there he was sitting with his elbows on the makeup table and hands clasped in front of him, quietly staring into the mirror.

For a few seconds, I witnessed a private moment until he suddenly saw me at the door.

"Hi, Bert, how are you today?" I inquired.

He turned toward me in his chair and asked, "Was I any good yesterday, Janis? I don't think I was very good."

At that moment, I could only defend Bert from Bert. My voice rising, I said, "Bert, you're The Cowardly Lion, you're perfect and always will be."

"Thanks Janis," he said, "but I'm worried about yesterday."

No words of comfort would reassure him. Why is our gift of talent so often filled with pain? Bert always gave us so much joy. How I wished at that moment that I could have shared it with him and made him believe it.

I left Bert there with my totally insufficient, "Well, all I can say is, I adore you, Bert, and don't you forget it."

As I headed for makeup, my thoughts were on Bert and why he didn't know how wonderful he was. I felt funny and maybe a little sad, but my brief meeting with him had disturbed me and I didn't know why.

When I sat down to be transformed in the makeup chair, my thoughts were traveling in and out about those ever-present, punishing self-doubts with a glimpse, perhaps, into my own.

I watched as the artists worked their magic, until I disappeared. Looking back at me was a clown.

There I stood, my nose a round and rosy red bulb. They had painted a typical clown mouth with the corners going up instead of down, and I had freckles in various colors. I stared into the mirror, making faces at myself as I admired my crazy wig.

Next came the mismatched, oversized clothing and gaudy striped socks, with the *pièce de résistance* being those huge floppy clown shoes. They were funny just to look at, but when worn, they produced an unusual and hilariously funny walk, especially from the rear.

One should have earned hazard pay, because the walk came from trying not to fall over those enormous round-toed things on your feet. You were already larger than life, so a little over-the-top behavior was not only welcomed but was expected.

I'm in here somewhere, I thought as I joined Bert, Boris "Captain Hook" Karloff, Eddie Higgins and our circus. The hairdresser stuck a little hat on my head with a flower standing straight up and waving on its stem.

"We're ready," someone said, and we were.

I can only write from my own experiences, but Bert's seeming inability to appreciate his work or to really hear my unabashed praise of him opened a door to a mystery still unsolved.

Through the decades that followed, I've seen and felt that same, self-deprecating doubt, undeserving and a too-modest acceptance of our often-amazing talent. I've discovered these same feelings in myself, as if I didn't deserve applause for sharing my gift.

The subject is too dense, its reasons too diverse to understand in one small short lifetime. I have, however, found one common denominator that seems to link us all together, and that's the price of talent. I never met anyone who wouldn't pay it over and over again.

Bert Lahr
August 13, 1895 - December 4, 1967

Sammy Davis Jr. and Ciro's

The ultimate mystery is one's own self.
                              —Sammy Davis Jr.

There are moments in one's memory that never fade. They are as alive today as if they happened yesterday. The body never forgets, and I can feel the nausea, the embarrassment and that unbearable loneliness when you are all you have.

The year was 1951. David Susskind had found me a manager, MCA was my agent and I had begun to put my life back into some semblance of an order and future.

I was living in New York City, and I had found a tiny apartment on West 55th Street next door to the beautiful old Gotham Hotel. It was a converted brownstone with two small apartments to each floor, a great landlady—and it was mine, all mine. The kitchen was windowless because it had been a walk-in closet. The elevator shaft took up most of the tiny living room. The other rooms were a tiny bathroom and a tiny bedroom overlooking a courtyard.

At the time, I was still supporting a lovely house in Longridge Estates as well as my mother's house in North Hollywood. Frank and I had separated, and while I was on the road working, he and his vitriol proceeded to take everything of value. He left me a bunch of old pots and pans, a braided rug and very little else.

When I finally had the opportunity to confront Frank, I asked, "Why didn't you split the silver, the china and the crystal? Half of it was mine. Why did you take it all? You're not fair. I have nothing here."

Frank came back with, "I didn't want this separation, you did! Besides, the silver has an 'M' on it!"

It was at that moment that I knew, no matter what I had or didn't have, I was free.

I bought a bed and that was it. The living room had no furniture, and the only practical thing I owned was an ironing board. You can't imagine what you can chop, slice and prepare on an ironing board. I also bought myself *The Good Housekeeping Cookbook* and finally began to live.

With the help of my manager Ruth Aarons and a talented writer, we put an act together, broke it in a few times and then got the offer to play the famous Ciro's nightclub in Los Angeles. I was scared to go back to California but at the same time excited and hopeful. *Maybe they'll rediscover me*, I thought. So many hopeful plans. So many maybes.

Opening night was packed. Jack Benny and Mary Livingston as well as George Burns and Gracie Allen were front and center. Everywhere I looked, there were celebrities. Tuxes, beautiful clothes, jewelry and elegance filled every table.

That was the atmosphere created by the age of nightclubs. Fortunately, they became a major part of my ability to earn a living. There was constant travel and constant employment, and entertainers were sometimes blessed with too much work.

The marquee read, "CIRO'S—Starring Janis Paige." Below my billing was "Sammy Davis Jr. with The Will Mastin Trio." I had worked with opening acts who were unknown to me many times. They were simply other performers I would get to know during the run.

We had two blessed weeks of work. I was back home where I started, and (thank you, God) starring at Ciro's. Life and the work that I loved were once again coming together. It was, in a word, wonderful.

"And now," the announcer began, "Ciro's is proud to present . . . The Will Mastin Trio with Sammy Davis Jr.!" Their music started, and one of the stellar lights of our profession was born.

Sammy did everything perfectly. Danced great, sang great, did impressions, told jokes and had the audience entranced, exhausted and completely hooked. They would not let him leave the stage.

Watching him, I began to die a little. Finally, when my name was announced and I sang my opening number, I could have phoned me in. The audience talked throughout my performance. I tried my best and kept going, but I wasn't necessary after Sammy.

I took my bows—such as they were—and finally made my exit.

When I came off the stage, what I saw was a kind of bedlam. I made my way to my dressing room through an already swarming group of photographers, agents and visitors.

"Sammy, over here, one with Jack Benny!"

"Mr. Hover, can we get a picture with Sammy?"

Not one photographer asked for my picture, and there was no knock on my door. No congratulations. Nothing but Ruth assuring me that the show was "wonderful."

"No one saw or heard me, Ruthie," I said, fighting back tears.

My body was a combination of shame, paralysis and a sickening feeling of failure. At that moment, I heard my mother's voice reminding me that I wasn't that good.

We waited in painful silence until everyone had gone and we sneaked out. No "Good show tonight, Miss Paige." No "See you tomorrow, Miss Paige." Those words were spent instead on Sammy Davis Jr., and they were right. He was sensational.

After a fitful sleep, I awoke to the thought, *Oh my God, I have to go back there again tonight!* I was sick. The hours seemed like years. There were no calls, nothing but my own convoluted thoughts going over and over the night before.

What went wrong? Was it me? Wasn't I any good? How can I go out there again tonight? I was trapped inside my head as the questions and insecurities swirled around.

But I had no choice. I had to go back. "The show must go on!" and all that bullshit. I was deeply hurt, terrified, ashamed, discouraged and felt a deep sense of futility. My hopes had been so high before and were now so low.

I made my way through the stage door to my dressing room. I began to put my makeup on, do my hair and get dressed when there was a knock on the door. I opened it to see Herman Hover, the owner of Ciro's, standing there.

Am I getting fired? I wondered.

Mr. Hover was curt.

"I think it best that you open the show from now on, Janis," he said. "You can't follow Sammy. I'll leave the billing as is, but you open the show."

My manager protested, but Mr. Hover was adamant. By now, the word had spread about this phenomenal young star, and the audience was breathlessly waiting—not for me but for Sammy Davis Jr.

Ciro's is opposite a short little street called Olive. I would leave early, park on the hill on Olive, and cry. I cried until I stopped. I would then make my way through that dreaded stage door to my dressing room and prepare to face what felt like a little death each night.

It was always the same. The audience couldn't wait for Sammy, and the energy and excitement in the room for Sammy made me feel superfluous. No, I *was* superfluous! I can honestly say that Ciro's and Sammy was the hardest, most degrading and most difficult job of my career. In my beautiful new Ciro's gown, I was invisible.

Of course, the fangs appeared and contrary to comments made by George Schlatter and others, such as, "Janis Paige could not go on after the first night. She couldn't follow Sammy!"

Well, where were you, George? Did you forget that I was there too, and I never missed a show? Remember me, George? I became the opening act.

Through the years, I wondered why you perpetuated this fantasy, George. I guarantee you, if I had not gone on each night, Mr. Hover would have sued my ass off and rightfully so. So, from the horse's mouth, George, I opened for Sammy for the full two weeks and I never missed a show! Now please, knock it off.

By the way, George, did you know that the great Sophie Tucker, among other headliners, found that they, too, couldn't follow Sammy either? And like I, they all had to swallow their pride and open for this phenom known as Sammy Davis Jr.?

Outside of Judy Garland, I had never seen anything like him. His talent was boundless. There was nothing he couldn't do as he owned every show.

I had prayed that Ciro's would open up a new pathway to movie work and a kind of new beginning. Instead, I tucked my tail between my legs, took what little courage I had left and escaped to New York City, vowing never to return to California again.

Herman Hover didn't even say goodbye.

After Ciro's, I got a two-week run at the El Rancho Vegas in Las Vegas. My run there enjoyed a packed house every night, helping to make up for my Ciro's debacle. I had fantastic reviews, did great business and began to find my guts again. Also, I finally made the decision to stay an extra month to finalize my divorce from Frank Martinelli Jr.

The El Rancho was owned and run by Beldon Katleman. When I asked if I could rent the little house that I had lived in during my two weeks in his club, he answered, "Of course you can, Janis. For how long?"

"I'll need a month," I said.

"Pay us when you check out."

During my two-week run there, food, rent and everything was picked up by Beldon. It's what he did for his stars. He was generous beyond words.

When I got ready to leave for New York, I asked for my bill.

"Everything's been taken care of, Miss Paige, you owe nothing," I was told.

"But, but, but, I can't accept this, I want to pay my bill."

"Compliments of Mr. Katleman," he said.

And that was that. There are people connected to times in your life who are never forgotten. He made that unpleasant and lonely month livable and even hopeful that my life was looking up.

When Mr. Katleman finally let me say "Thanks," his answer was, "Forget it, Janis, it's my pleasure. Good luck and come back."

You're long gone, Beldon, but never, ever forgotten.

I felt like the launching pad for the meteor that the world would know as Sammy Davis Jr. He found his fame that night at Ciro's—and I found courage.

Courage didn't announce itself, mind you. There was no skywriting. No noise. No visible change. But my life was altered.

I took me, my courage and my divorce papers and fled to New York City and freedom.

Through the years that followed, I would see Sammy in clubs or the theater. I watched him become this diamond-encrusted, gold-chained, driving-the-high-road racer, never seeming to come down from the hyperbole of his life.

Sammy denied himself nothing. Money was spent over and over again in his Rat Pack world of fun, fame, drugs and rock 'n' roll. He knew the great good fortune achieved by only a few.

Did it ever occur to him, I wondered, *that this couldn't last?* He would say, "I have to touch earth one day, I have to get grounded, I'm not Pegasus, and I'll burn up."

Unfortunately, something else stopped Sammy.

Somehow, during his fiery ride of a life, he gathered great wisdom. As the Rat Pack aged and waned, Sammy came to grips with what he missed, but was now gone. He had so much still to give that had nothing to do with his talent.

In the late Eighties, we had a very popular daytime talk program called *The Sally Jessy Raphael Show*. She was an excellent interviewer, intelligent, thorough and always kept the shows interesting and very watchable.

Clever, successful people find a label, a gimmick, something that sets them apart from the pack. Sally's identification was a pair of bright red-rimmed glasses that she always wore. Those glasses and her ability to personalize her guests brought her well-deserved fame for many years.

As I turned on her show one day, she was announcing Sammy. I hadn't seen him for some time, and as I watched, I saw a very different man.

Gone was the brashness, the manic and excessive behavior. He was quieter, more introspective, less everything-is-a-joke, and he looked different. Yes, he was older, but there was something else. I watched in fascination, remembering the Sammy that I knew. Comparing the one before me left me feeling a kind of sadness for the old Sammy.

We were having a soaring drug problem. Our young men and women were succumbing to a flagrant and tempting supply of narcotics, with addiction becoming rampant.

As I heard Sammy speak, an idea began to form. That very day, I wrote him a three-page letter, telling him how impressed I was with his interview and to please consider becoming the spokesperson against the epidemic of drugs facing our young people, not to mention our country.

"You've done it all, Sammy," I wrote. "You've had it all. You can reach these kids. You can make a difference. You can take everything you know and give it back. You can be a true hero. Please consider my words, Sammy. We need you."

The year was 1989, and my letter went unanswered—which surprised me. It was unlike him.

Every holiday season, Hollywood has a Christmas parade, as it did in 1989. Sammy Davis Jr. was announced as the grand marshal of the parade, and there would be a group of stars from various walks of show business life who would ride in the parade along with Sammy.

I was invited that year. There were rumors, talk and gossip, and the usual questions about Sammy's health. Throat cancer was what we heard. My disbelief and sorrow followed.

We were all getting our marching orders when Sammy came in. I was shocked at how he looked. He was drawn, older, with that awful implosive appearance that cancer brings. I felt sick.

Sammy saw me and walked over. With a hug, he said, "Jan, I got your letter. It meant so much to me. I read it several times."

"I meant every word of it, Sammy. If ever I saw your true self, it was in that interview. I was deeply impressed and moved."

"I'm sorry I didn't get back to you," he said.

I told him that everything was still open, and if he wanted to talk with me, he knew where to find me.

"I'll look forward to it, Sammy."

We rode in our parade that night. As usual, Sammy got his "Sammy" applause. Anyone who ever saw him perform never forgot him.

The last words I ever had with Sammy went like this.

"How are you feeling, my friend?"

"Oh, I'm okay. I have to go get ready now. Thanks again for that wonderful letter. It meant a lot to me. I'll see ya!"

"Take care of yourself, Sammy."

We climbed into our parade vehicles and waved our way through the route. "Merry Christmas, Merry Christmas, Merry Christmas," until the last "Merry Christmas" had been wished.

Another Hollywood Christmas Parade was history, and so was Sammy Davis Jr.

Sammy died five months later. He was only sixty-four years old. He will not be forgotten. No life ever went untouched if Sammy had shared himself with you. He left everything on that stage. If ever there was a consummate performer, it was Sammy.

Sammy Davis Jr.
December 8, 1925 – May 18, 1990

You always have two choices—your commitment versus your fear.

"Remains to Be Seen"

*I LISTENED TO THOSE WHO THOUGHT AND ACTED
BEYOND MY FEARS AND DOUBT. THAT'S WHEN I
LEARNED HOW STRONG AND SMART I REALLY WAS.*

—JANIS PAIGE

WITH MY LITTLE apartment in New York and my newly found freedom, I had no idea what was going on in our new home in Longridge Estates. But there was no way I was going to find out without a break and a breather.

The old phrase, "Hell hath no fury like a woman scorned" had never met my ex-husband. It should have included men, too. I never expected such vitriol and vengeance.

He was right again in his mind, so Frank felt completely justified in unleashing all of his pent-up emotional junk on me. At that point, I just wanted to get back to my tiny bit of heaven on West 55th Street and people who were glad to see me.

I was not yet prepared to handle the closed system that was my husband, so I always ended up feeling like the dimmest bulb in the bunch because of my inability to reach him. Between my mother and my husband, I felt like an utter failure.

But I just played Las Vegas to packed houses, I thought. *I'm a success somewhere.* I reminded myself of this as we landed at La Guardia Airport.

Along with my successful run at the El Rancho Vegas, I also had my divorce papers.

I dumped my bags and grabbed a cab to the MCA offices. I was now out of a job again, so I wanted to present myself, ready to work. MCA had a sensational theatre division. Their agents were men experienced in all facets of Broadway.

Maynard Morris was sitting behind his desk when I was ushered in.

"Hi Maynard," I said.

He looked at me, then jumped up and asked, "Have they seen you for *Remains to Be Seen*?"

I laughed and said I had just gotten off of the plane from Las Vegas and I didn't know what he was talking about.

"Can you audition if we left now?" he asked. "Oh, of course you can," he answered himself.

While I waited, Maynard made several calls, then said, "Let's go."

Everything happened so fast. Maynard took my arm and steered me out of the MCA offices and into a cab, and off we went.

"For gosh sakes, Maynard, where are we going?" I asked, a bit confused.

"To the Morosco Theatre," he replied. "I called everyone to meet us there, including your manager."

Maynard paid the cabbie, and we entered through the stage door. As I got used to the dark of the backstage, a man introduced himself as Wally Wagner, the stage manager.

With that, Maynard took me onstage and introduced me to a small group of men sitting in the first two rows. There was a work light on stage and nothing more. I could see that the Morosco was an ornate little jewel box.

"Do you know why you're here, Miss Paige?" someone asked.

"I was told that I was to audition for something. I guess Maynard forgot to tell me what for."

They laughed at that.

"We're doing a new play called *Remains to Be Seen*. The role is for Jody Revere. We know this is very short notice, but would you read a few lines for us?"

The stage manager handed me a couple of pages and began to read the other part. I read Jody, they laughed some more, gave me a little applause, thanked me and offered me the starring role right there on the spot.

My honest answer almost killed Maynard and my wonderful new manager.

"Thank you," I explained, "but I have to tell you gentlemen that I've never done a play. I don't know anything about Broadway."

From the wings I heard, "Oh my God!"

When I looked up, Maynard and my brand-new manager gave the motion for me to shut up. Then I heard one of the men in the audience say, "We'd like you to say 'Yes,' Miss Paige, and please don't worry about Broadway. We're here to help you in whatever way we can. We've looked long and hard for our Jody Revere, and we finally found her."

I was scared, but before I knew what was happening, I was Jody and I had my first play. I got a lot of hugs and finally found out who these men were.

Maynard and Ruthie took me to Sardi's to celebrate. When we were seated, Maynard turned to me and said, "Have you any idea how fortunate you are, Janis? You're supported by Broadway's best." Then he proceeded to tell me just how completely I had lucked out.

Each and every member of that production was sensational. All were Broadway pros and knew the pressures of a new play and our hopes for a long run.

Unfortunately, while the audience loved us, Brooks Atkinson did not. Without his rave review in *The New York Times*, we could not get enough of an advance to carry us beyond four months.

I had my first pre-opening performances in New Haven, Connecticut. I had a "little" emergency onstage that night. My character Jody was changing her costume when the zipper got stuck. A few seconds of panic, and then I called my costar Jackie Cooper to help me get unstuck. He entered as shy Waldo, freed my zipper and exited without once looking at me.

All part of the stage experience.

Thank God for my vaudeville training. It all felt so natural.

After that, it was on to Boston and finally New York and opening night. I can still see that dressing room and those illustrious and famous people who came to see us.

It didn't take me long to know what the Broadway experience was all about and why I wanted more of it. Maynard was right. I was one lucky young woman, and I never forgot it. Jackie Cooper was sensational in the show, and we even fell madly in love for a while. It was the cherry on the cake, I guess.

On October 3, 1951, we had that famous opening night party at Sardi's. Leland Hayward had taken over the upstairs, and I hadn't touched the ground all night, especially when we walked in and the entire room applauded.

I'd never known anything like that feeling in my entire life. We retired to our party room, drank champagne, ate and waited for the reviews. We had many papers in those days, but *The New York Times* was always the ultimate for the health and longevity of the show.

Unfortunately, Brooks Atkinson was not kind. He scolded the great Lindsay and Crouse for writing something so "frivolous" when they had previously done *Life with Father*, *Arsenic and Old Lace* and *State of the Union* and felt that *Remains* was beneath them.

Atkinson's review of me consisted of one line: "As far as the 'girl' was concerned, she has no apparent talent."

Part of me wanted to crawl somewhere, hide, lick my wounds and run as far away from Broadway as I could go, while part of me wanted to yell, "I may be new, I may come from motion pictures, I may be raw and you may not like me, but *no talent*? No way!"

Besides, everyone else loved me, including Marlene Dietrich. She should have written the review.

We ran for approximately four months and finished the show in Chicago with another two months. I played opposite Howard Lindsay, and it was a great and lasting experience. I'm deeply sorry that Mr. Atkinson didn't like the play. We had a marvelous cast and the audience seemed to love it. I was surrounded by the diamonds of the theatre. I could not have asked for more.

We were in *Life* magazine, and *Vogue* photographed me on two pages of its beautiful publication. I made lasting friendships and became a part of the Broadway community.

It was a very special time in my life and helped me to grow in all facets of my future. I adored New York City, walking to work down streets still living with its brownstones and history. I always felt safe there and never a stranger.

Ruth Anderson

Angels come in all colors.
—Janis Paige

When I was in rehearsal for my first Broadway show, *Remains to Be Seen*, my manager Ruth Aarons said, "We have to find you a theatre dresser, Jan. We'll interview three prospects today."

"Why do I need a dresser?" I asked. "I've always dressed myself, except when I was at Warner Bros."

"Well, this is Broadway, honey, and this kind of dressing you can't do by yourself and do the show, too. This is a very important relationship for you both, so be honest with yourself about your feelings. We'll meet in your dressing room and remember, with eight shows a week, you spend a lot of time together. So, feel comfortable with whomever you choose."

"I've never hired anyone, Ruthie," I replied. "It makes me feel funny."

"You're not hiring them, Jan," she insisted. "I am. Now. relax!"

We met the first two applicants, and both were more than acceptable. We thanked them and said we'd let them know our decision. We were waiting for the third and last of the day when there was a knock on my dressing room door.

"Come in," we said in tandem, and when the door opened, Ruth Anderson stepped in and stayed.

She was thin, neatly dressed and soft-spoken, with a calm, no-nonsense dignity—and clearly too old for the job.

We asked her to sit down, and Ruthie began the conversation. She was definitely not a kid anymore. Her hair was almost white, and the lines of age were well etched on her face and hands. I loved her on sight.

She began to answer Ruthie's questions about her work in the theatre.

"Well, Miss Aarons, my first job was in 1921 with Miss Vivian Segal in *The Desert Song*," she said. As usual, with my lousy math still alive and well, I subtly began to count the years on my fingers, trying to guess her age as she continued with her résumé.

"I loves the theatre, Miss Aarons, and I'd dearly love to help Miss Paige in her show," she continued.

I was hooked when she came in the door, but the look and the smile she sent my way clinched the deal for me. At that point, I would have helped her help me. I wanted her with me and no one else would do, age or no age.

"I hate asking you this, Ruth, but can you handle Miss Paige's fast changes?" my manager asked. "She has a few, and they are fast."

"Oh, Miss Aarons, that's the least of your worries," she assured. "I may not be young, and I know I'm thin, but I'm strong as an ox and Miss Paige is safe with me.

Ruth got the job, and I not only got my first theater maid but a friend, protector and teacher as well. She was unforgettable.

She adored the Brooklyn Dodgers, a.k.a. "dem bums," as well as fishing in Sheepshead Bay, her sister Nettie, and her little brother Charlie. They all lived together in Harlem, Ruth being the oldest.

My lifelong, undying and faithful love of the Dodgers began with Ruth. The only entrance I ever missed in my entire career was when Ruth and I were listening to them win the 1955 pennant. All I can remember was hearing the stage manager yell, "You're on, Janis! You're on NOW!"

I literally ran to the wings, trying to compose myself as I knew that I had kept the entire company waiting for my entrance. Although I apologized profusely and the company had fun teasing me, it took me years to forgive myself. Perhaps I never have. Even now, I can still feel that sickening fear at missing my entrance cue.

I was always early to the theatre and was putting my makeup on when I saw Ruth, two big shopping bags in tow, slowly making her way up the stairs to my dressing room.

"You OK?" I asked.

"I'm fine, Miss Janis. I been fishin' all day."

As she passed by my mirror, she peeked at herself. Down went the shopping bags, her hand flying to her cheek as she cried, "Oh, good lord, Nettie's gonna kill me, I got so sunburned today."

I stopped mid-makeup with a look that prompted her to say, "Oh, I know what you're thinkin'. You think black folks don't sunburn, but they do Miss Janis, they do."

We stared at each other and then I said, "You got me, Ruth. I was thinking just that and was too afraid to ask."

"Oh Miss Janis, you can ask me anything, you know that."

And I usually did.

I didn't grow up with "black folks," as Ruth described them. The Pacific Northwest was a rather isolated and ethnically mixed part of America, but our largest contingent of immigrants were Japanese, followed by German, Norwegian, Irish and Polish.

My father's family came from the Netherlands, so school was always a mixed-bag filled with hard-to-pronounce names like mine. We were a huge lumber, fishing and flour mill area. Where I grew up and where Ruth Anderson was born might as well have been on different planets.

Ruth's mother grew up as a slave on a plantation. That part was in a history book, but I couldn't have had a more loving, kind, tough and wise woman enter my life.

"How'd you get so much smarter than I am, Ruth?" I asked her one day.

"Well, Miss Janis, my mother had no education, but she taught us to never let hate in our lives, to always have good manners, work real hard and believe in ourselves."

"You're ahead of me, Ruth," I replied. "I wish she'd taught me. I still doubt myself in so many ways and I don't know why."

When she got me ready for the show that night, Ruth did everything perfectly, as usual. But I could see that fishin' all day in the hot summer sun had slowed her down a bit.

When I got the role of Babe in the forever hit musical *The Pajama Game*, my little piece of heaven on 55th Street was left for a larger apartment on Fifth Avenue.

One morning, Ruth showed up to clean my apartment and make my breakfast.

"You can't do this and work the show too, Ruth," I told her. "I'm more than grateful, but I need you at the St. James, not here."

"You leave that up to me, Miss Janis," she assured me. "You love these, so I brought you a sack. Thems Harlem donuts, Miss Janis, better than those puny things they sell on Eighth Avenue. They's not donuts!"

I was dressed for a date after the show one night when I heard my name called. I went out to see a man coming up the stairs toward me, with the doorman on his heels. Before I could move away from him, I was suddenly pushed aside and my Ruth stood in front of me, her arms outspread yelling, "You get back down those stairs and out the door before I beat you good!"

The man stopped in his tracks and Ruth just stared him down without a word. I still see that picture of her skinny arms protecting me as she hid me behind her.

The stage doorman and a couple of the dancers grabbed him, dragged him down the stairs and out to the street. Believe me, he was lucky that he didn't have to deal with Ruth.

When I left the show in 1955 to do my own TV series, I asked Ruth to come with me to California. As a matter of fact, I begged her.

"What am I going to do without you, Ruth? You're a part of me now."

"Oh, Miss Janis, I'll miss you so, but I can't leave Nettie and Charlie. They's my family and I'd be lost without them and they'd be lost without me. My life's in Harlem."

I was a sobbing mess the day we said goodbye. The West Coast became my home when I foolishly got married again for what seemed like a stormy and regret-filled five minutes, but it really lasted a stormy and regret-filled year.

My next show was not until 1963 and Ruth had long retired. Her sister Nettie came to help me, and like Ruth she was wonderful. Ruth never came to the theater again, but she was, without a doubt, the most unforgettable character I've ever met. She was from another time, someone who stole my heart the first moment I laid eyes on her.

My life was so much richer because she was in it. We never knew her age, nor did she ever tell us—and I never asked. I didn't want to know. To me, she was ageless and always would be. Like her age, I have no record of her death.

Life, logistics and the passing years detoured us, and we simply lost touch. But Ruth never lost my heart. She lives in there always.

Ruth Anderson
Fishin' Somewhere

HELEN HAYES

EVERY HUMAN BEING IS BORN WITH A TRAGEDY, AND IT ISN'T ORIGINAL SIN. HE IS BORN WITH THE TRAGEDY THAT HE HAS TO GROW UP. A LOT OF PEOPLE DON'T HAVE THE COURAGE TO DO IT.

–HELEN HAYES

It was October 1951. One of the crisp, clear and sunny autumn days in New York that I so loved. I had just survived my first opening night of my first Broadway show and was still three feet off the ground.

My manager and I were celebrating with lunch at Michael's Pub. It was the new restaurant face in town. Michael knew everyone, and everyone knew Michael. His delightful personality and wonderful food created an irresistible ambience. Comfort was the operative word as we all say respectfully visible at our table.

The restaurant was on the East Side of Manhattan and was always well represented with its many Broadway stars, some often dining alone. I always thought it has a West Side look, but perhaps that was what the East and West Sides loved. It was, in a word, Michael, who knew and was New York itself.

Michael had our table waiting for us as we settled in to order. Soon, two glasses of champagne arrived, "compliments of Michael in celebration of you," the waiter said.

I was still full of our opening night of *Remains to Be Seen* and my flower-filled dressing room, Marlene Dietrich's genuine hug and the sheer and heady excitement everywhere.

As I looked around the room of the restaurant, there I saw the wondrous Helen Hayes, First Lady of the Theatre, sitting alone at a sunny window.

"Oh my God, Ruthie!" I exclaimed, "there's Helen Hayes sitting right over there. I can't believe it, there she is. She's so beautiful!"

As I stared, the waiter brought her check, they chatted for a few minutes, and then she prepared to leave. There were two paths to the exit, one slightly to the right and one to the left. We were sitting on the edge toward the left.

"Oh gosh, Ruthie, I think she's going to walk right by us!' I whispered, trying not to be obvious but of course I was.

Suddenly, she stopped, introduced herself and said, "I was in the audience last night, Miss Paige, and I want to tell you how wonderful you were."

I felt as if the room were in a state of stop-action while I tried to find my voice.

She was elegantly simple, with no façade in sight.

"Thank you so much, Miss Hayes," I finally managed to say, "you'll never know what this means to me. I was in the audience and saw you in *Happy Birthday*, always loving you and that wonderful play."

Miss Hayes thanked me and left with the words, "I won't keep you from your lunch. Thank you again for a delightful evening, Miss Paige. Enjoy your life! Goodbye."

I was standing as she left. When I came back to earth, I realized that the room and seemingly everyone in it was smiling, too.

As I recount and relive this long, ups-and-downs life I've known, it's not the victories and defeats I recall first. It's moments like this that I remember and cherish most.

Helen Hayes
October 10, 1900 - March 17, 1993

If you rest, you rust!

∽

Marlene Dietrich

Once a woman has forgiven her man, she must not reheat his sins for breakfast.

—Marlene Dietrich

The year was 1951, and the opening night of my first Broadway show was now a tiny place in the history of the Broadway theatre.

The performance of *Remains to Be Seen* was over, and heady stuff it was. The dressing room was teeming with people. Flowers were everywhere. Telegrams were piled on my makeup table. Yes, I said telegrams. The internet had not been invented. There were no cell phones, hence no texting.

What we had were those wonderful sealed envelopes with their messages inside. Only a few were opened. No time before the show, so the sealed ones remained closed for a later, quieter time.

People everywhere were lavishing me with hugs and kisses and encouragements like, "I'm so proud of you!" The absolute thrill for me, coupled with disbelief, was that I had survived the tears, fears and at times absolute terror of treading the boards for the first time on The Great White Way.

In the midst of all of this craziness, there she was.

"May I come in?" she asked in that smoky, sexy voice belonging only to Marlene Dietrich.

I could not catch my breath. I was absolutely transfixed by this vision in front of me. My exact words were, "Oh my gosh, it's you! I can't believe you were in the audience tonight."

Classy, huh?

She was dressed in a pale shade called bone. A full-length mink coat, gorgeous, beaded gown (Jean Louis, maybe?). She wore bone-colored shoes, while a chic little satin beret crowned the famous blond Marlene Dietrich haircut.

Was she wearing jewelry? I remember diamond earrings, but the elegant, matching suede gloves covered whatever might be on her hands.

That famous aura surrounded her. To me, she was otherworldly.

Marlene gave me a strong hug, kissed me on both cheeks and then held me at arm's length and told me how "wonderful" I was. She thanked me for a "marvelous performance" and noted that she would be "watching for your next show."

As I stumbled out some words of thanks, she said, "I won't keep you, you have many admirers waiting to speak with you. Goodnight, Janis, thank you again."

And she was gone.

As I came back to the room, I realized how quiet it had become as all eyes and ears were on her. She was a perfect example of the word star.

The next time I saw her, I was well on my way to being a part of Broadway theatre. And there was nothing like it,

I was starring alongside the marvelous John Raitt and the irrepressible Eddie Foy Jr. in the massive George Abbott hit, *The Pajama Game*.

The year was 1954, and I was being invited most everywhere. Leonard Lyons, a very well-liked showbiz columnist on the *New York Post*, had wonderful parties, and I got an invitation for one of his famous Sunday gatherings.

He lived in The Beresford, a towering apartment building uptown on Central Park West. I used to dream of the day when I, too, would live at The Beresford or The Dakota. Frankly, I didn't care which, either one would do.

If I could live in one of those elegant places, I'd never leave. I'd just stare out the windows at Central Park while the world went by. I adored New York, and fortunately, it seemed to like me, too.

This particular soiree was on a Sunday, our "dark night" in the theater. (By then, I had learned a bit of the theatrical lingo. Dark meant that we didn't turn the lights on - hence, no show.)

I arrived by myself. When I entered, I could see that the party had definitely begun. Everyone was dressed beautifully. After all, it was 1954, and it was New York City.

The apartment was very large, with a lovely, marble-floored foyer. I could see about three rooms from where I stood. I hesitated, not sure where I should go, when suddenly I heard a voice calling my name.

"Janis, Janis darling, over here, come join us."

When I looked up, there sat Marlene Dietrich, surrounded by several men seemingly in rapt attention. She was sitting on an elegant high-backed stool as someone brought another for me and I sat down beside her. She was holding court, so to speak, dressed in what we now call our LBD (or Little Black Dress). Simple but costly.

Marlene had a beautiful figure, and her long-sleeved dress was unadorned except for pearls. On her feet were black suede pumps with high-curved heels. As I remember it, those heels were called French. In fact, they still are, and they're still sexy.

Last, but certainly not least, her world-famous legs were comfortably crossed and clad in pale, flesh-colored hosiery.

Marlene's audience consisted of the likes of Dr. Ralph Bunche, under-secretary-general of the United Nations; James Michener, one of America's most prolific writers; Lowell Thomas, world-renowned commentator; and four or five others, familiar but whose names escaped me.

Across the room, a piano was softly and lovingly tinkled by the quiet genius Harold Arlen. James ("Call me Jimmy") Michener brought me a glass of wine, and I joined this fascinating group, discussing everything from politics to Paris and beyond.

As I sat there, the old familiar memory of Tacoma met The Beresford, its guests, the elegance and the ease with which everyone seemed to move. I was in a kind of pinch-me awe at everyone and everything.

A voice said something about food, and I could see part of a large and expansive buffet. As the guests made their way to the table, I got up to join them when Miss Dietrich ordered, "Stay here, Janis. I'm going to get Harold a plate and I'll bring you one, too."

I protested, but that was that, and off she went, returning with our dinners. When we finished, she picked up our plates along with a couple of others she found and took them to somewhere out of sight. What an unforgettable image she was, juggling our used plates in her little black dress, her high-heeled pumps and those legs in their nude-colored hose. The legs won.

She sat down again, and we began to talk.

"May I ask you a question?" I began.

"Of course," she replied, but in the midst of my sentence, I heard her ask, "Do you see that man over there, in the next room?"

I eyed three men in deep conversation.

"Which one? I asked.

"That one," she said, pointing.

"That one" was Adlai Stevenson, former Governor of Illinois, three-time Presidential nominee and our Ambassador to the United Nations.

Governor Stevenson was considered an intellectual giant, but to me, sexual charisma would not be the words used to describe him. He had an oddly shaped head that looked to me as if God had crowded an extra set of brains into that vast expanse of baldness. His physique was obviously not built in a gym.

And yet, this goddess sitting beside me had seen and felt something the rest of us missed completely. The look on her face revealed a still-painful memory.

"I was mad about that man," she said to me. "I wanted to have an affair with him. I thought he was amazing and told him so. I threw myself at him, and he totally rejected me. What a damned fool!"

"Maybe he was afraid of you," I offered.

Her answer was an incredulous "Afraid of me? He could have had me in a second, the damned fool!"

There she sat, staring at him while I stared at her. A tiny, familiar feeling rumbled around inside me. The experience of rejection is always identifiable and interchangeable. I watched her emotional roller-coaster ride as she felt unzipped and raw, reliving her pain.

In the next few moments, this woman revealed bravado, denial, disappointment and the anger hiding the hurt. There she sat, open, honest and—for a few painful moments—so very vulnerable.

Governor Stevenson must have seen her but never came over to so much as say "Hello." When he left, he passed just a few feet from where we sat but never looked her way.

He may have been one of the world's great minds, but no amount of intellectual prowess can solve the fears and insecurities within us all. I remain convinced that he was terrified of the intimacy that she so openly offered him.

There was silence as she watched him leave. Then the moment passed with her words, "I see dessert and coffee. Harold, I'm getting dessert, do you want coffee?"

"I'll help you," I said.

"Oh, thank you, Janis, let's see what they have."

The curtain had fallen, suddenly, quietly and firmly.

When it comes to rejection, we all row the same boat. No matter what Stevenson's reasons for ignoring her offer, he was not the only one intimidated by her presence. She was impressive, to say the least.

I had now met two Marlenes. There was the beaded, be-gowned, minkcoated and stunning superstar at the door of my dressing room on opening night of my first Broadway show. Then there was the Marlene sitting next to me, pining away for what might have been.

Whether gowned or in her little black dress, she was forever elegant, intelligent, worldly, savvy, thoughtful and kind. Yet as someone once said long ago, "At heart, she is simply a German hausfrau."

Marlene left me a lasting gift as I remember the little black dress and the legs bringing dinner, clearing plates and her genuine caring and thoughtfulness. She remains an integral and unforgettable part of my memories.

Miss Dietrich and Governor Stevenson have both been gone for many years now. I never met him, but I did meet her, and she was crazy about him. I still consider that potential pairing odd at best, but she didn't, and I'd easily trust her choice.

We'll never know who missed the most, will we? But I'll put my money on him as the loser. I can still hear her say, "He could have had me in a second. The damned fool!" Through another of life's ironies, she had pulled herself together and was, once again, strong, feminine and human.

We ended that day with her asking about my original question. She had remembered, but I'd forgotten, lost in the Adlai Stevenson drama.

"What did you want to ask me, Janis"?

"Please forgive my curiosity Marlene, but though you're dressed in black today, your hosiery is a nude color," I replied. "I love the look, but most women would have worn black hose."

Before I could speak another word, Marlene quickly countered with, "Oh, Janis dear, I never wear black stockings. If you have good legs, you must show them. Black hides everything."

With advice from an expert, I have always worn nude hosiery. A bit of trivia, important only to me, perhaps, or those with good legs.

As I left that already eventful day, Dr. Bunche and James Michener joined me at the elevator. Dr. Bunche asked me if he could take me somewhere.

"Where do you live?" he asked.

"At 76th and Fifth," I answered.

"That's perfect," he said. "Jimmy and I are headed downtown. We'll be happy to drop you off."

I don't know what I expected in the presence of such elevated and successful company, but what I found was unexpected simplicity. Life overflows with one surprise after another.

Marlene Dietrich
December 27, 1901 - May 6, 1992

I am, at heart, a gentleman.

THE RAINCOAT

NEVER JUDGE A BOOK BY ITS COVER.
                              −ANONYMOUS

WHEN I WAS offered the starring role in the new Lindsay and Crouse play on Broadway, I won the cream of the crop, so to speak.

From the producer, director and stellar cast to the stage manager, it was first class all the way. I was one extremely fortunate young woman, now guided and protected by the best in her profession.

Heading the production was the one and only Leland Hayward. Elegant, sophisticated and highly successful, he would steer us through the countless problems and muddy waters of pre-production, including the jitters of a star in her first Broadway venture.

It was one surprise after another. And frankly, considering all of the diverse facets involved in reaching an opening night, we finally did on October 3, 1951.

Along with the nearly paralyzing "I can't remember my first line" nerves, there were the flowers, overflowing into the hallway outside my dressing room, and the ever-growing stack of Western Union telegrams on the table.

The organized bedlam of an opening night does not come along very often, if ever. So, speaking for myself, the mayhem fades and the anticipation of the audience, the well wishes, the "Break a leg!" tradition of the cast and a deep, abiding hope that we have a hit will hang around until my final closing notice is posted.

Fortunately, there were no emails then. Just piles of those pale, yellow things called telegrams and the warm, loving and tactile messages contained within those sealed envelopes. It was a time when we had time to stop and smell the flowers, when there was still time for civility and the excitement matching our own from a beautifully dressed opening night audience.

About two weeks after we opened, Mr. Hayward called and invited me to lunch.

"Have you been to The Colony?" he asked.

"No."

"Fine, we'll go there. It's my favorite place for lunch. I'll pick you up tomorrow at 1."

I immediately called my manager and said, "Ruthie, Leland Hayward is taking me to lunch tomorrow at The Colony. What do I wear?"

"It's not Sardi's," she said. "The Colony is ten percent show business and ninety percent New York Society."

"Oh my God, WHAT DO I WEAR?!"

"It's easy," she said. "Wear a black dress, shoes and bag to match, simple and not too much jewelry and you'll be fine. It's about time you saw The Colony. Call me later and tell me about your new adventure."

Mr. Hayward picked me up in a limo when we could easily have walked to The Colony, but I dearly loved riding in one of those eye-catching, wonder-who's-in-there vehicles—so I kept quiet.

He got out to help me when I saw how he was dressed. Everything about him was handsome, from his looks to his behavior to his easy acceptance of his place in the world. Here I was, as perfectly and safely dressed as I could be, but not so Mr. Hayward.

I didn't know what to do. So, of course, I did nothing, but inside I wondered about his coat.

To me, The Colony was scarcely visible to those walking by. It had a short flight of stairs and a small canopy with the words "The Colony" and a doorman who seemed to come from nowhere as we pulled to the curb.

From the bustle, excitement and just plain otherworldliness of the Broadway Theatre district, to the upper stratospheric ambiance of the East

Side, this was all heady stuff for me. But not for Mr. Hayward. Oh no, not Mr. Hayward.

He was wearing a raincoat that was, to me, just plain dirty. It was the famous khaki color so prevalent in raincoats, even those of today. You know, rather military in style with epaulets, double-breasted buttons, a belt and a collar resembling a James Bond-ish wardrobe.

The doorman greeted Mr. Hayward like an old friend, with a few niceties exchanged. Leland politely introduced me with, "You should see her in our new play, she is marvelous!"

"Oh, I will Mr. Hayward, looking forward to it," he said. "Enjoy your lunch."

The doorman sneaked not even a glance at Mr. Hayward's New York, black-sooted, needs-a-cleaning raincoat.

Leland took my arm as we headed inside for my first visit to this famous restaurant. A welcoming maître d' met us with, "Always a pleasure to see you, Mr. Hayward. I have your table ready when you are."

They shook hands and once again I heard, "I'd like you to meet Miss Janis Paige. She is starring in our new play at The Morosco and she is just wonderful. Don't miss it."

"My pleasure, Miss Paige," the maître d' said. "We'll always welcome you at The Colony."

All of this splendor, and all I could think of was that raincoat that looked as if it had come from a Goodwill pile of castoffs.

Little did I know that I would soon have my first lesson in how the rich and famous lived while I, obviously, was still in Tacoma.

Hatcheck closets and the girls who attended to the various checkable items that would be cared for during the owner's time without them were everywhere. They were also in the lobbies of the theaters.

The girl usually wore a cute little uniform befitting her station, and from hats to wet umbrellas to coats and shopping packages, the hatcheck girl would receive the items. In exchange, she would give a check or ticket to be exchanged when the items were returned to their proper owners. This service always silently involved a tip for her.

The Colony was no exception, as I watched Mr. Hayward approach the hatcheck girl's waiting arms. He knew her by name, and she knew him. He was most definitely a good customer and, I'm sure, a very generous tipper.

He loosened his belt, and as he began to remove his raincoat, a small but audible gasp escaped my throat.

"Oh my God," I whispered, "that thing is turning into a gorgeous, lush and very black mink coat. Good lord. No wonder he doesn't bother to clean it."

Mr. Hayward put his claim check in his pocket and said, "C'mon Janis, let's eat. I'm hungry."

Will I ever emulate Leland Hayward? No way, I thought, at least not in the near future. I'd be wearing the mink side out for all the world to see.

We were seated at Mr. Hayward's favorite table when he asked me if I liked caviar. I wanted to yell, "You're ordering caviar at The Colony with these prices?" But I didn't. I also didn't tell him that I absolutely adored caviar.

Instead, I remained the lady I had to be and politely told him that I liked it very much.

"Then caviar it is!"

I don't remember what else I ate after I saw the waiter bring a rather large mound of huge, grey caviar eggs on a silver tray accompanied by all of the caviar-istic trimmings one loves when savoring this delectable delicacy.

As the waiter cleared our plates, I noticed three or four eggs left on Leland's plate. If I were home, I thought, I'd spear those little darlings no matter who witnessed my bad manners.

I never went back to The Colony. I enjoyed El Morocco several times, had lunch and dinner at the famous 21 and felt right at home at Sardi's and Toots Shor's, but I always felt strangely wrong somehow at The Colony. Besides, how could I ever top my lunch with Leland Hayward and his "dirty" raincoat?

Remains to Be Seen ran for six months between New York and Chicago. My memory of Leland Hayward, The Colony, the caviar and his mink-lined raincoat has remained there for sixty-five years.

Leland Hayward
September 13, 1902 - March 18, 1971

The Colony
1923 - 1971

Marlon Brando

With women, I've got a long bamboo pole with a leather loop at its end. I slip the loop around their necks so they can't get away or come too close, like catching snakes.

—Marlon Brando

The year was 1952, and my thirtieth birthday was approaching. I had just finished my Broadway show *Remains to Be Seen* and I loved being a part of the theatre community. I also loved Sardi's, so friends had arranged a very small party for me there.

La Tour d'Argent in Paris had nothing on Sardi's. It was for the theatre, and that was the way it always made you feel: Welcome.

For days before, my friends had teased me with their gift of a surprise guest. Sardi's had arranged a table in the middle of the restaurant. They even had flowers for me. Fritz, my favorite maître d' in the world, wished me a happy birthday, as did owner Vincent Sardi and several of the diners seated around us. It was all very festive, friendly and fun.

About twenty minutes later, as we were all enjoying a glass of champagne, there in my line of sight suddenly stood Marlon Brando just inside the door.

"Oh my God," I said, "there's Marlon Brando!"

He proceeded to walk toward our table and my friends shouted, "Surprise!"

Believe me, I was shocked. We were introduced, there were hellos, and Brando sat down. In what was the longest and most torturous half-hour of my life, he never said another word to me. That beautiful face that drew unabashed stares and looked like it had been the model for an ancient Roman coin ignored me completely.

The man didn't even wish me a happy birthday. He made small talk with my friends, then suddenly stood, said "Goodnight" and exited center stage. Was this a joke?

I'd arrived that night feeling like my own birthday balloon, but it took the great and gifted Marlon Brando and his pitchfork to puncture everything, including the friends who got him there. I sat wordless, feeling demeaned, discounted and invisible.

Mind you, the feeling was sadly not unfamiliar. All of our individual emotions danced together at my birthday party until our true feelings about the beautiful Mr. Brando began to surface.

"That bastard!" one of them said. "What a mean SOB he is. I'm so sorry, Jan."

I was close to tears.

"Why did he treat me this way?" I asked. "I don't even know how to think right now."

I just sat there and disappeared. He simply took everything away from me. I couldn't even tell him to take his bad manners and go to hell! Here, in the center of a crowded Sardi's, at the beginning of my thirtieth birthday, I'd been demolished by the great Marlon Brando. I wanted to know why.

Everyone was stunned into silence, feeling sad and confused for me.

"We need some champagne," someone said, filling our glasses. I sat through the surface talk, mentally telling off the great Brando with every bad word I'd ever heard. I sure have plenty of guts now, I thought.

We were interrupted by Fritz bringing the menus and his recommendations for dinner. We ordered and things began to lighten up a bit, but the more I thought about the disrespect I received from this man on my birthday, the angrier I got.

We were in the middle of enjoying one of Fritz's perfectly-mixed salads when I said, "We've been talking around what happened to me tonight, and I doubt that we're going to forget it very soon. I know I'm not. Knowing myself as I do, I'll be trying to make some sense out of his craziness. Unfortunately, I have a tendency to blame myself for not making things work."

Then I said, "What do you call that thing that happens when you mentally and emotionally wake up? Somebody help me here, please."

"Are you talking about an epiphany?" somebody asked.

"Yes, yes, that's it! I think I'm having an epiphany!"

Fortunately, it would not be my last.

"In less than an hour," I added, "I've gone from embarrassment, rejection and not being seen or heard to good old-fashioned hurt. Sure, I'm pissed off at his behavior and my taking it, but I think I dodged a big fat bullet tonight. Thank God he didn't like me, and I definitely did not like him.

"Too many times in the past, I'd go after someone who ignored me. When I finally got what I thought I wanted, they were either lousy lovers or boring and full of themselves. Instead of recognizing the 'No Trespassing' signs, I hung around and got what I deserved."

I looked at my loving and slightly uncomfortable friends and said, "Dare I think that as my thirtieth year begins, I'm finally beginning to grow up? Either we saw the Brando game plan for women, or he's brutally rude. Both are painful. I began tonight with my Brando fascination and ended up with utter disillusionment.

"Thank God, he's finally not my type and obviously, I was not his," I continued. "Or was I? Believe me, I won't ever get close enough to find out. As usual, I'll have to re-live this tomorrow. I'll have to go through the self-doubts again, but for now, I feel pretty good."

Finally, I concluded, "It's my birthday! Let's send Mr. Gorgeous off with a toast. Ya ready? Here's to you, beautiful Roman Coin Face Brando. Here's to showing me the worst all-around bad manners that I have ever witnessed. In other words, thank you, gorgeous, for being such an all-around shit. At least I got a chance to see that face up close but not too personal, even while you were casing the rest of the room."

His brilliant talent never let us down. I've seen almost everything he ever did, but the mystery of Brando died with him. When I read his countless quotes, I found less mystery and more ambivalence in his confusion about life, truth and his own vulnerability.

Marlon Brando
April 3, 1924 – July 1, 2004

I put on an act sometimes and people think I'm insensitive. If there are two hundred people in the room and one of them doesn't like me, I've got to get out!

President Richard Milhous Nixon

It is safer for a politician to go to a whorehouse than to see a psychiatrist.

–Richard Milhous Nixon

Prophetic words, painful truth, sadly reaching fruition today. While he was still Vice President, Richard Nixon read Dr. Arnold A. Hutschnecker's book, *The Will to Live*.

In 1953, I showed up for an appointment with Arnold, only to be stopped by a man in an overcoat standing just inside the office door. There was another similarly-dressed man standing outside in the hallway. They asked me who I was, and Florita, Arnold's nurse, told them my name and that I was the doctor's next patient.

I turned to Florita and mouthed, "What's going on?" She imperceptibly shook her head, her eyes saying, "Not now."

About a half-hour had passed when I heard the door to Arnold's office open. Muddled "Thank yous," laughter and goodbyes were heard, then silence.

"Who were those men, Florita, what's going on?" I asked with anxious curiosity.

"They were the FBI," she said.

"Why, what were they doing here? Not anything about Arnold, I hope."

"No Jan. Vice President Nixon was here. He read Arnold's book."

"Oh my God, I can't believe it. There may be hope for the country yet," I concluded.

Therapy was poisoned meat to a politician. It took a lot of guts to brave this uncharted territory, and Richard Nixon rose in my estimation for his courage. There had been a couple of politicians who admitted getting "help," and they were vilified politically, never to surface again.

Needing or wanting therapy was the death blow to anyone with political ambitions. We take tests for everything except the most important job, that of running for and winning the Presidency of the United States of America. He was elected President in 1968, vowing to end the Vietnam War.

President Nixon had a lot of demons to slay and, unfortunately, a public forum on which to do battle. I know that he and Arnold became very good friends, and both were dedicated to a couple of far-reaching projects about peace and how to maintain it.

Because of the infamous Watergate scandal, and facing impeachment, President Nixon resigned in 1974. The picture of him leaving the White House for the last time, arms upraised in a victory sign, his head held high, is famous.

The picture of the President's wife Pat, however, is far less filled with bravado. I'll never forget the sadness that barely covered her stiff-upper-lip façade for everyone, but especially for him. So many hopes dashed on the sharp and unforgiving rocks of politics. He and his wife moved to their home in San Clemente above the Pacific Ocean.

My late husband, Ray Gilbert, was a Democrat who voted for Nixon. I remember Ray's words like I do Arnold's: "I've got a hunch, honey, that he can be a very good President. I hope people give him a chance."

The next words I remember were his, too: "My God, why didn't he tell us the truth? We would have respected him for it and forgiven him. What a damn shame! He shot himself in the foot and he shot the country, too!"

Some four years after his resignation, I got a call from Arnold.

"President Nixon wants to see me, Jan. Would you drive me to San Clemente?"

"Need you ask? I can't wait to see you. We can get caught up on the drive down."

At the Nixon estate on a cliff above the sea, I was instructed where to park, and we entered the outer office. There stood the famous "18 ½-minute missing tape" lady, the President's longtime secretary, Rosemary Woods. She was smiling and warm and said, "I'll tell the President you're here."

Miss Woods quickly added, "Please go in, doctor." I heard Arnold say, "Mr. President" and the reply, "Arnold, thank you for coming."

Then I heard the door close.

"Can I get you something to drink, Miss Paige?" Miss Woods asked.

'I'd love a cup of coffee if you have some ready."

That line came straight out of Tacoma.

"How do you take it?" she asked.

"Oh, just black, thank you."

From another room somewhere came a woman with a cup of coffee, who placed it on the table beside my chair. It was served on the White House china, and as I lifted the cup, there was a distinct chip on the rim. I found that prophetic and sad.

When we started home, Arnold said, "The President told me to thank you for driving me down to see him."

"Thank you, Doc. I'm happy to do it. How is he?"

"He was very glad to see me. Jan. We talked of our project and he had read my new book. We spoke of that, too."

"But how is he?" I repeated.

"Oh, Jan, there is such a sadness underlying that Nixon exterior. He could have accomplished so much for this country and for the world."

"You sound just like Ray," I said. "We'll never know, will we? Why is it so difficult to simply tell the truth? The American people deserved it. Political lies seem to be morphing into an art form. Our trust is badly damaged and it's dangerous for the health of the country.

"I respect the office of the Presidency," I continued, "but when you take that oath to serve and protect, the job ceases to be about one person and his ideology and neuroses. I know I'm naïve, Arnold, but the test of one's character to lead should come before he decides to take on such an awesome responsibility. How about *that* for a plan, Doc?"

"Unfortunately, Jan," he answered, "I'm afraid no one would try."

What was the uncharted, undiscovered and untrusting part of Nixon's psyche that forced his decisions and brought down his Presidency? We only have speculations now and very little of that as he fades into history.

In 1993, Arnold sent me a clipping from *The New York Times*. The picture was of a sobbing Nixon, tears rolling down his face, as he buried his wife, Pat. The caption, written in Arnold's hand, describes "the saddest day of Nixon's life."

President Nixon died in 1994. I knew that he and Arnold were great friends, but I'd never known that Arnold was also his therapist. I hoped it was true. I know that he helped the President greatly, but the mystery of Nixon remains just that. Whatever Arnold knew died with him in 2001.

Why is it so difficult, and oftentimes impossible, for people to simply admit a mistake? Dr. Phil McGraw calls them "right fighters." That phrase clarified and reduced this ugly and demeaning posture down to its truth.

I grew up being parented by a right fighter, and it left me with a sense that I was always wrong about something. They, of course, will claim to be right no matter how much they harm those whom they profess to love.

In therapy, I found that the constant hyper-criticism from my right fighter was my answer. It's only supposition on my part, but I believe that President Nixon also had this self-protective, self-defending right fighter belief system. With help, it's fixable.

Unfortunately, Washington, D.C. with its power-mad environs, is a perfect training ground for self-corruption and ego-bloated ideas with their names attached. President Nixon, after reading Arnold's book, must have had his own awakenings to prompt his visit that day to Arnold's office in New York City.

Now, if I were President, I would not only have my own emotional junk clarified and in a controllable condition, there would be a mandatory psychological test for anyone thinking of running this country. That would surely separate the ego-driven and power-riven from those who seriously take their oath to serve, protect and defend.

At the very least, we'd have a place to start.

I can hear them now as they accuse one American woman's feeble attempt at a solution for disinfecting the political fungus invading us. "Ho-hum, just a typical female's over-simplification of a complex problem."

Unfortunately, solving the seemingly unending and undying hypocrisy of today is as slippery as quicksand and just as dangerous for the preservation of our country.

The differences between a Nixon, Clinton, Bush, Obama or Trump are now so polarized as to be immovable. Gone is the day when a President Reagan could settle a political impasse over dinner with his Democratic opponent. Instead of a political platform on which to stand, understand, agree or disagree, we have an imitative arm of something called the press. A politically biased cult with abusive liars repeating their script of hate.

Sadly, I see and hear crazed, set-in-stone paralysis toward the needs of their country and the citizens who pay the bill for this unhinged behavior.

The gap between right and wrong and lies and truth has widened until we can no longer see the shores of either side. Shame on us for not holding the media's well-shod feet to a roaring fire until they fess up or get out.

Richard Milhous Nixon
January 9, 1913 – April 22, 1994

If, when the chips are down and the world's most
powerful nation, the United States of America,
acts like a pitiful and helpless giant, the forces
of totalitarianism and anarchy will threaten free
nations and free institutions throughout the world.

George Abbott and "The Pajama Game"

> *I MUST CONFESS THAT ONE OF MY MAIN DEFECTS AS A DIRECTOR HAS ALWAYS BEEN AN INCURABLE IMPATIENCE.*
>
> –George Abbott

In 1954, I was given the role of Babe Williams in *The Pajama Game*, the new George Abbott musical by Richard Bissell from his book *7 ½ Cents*.

It was the story of a pajama factory somewhere in the Midwest and the company's attempt to get a 7 ½-cent raise. Babe was the union rep. It also starred John Raitt as the new superintendent and Eddie Foy Jr. as the factory foreman.

Nobody thought we had a chance. "Is George Abbott crazy?" became an oft-heard refrain when they tried to raise money.

"Who wants to see a musical about a pajama factory and a union?" was also often heard. "Who wants to invest in a show like that?" But since this was a George Abbott show, investors still invested.

Mr. Abbott cast a wonderfully mixed bag of talented performers, and it showed onstage in our chemistry. The music and lyrics were written by the very new team of Richard Adler and Jerry Ross. It was choreographed by Bob Fosse (his first musical) and produced by Abbott, Robert Griffith,

Freddie Brisson and a very young Hal Prince. The executive producer and choreographer was the esteemed Jerome Robbins (*The King and I*, *West Side Story*, *Fiddler on the Roof*).

And so, we began.

Our first rehearsal was in a room above Danny's Hideaway, a much-loved restaurant of its day. I had just finished a Bob Hope show in Los Angeles, and while sitting in the airport saying a long and loving goodbye to the most important man in my life at the moment, I missed my plane!

I was absolutely mortified and immediately called my manager.

"Oh my God, Ruthie, I missed the plane!"

I could hardly get the words out. I'd never missed a plane in my life. A loud laugh followed my terror and her answer was, "Well, it's about time you miss a plane at least one time in your life."

"This isn't funny!" I said. "I'm probably fired before I start and I'm sick at my stupidity."

With that, Ruth told me to get the next plane out and not to worry. I did get on the next plane, and when we tried to cross Fifth Avenue, we ran smack into the St. Patrick's Day Parade.

Here I was, in a taxi on the east side of New York City, late for my first day of work with George Abbott and facing the *wearin' of the green* in full splendor.

After several tries at getting to the West Side, we finally made it. I arrived with bags in tow, apologizing profusely and wearing every nerve in my body.

This was how I began my first day in my first Broadway musical. Not only that, it was a George Abbott musical, a "Mr. Broadway" musical. I would soon find out that he was a tough but great teacher.

Mr. Abbott was most imposing. He was about six foot three or four, with silvery gray hair, a straight, slim physique and was what I would call elegantly handsome. He was then sixty-seven and not one to be easily forgotten.

I apologized again for keeping them waiting, and I could see that my constant worries, nurtured by my vivid imagination of being fired, had been unnecessary. Nevertheless, I meted out my punishment to myself for missing the plane and went to work. I met the entire cast and found out that they were just as nervous as I.

Will we ever learn that nerves, insecurities, praying to be great and trying to hide it all simply goes with the territory?

After a short time at Danny's, we moved to the St. James, where we would open in New York following our out-of-town tryout in Boston. I had done several movie musicals, but very shortly I realized that one had absolutely nothing to do with the other.

The rehearsals progressed and then the cuts and changes began to nibble away at the original show. One of the biggest changes was that of Poopsie, played by the one and only Carol Haney. She was amazing, adorable and a surefire hit.

It was then that I began to witness the George Abbott power in play.

As intimidating as he was, there was a reason for his legacy of successes. When he knew what he wanted, he wasted no time in putting it in the show and was unapologetic. When he discovered Carol's comedic abilities along with her dancing, he enlarged her role by writing out Charlotte Rae's part and letting her go.

We were on a break one day when I saw the sadness in Charlotte's face.

"What's wrong?" I asked.

"I just got fired," she said.

I felt as if someone had kicked me in the gut, because it was so sudden and, to me, so cold.

What a child I was. Mr. Abbott was doing exactly what Jack Warner had done to me when I was "too offbeat" to keep me. They were both responsible to their backers, investors, reputations and product. We were, therefore, replaceable.

John Raitt introduced the tune *Hey There*, and I was to reprise it on stage left in *One*. As time went on, I began to hear the rumors that Mr. Abbott considered my reprise a possible stage wait, and God forbid a stage wait in an Abbott show.

This possible decision was being made without his ever hearing me sing it. Was I too going to be a victim of changes to make the show better?

I was also aware that this musical was not the standard Abbott show. His romantic leads usually stayed in their own backyard, and the comedy leads usually had a bigger yard. Was mine beginning to shrink?

I knew that Babe certainly was not the typical romantic lead. She was tough, strong-minded, purposeful and determined to be her own person. There began to be little cuts here and little changes there.

All of the musical numbers had been staged except for my *I'm Not at All in Love* and the reprise. I didn't know what it was called then, but my old familiar actor's paranoia was finding its way in again.

I screwed up my courage and asked for a few minutes of Mr. Abbott's time, letting my manager know. I was told when and where and was very nervous when I knocked on his office door.

"Come in, Janis," he said.

He did not stand as I entered his office, nor did he ask me to sit down. He was sitting at a big desk. Standing behind him were his producers Bobby Griffiths, Freddie Brisson and Hal Prince. I was definitely facing a jury who looked as if they were about to give me a bad verdict.

"What can I do for you, Janis?" Mr. Abbott asked.

"I want to discuss the rumors I continue to hear about the reprise of *Hey There* and the possibility of it being cut from the show. Neither *I'm Not at All in Love* nor the reprise have even been staged yet, let alone seen. All of the other numbers are finished. I know rumors can be just that, but I'd like some clarification on where I am."

I stumbled out something else that I can't even remember and then, silence. What happened next is branded on my brain.

"You see that door over there?" he asked.

"Yes, Mr. Abbott," I replied.

"I want you to go through that door and shut it. You have five minutes to make up your mind if you're staying in this show or leaving it. Five minutes."

My eyes flooded with sudden tears, but I went through that door, shut it and quietly sobbed in humiliation.

"What are you going to do, Jan?" my manager asked.

I kept taking deep breaths to control the rage I felt at that moment. Finally, I said, "Why do I take this stuff, Ruthie? Why don't I just quit?"

"Because it's not in you," she answered.

As I dried my eyes, I said, "I don't understand what just happened to me. Maybe one day I will, but for now, not even George Abbott is going to make me tuck my tail between my legs and just disappear. I'm embarrassed, mad as hell and dying inside. I've watched everyone find their stage legs, while I can't seem to find mine.

"I may be different tomorrow," I continued, "but for now, I'll be damned if I'm going to die in this hallway. Somehow, I have to pull myself together as best I can and stay that way. How do I look?"

My manager gave me a hug and said, "Fine."

I took another deep breath, still fighting my way through the intense hurt, slapped my cheeks hard a few times for some much-needed color, and faced that closed door. With my last ounce of self-respect, I heard myself whisper, "To hell with you, George Mr. Abbott, sir. To hell with you!"

I opened the door with the words, "I'm staying!"

"Fine," he said, "now get back to work."

For the next two weeks, Mr. Abbott never spoke a word to me. I was completely ignored, even to being given stage directions. I didn't ask, he didn't give. I seemed to be invisible.

One day, he treated the entire cast to a short version of his dramatic flair. We were rehearsing a scene when suddenly he yelled, "Stop!" We did, and then from the first row he stood, raised his arms to the ceiling, and said, "If I could only work with the script, the lights, the props, the music, the scenery, but no actors!"

We stood in stunned silence. I don't think any of us had ever been compared to inanimate objects, and I don't think Mr. Abbott ever did anything without a reason.

Surprisingly, my feelings weren't hurt. The memory, however, remains, and I can still see the expressions and feel the tension. He sat back down and simply said, "Now do it again." And we did.

The day of our first run-through arrived. Our first time to see the show come together. Bobby Fosse ran through everything up to *I'm Not at All in Love*, Babe's first solo number.

We stood, quietly waiting, until we heard Jerry Robbins ask, "Where's *I'm Not at All in Love*, Bobby?"

Finally, the truth will come out. Bobby simply turned to Jerry and said, "It's not staged, Jerry, and it's my fault. I just don't know what to do with it." Without a beat, I heard Jerry say, "Everybody in this number on stage."

I dearly loved Bobby Fosse, but I had been between a rock and a hard place for so long. I finally took a deep breath of relief and thoroughly enjoyed myself, and the loving and talented female factory workers on stage with me.

The number was staged in about forty minutes, and it was simply wonderful. When we left the stage that day, one of my favorite and funniest members in the number squeezed my hand and said, "It's about time, Jan."

I dearly loved every member of that outstanding and supportive cast. We had each other's backs. They were spectacular!

As our run-through progressed, we got nearer the reprise of *Hey There*. I stood up, only to hear Mr. Abbott say, "Skip this and go on to the next." I couldn't believe what I'd heard. *I didn't ask for a battle*, I thought, *but I seem to be in one.*

I walked to the edge of the stage and in front of everyone said, "Excuse me, Mr. Abbott, but this isn't fair. I think that before you cut this out, you owe me the courtesy of letting me do it for you."

Silence. Then, "All right, Janis, do it now!"

I did, and it stayed exactly where it belonged in the show. I seemed to be winning a few battles, but would I win the war I never wanted?

Our pre-Broadway tryout began in the beautiful old Colonial Theatre in Boston. Every night, I went on and struggled to find Babe Williams. I looked around and, to me, everyone else was fine and defined, but not I. I went on every night in Boston terrified of our New York opening. I thought everyone was good except me.

Mr. Abbott was someone I came to not only respect but to admire and like as well. My first Broadway show had been filled with warm and fuzzy people. Mr. Abbott was the opposite. One would never describe him as warm or fuzzy, but he was brilliant, a master at his profession. uncompromising with what he knew and a strong and solid leader.

Thanks to the wisdom and generosity of one Rosalind Russell, Mr. Abbott and I also became friends. His 100th birthday was celebrated at the grand old Palace Theatre in New York City. The Abbott alumni flew in from all over to honor him. We performed the numbers we had done in our Abbott shows, and to see his body of work was astounding.

We couldn't have had a better or wiser captain to steer us into the enormous success that *The Pajama Game* has enjoyed for over sixty years.

George Abbott
June 25, 1887 – January 31, 1995

Rosalind Russell, a Beautiful Soul

> *Acting is standing up naked and*
> *turning around, slowly.*
>
> —Rosalind Russell

We had about three nights left on our out-of-town tryout for *The Pajama Game* before we closed in Boston in 1954. Our next stop was the St. James Theatre and the opening night of the show on Broadway. If you don't remember it, you're too young, not born yet, or dead.

This particular night, I had just come off the stage and, as usual, sat down at my dressing room table, staring at the face in the mirror, saying, "Where are you in there? Everyone seems to have their characters in place except you, Jan. Who the hell is Babe?"

During a conversation one day, Stanley "Stash" Prager—one of the actors in our show—had mentioned that the great dean of critics, Brooks Atkinson of the prestigious *New York Times*, seldom reversed his first critical review of a performer. His words were like a knife in my heart as I recalled his review of me in my first show, *Remains to Be Seen*.

"As far as the girl is concerned," Atkinson wrote of my performance, "she has no apparent talent."

Apparently, I was talented enough to win the role over hundreds of other actresses. I was talented enough for some of the most respected and famous Broadway luminaries to hire me. I was talented enough for the rest of the press to like and accept me. But that first critical voice of my mother was all that I heard.

I had a long way to go before I understood this deeply buried part of myself.

I was scared to death and feeling like I was going to meet my embarrassing demise on the stage of the St. James when there was a knock on the door, jolting me out of my sad reverie. When I opened it, there stood Rosalind Russell.

She was a vision in pale beige, from her beautiful suit to her shoes, gloves, silk blouse and a little hat with a tiny veil perched on the side of her head. I stood there, dumbfounded, when I heard that no-nonsense voice of hers ask, "Well, can I come in?"

All I could blurt out was, "You took my breath away. Forgive me, Miss Russell, please come in, sit down."

"Call me Roz," she said. "Now get dressed, we're going for a glass of wine and a bite to eat. I want to talk to you."

We all knew that she was married to Freddie Brisson, one of the producers of the show, but to my knowledge no one had seen her. She simply hadn't been around. She sat there, long legs crossed, while I nervously got dressed, wondering why she was here.

I had a knot the size of a balloon in the pit of my stomach as we left the stage door and wandered up the alley.

"What's close by and quiet?" she asked. "What about that one across the street?"

With her hand at my back, Roz maneuvered us through the traffic to the other side. The restaurant had tables, no booths, but she looked around and steered me to a quiet place away from the others in the room.

As we sat opposite each other, I felt the tears welling up. The waiter brought the menu and left it for us. Roz stared at me for a moment, and then, putting her hand over mine, spoke those words I'll never forget.

"I've been where you are, and I want to talk to you about it."

I started to cry, tears silently rolling down my cheeks.

"And I've been there, too," she said as she grabbed a paper napkin for my eyes.

"I'm so sorry to do this," I blubbered. "I don't know what's wrong with me. The New York opening is just a week away and I still can't seem to find Babe."

"Well, that's why I'm here," she said, "to tell you that there's nothing wrong with you. There's everything right with you, dear Janis. I want you to hear this. You and your presence on stage drive this story and everyone knows it except you."

"Does it show out there, this insecurity I feel?" I asked.

"Of course not. That stuff's in you. Listen, we have a big hit here, and you have just as much right to enjoy it as everyone else. Now, between bedtime tonight and your performance tomorrow night, you gotta find your backbone. When you make your entrance, claim your absolute right to be there. You've earned it!"

Roz continued, "Believe me, you *are* Babe."

I didn't have a "But...but...but..." left in me.

"Now," she said, "I'm hungry and you must be, too. Waiter, we're ready to order. Two hamburgers, please."

I needed a Roz Russell that night—and I got her.

When I could finally speak, I said, "You're the only one who's said anything to me, Roz. Mr. Abbott and I had a confrontation that was unlike anything I've ever known. I've heard nothing from him. Nothing good, nothing bad, just nothing, and that's the way I've felt. He didn't even speak to me for two weeks. I'm sure I didn't endear myself to him when I stood up for my actor's rights a couple of times. He was big enough to admit that I was right, and I always respected him for that.

"I still can't believe you're here. I can even call you Roz. Like everyone else, I've always adored you, but to finally meet you...."

"Oh, pooh," she said.

"No, no, please, let me tell you how grateful I am. Thank you is simply not enough and never will be."

"You want to thank me?" she asked. "Enjoy this show, your talent, and your life. Oh, and don't forget to thank yourself once in a while. Now... here's to you, dear Janis, and here's to us. We deserve it!"

What she said made all the difference in the world to me. Nothing changed, except my attitude toward my work and myself. I was lost until a major human being shared her pain of growing a new person while trying to hold on to the familiar one. The one you think you know.

During the closing night in Boston, Mr. Abbott knocked on my dressing room door.

"Can I hang my coat in your closet?" he asked.

"Of course."

I took it, hung it up and, when I turned around, he put an envelope in my hand and said, "This is for you. Read it later." He wished me luck and after he left, I opened his note. I couldn't wait.

"Dear Janis: I'm so proud of you and how hard you worked to become Babe. You have my appreciation and gratitude. Love, George."

Not "Mr. Abbott" but "George"—though he would always be Mr. Abbott to me.

What a way to leave Boston and what a night that opening was. Everything we did was a showstopper. I've never seen anything like it. We were all in a daze, not touching the ground.

"Did you hear that? They made us do an encore. They don't do things like that in the theatre, do they?" and "I can't believe what's happened to us tonight" and on and on. There were no words to express that opening night. And the ensuing reviews!

Oh, by the way, they were all wrong about Brooks Atkinson. His review of me was, "Her shape is almost as exhilarating as her voice."

Pajama Game is now a 65-year-old show and has been revived on Broadway over and over. It still has legs and heart and fun and remains unforgettable.

It was worth all the heartache, the tears, the fears and the doubts because I had my guardian angel, who never lets me down. This time, she came in the form of one Roz Russell.

"It's all there, Janis, just believe it," she told me. Roz unlocked a door for me that night, and as long as I live, I will never forget her generosity, sensitivity and caring that prompted her to talk to me that night.

Without thinking too much, a few words come to mind that best describe Rosalind Russell. Elegant, funny, generous, genuine, openhearted and definite, definitely definite! She was all of that and so much more.

Roz Russell turned the key that opened the door to a whole new world for me. She made a difference in my life, one that has stayed with me through life's obstacle course with its ruts, hills and valleys, bumps and bruises, rejections and self-doubts. Through it all shines the joy and the victories. I'm talking about the real ones, the victories over yourself. That's true freedom!

So, here's to you, dear Roz. For you and all of the guardian angels who see a need and step up to the plate. I can still see you and will always feel your dynamic presence, accompanied by your amazing truth.

I've been able to emulate you several times through the years involving performers. Your words—"I've been where you are, and I can fix this"—have been repeated countless times.

Rosalind Russell
June 4, 1907 - November 28, 1976

You are always in my heart.

Postscript: For all of you budding actors and those of you who have bloomed, I suggest that you rent His Girl Friday. *It stars the late and unforgettable greats, Rosalind Russell and Cary Grant.*

From the moment she appears, she is "in the moment," and the result is stunning. Displaying her famous Roz Russell bravado, she begins a walking and talking scene that was completely uncut. There were no close-ups to stop or impede her amazing ability to let us know her, and that Cary will soon meet his match. She was an example of what it takes to be the epitome of a star.

"The Pajama Game" Meets the Queen Mother

To curtsy or not to curtsy, that was the question. I practiced, but then I forgot.

–Janis Paige

There was an electric excitement in the air as I went to work on *The Pajama Game* this night.

"The Queen Mother is seeing the show tonight!" someone said.

I ran to peek through the curtains and saw her seats roped off and several security men lining the aisles. There is something awe-inspiring about Americans meeting royalty. To curtsy or not to curtsy, ah, that is the question.

Needless to say, our question went unanswered as we awaited Her Majesty.

I had the largest dressing room, so we were all scheduled to meet there and have champagne during intermission. I was waiting for the cast when Hal Prince told me that Her Majesty was on her way. Once she was settled, we would all come in to meet her.

With that, Hal told me to hide until everyone arrived.

"Where do I go, Hal?" I asked.

"Go in the bathroom and I'll come and get you."

Naturally, my bathroom was small, with only the facility and a sink. There was one of those vents with slats in the bottom of the door.

Suddenly, I heard her beautifully modulated voice utter, "Loving the performance." I quickly got on my knees in front of that vent to see beautifully well-shod feet passing by.

I could hear a few other elegant English voices along with Hal's. Then John Raitt entered with Eddie Foy Jr. and Carol Haney. Damn, did he forget me?

There I was, on my knees trying to at least hear through the vent. As I listened, there was champagne being served. Damn! Hal *did* forget me! Well there was no way I was going to miss the Queen.

I gingerly reached for the doorknob and started to come out when a man stood over me with a gun asking who I was.

"J-J-Janis Paige," I managed to stammer out. "I'm in the show! This is my dressing room!"

Just then, Hal ran over and said, "Oh Janis, I'm so sorry, I forgot you!"

"No kidding, Hal," I whispered as I quickly gathered myself to meet Her Majesty.

Inside, I'm thinking, "That's okay. It's only Her Majesty The Queen of England. No big deal."

I finally met the Queen Mother, her Lady in Waiting and a gentleman who accompanied them. She did not disappoint. She was dressed in a lovely, long gown, some of it with a subtle sparkle. She also wore a small but gorgeous diamond tiara.

As I quickly tried to remember everything, my eyes found her pearls. I adore pearls, but never in my life had I seen such gigantic, perfectly shaped gems as those she wore around her neck, reflecting her flawless skin.

From her warmth, her graciousness and her ability to keep the conversation going when none of us knew what to speak about, Her Majesty was amazing. She gave us all a feeling that she was truly interested in us as we tried to answer her soft and modulated questions.

It's an experience I'll never forget.

Damn, I forgot to curtsy!

Elizabeth, The Queen Mother
August 4, 1900 – March 30, 2002

James Michener

Character consists of what you do on the third and fourth tries.

—James A. Michener

When I met Jimmy Michener, involvement was the last thing on my mind. He was definitely not my type, and types were a big part of attractions then, so a relationship was never in my sight.

As I write about my immaturity of yesterday, I'm amazed at how long my learning road is in this ever-changing, ever-challenging process called life.

In 1954, I found myself starring in one of the biggest musical hits ever to reach the Broadway stage, *The Pajama Game*. With glowing reviews, SRO audiences and countless admiring men at my door—not to mention the special fame that comes with a Broadway hit—it was very heady stuff!

I was naïve about myself, about the spectacular life I was sharing with that kid from Tacoma and an intoxicating New York City. In other words, I was still an amateur human being.

As usual, I just flew by the seat of my pants through two vastly different generations. Success, excitement and fame were all mine, but I was living on the edge of hyperbole and I made mistakes. A few of them taught me to know how it felt to be scared to death.

The art of finding my balanced life was still in its infancy. Oh, once in a while I'd have a flash of something called an epiphany. Its arrival was sudden, thrilling and puzzling, but most of my emotional education was a combination of intuition, perseverance, intense curiosity and a seemingly unstoppable love of life.

My few but precious vaudeville years had enriched qualities in me that were so necessary to stay afloat in life's sea of ups and downs. Surprises, however, always lurked nearby to remind me of what I had yet to learn.

For the first time, I was learning to live entirely alone. I was somewhat protected by my right-and-wrong upbringing, but at times temptation got in the way of my basic good sense. I certainly had the talent to earn my living, that was a given. But the skills needed for an integrated life were still a long way off.

Being in a hit show does not an adult make, and I had a long road to travel before I could reach that lofty position where I could really take care of myself.

James Michener was one of a number of teachers throughout my life. I just didn't know it then.

I met Jimmy the night I sat next to Marlene Dietrich, with the two of us surrounded by famous men of the day. Miss Dietrich held court with her usual grace and sophistication, not to mention her perfect legs, while I sat completely entranced by my surroundings. Leonard Lyons' beautiful apartment in the famous Beresford, way Uptown, was the setting for this soiree. It was my first!

As I sat there, the constant memory of Tacoma, the Great Depression and just plain survival met the Beresford, the guests, the food, the elegance and mostly the ease with which everyone seemed to move and speak.

When it came time to leave, I got my coat, said my thanks for the lovely party and made my way to the elevator. Waiting there, too, were Dr. Bunche and Mr. Michener.

Dr. Bunche asked if he could drop me somewhere, as they were heading Downtown.

"So am I," I replied, "and thank you very much."

Good lord, I was chauffeured home by the head of the United Nations, and the world-renowned author of *Tales of the South Pacific*, James Michener, was my doorman.

Goodnights and pleased-to-meet-you's were exchanged, and I was home. My feet scarcely touched the ground.

The next day brought a call from Mr. Michener. I was completely surprised and rather flustered.

"First, call me Jimmy," he said, "and I'd love to take you to dinner."

Now the man I met the night before was quiet, not talkative, but polite and a listener. At least that was my impression. He was academic and introspective, and I simply wondered if there could possibly be a common thread of conversation and what I should do if I couldn't keep the evening interesting.

Why this was *my* responsibility flashed through my brain, but it was quickly gone. As usual, sophistication and security were not my strongest suits. I wasn't even aware of how underdeveloped those qualities were in me.

"I'd love to spend some time with you and find out why you enjoy your life so much," Jimmy said to me.

Well, I was hooked with that flattery and said, "Thank you, I'd love to have dinner with you and ask you about *Tales of the South Pacific*. I read it a few years ago, and I simply adored that perfect musical called *South Pacific*, based on your book."

We went to Sardi's, my absolute favorite restaurant—and why not? If you were on Broadway and you entered Sardi's, someone would inevitably applaud in appreciation of your work. I felt very special, and here I was on the arm of one of the world's great writers.

I needn't have wondered if we had something in common. The something in common was *me*.

During dinner, Jimmy asked me question after question about my childhood, my hometown, my parents, the Depression, school, singing, marriage, but mostly how and why I loved life so much. I told him that I had much to be grateful for: A hit show, security for a while, my talent that had brought me so far, the surprises that seem to wait around every corner—and being born in America.

"I love my country!" I beamed. "And meeting you, Jimmy, this is a thrill for me."

Jimmy was so attentive that I found the idea of him not being my type fading and this non-type finding a place in my life.

We began to see each other often. The questions continued, but when I tried to ask him about him, he was not forthcoming. He did say that he had been adopted but would not go further. It didn't mean as much to me then as it would now.

It didn't matter. I felt close to him. I trusted him. I enjoyed him. He also bolstered my own lack of something I had always admired: The world of academia.

One night over dinner, Jimmy looked at me and out came the words, "When are we going to sleep together?"

A million thoughts sped through my head at that question. *Oh dear,* I thought, *sex, with its bag of tricks, is going to ruin what up until now has been a good relationship. If I say 'No,' will he be gone? Will everything be over?*

My decision was all about him. I never gave a thought to how I was feeling except to wonder if he would like me. Not if I would like him. So, I buried my own truth and simply said, "I guess it's time, Jimmy."

The relationship became "They're seeing each other." One night over dinner, he mentioned that he was from Doylestown, Bucks County, PA.

"I need to take care of some business there," Jimmy said, "and I'd love for you to go with me this coming weekend. I'll pick you up Saturday night and we can drive down after the show."

Now this was suddenly very different. A kind of queasy feeling materialized in my stomach, and the first thing I thought of were those firmly taught childhood rules. I had already broken many of them, but this one was holding fast.

I felt guilty, out of control and kind of trapped.

"Is there a problem?"

"No, Jimmy," I lied, "I'm just surprised, that's all. I've heard so much about Bucks County. I've wanted to see it. I understand it's beautiful."

"Well, I'll show it to you."

Once again, I pushed aside any investigation of how and what I truly felt and ignored those all-important inner questions. The difference between pleasing and being a pleaser was, as yet, unknown to me, so I remained dishonest to myself.

I hated the feeling, but the possible consequences of honesty intimidated me. So I buried my true feelings and carried on as usual.

It took me a long time and years of good therapy to help me finally understand the complicated relationship with my mother that continued to keep me in the dark about myself. My opinions, needs and struggles were never validated in any way or for any reason. I was too young to know how her behavior would influence the future events in my life. They just did, and I simply knew no difference.

We left the St. James Theatre about eleven-thirty on that Saturday night. The drive was pleasant and uneventful. Jimmy's usual questions were prevalent, and I laughed and asked him what more he thought he could uncover about me.

"I envy your ability to enjoy life as you do. I don't have that quality," he admitted.

"But Jimmy, you have a great life."

He didn't answer as we drove up to a house. I asked him if this was his home.

"No, it belongs to an old friend of mine. I always stay with him and his wife."

My heart sank and I felt suddenly sick with disbelief. Did he lie by omission or could he possibly be so insensitive as to not value my feelings, let alone my privacy?

"Do you mean they are here now? I'm very uncomfortable, Jimmy. I've never done anything like this."

"They are my oldest friends, Jan. Stop worrying."

"My God, don't worry? I'm sick with worry," I replied.

His friend opened the door and I wished that the floor would swallow me up and I could end my embarrassment. After introductions and pleasantries, I heard the words, "Jimmy, you know where to go, sleep well, yell if you need anything."

We climbed the stairs, not up to a bedroom but to the attic. A single bed stood quietly waiting. I was stunned that he had so blatantly betrayed me with not a thought as to the consequences. I hated both of us.

"Why didn't you tell me the truth, Jimmy?" I fumed. "Give me a choice! I'm so uncomfortable and ashamed!"

"But they're my oldest friends, Jan."

"But they're not mine."

I gritted through my teeth. We slept and nothing more. I saw Bucks County the next day while hiding all of my feelings. I simply did not have the words for a confrontation with him. I'd only end up wrong again, I thought.

I got through another night in that attic and that single bed, but I was finally awakening to my own unimportance. Jimmy had said that he thought my feelings about the weekend were "unimportant."

"If they're unimportant," I insisted, "why do I feel so terrible and so sad?"

The drive home was uneventful. I sorted and re-sorted my thoughts while keeping everything else normal, whatever that was. Things were in fact far from normal.

The relationship phased out. Relationships are littered with expectations, and most of the time, these expectations are known only by the one doing the expecting. Of course, that's not fair to the other guy, but two play this game.

I expected trust from Jimmy, and he expected unquestioned acceptance. We were both dishonest and both unsure of our still-shaky ability to be honest with one another. After all, truth could mean rejection, hurt feelings, anger and retribution. Why risk it?

I wasn't wrong about my queasiness, the single bed, the attic and Jimmy's so-called best and oldest friend. The "friend" wrote a book about their relationship and had the insensitive gall to send me a copy.

There, in its own little niche, were Jimmy and me, the attic and "how did they manage in that single bed?" among other things. Of course, I expected nothing less from this amateur voyeur.

I found this published information extremely disloyal to Jimmy. He owed me nothing except common decency as a guest in his home. Instead, I received his lascivious, nasty and titillating paragraph about that single bed and my supposed behavior. The result was just some stupid celebrity gossip that I did not deserve from Jimmy's "oldest and dearest friends."

Many years have passed since we met, but still I realize how little I knew about the brilliant but hidden James Michener. He never did see the problem with the Bucks County weekend.

I screwed up enough courage to talk to him about it, but after a few tries a wall went up and I stopped trying to climb it. Jimmy was incredibly complicated as well as enormously talented and prolific, and I realized some years later that he was, at least to me, emotionally unavailable.

Whatever it was, when the conversation turned to him and his questionable behavior, he simply faded into a frustrating silence. He could question me forever, but never himself.

Jimmy married in 1955. He stayed married for 39 years until his wife's death in 1994. He continued his philanthropy and his writing, receiving countless awards including the highest his country could give him, The

Presidential Medal of Freedom. He also died never knowing, and never discovering. his biological parents. When I heard that, it spoke volumes about the man I knew.

The last time I heard from Jimmy was in 1971. I was starring in the first international company of the musical *Applause* in Johannesburg, South Africa.

We hadn't spoken in years. Logistics and the usual life changes sent us our separate ways. When I picked up my mail at the hotel, there was a note to me, written in a very recognizable hand. When I opened it, there was that familiar writing.

"Janis dear," it began, "I read of your success in the paper and I was hoping we could see each other. I am leaving to continue my research on Africa. If you get this note, please give me a call. Love, Jimmy."

I called immediately and missed him by an hour.

When I got home, I dropped a note to him in Austin, Texas, where he lived. I heard nothing back from him until March 1992, when I received a copy of his lovely and last book, *The World Is My Home*.

It was beautifully inscribed to me with his final sentence, "Keep going, Jan, we need you. With deep affection, Jimmy Michener."

When you look at his prolific body of work, the world was definitely his home.

The last years of Jimmy's life were spent on a dialysis machine. When he began to get worse and the prognosis not good, he made a decision. He bid his friends goodbye, had the machine turned off and awaited the rest of his life and ultimate death. He died as he lived—his way, with no apparent frills, just his courage and readiness to accept his fate.

Jimmy died on October 16, 1997. He was a great teacher. I learned much about myself and traveled many hills and valleys with him. Perhaps his greatest and most enduring gift to me was the knowledge he instilled in me that I was "special." His word, not mine.

You had a love of life, Jimmy. It lives in your books as we travel the world with you, my friend. We rubbed off on one another. It was a pleasure and a gift to know you.

James Michener
February 3, 1907 - October 16, 1997

Lucille Ball and Desilu

Luck! I don't know anything about luck. I never banked on it, and I'm afraid of people who do. Luck to me is something else: Hard work and realizing what opportunity is and what isn't.

–Lucille Ball

In the summer of 1955, *The Pajama Game* was playing to standing-room-only audiences and continued to be the light of our lives. We were such a happy bunch that it was just fun to go to work.

During that time, my agent called, saying that there was a TV series offered to me and that the writer would be seeing the show that evening.

His name was Arthur Stander and his background was stellar. He had written for *The Danny Thomas Show*, a huge hit at the time, and countless others. He would produce and be head writer on the project.

Naturally, I was excited and was advised to take advantage of the opportunity in front of me. I had been in the show for a year and four months, but my closing night tore me apart when I had to leave. and say "Goodbye" to those who had been so close and dear to me.

I cried my eyes out as I left the theater that night.

Here I go again, I thought, *I'm on the road again.*

Danny Thomas himself was crazy about the script and, fortunately, about me as well. He also owned half of the show. We got the cast together, the director, the musical conductor, writers, guest stars, etc., and we filmed at the now famous Desilu Studios, the joint venture of Desi Arnaz and his wife, Lucille Ball.

I Love Lucy was produced and filmed there, and it was a very busy studio. Lucy and Desi proved to be excellent business partners. They continued their success, not only with their own worldwide hit, but also while producing and filming many other television shows.

One day on my way to work, I met the great Vivian Vance outside the soundstage door. She was leaving and I was going to work. There she was, Lucy's famous and funny sidekick.

"Janis, I just love your show," Vivian said. "You are wonderful, and I love your song every show."

Well, would you have ignored Vivian Vance, even if you were a few minutes late for makeup? I don't know what you would have done, but I was too scared and intimidated to say I was late, so I spoke with her. We weren't there very long when I thanked her and ran to makeup and hair.

No one said anything to me, but there was obviously a rushed feeling.

"I'm sorry I was a few minutes late this morning," I said as I related having run into Vivian. By the time I arrived on the set, I was about a half hour late and embarrassed. I apologized profusely to everyone.

We broke for lunch and the assistant director said, "Lucy would like to see you. She's in her office."

"Now?" I asked.

"Right now."

As I made my way to see Lucy—whom I had never met—I pondered why I was being summoned at lunchtime. We had only an hour.

The secretary ushered me in, and there she sat. The fabulous Lucille Ball. Bright orange-pink hair, wearing a blouse and slacks, no makeup and stunning!

"Sit down, Janis," she said.

"Thank you, Miss Ball."

"Call me Lucy," she answered. "Have you ever heard the phrase 'Time is money'?"

"My grandfather used to say it," I assured her.

"Well, you cost the studio money today when you were late. Time is money, Janis. Please don't be late again."

I sputtered out my apologies, close to tears, and again tried to tell her what had transpired that morning. She knew all about Vivian stopping me to talk, but my responsibility was to my work.

I apologized again, thanked her, and assured Lucy that it would never happen again. She walked around the desk, gave me a hug, and said, "Grab a bite to eat. Now go!"

I wanted to tell her that I was never late. I was brought up to be on time. I was never late for school, church, classes, home or anything else. It was something that happened, and it was my fault. Never again!

The President of the United States could have stopped me, and I would have said, "Not now, Mr. President, I'll be late for work. See you later, give me a call."

With her spectacular looks and array of seemingly endless Lucy faces, Lucille Ball was innately a clown. When I watched her, I saw Emmett Kelly, Gene Sheldon, Red Skelton and the countless clowns I had seen through my years in vaudeville.

None of this would have been captured without Desi playing the perfect and endlessly innocent foil of his wife's crazy choices. Each episode usually followed that wide, open-mouthed cry of, "I didn't mean it, sweetheart!"

In his famous Cuban accent, Desi would often counter with, "You never 'didn't mean it!'" To me, they were the Laurel and Hardy of their time.

No one even came close to the rare and often mysterious combination of plot, writing, directing, supporting cast and the magic of the stars whose talent brought it all to everlasting life. Lucy was a clown, and Desi her straight man.

Lucy's support of me never wavered. In the early Sixties, I got a call from her wanting to do a series with me. Needless to say, I was thrilled at my good fortune. She wanted her writers to write the pilot, so meetings were set up, the great Jack Oakie agreed to play my father, and all was a "Go."

The "Go" came to a screeching halt when, out of the blue, I got the mumps. The sad ending was just that. I was gone for six weeks, we lost Oakie to another role, and I accepted a movie to be filmed in France. We could never pull everybody together again.

I lost my opportunity to work with the one and only Lucille Ball. I also lost my chance to soak up everything that she could teach me. I don't have a lot of regrets, but I have this one. Through it all, she remained my friend and supporter and never forgot to say, "One of these days, Janis, we're going to do that series."

There's an old adage that warns us to strike while the iron is hot. We did, but so did the mumps. And while I was getting well, the iron cooled off. She never did, however, and like everyone else, I'll love her forever.

Lucille Ball
August 8, 1911 - April 26, 1989

Nearly 70 years after it premiered, every day, twenty-four hours a day, somewhere in the world, someone watches an I Love Lucy *episode.*

Fred Astaire

I JUST PUT MY FEET IN THE AIR
AND MOVE THEM AROUND.

—Fred Astaire

After I finished filming my TV series, *It's Always Jan*, in 1956, I had an offer to return to Las Vegas and the New Frontier Hotel. By now, I had two dancers, an orchestra leader, costume changes and a show worthy of The Biggest Little City in the World.

Las Vegas was nothing but wall-to-wall talent. The word "superstar" had not yet been invented, but we didn't need it. Las Vegas always had the greatest stars of the day—Frank Sinatra, Sammy Davis Jr., Lena Horne, Jack Benny, George Burns and Gracie Allen and Tony Bennett, to name but a few. If you were an entertainer, your ultimate destination was Vegas.

If my own shows were timed correctly, I could run across that two-lane road we called Las Vegas Boulevard and catch the star at The Desert Inn or The Tropicana or The Sahara or El Rancho Vegas.

That little Strip was packed on both sides with clubs and their stars. Even the opening acts were so good that some of them became stars in their own right. Playing Las Vegas was the top of the heap, and I couldn't wait to see it again.

Like vaudeville, playing the clubs offered the opportunity to perfect your act as well as your ability to know and understand an audience.

We not only did two or three shows a night but also learned to handle food and drink service during the show, noisy dishes, a talkative diner, the occasional dreaded drunk and myriad other possible problems that could and often did occur during one's act.

The one thing you could not do was lose control of the audience. Consequently, diplomacy wrapped in a great sense of humor was the answer. We always had to find a way to make lemonade out of what could have been a lemon of an evening.

I got my first solo record album during my New Frontier run and an offer to play the Cocoanut Grove in the gorgeous and very ritzy Ambassador Hotel in Los Angeles.

It took me six years, but I was finally going home a winner. I'd done my time (so to speak) crisscrossing the country, and I was more than ready for Hollywood. Besides, I didn't have to follow Sammy Davis Jr. this time.

The room was ultra-chic and quite beautiful, encircled by its enormous white palm trees. The band conducted by Freddie Martin was equally famous, as was his band singer, Merv Griffin. Yes, *that* Merv Griffin, who went on to great fame and fortune as host of his own long-running talk show.

Merv also owned the Beverly Hilton Hotel and created the iconic game shows *Jeopardy!* and *Wheel of Fortune*, series still running today. He, like Bob Hope, was born to be a mogul. They were both fascinating men.

This was 1957, when an opening night was filled with tuxes and women in little black dresses and jewelry from the finest stores that money could support. It was spectacular and a thrill for me to come back to where I started, having left Ciro's defeated, rejected and vowing never to return again.

I was more than ready for the Grove, and they got their money's worth that first night. I'd had plenty of time and opportunity to sharpen my skills, putting on a great show. The audience showed its appreciation with three encores!

After the show, there was a knock on my dressing room door. The maître d' told me that Arthur Freed was in the audience and would love me to join him at his table.

Arthur Freed was perhaps the best musical motion picture producer Metro had at that time. He had an innate flair for his work and was highly respected. Of course, I accepted.

When I joined him, Mr. Freed gave me a hug, told me how wonderful I was, introduced me to everyone and asked me to sit. He put his hand over mine and proceeded to tell me that he had a film he wanted me to do.

"A film?" I repeated, surprised at the offer.

It was the last thing I expected.

"I'm filming the Broadway musical *Silk Stockings* starring Fred Astaire and Cyd Charisse, and I want you to co-star," he said. "You'll have a musical number with Fred."

"Mr. Freed," I said with complete honesty, "I'm not a dancer."

He interrupted me with, "Janis, you know Metro. You may not be a dancer now, but we'll have you dancing in no time. What do you say?"

Of course, I said "Yes!"

I didn't even have to audition, but come to think of it, I guess I'd just done that on the stage at the Cocoanut Grove.

The first day of rehearsal arrived, and I was ready. In 1950, I'd had to sell my car to pay some bills. Being from California, a car was an appendage but a much-needed extension of our lives. Not so in New York City, so it had to go.

When I got my first paycheck from *Pajama Game*, my manager and her brother said, "You've always missed your car, so we want you to take this check and buy a new one. You don't have to worry now, so begin to enjoy yourself."

"Oh, Ruthie and Lisle, I saw a picture of a Ford convertible I loved," I told them. "Do you think I could get one of those?"

Lisle said he'd find me one and let me know.

A few weeks later, he called and said he'd found my car in Brooklyn.

"It's pale blue with white leather seats," he said. "I'll take you out to get it."

"I know you're going to think I'm crazy," I responded, "and I am, a little. But I want it painted a certain color."

"Jan, it's brand new and you want it painted before you see it?"

"When I was finally through 1950," I said to Lisle, "I was in Mark Cross one day. They had such beautiful things and I saw a very large pink silk chiffon scarf that I adored and bought. I wear it all the time and I want my new car painted the color of that scarf."

Silence on the other end of the phone.

"Are you there, Lisle?"

"Barely," he said. "Do you want to think about this, Jan?"

"No, I don't, Lisle. Would you help me get this done? When it's finished, we'll go to Brooklyn together and drive it back."

Another silence, and then, "Of course I'll get it done. Can I pick up the scarf so I can get it to the dealer?"

"I have a matinee tomorrow and I'll have it at the St. James. I love you, my friend."

I had a phone in my dressing room, and two days later I started to get phone calls from not only the dealer but also from the guy who would paint the car.

"It's beautiful now," the dealer said. "Are you sure you want to do this to the painter who said that my request hurt him?"

Then, from the painter: "I don't want to paint this beautiful car this weird color. I've never even seen this color."

"But I have," I insisted, "and I want the car the color of my scarf."

The day came when I got the call that it was finished.

"How does it look?" I asked.

"Well, it's not for me," the dealer said, "but I have to admit, it's kinda pretty. Anyway, it's ready and your scarf is in the glove compartment."

"Thank you so very much," I said.

"We'll see you tomorrow."

It was parked outside his business—and it was gorgeous!

However, I wasn't ready for the reaction of the public and other drivers. My pink car hit the columns with a variety of remarks, but I loved that car, especially in the summer when the top was down and the white seats set off that Schiaparelli pink color. All of this splendor was finished off by its white-rimmed tires.

The following year, the painter called to tell me that Ford Motors had called him to find out the "recipe" he used to paint my car. He said that he didn't give it to them, but the next year, Ford came out with its first pink car.

Even today, one can buy a pink car if they choose, but I did it first!

It was that car that I drove to Metro the day I met Fred Astaire.

My mind kept traveling back to the Thirties when I was about twelve and we could finally afford to go to the movies. My first Fred Astaire film was *Flying Down to Rio* (1933) at the tiny Proctor Theater in Tacoma, and he became my hero.

I remember sitting transfixed as Fred and Ginger Rogers danced us to Paris, London, Rio and Broadway, and he danced his way into our hearts. He, in top hat, white tie and tails, and she in feathers, satin, rhinestones and high heels.

Now, here I was, driving to meet and begin working with the one and only Fred Astaire. Go figure life, if you can.

I had allowed an extra hour to be early on the set and have time to pull my nerves together, stare at him, screw up my dancing courage and get comfortable, if there was such a thing on a day like this.

I drove up to those wrought-iron gates at Metro. The guard welcomed me, asked where I was going, congratulated me on my good fortune and, as I started to leave, shouted for me to stop.

"What else do you need?" I asked.

"There is no drive-on pass for you at this gate," he explained.

By then, I was so nervous and afraid of being late that instead of asking him to call Mr. Freed's office to fix the problem, I asked him what he wanted me to do.

"I'm sorry, Miss Paige, but you'll have to park off-lot. I don't have an assigned space for you."

Can you believe how scared stupid I was? All I had to do was to have him make a phone call and I'd be on my way to the soundstage, but did I do that? Of course not.

Instead, I quickly turned around and began to look for a parking space off the lot. Now it was getting late, and the time looking for a place to park was eating into my hour-early promise I'd made earlier.

Oh my God, is it possible that I'm going to be late for Fred Astaire? Good lord, I'm never late for anything, why today? I finally found a space down by the train station.

I locked my pink car and began to run. I ran past the guard at the gate and kept running until I reached the soundstage. I swung open that heavy door with its familiar "whoosh" sound, and the first thing I saw was Fred kind of pacing and glancing at his watch.

There stood Fred, Hermes Pan, his famous choreographer, the piano player, the drummer and the assistant. I was almost a half hour late, and I couldn't breathe.

As I started to apologize, the floodgates opened, and I began to cry. I must have scared poor Fred because he ran up to me.

"What's wrong, Janis?"

Through trying to catch my breath, being late, being nervous and just plain terrified, I blurted out what had happened at the gate. He listened while someone brought me a chair and a glass of water. Then I heard, "I'm so very sorry this happened to you, Janis. it won't happen again. May I have your car keys?"

With the keys in his hand, I watched Mr. Astaire go to the phone and speak to someone, all the while twirling my keys on his finger.

Then, I actually *saw* him!

There stood my childhood hero, looking exactly like Fred Astaire. He was dressed in a pair of gray flannel trousers, pristine white shirt, cuffs rolled up to reveal a gorgeous gold watch, one of his famous ascots at his neck and a soft pink and French blue repp tie at his waist, where anyone else would have worn a belt. It was knotted with its ends hanging loosely and oh-so-right on Fred.

The next things I saw were his socks, They were a soft shade of dusty pink to match his tie, and he wore those great looking black and white oxfords with his taps.

Everything standing in front of me was the one and only Fred Astaire.

He hung up the phone, knelt by my chair and said, "Tomorrow, you come through the gate down to the soundstage, and there will be a parking place with your name on it right outside the door, next to mine. This will be your permanent space through the film. Now, if you'll tell them where you left your car, we'll pick it up and bring it here."

"It's over by the train station," I replied, "and it's pink. You can't miss it."

Fred gave the keys to a man nearby, told him where the car was parked, then said, "You can't miss it, it's pink." And he didn't.

Fred Astaire was patient, kind, helpful and always appreciative of my hard work on *Stereophonic Sound*. Each day, as I learned one part of the number, he would show me another and always asked, "Do you think you can do this?"

"Of course, Fred!"

I never said "No," and the black and blue marks on my body from "swimming" up and down that conference table several times a day were proof that I could not ever turn down Fred Astaire.

One of the unforgettable memories I have of that time occurred when Fred and Hermes Pan would invent and work on the next steps. They not only moved alike; they looked alike, too. Both were soft-spoken gentlemen with a mutual respect for one another.

I loved watching them work together, closing everything and everyone out until they had it right. What amazing people they were and how lucky I was to be a part it all.

One day near the end of the number, Fred came to me with an idea for the ending.

"Janis, when we finish the last turns on the table, I'm going to send in a big chandelier on cue," he said. "We'll both grab it, swing out over the heads of the press on the floor in front of us, let go and then slide on our knees à la Jolson to the finish."

Now how am I going to do that? I thought. But I didn't say it, of course.

"That sounds wonderful, Fred! I can't wait to try it."

There was no way to rehearse the ending, so we counted everything out until the day came to film the entire number. All I could think of was the knee slide that we hadn't done yet.

Everything was lit, camera ready, cast and playback ready.

"We'll go through the whole number once without stopping," Fred said.

The music started. We sang, danced and came to the end we had not rehearsed. The chandelier came in on cue, we grabbed it on cue and hung on until we let go and slid on our knees à la Jolson to a perfect finish and applause from everyone around.

I could not believe that we had done it all the way through for the first time. Fred was more than pleased, as was everyone else.

I loved making that film, but the wonder of it all was remembering that twelve-year-old kid I once was, watching *Flying Down to Rio* at the Proctor in Tacoma, never even dreaming that one day I too would be dancing with the great Fred Astaire.

He was always ready, always the total professional. What I didn't know was that he was a worrier, and I'd never seen that side of him.

One day, I was watching him film a scene when he began to blow his lines. Each time he tried again, something would happen that would cause him to stop. The harder he tried, the more difficult it became for him to finish. He was angry at himself and probably embarrassed with the cast and crew watching.

I felt so sorry for Fred until our director finally yelled, "Print that one!" It was his twenty-first take. He immediately said, "Let's try it again," but they had what they needed, and the torture was over.

My heart went out to him that day. I knew how he felt. They could have printed several out of the twenty-one takes, but Fred insisted that he "get it right." It took me a long time to finally learn that blowing your well-learned lines over and over again could be caused by something outside of the day's work.

In therapy, I learned a word called "fragmentation" and the tools used to get out of it. We fragment in so many ways and for so many reasons not known to us at the time we do it.

Fragmentation is a body feeling, but if we aren't taught to be aware of and awake to that warning, we don't stop it before we go completely off the rails, as did Fred that long-ago day. This knowledge has been a godsend for me, but as much as I know, I still fall into the trap and get fragmented.

The difference is, now I know how to get out.

Fred Astaire
May 10, 1899 – June 27, 1987

Top:
With Howard Lindsay, one of the great playwrights of all time, in a scene from my first Broadway hit, Remains to Be Seen, *in 1951.*

Middle:
A scene from Remains to Be Seen. *under the table. This is in the middle of a massive fight with guns. Someone was being arrested, and I was saying, "Will you shut up over there? I'm on the phone!" It got a huge laugh every time.*

Bottom:
Jackie Cooper and I are here with Madeleine Morka in Remains to Be Seen.

Above:

Singing "7 ½ Cents" from The Pajama Game, *my biggest hit on Broadway. It opened in 1954 and won the 1955 Tony Award for Best Musical.*

Below:

Performing "I'm Not at All in Love" in The Pajama Game.

Above:
In Pajama Game *with my costar John Raitt, singing "There Once Was a Man." John was a marvelous singer and performer.*

Right:
During the knife-throwing scene in Pajama Game.

Above:
In The Pajama Game *with John Raitt and a dancer. It's the first time I meet John's character onstage.*

Left:
With John Raitt performing the song "Small Talk" in Pajama Game.

Above:
With Stanley Prager and the ensemble doing "7 ½ Cents" in Pajama Game.

Right:
The great George Abbott, who wrote the book for and directed The Pajama Game, Damn Yankees *and so many more.*

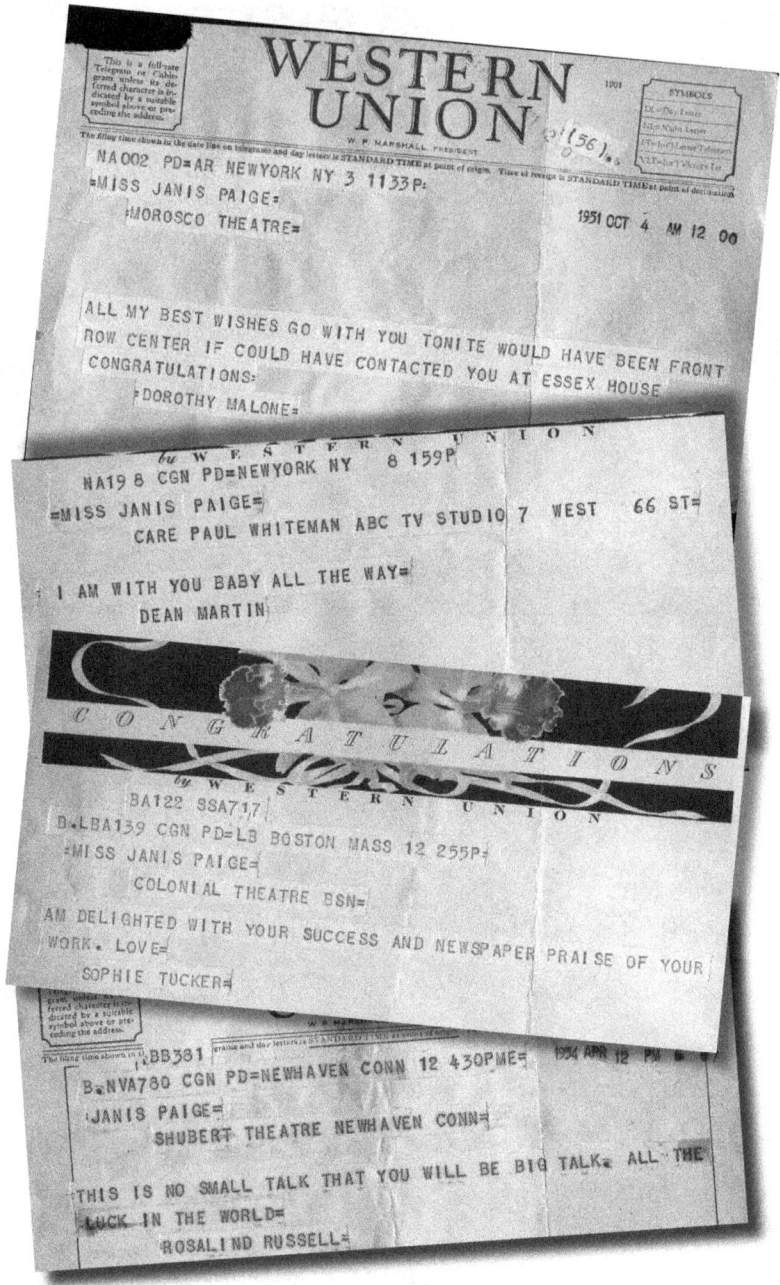

During out-of-town previews of a show or in advance of opening night on Broadway, one of the great traditions used to be receiving telegrams of support. Typically, I received literally hundreds of them. Those days are gone – but it was wonderful while it lasted. Here, I'm given best wishes from Dorothy Malone, Dean Martin, Sophie Tucker and Rosalind Russell. Some pretty fine company to be in.

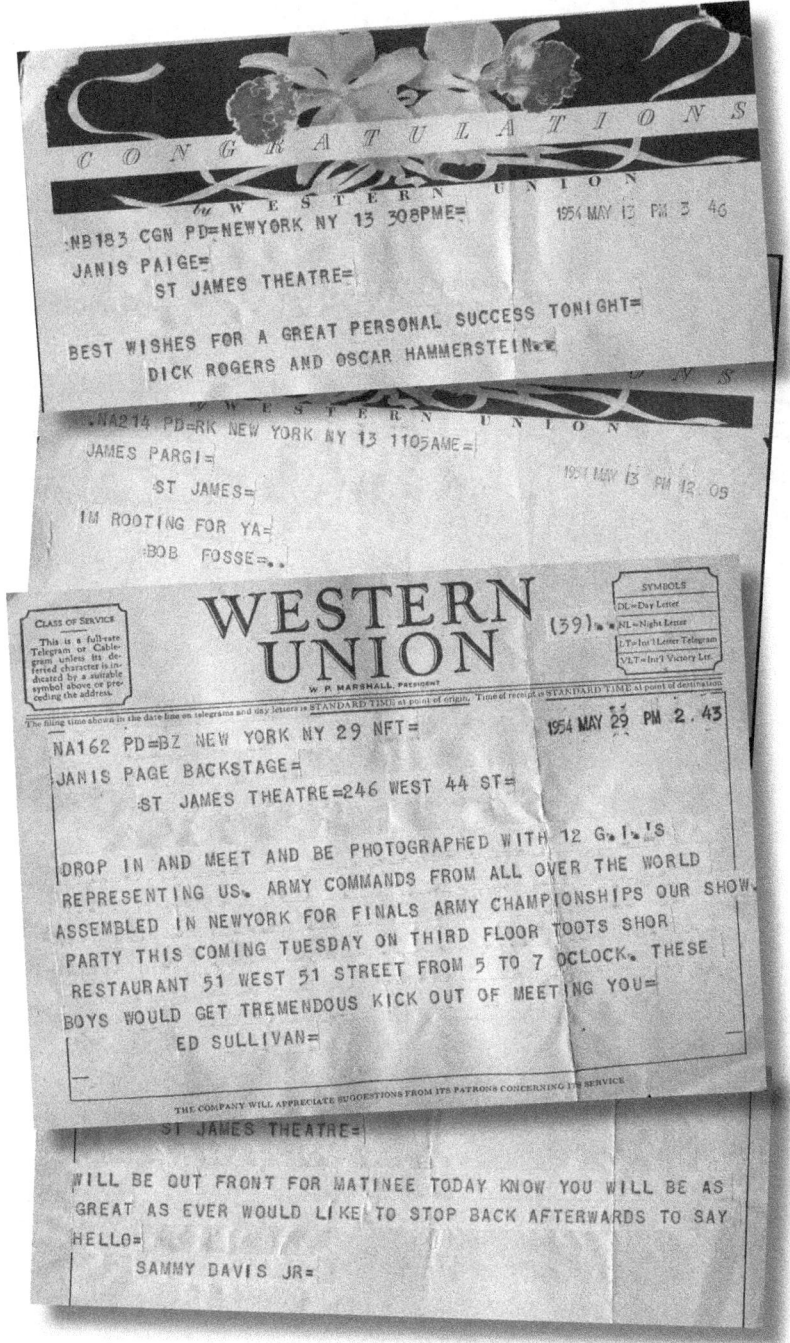

Leading up to and during my run of The Pajama Game *on Broadway in '54, I received some magnificent telegram correspondence from some names you may have heard of: Rodgers and Hammerstein, Bob Fosse, Ed Sullivan and Sammy Davis Jr.*

Left:
In my New York apartment, a tiny brownstone with no window and a walk-in closet that turned into a kitchen, at 14 West 55th Street. In the 1950s. The dog is my first Jody. I called the place Heaven.

Right:
Posing for my first cover of TV Guide *in 1955.*

Right:

On the cover of Cosmopolitan *in September of 1955. It says that I have "everything but a man." I would marry Arthur Stander the following year and divorce him in 1957. I wouldn't marry my true love until 1962.*

Left:

The cover of TV Guide *in 1956.*

Above: *From my comedy series* It's Always Jan, *which ran during the 1955-56 season on CBS. Left to right, that's my costars Patricia Bright, Lauri Anders and Arte Johnson. Sid Melton is on piano.*

Below: *Pat Bright, me, Arte Johnson and Lauri Anders in my sitcom* It's Always Jan. *Arte would go on to great success on* Rowan & Martin's Laugh-In.

Left:
Performing at The Cocoanut Grove in 1957. It's the night that producer Arthur Freed offered me a starring role in the film Silk Stockings. *I had a great act, and the Grove was a beautiful nightclub.*

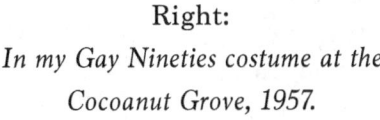

Right:
In my Gay Nineties costume at the Cocoanut Grove, 1957.

Left: *In Las Vegas at the New Frontier Hotel, 1957.*

Below: *With Fred Astaire in* Silk Stockings *(1957).*

Can it possibly get better than dancing with Fred Astaire? Here I am doing it in Silk Stockings.

Section V
The 1960s

Robert Mitchum

Maybe I was wrong, and luck is like love.
You have to go all the way to find it.
—Robert Mitchum

The Santa Barbara Horse Show was important for anyone involved with horses, and Flintridge Riding Club was no exception. As a member, I was on my way to try to win a ribbon. Instead, I wound up taking one for the team.

It had been raining, and unfortunately the ring was muddy and slippery. I was a little bit apprehensive, but not enough to give up. I knew how to ride and jump, and I was on my dependable Adam.

"Ride him the same as always, Jan, you'll be fine," my multi-winning, beribboned teacher said as I entered the ring.

We picked up a canter and got over the first jump when I felt Adam slip. It didn't bother him, but it was enough for me to lose my attention approaching the next jump. Adam jumped, but I hit the mud.

Along with my embarrassment, I was a muddy mess.

Back at my hotel, still nursing my silly ego, the phone rang.

"It's Marge Durante, honey, how are you?"

"Finally clean," I said, "but feeling pretty dumb. I'm going to have a hot bath with a whole box of Epsom salts and go to bed."

"Do that later," she said. "We're having dinner with my good friends, Dorothy and Bob Mitchum. Now get dressed, I'm picking you up at six.

Jimmy and Marge were my neighbors, and their daughter Cece was also a member of Flintridge, so Marge and I saw one another often.

Gone now was the memory of my fall, the mud and my bath with the Epsom salts. I was going to have dinner with the Mitchums! Oh, life was good.

Robert and Dorothy lived in a lovely home in Montecito.

"They are in the throes of remodeling their home," Marge said. "I've known them both for many years, and they are simply wonderful people."

Marge knocked and then opened the door with "It's Marge." I met a smiling and warm Dorothy Mitchum, who promptly asked me how I felt after my fall.

"Bob's watching television, Marge," she said. "You know the way."

"It's Marge. Bob, meet my friend Janis Paige."

He was sitting cross-legged on the floor, his back braced against the front of a sofa, watching television. He was shoeless, his feet encased in thick, white athletic socks, his legs in well-worn jeans, his upper half in a white t-shirt. He quickly unfolded his long legs, stood up and said, "Welcome, Janis. I'm glad you could join us."

Everything, including the room, looked lived in.

"Would you call El Encanto, Bob?" Dorothy asked. "Tell them we need a table for six in about forty-five minutes."

In a short time, Bob returned wearing a beautiful gray suit, white shirt, tasteful tie and highly shined moccasins. He looked like he could run a studio.

When we entered the dining room, it was obvious that the Mitchums were no strangers to El Encanto. While Dorothy and the maître d' were deciding on dinner, Bob chose the wine. He turned to me, asking what kind I would like.

I was not unfamiliar with wines and I asked about the chardonnay. He read off a list of names and finally I said, "I like that one, but you choose, Bob."

"I couldn't do it better," he said. "Now choose a red one, too." I chose a California label I knew and again he agreed.

After he'd ordered, he asked me about my choices in wine. I told him about marrying into the Martinelli family and their sophisticated life. My gourmet in-laws introduced me to so many firsts in my life. First freshly ground coffee and fine wines, especially from California's growing industry.

I love to learn, and like a sponge I'd soaked up everything they had to offer. The marriage didn't last, but the education opened a whole new world for me.

As Bob and I spoke about books, music, travel, etc., I was amazed at how erudite he was. He seemed devoid of the artifice so prevalent in a profession filled with it.

I remember asking my production manager friend, Max Henry, about Bob when they did a movie together in Chile.

"He's the greatest, Jan," he said then. "Just an all-around good guy and everybody feels the same about him."

His diversified talent was always admired and highly praised, but he seemed unfazed by fame.

He also had a smoldering sexuality which was lost on no one, including me. There was nothing overt or obvious about it. It was just there in whatever he did, including walk across the screen. It was a part of Bob like his height or that unforgettable cleft chin.

Bob was a flattering listener, interested and interesting. He was focused, awake and at ease with himself. After watching Laurence Fishburne for the first time years ago, I heard my friend say, "He's got the secret, Jan."

"What secret?"

"I don't know, sweetheart, it's a secret," he said with a laugh. "Every good actor has one."

Perhaps those qualities and the mystery of what we didn't know made Bob irresistible to audiences and women everywhere. I was both, and speaking for myself, it would not have been an intellectual conversation about his secret that would have attracted me. Not when you were in the presence of a man who made "What time is it?" sensually provocative.

There was always gossip about Bob and his leading ladies. Oddly enough, the talk came from the women involved and not Bob. As he once said, "I don't mind questions, but don't get upset if you don't get an answer."

Dorothy and Bob had been married for fifty-seven years when he died of lung cancer at seventy-nine. The fact that they stayed married all of their lives is to me a tribute to them both. In a profession famous for its noisy divorces, they were rare birds indeed.

As we all shared the evening and great dinner conversation, I saw a wonderful ease between these two. That quality only comes from knowing one another, knowing oneself and the patient attention it takes to keep it going.

When we said our thanks and goodnights and drove back to our hotel, I said, "Thank you, Marge, for an evening I won't forget. I feel like I've known them forever."

"Oh Jan," she said, "they're like a pair of old shoes you can't wait to wear again. I love them both."

"So do I, honey. So do I."

Dorothy lived on and passed away on April 12, 2014. She was ninety-four.

Robert Mitchum
August 6, 1917 – July 1, 1997

Meeting Ray Gilbert

> *Sometimes when you meet someone, there's a click. I don't believe in love at first sight, but I do believe in that click.*
>
> —Janis Paige

THE DECADE OF the Sixties became an embarrassment of riches for me. I had to pinch myself to realize that for now, everything was better than it had ever been.

Indeed, I was, for the first time in my life, turning work down and trying not to worry about it. The momentum for this creative and very busy life I was enjoying began during the last half of 1951 and kept steadily building toward the stage megahit *The Pajama Game*.

The last half of the Fifties decade brought my own series on CBS (*It's Always Jan*) to another stint in Las Vegas, my first solo vocal album, a second marriage that was over before it started and the cherry on the cake, starring with Fred Astaire and Cyd Charisse in *Silk Stockings*.

The painful memories of 1950 were finally put away alongside the scarred recollections of having survived that sad time in my life. The highs far outweighed the lows now, and I did not forget to take stock of my great good fortune.

I had found a business manager who made each of his clients buy a house instead of throwing their money away in rents. I listened to him, and 1960 began with a brand-new house, bought and paid for by me.

When I wrote the check for the down payment, "What if you don't work again?" loomed large for a minute or so in my mind. But a deep breath exhaled it out, and I've never regretted my decision. I still live in that house today, although it's grown up and out along the way.

When I finished filming *Please Don't Eat the Daisies* in 1960, with David Niven and Doris Day, my agents at William Morris called to say that they had two offers for me.

One came from Las Vegas. Playing Vegas was like catnip to me. I loved being a part of that crazy, we-never-sleep, exciting little place for a few weeks, but I needed a new act. My manager found someone highly recommended to write and direct my show. His name was Ray Gilbert. I had seen his daughter, Joanne Gilbert, do her act and she was sensational.

We made a date to meet the following week.

The second offer was a fantastic opportunity for my future. Lucille Ball and Desi Arnaz, who founded and owned Desilu, wanted to produce a new series for me if we could come up with an idea. Desilu had filmed my first series, but to have the *I Love Lucy* writers involved was enough to even make me forget that nasty old phrase, "This can't last."

In the meantime, my manager Ruth Aarons and I headed for our first meeting with Ray Gilbert on my new act. I was enjoying a variety of male relationships at the time, and the idea of anything serious, much less another marriage, wasn't even a thought in a very far off and distant future.

What's that old parable about the best laid plans, etc. etc.?

My potential writer and director opened the door, and I wasn't ready for the response I felt. I don't know what I expected, but Ray surprised me.

His face was interesting to say the least, with a charisma to match. He wore a perfect Van Dyke beard, accompanied by beautiful brown eyes that held what I remembered as a kind of soft sadness. He wasn't very tall, five-foot-nine or so, but with a strong physique.

That very attractive face was set in a bald head, which only added to his look of someone from another time and far-off place. When we'd travel throughout Europe, I'd often say, "When did you pose for that one, honey?"

"Oh, about 1690," he'd reply.

We discussed a few ideas for the act, and I liked them. I felt good about working with him and I left with Ruthie to discuss the cost. I wrote him a check for $3,000, with two more to follow as the work progressed. We said "Goodbye," and when I got into the car, I turned to my manager and said, "Ruthie, I'm going to marry that man."

"What happened to your new freedom?" she asked.

"I didn't say *when*, Ruthie," I answered. "I didn't say when."

The longer I live, the less I believe in accidents.

It was exhilarating to be alive in 1960. Up to that point, I had paid my dues, so to speak, to a profession I loved but that I also knew could suddenly end. I knew those feelings very well.

As exciting as my life was, I made sure that buried deeply inside was that room, waiting for me to open the door once again. In a way, it kept me grounded—but not too grounded. There was still much to learn from those teachable mistakes to come.

While waiting to hear from Ray on the act, I had my first meeting with Bob Carroll and Madelyn Pugh, the famous *I Love Lucy* writers. We discussed the format, and someone mentioned the great Jack Oakie to play my father.

"I grew up with him. Are you kidding? Would he be interested?"

"He is very interested, Janis, and would love to meet you."

When we met a few days later at my agent's office, I felt like bowing low. I remember being a little speechless, but he was the great Jack Oakie that I remembered, and he made everything easy for me. I was simply thrilled beyond words at the prospect of working with him. How lucky could I be?

The next day, I woke up not feeling well. Nothing to put my finger on, just something. I had another meeting at William Morris with the writers to hear some ideas they had on the pilot, and I was not going to miss that.

On the drive to my agent's office, I began to feel even worse. I was there for about a half-hour and I started feeling nauseous.

Oh my God, I thought. What do I do now? My stomach was telling me that I had no choice. Good lord, I can't get sick in my agent's office, I realized, so I simply told everyone the truth and with, "I'm so sorry, I'll call you" I excused myself and began to run to my car.

As I hurried down the hallway, I ran into the man who would be my future husband. Of course, I didn't know it then.

Ray would hang around throughout my convalescence with the mumps. During this utterly miserable period, this man always seemed to be nearby. My housekeeper would say, "Mr. Gilbert came by to bring you some fresh Danish and warm bagels." There was always some thoughtful surprise.

"Can't I do something to repay you for all the time you spent here with me and my mumps?" I asked Ray one day.

"As a matter of fact, there is," he said. "I'd love to take you to dinner and go over my ideas for your Vegas act. Only, of course, when you feel well enough."

"How about next week?" I asked.

During the month of recuperation, Bob Hope called to ask me to go to Guantanamo, Cuba for his Christmas show. Fidel Castro had declared a revolution in his country, and America was now the enemy.

I'd already done a few shows for Bob, so of course I said "Yes!" Between rehearsals, wardrobe fittings, shots and preparing to leave, everything else was on hold. As I write about it, I vividly remember what an insanely hyperbolic time it was. We did not return home until the end of December.

In 1961, I was offered the role of Marion in the film *The Caretakers*. You know the old saying, "When it rains, it pours"? That was me.

The film was based on a fictionalized but true account of mental patients in Menninger's Clinic. It was a life-changing step for me, but I had to choose between the film and the Desilu series. I chose the film.

I'll never know if my choice was good or bad for my career, but the experience of doing this role was formidable and pushed me into a new facet of my career.

It was, however. an uphill climb for Hall Bartlett, who was the producer and director. The money people didn't want me.

They rejected me because I was a comedienne. But Hall stuck to his guns, however, and they eventually gave in and I got the role.

There were a couple of the leading actors in the film who felt the same way about my participation. One of them was Robert Stack. Hall never told me, and after a few days' work, Bob asked to speak with me.

"I want you to know, Janis, that I did not want you in the picture," Stack admitted. "I truly love your work, but I always looked at you as a comedienne. I was dead wrong, you're great."

Not everyone had Bob's sense of decency. He was a classy guy.

One morning, Hall came to me and asked how my interpretive skills were.

"Do you mean ad-libbing?" I asked.

"Well, that's a simple way of answering my question, but yes, that's what I mean," he said.

"What do you want me to do, Hall?"

He explained the scene and what he wanted from me. There were no lines, just an idea. I remembered back to my vaudeville days, when I had to get by on my improvisation.

"I'll try it, Hall" I said, "but please, don't let me go too far and make a fool of myself. Promise me."

"You have my word, Janis—and my appreciation. Now go get familiar with your props. There are a lot of them."

I quietly rehearsed handling the props and then said, "I'm ready, Hall."

My character Marion was a hell-on-wheels and a constant irritant against rules of any kind. She was completely compulsive. This scene was about me making booze out of rubbing alcohol. My fellow inmates brought cans of juices to mix with the alcohol, and I was the bartender.

All of this was done by Marion's destructive nature, of course, and the scene takes a tragic turn in the script. When we finished, I was surprised by the applause I got from those around me. Just one take. It worked.

As I went to my dressing room, I was stopped in my tracks by these angry and accusatory words: "Don't you *ever* let a director demean and denigrate you again."

The memory of their applause faded fast with this criticism of me. The criticism continued, "You should never have done that scene without a script. What were you thinking, Janis?"

With that statement, she walked away, leaving me there with those "old voices" reminding me once again that I'd never be good enough. I had tears in my eyes as I drove home that evening.

Ray had brought Chinese food for dinner and when he saw my face, he said, "What's wrong, Jan?" I related the day through my suppressed tears. He listened without a word and when I'd finished, he very quietly said, "My God, you must have been good."

I just stood there, staring at him.

"You forgot the applause and the thank-you's and the pleasure you felt and with a few hostile, angry and envious words, she flattened you," Ray explained. "What are we going to do with you, honey? Life is too short not to enjoy your victories. Can't you see that the problem was hers and had nothing to do with you?"

Ray had an immense amount of wisdom, I quickly realized that I'd be nuts to let him disappear.

My second marriage was over and never should have started in the first place. I remember standing in front of the justice of the peace, the guests, our agents, my manager and the press wishing to God that I'd had enough courage to say to one and all, "I'm sorry, I don't want to get married and neither does he. Let's call the whole thing off!"

But, like Jimmy Michener and that terrible weekend in Bucks County, I was too embarrassed to tell the truth and once again, did not take care of myself. In a very short time, I faced another divorce. At least we agreed and stayed friends instead of divorced enemies, and the all-too-frequent vitriol that follows.

Like a terrifying roller coaster, the Fifties had taken me from the depths of despair to the peak of success on Broadway. I'd filmed a television series and gone from that into starring with Fred Astaire and Cyd Charisse in the MGM musical *Silk Stockings*. I'd played Las Vegas again and had recorded my first solo album.

This eventful decade had ended on a high and seemed destined to continue.

DAVID NIVEN

*KEEP THE CIRCUS INSIDE YOU GOING. KEEP IT
GOING. DON'T TAKE ANYTHING TOO SERIOUSLY,
IT'LL ALL WORK OUT IN THE END.*

–DAVID NIVEN

WORDS ALWAYS FAIL me when I'm asked about David Niven. "Irresistible" comes to mind, but who am I, a mere mortal, a smitten female, to describe the man? Frankly speaking, it's an impossible task, but I'm more than willing to try.

His charm oozed out of every pore in his body as it took its place alongside his honesty, generosity, wit and humor. He wore the sophistication of a citizen of the world with an ease that fascinated me. After all, I was still finding mine.

When I looked at David, I always saw the circus inside, with a kind of suppressed laughter at the ready. His eyes smiled. They could also take on a kind of far-away sadness. I never knew him well enough to ask about what I saw, but it was most definitely there, hidden away in a place he visited often.

The year was 1960. MGM sent me the script for a film called *Please Don't Eat the Daisies*. Doris Day and David Niven were already signed. I loved the role and of course said "Yes!".

MGM was still the big, beautiful, bustling, busy, technicolored place I remembered so well. The role I played was that of a big Broadway star who had been given a bad review by a critic, played by David. Doris played his wife.

Naturally, there were gorgeous clothes designed by Morton Haack, and everything was up to the usual Metro production standard. Fittings were over, hair color and style were okayed, and the first day of work arrived for me.

Believe it or not, David and I were meeting for the first time—and I had to slap his face! We met and rehearsed the scene without the slap. I apologized profusely for what I was about to do, and they yelled "Action!"

I had not been instructed in how to pull my punches, so to speak, and I let one fly. Poor David did not expect it, and I left a lovely rosy palm print on his cheek. Without a word, he looked at me and said, "You work out, don't you? Next time, remind me to duck!"

I was mortified at what I'd done and began a series of "I'm so sorrys."

"Forget it, we got the scene in one take, didn't we?" David replied. "I wouldn't want to do it again."

I should add "gracious" to my list of adjectives for this remarkable man. Of course, I immediately adored him.

After so many years, as I write about him, I can still feel the sexual pull between us, buffered by a lot of laughs, subtle flirts and that age-old feeling that has nothing to do with your mind.

We were waiting to perform one day—you know, lighting, camera moves, etc. David said that he was having a few friends in on Sunday and he would love to have me join them.

Now, to say that I was attracted to this man was putting it mildly. There was so much chemistry going on between us, but still I answered by saying, "You're married, aren't you, David?"

"Well, we're separated and not for the first time," he replied. "She is living in her own place, and I live in mine. Please come, and don't worry. I would never make you feel uncomfortable."

"In that case, yes!"

Are you in trouble Jan? I thought. *Don't be silly, of course you are!*

David was "sex-nip" because he didn't have to try. Like his other attributes, it was just a part of the whole package.

The "few friends" David had over turned out to be Richard Burton, whose voice preceded his entrance; Sybel, his first wife; and Mitzi Gaynor and her husband, who arrived shortly after. They were followed by a couple of directors and their wives (and producers too). There was also an agent and a couple of writers mingled with some faces I'd never seen.

It was a mixed crowd, to say the least, all of them David's adoring friends. As I watched him chatting easily with everyone, I was in awe at the gift he had. A gift that comes with someone who is totally at ease with himself, in his own skin.

In my entire life, I never met anyone with David's ability to make you his friend. Whoever coined the phrase, "If you want a friend, you have to be a friend" must have had David Niven in mind.

Burton had found a table, and it didn't take long for that masterful raconteur to begin "raconteur-ing." He had a million stories and he held complete court while everyone listened intently and laughed loudly at his raucous storytelling. He obviously enjoyed this role, and I wondered what it must be like to be married to such a bright light. How could you not feel intimidated by living in his shadow?

Most of us were listening to Mr. Burton when some of the talking began to stop and finally faded out. I turned around to see a very tall, very thin woman standing in the patio area. I didn't know who she was until I heard David say, "What are you doing here? Everybody, you know my wife, she wasn't invited, but here she is!"

She was in a bathing suit with a jacket thrown over her arm. Her legs had several bruises on them, and David, with his usual aplomb, asked, "Who's been beating you up, sweetheart?"

Mrs. Niven said nothing, but her discomfort at crashing his little party was obvious. Then I heard a woman behind me say, "She must have heard about Janis because here she is, protecting her territory."

I knew there had been talk about David and me, but there's always talk about stars who work together. Besides, it wasn't true. Yet.

Suddenly, I felt exposed. An object of gossip, the unspoken subject of the evening—and I was having none of it. The price was too high. I cared about my reputation but, I'll admit, I was quietly pissed at her while at the same time feeling sorry for her.

I could see how uncomfortable David was, and when I had waited an adequate amount of time, I excused myself. As David walked me to my car, I told him not to worry about anything.

"I did not invite her, she just showed up," he explained. "Believe me, I didn't plan it this way."

"I know that," I assured him, "and I'm sorry too, very sorry. But all is not lost. How else could I have met Richard Burton? See ya, Gorgeous."

I became The Other Woman that day, and I didn't even get a chance to deserve it, let alone enjoy it. The word "unrequited" came to mind as I drove home.

Two years later, I was standing in the lobby of the lovely old Negresco Hotel in Nice, France when I heard, "What the hell are you doing here?"

The year was 1962. I remember feeling a skipped heartbeat as I turned to look into the face of one tanned, tall, terrific-looking David Niven.

He gave me a bear hug and repeated, "What are you doing here?"

"I'm filming a movie for Metro called *Follow the Boys* and I'm living here until I find an apartment," I said. "Oh David, what a beautiful place to see. I don't even want to sleep. I'm afraid I'll miss something! I just passed by Napoleon's house, or one of them. I still can't believe I saw it!"

I was chattering away, and he was listening as he always did, when I asked, "By the way, what are *you* doing here?"

"I live here," he replied. "I have a home at Cap Ferrat. I'd love for you to see it. My boys and I are here for the summer. Please, can I take you to lunch? You'll meet my boys and see the house and we'll have a bite at a little café I know. Have you seen Cap Ferrat? Have you had a chance to see anything yet?"

David was two years older and two years more attractive, if such a thing could be possible. He had a glorious smile set off by perfectly shaped white teeth.

He had always lived a diversified life, but looking at him that day in the lobby of the busy Negresco, he could only be a movie star.

What are you going to do, Jan? I thought. *How could lunch be dangerous?* I found myself telling him that I had little time to explore. I desperately wanted to take my healthy per diem from Metro and spend it on an apartment instead of blowing it on the hotel.

In fact, I had found a place that morning and I was excited at the prospect of moving.

"Life is so good right now, God," I said to myself. "Please don't send this problem my way, not now."

"But what about lunch?" he asked.

Oh David, I thought, *maybe if I had allowed myself to be available through your separations, I would have ended up not liking you, myself or any of the other scenarios I might have written. Maybe if I had stayed, I wouldn't have the conflict I have at this particular moment.*

There is unfinished business here and I need to clean it up. Why do you have to be so damned you, David?

I said, "I'd love to see your house and meet your boys and have lunch. Give me ten minutes. I'll meet you back here." Conflict or not, as Scarlett would say, I'll think about it tomorrow."

I had fallen in love with the South of France. The air, the light and the sun glistening on the Mediterranean were all hypnotic. Where else could you find the yacht belonging to the billionaire Stavros Niarchos regally drifting like a beautiful and mysterious black swan?

There, too, was Ari Onassis' yacht, with its crew bustling about serving the guests most anything they wanted. It was a life so distant from mine as to be inter-terrestrial. The world seemed so far away, and there was only Provence with its bread, cheese, rosé wine and its stratospheric living. I was a long, long way from Tacoma, Washington, and I was sure I'd found Oz.

David was waiting for me and off we went with the top down, winding our way through the quaint little villages to Cap Ferrat. The first thing I saw as we walked toward the house was an Olympic-sized swimming pool.

"What do you need this for with the Mediterranean close by?" I asked.

Stupid question, Jan.

"Doesn't everyone have an Olympic-sized pool next to the sea?" David inquired impishly.

We visited with his sons as he showed me the house. It was lovely and sun-filled and then, "Are you hungry? I am. Let's go."

He ordered two glasses of that lovely Provence rosé` wine, a salad and, of course, it was served with their addictive French bread, crusty on the outside with a soft and tender inner core. I would have been completely satisfied if I could have had nothing but the wine, the bread and a plate of their heavenly, soft cheeses. But I behaved and ate the salad, too.

We talked of almost everything, laughed a lot and, as the afternoon deepened, I suggested that we head back, as I'd been gone most of the day.

There was an indescribable ambiance to the South of France. Not only the light, the life and the food, but the way the women put themselves together in their own, effortless, French way of dressing. No matter how I tried, I never got it. I always looked like an American.

There was so much to see and to talk about, from the Saracen city of Ez to the Van Gogh country (Arles) where that genius had lived and painted. Hemingway said that "Paris was a moveable feast," but to me, it was the South of France and I was eternally hungry.

"What are you doing for dinner?" David asked suddenly.

He snapped me out of my Provence reverie.

"Didn't you have enough of me today?"

"No, and what about dinner?"

"I'm probably shooting tomorrow," I said, "and if I have my schedule, it's an early night for me."

"And if you don't have to work tomorrow," David persisted, "how about dinner? There's an old, fascinating place on the High Cornish that you'd never find. Great food, spectacular view, you have to see it! How about dinner?"

I took a deep breath.

"I've had a busy and fulfilling life since we last saw each other. David." I took another breath and then added, "I met someone. We're going to be married here in Nice at the end of the month."

Without a beat he answered, "Why do you want to do a damn fool thing like that?"

"We'll talk about it over dinner."

"Maybe I can talk you out of it. I'll pick you up in an hour."

With a wave, he was gone.

David was true to his word. The High Cornish drive was spectacular, with breathtaking vistas of the light making rainbows on the sea below as we climbed higher and higher.

Suddenly, we pulled off the road and parked in front of a very old stone building.

"This was once an Abbey," he said. "It's my favorite place; I know you'll love it!"

He took my arm and walked me in to the most amazing place I had ever seen. It was all rough-hewn stones. No measured perfection here, just the beauty of its age. The floor was worn from thousands of footsteps through its countless years of life. Candles perched in the necks of empty wine bottles, and their flickering light, mixed with the fading light of Provence, made everything seem slightly out of focus. Or was it the way I felt?

The *pièce de résistance* was the gentle, almost silent cats, tenderly weaving their welcomes through our bare, sun-tanned legs, their soft fur caressing you under the table.

At that moment, I felt as if the world had its arms around me.

"Oh, thank you, David, thank you for giving me this heavenly experience. I'll never forget it, or you."

He ordered us a glass of dark, red wine accompanied by a platter of crudités and we toasted the day. As I took a sip, breathing in its aged aroma, I wondered, "Have I died and gone to heaven?"

"What do you think?" he asked.

"I feel like I'm in *Brigadoon*," I laughed, "and everything will ultimately disappear in an all-too-short one day a year."

David fixed us a plate of crudités and then asked, "What happened to you? Where did you go after the film?"

"Life's been good. Lots of television, two films in a row, and now living in the South of France. I'd be ashamed to ask for more."

"Now tell me about this man in your life," he probed. "Where did you meet?"

I told him that we first met on the possibility of working together. I needed a new act for my next appearance in Las Vegas and wanted to know if he was interested in writing it for me. He was, and the deal was made that day.

I continued to relate the story.

About a month later, I was at my agent's office, meeting with Lucille Ball's writers on a TV series she wanted me to do for her at Desilu. I had felt oddly queasy for a couple of days, but it was an important day, so I chose to ignore how I felt.

I ran into Ray in the hallway at William Morris while beating a hasty retreat from my meeting. He saw I looked terrible and offered to drive me home. As we wound our way up the hill toward my house in his car, I got worse and wondered if I was going to make it. Please God, let me out of this car. As he pulled up to the driveway, I opened the door—but that was as far as I got.

I aimed for the driveway but threw up all over Ray's beautiful new car door.

I don't remember much after that, as I ran to the bathroom and then threw myself on the couch. He called my doctor, who paid me a visit and informed me that I had the mumps.

"Mumps," I moaned, "little kids get mumps."

"And if you never had them, so do adults," the doctor said. "For everyone who never had the mumps, it's gamma shots immediately."

"The writers, too? I asked.

"Everyone," he repeated.

"They'll never hire me again," I whispered.

Until I heard him laugh, I'd forgotten Ray was still there. "Oh, your car, your beautiful new car! Did you get it cleaned? I'm so sorry about your car. I'm so sorry I got up this morning."

Ray just laughed. "Don't worry, I hosed everything off," he assured.

"I kept saying, "I'm so sorry, I'm so sorry."

"I know you are," he said, "I'm convinced!"

Through the next two weeks of the miserable mumps, high fevers, hallucinations and wondering if I would live, this man, whom I did not know, would leave and come back. Lord knows he saw me at my worst but remained devoted to getting me well.

I related all of this to David, who was quiet.

"He also had a fantastic sense of humor that had me laughing through it all," I said.

"He sounds like quite a guy, but why the rush?" David asked.

"Because it's time, David. It's time for me to settle down and stop thinking that I'm going to be thirty-eight forever."

We were interrupted by the waiter refilling our glasses and serving our food. Like everything else, it was delicious. A few more sips of the wine were followed by an unforgettable dessert. The waiter called it chestnuts in cream, and from a glazed crockery pot, we were treated to something made only for the gods.

I have traveled this world, from Africa to Asia, and most everything in between, but I have never found that delectable treat again. Perhaps, like *Brigadoon*, I came to life once a year, lived for a day like this, and then disappeared along with the chestnuts in cream.

Silence again followed, and then I heard David ask for the check. It's over, I thought. This place, the cats, the wine, the food, the view, the ambience and the company. Now begin the memories.

We walked arm in arm to the car. Everything was the same. Oh, that's not true, everything was different. We started down the mountainside to the earth below and reality.

"I'm happy for you, Janis," David said. "I hope life works out for you, I really do."

"Thank you, David," I said, "I appreciate that. I wouldn't expect anything less from you."

We sat in silence outside the hotel. It seemed like an eternity before I finally said, "Goodnight, David. Knowing you will always be a gift to me."

He opened my door, we hugged and then, "Take care of yourself."

"You too." I replied, and his little car roared away, gears shifting into the night, like a cold wind slapping me right across the face.

What up until then had been a remote and distant possibility was now just a fading fantasy. It would eventually find its place among all of the others in my life, gathering dust in some far off, tucked away mind closet. They would be closed to everyone and everything, except my memories.

David Niven
March 1, 1910 - July 29, 1983

Bob Hope and the U.S.O.

I've seen what a laugh can do. It can transform almost unbearable tears into something bearable, even hopeful.

–Bob Hope

How do I begin to describe Bob Hope? I'll start with bigger than life. Bob and I began working together way back in 1950. Up until then, television was broadcast in black and white. Now, the first coast-to-coast color broadcast would be aired, and Bob would star, with me as a guest. Television history was being made, and we were a part of it.

The filming instructions were fierce. You couldn't wear black, white, yellow, stripes, checks, prints, dots and I don't remember all of the other no-nos. Our makeup was an otherworldly color resembling death warmed over. But dressed in our appropriate colors, we proceeded to do the show—LIVE!

It was *all* live in those days, and everything was a combination of heart-stopping excitement and a similar kind of fear.

"What if I make a mistake? What if I forget a lyric, or a line, or a dance step? What if I don't hear my cue?" When that red light went on, there was no stopping, no editing, no cutting and no starting over. It was an invaluable, unforgettable and character-building experience, and it was simply a progressive and new way of getting my showbiz feet wet.

Early live television was all about waiting for that red light warning us to "Stand by, it's show time! You're on!"

Working with Bob was extraordinary. Not only was I beside a world-renowned performer, he knew what he expected from everyone around him. He had the best writers who knew how to make us all shine, and they did. I always loved comedy and working with Bob was a constant lesson in improving my skills.

His home was lovely. It was a large two-story house in a Valley neighborhood called Toluca Lake. Bob's love of golf was as famous as he was, so he had a nine-hole course built on his property. It was impressive, to say the least.

Bob also built a lovely studio near the main house where we'd rehearse parts of the show with the writers and producers present. The phrase used was "getting it on its feet to see what we have."

The studio also held his countless awards, honors and undying thanks from the military. His visits to our troops throughout the world during WWII was a vivid part of my life then as I grew into young adulthood and began my own career.

We were on a short rehearsal break one day when I saw Bob standing at his desk, opening a letter. He called me over and said, "Look at what just one little old oil well brings in."

He showed a check and I almost fell over. I gasped and asked if it was real. He laughed and said, "Nice, huh?"

"Nice?" I said. "Nice? This is for $350,000. I can't even wrap my head around that much money, Bob. You could run a corporation. How about General Motors or Standard Oil? Oh, my gosh, Bob, you could even run for President. Everybody knows you and you could loan the country some money when we need it."

He gave me that famous Bob Hope take as he put the check back on his desk.

"Break's over," the assistant called out.

"I mean it, Bob. Have you ever thought about running for office?"

"No. It's a terrible idea. What would I do for laughs?"

A few years later, we did his show from New York again. One of the great beauties of the day was a guest star. We began rehearsals, and as the days went by and we got closer to the night of the show, she had not shown up. Gossip was that she was having a love affair with a handsome, often bedded, Latin lover.

Now, I realize that affairs can really screw up working for a living, but a contract is a contract. When I asked where she was. I was told that she'd be there for the rehearsal run-through but she was still a no-show.

I had some smart-ass thought about, well, maybe she's having trouble getting out of bed. What was going on? If that were me, I'd be scared to death that I'd never work again. What's the matter with her?

I was dressed and getting ready to go home when someone knocked on my dressing room door. When I opened it, there stood the producer, the director and one of the writers. All they said was, "She's not doing the show. Bob asked if you'd learn her part and go on for her tomorrow night."

A long pause, and then, "I'll learn it, but what about wardrobe and my own skit with Bob, plus my dance number? How will I get it all done in an hour show?"

"Wardrobe is easy," I was assured, "and you let us worry about the rest. Thanks a million, Janis."

Of course, we got it done, Bob thanked me and we said, "Goodnight."

When my check arrived a few days later, there were two, mine and hers. I never expected it, but it was a generous way for Bob to show his appreciation. His note read, "What would I do without my Bladder Baby?"

If anyone's left out there from the burlesque world, they'll know what I'm talking about.

Being a part of a Bob Hope show was always a life-changer for me. He hired me many times and always gave me an opportunity to shine in my own way. I always knew that I would have a song, a dance number, a sketch with Bob, maybe that tricky soft-shoe with the twisted heels thing and anything else the writers and Bob would throw my way.

My first Christmas show with Bob was in 1960. Fidel Castro had taken over Cuba and we suddenly had an enemy ninety miles from American shores. Of course, Bob wanted to go to Guantanamo, our military base there. Our guest stars were Andy Williams, Zsa Zsa Gabor, and yours truly.

We rehearsed, wardrobe got the variety of shots needed, and we were on our way, not knowing what to expect. The show was transported in two planes. One carried Bob, the cast, producers, director, writers, band and press. The second plane hauled the equipment, the crew and anything pertaining to filming the show.

It always amazed me how these people got such a professional production accomplished under some very difficult and at times seemingly impossible circumstances. There was no way to figure out everything. After all, we were not working at NBC in Burbank. It was a lesson in self-control and pulling your own weight, along with helping others if necessary.

In 1964, we were in Thailand on our way to Vietnam. There was a small American air base in a God-forsaken place called Takhli. Bob loved and respected all of the armed forces, but he had a special affinity for pilots.

"They have an amazing live-for-today attitude, and I love that in them," he once told me.

One day, I found myself in what was called a banana helicopter. We were headed for an airbase deep in the jungles of Thailand. I was strapped in with some of the other members of the show with the now old-fashioned seat belt, lap only, no shoulder belts.

We sat side by side, lengthwise, and I happened to be in the middle, in front of the big sliding door that was wide open. Suddenly, we rose, banked, and I felt my back, butt, and anything else that might be attached leave the seat, slightly suspended, with only that lap belt keeping me from falling into that dense, vast, snake-infested jungle below.

When the pilot straightened out the bank and I felt the seat once more, I began to breathe again. My heart finally left my throat and settled back where it belonged. I'm not good with heights but staring even briefly at the top of that jungle scared me to death.

The big burly sergeant opposite me, one foot casually hanging out of the copter with no seat belt, prompted a question.

"Aren't you afraid you might fall out one day?" I asked.

He chuckled, polite and cool as the proverbial cucumber. "No, Miss Paige, I never think about it."

"Well I do, I'm worried sick about you."

"Thanks, Miss Paige, but you don't have to worry, we're used to it!"

Oh my God, I thought, used to the constant, unrelenting dangers? The war, the jungles, the deadly snakes, the bugs, the oppressive heat, the what's-next fears?

Till the day I check out, the memories of those Christmas shows are with me always. My memories are still so acutely available and unforgettable.

One day, we were getting ready to helicopter to another base somewhere when Sil, one of our producers, told me that Bob wanted me to fly with him. I said fine and proceeded to Bob's plane, sat down beside him and fastened my seat belt, all the while wondering what I was doing there.

As we took off, I was chattering away when I heard Bob say, or thought I did, "Why the hell can't you get that soft-shoe step right?"

He was looking out the window, not at me, but there was a definite, "I'm not kidding" sound in his voice. I'd heard it applied to others, but this was the first time his displeasure was aimed at me. Then he turned to me and repeated his statement. He meant business and I knew it.

I had worked on that twisted-heel thing that he did, but I couldn't seem to get it.

"I don't know what's wrong, Bob, but I can't do the soft-shoe your way," I admitted. "I can't seem to figure it out and I want to do it right. I'm so sorry."

In that same cold, quiet and now distant voice, I heard, "Work on it and get it right. We do it in the next show."

No laughs now. I was scared, apologetic and defeated. I assured him that I would get it right but wondered how I would.

When we landed, I ran to Peter Leeds. Everybody always ran to Peter Leeds, and I repeated that awful, interminable ten minutes with Bob.

"What am I going to do, Peter? Now I have a mental block on the damned thing and I'll never get it. The more I try, the more I screw it up, and now I'm scared of him!"

"C'mere, Jan," Peter said. I stood beside him and he hummed the music while he did the step perfectly.

"For God's sake, Peter, even you can do it."

"So can you," he assured me. "Let's go!"

Five minutes later, I got it, never to lose it again.

An hour or so later, I was dancing it with Bob.

"Great, kid," he whispered over the applause, and that was the end of it. No mention, ever again.

Nothing escaped Bob. He saw everything and everyone, and he wanted his show to reflect his standards. He had a huge staff working for him, but the big gun was always Bob.

Sometime in the Nineties, I got a call from Bob. I was surprised but glad to hear from him.

"What's new?" I asked.

"Let me ask you something, Jan," Bob replied. "Did we ever have a thing together?"

"No, Bob, you were never my type and I don't fool around with the boss."

He laughed and then said, "I'm sorry I have to ask that, Jan. but The Enquirer is doing one of those trash stories on me and I hate telling you, but you're in it."

"Oh my God!" I gasped. "I'm so sorry, but it's attorney time for us all. Who's behind this, Bob?"

He mentioned one of his employees and the rumored amount of money she got for her disloyalty.

My attorney demanded a retraction, but of course none came. It was the typical hatchet job, and on the advice of my attorney, I was advised to let it hurt for a while and then drop it.

I saw parts of this world that I never would have or could have if it weren't for Bob. Cuba, Panama, the Bahamas and the missile-tracking stations, Puerto Rico, Korea (twice), Japan, Thailand (twice), Guam, Okinawa, Taiwan and then Vietnam.

I knew I was in a war the first time I saw the piles of supplies and ammo at the airport. Guards, guns, protection everywhere, but the armed forces made us feel safe and that was all we needed to do the shows.

It was never too hard. At Camp Casey in South Korea, those men sat in the mud and waited so patiently to see Bob and his troupe of players.

Somehow, in Pleiku, Vietnam, they got mirrors in so that the women could make up and see how they looked before they went onstage.

One time in Korea, it was freezing cold and snowing a little. I had to pee, and then I saw where I had to go, in costume, to complete the dastardly deed. The mud was so thick they built a walkway to the portable john at the end.

It was a good 50-foot walk, and I wondered if I could hold everything through the dancing and singing and cold, and I knew that I had to make that walk, in costume, in front of those G.I.'s. Somebody threw a coat around my shoulders and I began that trek that started with applause, whistles, woo-woos and anything else they could think of until I got through the door.

I knew I had to walk back, so when I stepped out, they gave me a big ovation and I turned to all 5,000 of them and took a bow. I'm grateful they had a couple of hours of fun and joy and Christmas memories, because so many of them never came back.

I did three of Bob's overseas shows and had experiences and relationships I would never have even come close to had it not been for Bob.

At his invitation-only memorial, it became three days of seeing old friends and some of the service men and women who had been there with us. Performers, guest artists and his children and grandchildren spoke. They were beautifully and perfectly orchestrated, culminating in a filmed retrospective of his life and work.

I'm proud and grateful to have been a part of Bob Hope's remarkable career, and to call him my friend. He certainly was a friend to me.

Bob Hope
May 29, 1903 – July 27, 2003

The good news is that Jesus is coming back. The bad news is that he's really pissed off.

CHRISTMAS WITH CASTRO

DICTATORS FREE THEMSELVES BUT THEY ENSLAVE THEIR PEOPLE.

—CHARLES CHAPLIN

IN 1960, WE not only had a handsome, young and vital new President but also saw a despotic America-hating dictator conquer the island of Cuba, 90 miles off the coast of Florida.

Our naval base there was called Guantanamo. It was all that was left of our relationship with the Cuban government. Of course, Bob Hope was ready to go and I, along with Andy Williams, Zsa Zsa Gabor and Bob's complete company, took off for his Christmas show, entertaining our troops stationed there.

Fortunately, the only war we faced was the one with Miss Gabor—but I digress. (What a good idea, Janis.)

Alabama was our first stop, then Panama and a hellhole called Camp Davis, where they trained jungle fighters. Along with the gigantic bugs and intense and unrelenting heat, we did our best to give those poor guys a sense of home with high heels, makeup, costumes and a little female behavior. It was a punishing place to be, but we could eventually leave. They couldn't.

This was my first Bob Hope Christmas show, but it was not my last. If it hadn't been for Bob, I would have missed a huge part of my life experiences.

From Panama, we stopped at the missile tracking stations in the Caribbean. We'd island hop, land, do a show and then go on to the next, with Cuba as our final destination. A whole new world was opening for me, one that was exhilarating and extremely difficult (often at the same time).

Fidel Castro had isolated Cuba in his tyrannical grip. No one spoke of it, but there was a quiet nervousness as we approached the base.

I was sitting across the aisle from Bob when I heard him ask, "What the hell is that?" We looked out the window and on either side of the plane we could see two Cuban fighter planes, flying so close we could make out their faces.

We held our collective breath for what seemed an eternity when suddenly they peeled away, replaced by four of our fighters giving us the "Thumbs up" sign. When we began to breathe again, our collective exhale was audible.

My quarters were in an officer's home, but I never saw it. When Miss Gabor found out that she was sleeping in a quonset hut, all hell broke loose and she threatened big time that she would not do the show and sue everybody in sight.

Bob asked me if I would change places with her to keep peace and get the show on. Of course, I said "Yes," and the following nights were spent fighting off the huge bugs that would fall off of the ceiling onto my bed. I finally slept in a chair with my feet off the floor. I didn't dare investigate what I might find there.

We spent Christmas with our troops, and that experience was worth everything. If you were fortunate enough to experience one of Bob's Christmas shows, it stayed with you always.

My review of the abusive and filthy-mouthed Zsa Zsa is short. After hearing her call everybody in sight a "beetch" or a "son of a beetch," I'll leave it with this: What a *BIX!YT#!* "beetch" she was!

When Anita Bryant closed the show by singing "Silent Night," the voices of our troops joined in. It was moving and deeply emotional. Many had tears running down their cheeks with the memories of a holiday past. We'd wish them a "Merry Christmas" with what was always a painful and tearful goodbye.

Writers, Writers, Writers

To gain your own voice, you have to forget about having it heard.

—Allen Ginsburg

Along with my intense curiosity has come a voracious love of reading. Many a morning broke with my nose still in a book, hating to know the end was near. The writer's ability to paint word pictures carrying me along to far-off places fascinated me.

Robert Ruark helped me to see Africa until I finally got there. Ian Fleming became my friend from a drugstore paperback my husband found on a rainy day in Bermuda. Before I finished it, I had ordered every one of his unforgettable books in hardcover. *You Only Live Twice* remains unfinished today.

I was halfway through it when Ian died suddenly. After I'd cried my eyes out, I kept him alive by closing the book where I'd left off. My rationale was, if I don't finish, *he's* not finished. After fifty years, my bookmark still lives there.

If my eyes would still let me read, I'd start all over again. From John Steinbeck's *The Winter of Our Discontent* to Alan Paton's *Cry the Beloved Country*, I'd read my United States history books again as well as the newer ones on the Presidents and their lives.

There were also Pat Conroy's *The Prince of Tides*, John Irving's *The World According to Garp* and the book that helped me through the loss of my husband, Robert Pirsig's *Zen and The Art of Motorcycle Maintenance*. Shortly after Ray died, a guardian angel, disguised as a friend named Hannah Russell, gave that one to me.

"This will help you, Janis, I promise," she said.

Pirsig's ability to write about the finely tuned affinity of caring for oneself and caring for a motorcycle was beyond anything I had ever experienced—and Hannah was right!

These writers' diverse and soaring talents were a magic carpet ride for me, and I miss them every day. I admire and appreciate Bill O'Reilly's magnificent and unique history books as well, but I now have to "read" them through audio books. I'm grateful for them, but I sorely miss the tactile pleasure of turning a page, then going back to read once more some piece of wisdom I'd missed.

Once around this thing called life is never enough. Are we products of nurture or nature? At my stage of growth, I'd say it's both.

Whatever the answer to this ever-puzzling question may be, I know it'll be found in some book, sometime, somewhere.

The road to hell is paved with adverbs.

- Stephen King

Michel-Marie Poulain

J'ai Choisi Mon Sexe
(I Chose My Sex)
–Michel-Marie Poulain

In June of 1962, I flew to Nice, France, to film *Follow the Boys* for Metro Goldwyn Mayer. Needless to say, I fell in love with everything the South of France had to offer. Provence and its ambiance were simply magic to me.

Our cast, except for the late French actress Dany Robin, were Americans. The crew was French mixed with a few English, and all in all it was a great experience.

I took my generous per diem from Metro and found a spectacular apartment overlooking Nice and its harbor. Why waste it on a hotel when I could begin my day watching the yachts belonging to Aristotle Onassis and Niarchos? One was white and one black, floating like giant swans in the morning Mediterranean.

The studio car picked me up at five-thirty a.m., and I would remember my high school book report on Napoleon earning me an A as we passed his home in Nice. *Was life just one big plan after all?* I wondered.

My future husband was joining me in August to post our bonds, which was compelled under Napoleon's Marriage Vows. We met with a magistrate who very soberly asked us our intentions.

"To get married," Ray said, shooting me an "Is he kidding?" look.

After more questions, the man issued us a license to marry. In 1962, those same vows had been in effect for 150 years, giving men power over women. In 1965, they were finally dispelled, and women were given their own independent power.

On August 28, 1962, we were married. The very handsome mayor of Nice presided, and all of Nice waited to throw rice and wish us well.

What continued to amuse us, however, was the plethora of lovers and mistresses operating under the strict laws of Napoleon and the Papal laws of the church in both France and Italy. Perhaps that old adage about laws being meant to be broken fit this bit of hypocrisy.

Near the end of filming the picture, my French dresser told me about an artist "you simply have to meet." She told me her name was Michel-Marie Poulain, and "she" lived south in the village of Èze.

"You'll never forget her," she added.

"Michel is a *her*?" I asked.

"She's both," she replied.

As she related what she knew about this intriguing figure, I sat mesmerized in a combination of disbelief and awe. A million questions filled my head as she continued.

"He joined the army during WWII, was a French Freedom Fighter and was honored by the French Government for his heroism against the Nazis," she explained.

When asked what a grateful France could do for him, Michel answered, "I wish to live the rest of my life as a woman." His wish was granted, and in spite of his lifestyle, he stayed married and continued to be a father to their daughter.

People have related seeing Poulain dressed as a woman, walking arm in arm with her daughter as the daughter called her "Papa."

Ray and I began our honeymoon during the first week of September. Needless to say, our first stop was the ancient Saracen village of Èze to meet a person I would not forget for the rest of my life. No cars of any kind were allowed on those still-cobblestoned streets, so we parked outside and walked into medieval history.

We were on a time schedule, so we promptly asked for and found Monsieur Poulain's gallery.

"She's on her way," the woman said. "Please wait."

There was a tiny square with tables and chairs, so we ordered coffee and waited in the gorgeous Côte d'Azur sunshine.

I heard her before I saw her. As she walked toward us, my mind snapped a picture I'll see forever.

She was tall, deep-voiced, broad-shouldered and muscular. She had shoulder length, bleached blond hair. Pancake makeup covered her face with too much rouge. She was dressed in a pale blue women's tailored jacket, skirt and white silk blouse with a soft, feminine bow.

As I traveled down to her feet, I noticed that she had calves that matched her huge hands. She was wearing sensible women's shoes with a strong heel. Those cobblestoned streets demanded nothing less. It was all topped off by a bracelet, ring and earrings. She was, frankly, magnificent in her own warm, unique persona.

Time schedule or not, Michel-Marie insisted on ordering some delicious little something as she asked how she could help me. I told her how I had found her and that I would love to see her paintings.

"My gallery is a few steps away," she said. "I'd be happy to show them to you."

Then she began to ask numerous questions about me while Ray sat silently but intently listening to our conversation. Lunch was over when Ray reminded me that it was getting late.

As we entered the gallery, Poulain introduced us to the same woman we'd seen before. I wondered if she was her wife. As we toured her beautiful work, I found it as diverse as she: exquisitely colorful, sensitive yet strong.

We bought a still-life and her "Sailors and Girls" that day, and after living with them for over fifty years, I treasure them now as I did that day in Èze.

After we said our goodbyes and were quietly walking to our car, I asked, "What do you think, honey?"

As usual, Ray's answer both surprised me and clarified a feeling I'd had while being "interviewed" by Monsieur/ Madame Poulain.

"Were you aware that he was flirting with you?" he asked.

I stared at him.

"I was fascinated watching you bring out the male in her."

"I didn't do anything, honey," I said, "but I did begin to feel uncomfortable. I thought it was because he was ignoring you as if you were invisible.

"I wouldn't have missed watching you for the world," he said with a laugh. "You just didn't get it." He was right again.

Most of my life had passed before I began to write this book. When I recalled Madame Poulain, I wanted to know more, so I spent a great deal of time researching her. I found her history lacking in content, but the following filled in so much of my unfulfilled curiosity and, perhaps, yours too.

She was born a male in 1906 but soon began to intermittently dress like a female. This behavior continued until high school, when he began to wear skirts and women's clothing. His choices often brought out the teasers, harassers and bullies, and he was shunned by his classmates.

Women's attire or not, Poulain grew to be enormously strong and muscular. While in school one day, his peers made the mistake of taunting him/her again and she promptly flattened them. The cruel behavior stopped abruptly, replaced by a healthy fear of those powerful fists.

In 1932, he visited Dr. Magnus Hirschfeld at his clinic for trans-sexual studies in Berlin. Perhaps even then, Poulain was interested in a change for himself. However, in1933, the Nazis destroyed the clinic and the doctor escaped with his life. He died in 1935.

Michel became a performer known as Mickey, even owning his own club. He married Solange, a fellow performer, and had a child named Michele. In spite of her lifestyle, the pair remained married for the rest of her life.

When Poulain joined the French Army to fight Hitler, he cut off his hair and lived as a man. He was a sergeant in the paratroopers and, after countless heroic acts, was captured by the Nazis. During his imprisonment, he castrated himself.

After the war ended, the French Government honored him and his request to live as a woman.

Not only was she a performer, but also a high-fashion model, a successful painter and a stained-glass artist. As I studied her pictures, I saw a different Michel than the one I'd met. Gone was the yellow-blond hair, the excessive makeup and the bigger-than-life persona. Her hair was now natural, her makeup subtle and her clothing tastefully simple.

If she had medical help with her newness, I may never know, but there was no disguising her still powerful arms and hands. She bravely lived life her way and still remains the most unforgettable character I've ever met.

Michel-Marie Poulain
1906 – 1991

À vaillant coeur rien d'impossible.
(For a valiant heart, nothing is impossible.)

Two for the Road

*MAYBE YOU DON'T NEED THE WHOLE WORLD TO
LOVE YOU, YOU KNOW; MAYBE YOU JUST NEED ONE.*

—Kermit the Frog

WHEN RAY AND I left Èze and Madame Poulain, we headed for Lugano, Italy, our first stop on our honeymoon. In order to make up some time, we drove without stopping until hunger pangs made us look for the first place providing food.

As it started to get dark, I said, "There, honey, that little place on your right."

We joined two other cars, one of them being the twin to my Alfa Romeo.

"There's my car, honey, same color, too," I observed.

Ray was then very hungry and a little grumpy, so at that moment food was primary.

We climbed a flight of stairs to face an empty restaurant, except for two men sitting and talking. One of them rose to greet us.

"Are we too late to eat?" I asked.

"No, *signore*, come in."

"Don't worry about the food, sweetheart," I said. "There is no bad food in Italy."

We were seated and immediately brought their soft, crusty bread, sweet butter, two glasses of Chianti and the menu. There was nothing as good as that first bite of bread, a sip of wine and that sigh of relief one feels when fed something. Until the next time.

Leave the door of life open and you never know what will come through. My curiosity got the best of me and I asked the lone gentleman still at the other table, "Excuse me, but is that your Alfa Romeo outside? I have one just like it, same color too, and I love it!"

"Yes it is," he answered. "I always drive an Alfa."

The waiter brought our delicious food and our new friend asked if he could join us.

"Please do," we said in unison.

He had already eaten and was drinking coffee. He told me that our Alfas were rather rare, in that not many had been made for our year. He was dressed casually but had a kind of elegance about him. Charming was the word that fit him best.

The man asked about us, and we told him we had just been married and had two weeks to travel.

We spent a lovely hour together, but it was getting late and Lugano and our reservations were waiting. We exchanged names and addresses and when I saw the name "Galliano," I stared and said, "I have this fabulous liqueur in my home. It's my favorite. I first had it in Rome several years ago."

"*Grazie*," he said, "my family has been making it for almost seventy years."

Ray asked for our check, only to find that our new friend had quietly paid for our dinner. Ray protested, but it was done.

"It's my pleasure to have met you," he said. "I wish you a long and happy life."

We thanked him and I called out "Ciao" as he turned one way and we the other on our way to Lugano and the next surprise always waiting.

"What does that word mean, sweetheart?" Ray asked.

"'I'll be seeing you,' or 'See you soon,'" I said.

"What a nice word," he answered. "I hope we do."

When we got back home from the honeymoon, there was a gift-wrapped package of three bottles of Galliano Liqueur with a lovely note. Unfortunately, "Ciao" didn't come through this time. We never saw him again.

Often, climbing into my little yellow Alfa, I quietly said, "Hello." If you're fortunate enough to still own one of the original Galliano bottles, by the way, they're now worth $150, empty. If there is a little liqueur left, it brings it up to $200.

Driving down the mountain into Lugano was breathtaking. Every light seemed to be reflected in the waters of the lake. The hotels still had their own ambience, a combination of age, service, beauty and, most of all, assuring the comfort and care of their guests. None of the cookie-cutter places of today.

We checked in and when shown to our rooms, we saw a big basket of fruit, sweets and a chilled bottle of champagne. The note said, "Dearest Janis and Ray: May you have the same happiness that Al and I have found. Love to you, Joan (Crawford)."

I couldn't believe it! She was never anything but kind to me.

We had a lovely little balcony overlooking the lake, but the *pièce de résistance* was a giant mountain of goose down covered in white linen. Without a word, I dove into its center and was enveloped by a down cradle.

We toasted Joan, our Galliano friend, our journey and us. We barely brushed our teeth before we were both falling asleep under a lighter-than-air comforter.

When I finally go to that big sleeper in the sky, I hope a comforter is waiting for me.

After our continental breakfast on our balcony, with both of us feeling that we'd like to move to Lugano, we left and trekked toward our destiny: Berlin and The Wall. Ray had no sense of direction, so he drove, and I read the map and our wonderful Michelin Guide. In fact, the only time we got lost was when *I* drove, and *he* read the map. We went ten miles out of our way before I had to turn around, go back and take the correct turn.

As we drove, I remembered the words of Ray's daughter Joanne. He parked in Beverly Hills one day so that he could walk and write. When he got ready to go home, he forgot where he'd left his car. Joanne happened to drive by when she saw her father standing on a corner looking one way and then the other.

"Did you lose the car again, Daddy?" she asked.

"I guess I did, Woots. Can you drive me around until we find it?"

She did, and he found his way home.

"Don't worry, Jan," she said, "he always loses his car when he walks and writes."

Traveling with a Michelin Guidebook not only got you to your destination, but the historical information was also a part of that amazing gift to travelers. Sometimes, we'd stop at a *charcuterie* or *fromagerie*, buy that heavenly bread, cold meats, any French cheese, a bottle of the local wine and find a picnic spot.

Often, I'd make us driving food so that we didn't have to stop. No matter the place or the chef, the food was always spectacular.

We were both hungry and tired when we reached Berne and checked in to another of those elegant old hotels. Our Miniature Schnauzer, Jody, had been fed, so we left her in the room and made our way to the only place open for food.

The Rathskeller was almost empty when we found a booth near the door. Only three tables had customers. There was a maître d' and a waitress, and everyone had been served. After about fifteen minutes, no one came near us.

"Where is everybody?" Ray asked. "I'm starved and tired."

He finally asked the passing waitress for a menu. She never answered but on her next pass dropped two menus on the table and kept going.

"Good God," he said, "what does it take to have someone say 'Hello, can I take your order?'"

We'd been waiting for over half an hour when in walked five people. They were seated in the middle table and were given menus and greeted with friendly banter along with taking their orders.

My husband was slow to burn, but he was beginning to get angry. I was already ahead of him as I remembered my own disgusting moment at being refused service.

In the 1950s, I was playing a club in Birmingham, Alabama. A longtime member of a posh country club nearby had invited me to dinner. My friend's wife and I stood apart while he spoke to a man at the desk.

"My goodness," his wife said, "I wonder what the problem is."

When the doctor came back to us, his face was flushed,

"Let's go," he said.

"Does this have something to do with me, Doctor?" I asked.

"I apologize for this, Janis, but it does," he replied. "I've just been told, 'We don't allow blacks, Jews or show folk in the dining room.'"

Ray's "This is ridiculous!" fit the moment as he turned to the desk asking, "Can we get some help over here?" No "Hello," no "I'm sorry to keep you waiting," just a cold "What can I get you?"

We gave the waitress our order, and when she left, my Jewish husband said, "My gut is telling me that I'm not welcome here, honey. Let's go!"

"I feel the same way," I agreed as I followed my husband out.

I had to pass in back of the maître d', still writing food orders. Suddenly I whispered, "Heil Hitler!" and left.

Ray was intensely angry, but I had a kind of quiet rage. We started to climb the stairs to the lobby when Ray heard, "Mr. Gilbert, please wait, please wait."

We hadn't seen this man before.

"What's going on here?" Ray asked as he reiterated our experience.

"I am Swiss, sir, never a Nazi," the man explained. "I know that Berne has a bad reputation for the Neo-Nazi movement, but I am not one. I run the dining room, which is closed, but please let me make you some food. I feel terrible about how you were treated."

We sat alone in this big empty room, being served dinner. We asked our maître d' to sit with us, which he did. We not only got an education that night but a friend as well.

When we got back to our room, Jody was missing and we were frantic. I called the front desk, only to be assured that she was fine and waiting in the baggage room.

"What's she doing in the baggage room?" I asked.

"She was howling so loudly that the guests were complaining," I was told.

"I guess Jody doesn't like Berne, either," Ray said as he bailed her out of dog jail.

We drove through the breathtaking beauty of Switzerland, stopping at times to simply grab a memory of a place we had to come back to. I finally lost track of all the memories we planned to revisit.

One's imagination was stretched constantly as we planned what could only become a fantasy future as we caught up with the real world once more.

When we crossed the border into a new country and a new culture, the food, too, followed suit. To Ray's delight, the light-as-air bratwurst floating on our plates began to appear. I'd had sausages before but never anything like this. When I found out they were made from veal, I never touched another brat in my life, to this day.

When we pulled up to the Hilton Hotel in West Berlin, it seemed to be the only lodging for miles. It was new and strangely solitary in a sea of intermittent spaces. I never saw another in that allied bomb-flattened city rising from the ashes of post WWII Berlin.

That final battle that ended the war had also ended almost any vestiges of what was once one of the world's great cities. But Ray and I were able to arrange a tour of East Berlin.

En route, we passed Hitler's bunker where he and Eva Braun died. It was now just a huge mound of grass-covered soil. Like the Nazi concentration camps and the annihilation of the Jews, it seemingly had to be cleansed from German history. We saw the same attempt in Dachau.

Preparing for our tour, we approached Checkpoint Charlie, the military post dividing East and West Berlin. The first thing I saw was the American flag flying and waving in the wind.

The dichotomy separating the two Berlins was at once stunning and deeply sad. West Berlin was a bustling new, revitalized city, while East Berlin was unsmiling and seemed to be colored a dark, forbidding shade of gray. Even the sun looked different.

The small tour bus was waiting for us at the military gate separating the two halves of the city. We had a mixed bag of tourists, fascinating in a kind of James Bond-ish atmosphere. I expected to see Humphrey Bogart or Peter Lorre as we found our seats.

A sober-faced and rather intimidating East Berlin soldier boarded the bus and immediately began to say one word only: "*Passaport, Passaport,*" as we traded our precious identities for a 4x5-inch yellow card. Then we were asked to declare all of the money we had with us that day. Everything had to be counted and noted.

I had very little cash, and as he turned to my husband, I heard Ray counting out his money in Yiddish. I had no idea that Ray could speak or even understand Yiddish.

I felt the entire bus stiffen as he counted each coin into the palm of the East Berlin soldier's hand.

Ray's smiling and polite behavior did not go unnoticed, nor did the flushed face of his impatient recipient. When he left, our passports in his hand, we began our journey-in-shades-of-gray tour.

When one is born and raised in the freedom of America, it is inconceivable to even imagine another way of life. The infamous "Wall" was built the year before to keep its citizens from fleeing to the West and beyond.

East Berlin was now under Russian rule, and an atmosphere of oppression lay thick in the air. Our smiling female tour guide kept up a running praiseworthy description of how wonderful and progressive East Berlin was and avoided any discussion of their imprisonment behind that ugly wall watching us.

Watching was indeed the operative word because The Wall itself was actually armed. At certain angles, we could see the barrel ends of the guns.

As we drove, our bus and the city with its human contents were completely unaware of the famous tunnel being dug to freedom beneath under the street and the despised Wall. Many people escaped until the tunnel was discovered and closed.

Between my curiosity and the boring litany of our guide, I was moved to ask some questions. I kept them to what I'd read in the papers and what I'd seen in the newsreels before the movie began.

Not one word of these recent headline news stories had been mentioned by our guide, so I did. She simply ignored me until I politely insisted and finally got an answer. I felt a woman behind me poke me in the back with, "You're going to get us in trouble with your questions. Be quiet!"

We were finally approaching Checkpoint Charlie and the end of our tour of what they wanted us to see. I turned to the woman and said, "Shame on you. If America had stayed quiet, we Americans might be living behind a Wall of our own."

That seemed to shut her up.

I always had my Nikon camera with me, but I wasn't allowed to take any pictures during our tour. When we stopped, I walked to the front of the bus and walked down one step only to have a baby-faced soldier raise his rifle at me to "Get back."

"Please don't do that," I said. "I just wanted to take your picture."

I sat down and waited for my passport. The man who took them also brought them back. As he passed them out, he asked us to return the yellow card.

When he reached me, I held up my card and pleaded, "Souvenir, please. Souvenir?" I got a gruff "No."

"Please?" I repeated.

This time, a firmer "No, no!"

"Give it to him, honey," Ray said, "I'm hungry."

I got my passport back, and when he'd finished, he walked to the door of the bus to leave. Suddenly, the man stopped and fished something out of his pocket. When he found what he wanted, he turned back to me, took my hand and folded my fingers around an East German Mark.

"Souvenir," he said smiling before walking away.

If I'd kept quiet, I wouldn't have seen his smile or the twinkle in his eye as he presented me with my souvenir. I still have it, and the clear-eyed memory when there was no Wall, just a tiny touch of humanity between the East and the West of life.

When we reached the American side of the checkpoint, a tall, uniformed lieutenant approached us.

"Excuse me," he said, "but would you like to have your picture? I saw what happened. I can take it for you."

From the rather ill-fitting and unimpressive uniforms of the East side, I now stood before an immaculate version of a poster child for the United States Army. He resembled a young Sterling Hayden, which was about as far as you could go in the handsome men department back then.

This lovely man took my camera, walked to the edge of our side and clicked the picture. As he did so, the guard on the East Side raised his rifle. Our lieutenant simply took more pictures, including the gun.

"Thank you so much," I said.

"We were worried about you," we replied. "We're used to it. They do it all the time."

"Having that rifle pointed at me made me mad," I told him, "but I wasn't going to argue with it."

"You did the right thing," he answered.

We thanked him again, wished him a safe and great life and finally said our goodbyes. As we walked away, I said to Ray, "Aren't we lucky?"

"We sure are, honey," he replied. "I'm glad we were at Checkpoint Charlie. I thought you were going to be arrested and spend the night in an East Berlin jail."

"You'd never let that happen to me," I said with a laugh.

"No," he agreed, "but it was comforting to see the United States Army nearby, ready to help in case you couldn't charm your way out of it."

Over lunch, recalling our eventful visit, I asked Ray about his counting in Yiddish.

"I don't know where that came from, Jan, maybe my childhood," he admitted. "I'm still a Jew, honey, and I still have my voice. I guess I wanted to use it as a Jew in Germany.

"Maybe," Ray continued, "his arrogant attitude or his ill-mannered and curt demands made me do it, but I got mad and I wanted to get to him. It was my Yiddish with a smile that we both understood."

Ray continued, "And by the way, how did you know that was Yiddish?"

"I know a few words from all the Jewish comics I worked with during my nightclub days," I replied. "I know it when I hear it."

"I guess it rolled up from my childhood," Ray said. "My dad spoke it all the time, and that guy reminded me of my rotten and disgusting father. At least you got a souvenir."

"We both got a souvenir, honey," I pointed out. "We could leave, and they can't."

During the next couple of days, we saw what was left of old Berlin and the unstoppable economy of this new one. The night before our drive to Paris, we dined at a restaurant recommended by the Hilton's concierge.

It was not new, perhaps even a survivor of the allied carpet bombing of Berlin. Its familiar dark wooden booths faced us, and we simply sat down, enjoying the hunger-making odors coming from the kitchen. There were several tables of American businessmen mixed in with some armed forces and German citizens.

We ordered a delicious, ice cold beer and began to scan the room. It was noisy with the chatter of English mixed with German. While waiting for our food, I noticed a man sitting two booths from us, obviously getting ready to leave.

"Look at that man over there," I pointed out to my husband. "He's so angry that he's scary."

By then, this man was muttering something to the room as he got up to leave. The booths were short, so there was a view of every diner.

As he neared the door to leave, he suddenly wheeled around and violently spat at everyone. I'd never seen such rage as he screamed it out in German, ending his wrath with "*Amerikaners! Amerikaners!*" We didn't have to understand German to know what he said.

Silence followed, interrupted by our food and an apology from our waiter. The room came back, returning to its conversation and food while my hungry husband tackled his favorite bratwurst dinner, again.

We left very early the next morning for our drive through France to Paris. We navigated a part of France we'd never seen and were grateful for the opportunity to experience the history and beauty of Burgundy.

To me, everything seemed to resemble something from the magnificent impressionists of the nineteenth century. We made three stops, and if Ray had not put his well-shod foot down, I'd still be in some twelfth century cathedral.

We visited the home of the great Louis Pasteur, who discovered pasteurization. saving millions of lives. Everything was still personal with his nineteenth century bicycle, his books and his life for visitors to share.

We stopped for the night in the little town of Dijon, familiar for their mustard. The hotel was a far cry from the Hilton but was clean and comfortable in an ultra-simple way.

Starving as usual when we arrived, we asked where we could eat.

"Across the street," the man in the hotel said in French. We followed directions to a two-story house, opening the door to see a very large room with a long table. There were diners eating and a few empty chairs with place settings.

A busy woman motioned for us to sit down, and we did.

"It's family style, honey," I said to Ray. "It's out of my childhood. There's a place in Hoquiam, Washington, just like it. Great food, with a French accent, too."

Someone poured us a glass of very deep, dark red wine with the most heavenly and soft aroma. Maybe it was the unexpected and delightful dining experience, but we soon began to interact with the other people there, they speaking broken English, we speaking broken French and all of us laughing at the various translations of both.

We had our first Beef Bourguignon ever, and the wine with no label.

"They make it here," my dining neighbor said.

In my limited education of wine, in today's market, that no label bottle of Burgundy would be worth a small fortune. Dijon, family style, proved to be our favorite.

Our last stop was a twelfth century cathedral in a lovely, storybook town called Auxerre. It was simply enchanting with its lovely river Yonne, its bridges and its availability to all.

Back in 1962, it was a time of a slower pace, longer days and the feeling that an hour was an hour. We'll never see it again, and fortunately or unfortunately, you'll never know what you've missed. Most of all, I grieve for the natural civility we enjoyed. For the most part, it seemed then to still be a part of our DNA.

The truth (or old wives' tale) we were told was that Joan of Arc had worshiped at the cathedral in Auxerre before she went into battle. I don't doubt it for a moment. It stood on a hill overlooking the city. At the time we visited, it was in its eighth century and like nothing I'd seen before.

The first thing you noticed was the silence. There were a few people inside, but all we heard were muted echoes off the thick and barren walls. The only color came from the gigantic stained-glass window.

There was something that made one reverent of just walking on the worn floors of this living, breathing example of Gothic splendor. It was simply unlike anything I'd ever seen, even Notre Dame.

Sun poked through the stained-glass window, sending its pattern of color over parts of the gray stone floor and the rather primitive pews. All of this was seen through the filter of a fine layer of dust, giving it an ethereal aura. The ancient cathedrals, like the ancient castles, contained lives of their own, and I loved breathing in their history.

We continued on to Paris with our pack flat little dog, Jody. She loved nothing more than being with us, her curious little nose experiencing all the new smells carried on the winds of a new country.

As we neared Paris, we saw signs that read "Versailles."

"We can't go by without seeing the palace," I said.

"It's four-thirty, honey," Ray reasoned. "I'd like to see it too, but it's getting late."

It wasn't far from where we were, but as we ran to the gate, we saw that it was closed. "Open 9:00 to 5:00," the sign said.

We found ourselves in front of a huge and beautiful gate. On both sides was a tall and luminously decorated metal fence, enclosing the magnificent palace, its size indescribable.

As we stood there, gaping at what lay beyond, I saw Jody on the lawn inside while we remained on the outside. She was casually investigating this new space while I was becoming frantic at the thought of losing her at the Palace of Versailles.

Jody was paying no attention to our calls, just sniffing and drifting. All I could think was: How do we reach her? Suddenly, she squatted, left her mark at Versailles, and trotted back to us, easily squeezing through the gate again and completely ignoring palace decorum. She was, after all, a dog.

Ray had never been to Paris, let alone driven there. On the way to our hotel, he got caught in the Place de la Concorde's traffic. All we heard were brakes being pressed and drivers screaming in French, but we finally made it to the other side.

"Don't they have traffic lights in Paris, honey?" Ray asked. "What's the Parisian secret to getting to the other side of that craziness while still in one piece?"

Next was dinner at the famous Tour d'Argent with Jody at our feet, politely ignoring all the other dining dogs. We never heard one bark or growl that night as we all enjoyed the lights of Paris, magnificent food and wine and my favorite dessert ever: Chocolate Soufflé.

Jody enjoyed her bits of our dinner, too. We were all very civil and appreciative of our surroundings and the bill.

We left for London the next day. Jody's limo and driver were waiting for us at Heathrow, and we had to give her up to a lovely English gentleman who assured us that she would be well taken care of. If you travel to England, all animals have to be quarantined for the length of one's stay.

"We'll bring her back to you safe and sound," he promised. "Please don't worry." He was right.

It was a far different postwar London that I encountered with my husband Frank in 1949, prior to leaving for America. Those wonderful English movies were my only introduction to the city. I got a shocking view of a still war-torn city four years after hostilities ended.

In every direction, there were clean but barren neighborhoods once shared by buildings, homes, shops and people's lives. A view of sterile nothingness stared back at me. There would be a building or flats still used and then nothing again.

When I asked our British cabbie about the empty spaces, he cheerfully said, "We couldn't let our citizens live with the rubble of their lives and the losses they'd suffered from the German buzz bombs. We cleaned everything up as quickly as we could and carried on."

No newspaper or verbal accounts of the bombs that fell on these cities could ever adequately convey the emptiness where life once teemed.

Winston Churchill's famous "We will never surrender!" guts that live in the British were still very much alive in everyone we met as they struggled to restore London's greatness.

Suddenly, our cabbie pulled up and parked alongside many other cabs.

"Have you tried our fish and chips yet?" he asked.

When we said no, he replied, "It's my dinner time, I'll treat you, follow me."

We entered a large, square room with old tables covered in newspaper and obviously well-loved by cabbies, as we were surrounded by similar versions of our host.

We were quickly served pieces of hot, crisp fish and chips, a.k.a. the British version of French fries. Everything was dumped on the clean newspaper and we enjoyed the most delicious food since arriving in postwar London.

When we were finished, our waiter simply picked up the used newspaper, replacing it with a fresh one. No matter how hard we tried to pick up the check, our dear cabbie would have none of it. We left him a very healthy tip when we said, "Goodnight and thank you so much for your generosity."

We sailed for America the very next day. It was my first and my last voyage on a ship of any kind. I'll leave the water to the Pisces people and their fish. Being a Virgo, I'll stay firmly planted in my Zodiac's sign for "Earth."

Back again in 1962, on the day we were to leave to return to America, Heathrow was anything but orderly. Storms had forced landings from various parts of the world and there was a kind of bedlam in the air, English style.

Ray had to pick up Jody and there were bags to take care of, not to mention the check-in desk and the lines. Ray was worried about me and the bags when our lovely, soft-spoken cabbie said, "Don't worry about Mrs. Gilbert and the luggage. I'll stay with her while you take care of other things."

True to his word, this cabbie stayed with me until we had Jody, our boarding passes and our luggage stored and were ready to go.

Ray had paid the driver when we got out at the airport but never realized the time it would take inside. When Ray tried to give him a very generous and deserving tip, our cabbie raised his hands in front of him saying, "No, thank you sir, I am quite content."

Even when my husband reasoned with him and tried to give him the money, he refused. We never forgot him and spoke of him for years afterward. He made our lives so much easier during that hectic day at Heathrow.

Lana Turner—Korea 1962

*I FIND MEN TERRIBLY EXCITING, AND ANY GIRL WHO
SAYS SHE DOESN'T IS AN ANEMIC OLD MAID,
A STREETWALKER OR A SAINT.*

—Lana Turner

When the Korean War ended, the United States left thousands of men there to protect the 38th Parallel. It was a short but bloody war, with Russian, Chinese and North Korean Communists in the mix.

Finally, in 1953, a shaky truce was signed and the 38th Parallel separated the North from the South.

In 1962, Bob Hope decided to take his famous Christmas extravaganza to the troops in Korea with a show or two in Japan and Thailand.

That year, Bob chose, besides me, the famous and fabulous Lana Turner. Bob, Miss Turner and I had filmed *Bachelor in Paradise* the previous year, and Miss Turner was a lot of fun and great to work with.

How she was going to survive the Christmas show and Korea was debatable. Everyone does his or her best to make you comfortable, but being ready for the freezing and muddy wilds of Korea was always a shock.

Fortunately, Miss Turner was patient, appreciative and just plain amazing.

Our first show was in a large camp somewhere in Korea. The soldiers had put up a tent for the women. They'd built a wooden floor and even set up little make-up tables and small mirrors for us to use. It was bitter cold, but we had a couple of electric heaters that made everything seem kind of cozy.

Often, there was either snow, threatening snow or an active snowstorm. I often danced with the snowflakes sticking to my hair and face, shivering in my skimpy little costume.

But there was never a thought about being cold or the miserable weather because our military audience waited. They would sit for hours, wrapped in tarps against the snow and the infamous Korean winters. Falling snow was always lovely to see, but the real beauty was in the faces of the young men sitting before us on the frozen ground, or in the mud.

From Bob, wearing his Korean hat and carrying his ever-present golf club, to the lovable and generous Jerry Colonna and his skits with Bob, the boys roared with laughter. Les Brown and his Band of Renown were always a big part of Bob's show. They were funny and played the show through anything Korea could send our way.

There was always a tap dancer, the current Miss World winner, Miss Turner's skit with Bob, and my song-and-dance and skits with Bob. For a short time, we were able to help them forget where they were. Their expressions of joy and wonder stay with me forever, as it did with Bob.

The end of the show always brought the lovely voice of Anita Bryant. We would all gather onstage, and Anita would sing "Silent Night."

It was then that the tears began to fall. We all knew the show was over, but the emotion was so much deeper. To see the lonely "I miss Christmas and my family" tears welling up in our young soldiers' eyes and often rolling down their cheeks was always heartbreaking.

I used to wish with all of my heart that I could wrap my arms around them and bring them all home. Those feelings are still alive in me today. I can still see them there, loving everything we did. They were not only the greatest audiences in the world but the most appreciative as well.

Christmas of 1962 was spent on the base outside of Seoul. We had approximately 5,000 men stationed there, give or take a few hundred more or less. That was the number I was given when I asked about the troop numbers.

The base was a big and busy place. The women in the show were housed together in a warm and welcoming dwelling on the base. It had two stories, a fireplace complete with a fire, and we each had our own bedroom with very comfortable beds.

It was surprising to find such cozy quarters for us and we loved it. It reminded me of a mountain cabin. Lots of wood, simple but very hospitable. There was Miss Turner, her hairdresser Helen, Miss World, Anita, our tap dancer—and then I brought up the rear, so to speak. It was the first real privacy we had had. We could unpack, hang up our clothes, take a shower and begin to feel feminine again as well as warm.

I had an opportunity to observe Miss Turner under some very trying circumstances, and she always looked like the superstar she was. There were times, however, when I thought she wasn't feeling well.

We start out as strangers when we begin the tour but end up very close to one another by the end. The experience alone brings us together, and when you're forced to take care of yourself, you also help the other person to do the same.

There is always the nervousness of performing, but there are so many other factors influencing your commitment to Bob and the audience. We always found time to help each other.

Miss Turner and I laughed a lot. She had a great sense of humor, was never late and I never heard her complain about anything. When she walked out in front of those troops, you could hear the roar into the next country. She was Lana Turner with those dimples and her stunning figure. Her skits with Bob were very well done, and her comedic timing was right on. To me, she was an ultimate professional, never asking for anything the rest of us did not get.

The two of us became good friends, and when we would return to our quarters, our doors were left open and we would sit on our beds, talking and unwinding. Sometimes these sessions would last into the night, when we should have been sleeping.

During one of those "girl talk" times, I asked her about her health.

"Sometimes I don't think you're feeling well, honey," I admitted to her. "It concerns me."

She answered without hesitation.

"I'm not feeling so hot, Jan, but I don't want anyone to know," Miss Turner said. "Helen knows, and now you know, but please, keep it here."

She went on to explain that when she got home, she would have a hysterectomy immediately. I told her how sorry I was, but beyond that, she just waved any more concern away.

"I didn't want to miss this opportunity with Bob, and now I know you. I'm so glad I made it."

One night, Miss Turner wanted to talk. She asked me if I was tired. I told her that I was both a night person and a day person but we had our last show the following day so we can't stay up too late. She had twin beds in her room, so I sat on one and she across from me on the other.

I listened as Miss Turner spoke about a part of her life that I only knew from the scandalous headlines. She cried at times as she continued to unload what must have been the heaviest burden of her life. I sat quietly as she continued to express regrets, sadness and more regrets.

The next time I looked at the clock, it was three-fifteen a.m. She was tired and so was I. We bade each other goodnight, and I left wondering about the emotional and physical burdens we carry, and how we still function. There are times when I can't wrap my head around the amazing strength that we human beings possess.

Christmas Day was a festive affair, with everyone looking like they could have been in some fancy hotel in New York City. There was a band, a Christmas tree, lovely food and wine and the officers dressed in their best.

I remember that the brass on their uniforms shone so brightly, it reflected the Christmas tree lights. I was privileged to be a part of this special Christmas time and to be helping in some small way to make the season brighter for all.

Bob was already there, along with Les and the band, Jerry Colonna, the entire cast and crew, but no Lana Turner. I heard Bob ask, "Where the hell is Lana?"

We were all chatting away, sipping our wine, when I looked to see her standing in the entrance looking absolutely gorgeous. She was on the arm of one of the handsomest young men I had ever seen. Blond, built and movie star looks. I noticed he wore captain's bars on his shoulder as they began to walk toward Miss Turner's place at the table.

Miss Turner was late. She made an entrance and she was every inch the star. Her escort seated her as I watched her squeeze his hand. I could see that he was completely over the moon about her.

All through dinner, Miss Turner flirted with him until I began to feel sorry for him. They danced and laughed their way through the evening, and they were still dancing when I left. I often wondered if that poor, smitten captain ever got over his evening with the famous Lana Turner. I must say that I enjoyed her seductive performance thoroughly. We all did.

Through the years, I would witness other late to very late entrances by Miss Turner. Whatever the affair we both attended, her chair remained empty until the room was asking, "Where is Lana?" Then, from somewhere near the entrance, all eyes would be fixed on a slim, beautifully coiffed, elegantly dressed woman in a gorgeous gown with her diamonds blazing in the lights.

She always stood for a few minutes when the applause started, as if to ask, "Oh, this isn't for me, is it?" She was masterful at either playing or being the one-of-a-kind star that she was.

The Lana Turner I knew with Bob Hope in Korea was an uncomplaining, totally professional performer who earned our complete respect and admiration. She was a pleasure who never disappointed, and I'm grateful to have known her.

Lana Turner
February 8, 1921 – June 29, 1995

"Here's Love"

> *I don't like phonies. Actors who can't act, directors who can't direct, hack politicians. My circle of friends gets tighter and tighter. I'm eliminating the phonies. My friends and I sit . . . and tell the truth to each other.*
>
> —Robert Preston

From *The Pajama* Game to my own TV series *It's Always Jan*, my new Las Vegas nightclub act, *Silk Stockings* at Metro, living coast to coast and working constantly, I was enjoying a penthouse view of the world and my life.

I had not yet learned to get off the edge of hyperbole, so the highs would be followed by a few lows when my exhausted emotions would self-adjust, and I'd be headed up again.

Within the first two years of the Sixties, I bought my first house, did three films, copious TV—and got married.

I never knew until years later that there was even a word called "misogynist." I didn't know how to stand up for myself and what I knew to be true in the musical *Here's Love*, I just somehow made things work each night. I stood up for what I believed to be true and was called a bitch for it.

From growing up with intimidation, it was familiar territory to me. It may be dressed differently, but underneath it's the same—with the same reaction from me. I give in and hate the intimidator but hate myself more. I made myself a victim. I didn't know how to do it differently then. Instead of accepting where I was at the time, I'm still kicking myself for not being different.

In 1963, Meredith Willson asked me to do his latest Broadway musical, *Here's Love*, based on the famous film, *The Miracle on 34th Street*. It's a story of the true spirit of Christmas, and it was written by The Music Man himself.

We were fortunate to be directed and guided by someone we all adored, the talented and inventive Norman Jewison. My co-stars were Craig Stevens and the marvelous English actor, Laurence Naismith, who played Santa Claus. The company was stellar, with great voices from Broadway pros. We even duplicated the Macy's Christmas Day Parade, giant balloons and all.

At six o'clock, I walked into the theater, ready for our run-through before we left for Washington, D.C. and our out-of-town tryouts before opening on Broadway. I went to my dressing room. I waited for what seemed an eternity before there was a knock on my door. It was Stuart Ostrow, Meredith's producer.

"We're late, what's going on?" I asked.

"We've replaced Norman," he said.

Until that moment, we'd had no clue.

"My God, Stuart. we leave for Washington and we still have work to do."

I felt sick and was trying to take all of this in.

"What happened? Why now at the last minute?"

"Meredith and Norman didn't see eye to eye," he said.

"We need a director," I reasoned, "who's going to replace him?"

A long pause and then, "I am."

I couldn't believe my ears.

"But Stuart, you've never directed before."

Another pause, and then, "Don't you trust me?"

"Should I, Stuart? Should I?" I pleaded. "Put yourself in my place for a moment. Norman's career has been in directing, mine in years of performing. We know our craft well. Trust has nothing to do with it, but now I have to trust that you and Meredith know what you're doing."

We were in Washington for several weeks, cleaning up financially. D.C. loved the show, and they were making nothing but money. So, we stayed for what seemed to me a very long time.

I had asked to make some changes concerning two of my scenes. But with our huge Washington success, why mess with a good thing? So, the scenes remained as they were. I wasn't asking for the moon, just to use the pre-Broadway time to try what I felt needed fixing.

Of course, I could have been wrong. On the other hand, I could also could have been right.

Meredith had finally written a kind of soliloquy for my backstory in a scene with my daughter. It greatly aided what I felt was missing in the scene, and the day came when I was to sing it for Meredith. I had my Broadway voice as well as my operatic-trained soprano all ready. The former was the one I had used for Broadway and was using in *Here's Love*.

It was a dramatic song, sung as I put my daughter to sleep, denoting the history of the betrayal by her father and my reasons for turning away from life. I was thrilled with the opportunity given me until the day came when I was to finally sing it.

My voice spanned three octaves. Warner Bros., however, did not need opera, so I sang Gershwin, Porter, Green and the rest of the great songwriters of their day. Films were miked, nightclubs were miked, but when I went to Broadway in the Fifties there were no mikes onstage. We had to be heard over a full orchestra to the last row in the last balcony. Like Ethel Merman, we had to become belters.

I began to make adjustments to the Broadway stage and no mikes. Of course, there was no training in how best to accomplish this.

Using my belting voice more than my soprano voice brought a different sound to my upper voice, and the score was written for my lower voice—which I used throughout the show. We had one microphone stage right and one stage left. When we needed them for ensemble work, they rose and lowered as needed.

When I asked that the key be lowered, however, Meredith said that he wanted me to use my soprano voice for this song.

"But Meredith," I reasoned, "I'm singing everything else in my stage voice. You'll have two different vocal sounds. Just lower the key for me and I'll be fine. I'm terribly uncomfortable right now and I don't understand your thinking on this."

"Would you just let me hear it the way I wrote it, Janis?" Meredith asked.

Oh, there it was, that Meredith Willson smile behind his "I mean business" tone. Meredith was a rather handsome man with a big, open smile. He was also the last word. Charming but, when needed, that faint but decidedly present sense of impatience and intimidation appeared.

"Please, Janis, just sing the song the way I asked," he insisted. "At least let me hear it once."

"All right, Meredith," I said.

I knew I'd lost, and when I'd finished, I knew what he'd say.

"That's beautiful, Janis, exactly as I wanted you to sing it."

I left the stage that day feeling beaten down, alone and consumed with that age-old actress' dilemma: To be or not to be a bitch.

It wouldn't have mattered, anyway. My position had already been established. I dared to question Mr. Willson.

I'll never know his reason for the intimidation, but it became chronic and I had lost the enjoyment and pride of being a part of Broadway again. Before we opened in New York, Ray flew in to D.C. to see the show. When he came back to my dressing room, his face said it all.

"Quit, honey," he advised. "You're still out of town. Quit before you ruin your voice."

"I don't know how to quit," I admitted. "I've never quit anything."

Michael Kidd's choreography was, as usual, innovative and brilliant. There was one number in particular that prods my memory. Of course, we had marvelous, athletic dancers—a constant in a Kidd show—but the one I loved to watch was when the toys came to life, all dressed as we'd always known them.

One of the dancers was named Michael Bennett. He danced Raggedy Ann along with Andy, and the audience loved it. He got injured, however, and had to leave the show sometime after the New York opening.

Little did we know then that he would go on to become Michael Bennett of *A Chorus Line* fame. Finally, a dancer put those hard-working, back-breaking, dance-loving and tireless gypsies onstage in "One," and anyone who ever saw it never forgot his gift to the all-deserving chorus lines everywhere, for all time.

This was a time when the country was at once wary but hopeful. We had elected a fresh, young and positive President who inspired a nation to "Ask not what your country can do for you, but what you can do for your country." He had moved us into a new way of thinking and a new way of being American.

John F. Kennedy had been tested early in his first term when, in 1962, he faced the Cuban Missile Crisis and stared down Khrushchev while we held our collective breaths until Russia blinked and removed their deadly missiles ninety miles off the coast of Florida. A deep sigh of relief and pride followed President Kennedy's actions.

While in Washington, we had the great good fortune to hear the unforgettable, soaring-voiced Martin Luther King Jr. and his famous and deeply moving, "I Have a Dream" speech. Anyone on that packed Washington Mall that day in August, 1963 was changed, whether they knew it or not.

We leased an apartment for the run of the show in New York, and Ray became bi-coastal. We had barely been married a year when the show opened in October and he lived between his career at home and mine in New York City.

Due to Willson's megahit *The Music Man*, we'd had a very healthy advance playing to packed houses, especially as we approached the Christmas holidays. I loved my years as a New Yorker, but never as much as when the crisp, cold air was filled with the spirit of Christmas.

I walked to work each night and could never get enough of the lighted, animated windows of Saks Fifth Avenue, Lord & Taylor, the beautiful old B. Altman and Bonwit Teller, each storefront outdoing the other.

Music played over the traffic sounds, and when I'd reach Lord & Taylor, I'd go in to see the decorations and take the side door out toward Broadway, the Shubert and the show that night. The holiday atmosphere was everywhere. There was time to be polite, time to have time for so many little things I miss.

Unlike today, we could look in one another's eyes for support, warmth and human contact that were such an integral part of sharing life. For a tiny blip on the radar screen of history, we shared a place called Camelot—but our country's Impossible Dream ended on November 22, 1963.

I was on the second floor of Bergdorf Goodman's, happily Christmas shopping, when I heard a piercing scream. We saw a woman fall to a chair and begin to sob through the words, "The President's been killed!"

I stood in stunned disbelief, and then I began to run.

"Is it true?" I asked strangers going by as I ran to the street.

Everyone was running somewhere, yelling for taxis, but their empty lights were off as we scattered in a kind of crazy-quilt panic. I started to run home toward 69th and Central Park West and my Ray when a cabbie pulled up.

"Where are you going?"

"I have to get home!"

"Climb in and I'll drop you off," the taxi driver said. "I'm going home, too. Everybody is. I feel like I've been kicked in the gut. I can't breathe."

When I tried to pay him, he answered, "Not today, not today."

For a moment, I threw my arms around the neck of this stranger who was, like I, just trying to get home. I thanked him and told him to take care of himself as he pulled away.

When my husband's arms soon wrapped around me, I sobbed my heart out on his shoulder.

The theater went dark for two days, the lights dimmed as Broadway mourned. A few days later, the company of *Here's Love* simply sucked it up and did what we always did. We made the show go on.

One night, shortly before Christmas, ex-Vice President Richard Nixon attended a performance of our show. Secret Service was everywhere. What no one knew was that ex-President Harry Truman was also in the audience.

Without fanfare or publicity, the President showed up with his daughter, Margaret. President Truman was renowned for his lack of time-wasting diplomacy. Witness the famous sign, always on his desk in the Oval Office, stating, "The Buck Stops Here."

To be sure, there was no love lost between these two men. Craig Stevens, Laurence Naismith and I were summoned onstage to meet and have pictures taken for the press. Vice President Nixon was charming, warm and well-practiced in the art of politics and people. President Truman was the opposite. He stood for the picture, told us how much he liked the show and then said to Margaret, "Let's go."

"Goodnight Mr. President, and thank you," I said.

As President Truman and Margaret passed by me, one of the photographers yelled that famous last line, "Please, Mr. President, one more please."

I was the only one close enough to hear him mutter his next words, spat out in typical "Give 'em hell, Harry!" style.

"One picture is enough with that son of a bitch!"

And out the President strode into the December night.

My grandmother had a favorite saying when faced with a dilemma she found difficult to solve: "Well, I'll just have to make do." And to my young eyes, she would. *Here's Love* became a "make do" kind of show for me, and I finally had no choice.

The Sixties were a roller-coaster ride with no dips. Ray had begun to write with the "Girl from Ipanema" writer, Antonio Carlos Jobim, and I had done three films before we were married in 1962.

I stayed in *Here's Love* until May of 1964, when I simply could not do it anymore. The late Lisa Kirk replaced me—and yes, Meredith lowered the key for her.

Vietnam

> *One of the greatest casualties of the war in Vietnam is the Great Society... shot down on the battlefield.*
>
> —Martin Luther King Jr.

Anywhere our boys needed a laugh or a bit of home, Bob Hope and his ever-present golf club showed up for them. Even in Iraq, at his decidedly advanced age and generations apart, they knew him and loved him when we landed.

Bob had, for many years, devoted his Christmas show to entertaining our armed forces throughout the world, often in times of crisis. I was a guest star on many of his shows, and in 1964 I was called for his Christmas show again.

This time, it was in a place called Vietnam. Of course, I'd heard of it and the rumors of a pending war, but like millions of other Americans, I knew little of the truth.

The Army took over to gather our necessary travel papers, schedules and shots. They were given at NBC Studios in Burbank, and in true Army fashion they gave two or three at a time in the agile fingers of a trained noncom.

Naturally, one is not ready for those three needles deftly placed between three fingers. Before I knew what had happened, I had three shots at once. And this time, whatever they inoculated me with made me sick.

We were facing a whole new batch of diseases, including the plague, yellow fever and lord knows what else. We didn't worry about what we didn't know. We rehearsed, I learned my song and dance number and skits with Bob, and the rest of the cast did the same.

Everything was done as if we were performing it at NBC, except that we were flying across the Pacific Ocean to a land somewhere in Asia.

The amazing part of these Christmas shows was that they could be done at all. The shows that Bob did from NBC in Burbank for so many years were the same ones we brought to our Armed Forces.

For a short time, we were essentially in the Army and were kept on a tight schedule for our safety, if nothing else. We traveled on two planes. In those days, there were no jets, so we placed ourselves in the skillful hands of those tireless pilots who got us where we had to go and back.

Once in a while, the pilots flying the plane let us go into the cockpit and view the world from a much different seat in the sky. If I allowed myself to wonder why we could fly and what kept us up there, I quickly turned my thoughts to something or someone else, anything to keep me from pondering what could happen.

I remember flying over that unending Pacific Ocean at night when I awoke and looked out to see no lights for the longest time. It was then that I quietly said to myself, "If we go down, they'll never find us."

More than ever during those moments, I missed my husband and my dog waiting for me at home. I felt so vulnerable and lonely.

When we landed in Vietnam at Tan Son Nhat International Airport, the armaments of war were all around us. Each of us was placed in a car, followed by an armed Jeep. My escort was General Benjamin Harrison, who immediately said, "Call me Ben, Janis." We were in a huge convoy heading toward our hotel when I heard Ben ask, "What the hell is *that*?"

Up ahead was a big black billowing cloud of smoke rising in the air from our hotel. The next few moments are a blur. As we arrived, we could see glass strewn everywhere and men with blood on their faces. Everything happened so fast that I only remember havoc—sirens and people running everywhere.

I was pulled out of my car, shoved in the back and someone yelled, "Go, Miss Paige, go!" Two or three more GI's got me into an elevator and quickly down a hall into my room.

"Stay here, Miss Paige," they commanded, "and don't open the door to anyone but us and don't leave!"

As Bob would chillingly observe later, "The Viet Cong had targeted me and our entire troupe for death. Our lives were in constant danger over there. And when we arrived, they missed getting us at the hotel by only ten minutes!"

The door to my room at the Brinks Hotel was locked and the men were gone to the mayhem outside, I guess. I was sitting on my bed when they returned.

"Bomb Squad, Miss Paige!" they yelled. I asked their names and opened the door.

"We'll be here twice a day to check your room for bombs."

"Bombs?" I asked.

"Let us do this," they instructed. "Don't do this yourself. We know what to look for and where. This is Vietnam, Miss Paige. Our friends and our enemies all look alike."

They inspected everything in my room, including the back of the toilet tank, looking for bombs. Each day was harrowing and exciting at the same time. The Army did everything to protect us, but hidden danger seemed to lurk everywhere.

One day, we were on our way to a place called Pleiku. I was told that we were flying in General Westmoreland's plane called The White Whale. During our flight, I suddenly saw flashes of light below.

"What is that?" I asked.

"We're flying over a battle, Miss Paige," he calmly replied.

When we landed, pieces of shrapnel had punched a few holes in the bottom of the general's plane. As we deplaned, a worried medic met us.

"What are you women doing here?" he asked. "This place is full of malaria."

We were given two huge quinine pills.

"Take this one right now and one later. Don't forget it," he warned.

There were hazards seemingly around every corner in Vietnam. We saw piles and piles of sandbags and armaments everywhere for this purported "holding war."

While preparing for one of our shows, a scouting party found a mortar aimed at our stage a half-hour before our show was scheduled. Someone was trying to kill us. We simply moved inside a hangar and did the show there. It was, after all, a war, and that fact got clearer every day.

For good reason, each of us had a guard. Often, there was a Jeep mounted with a 30mm gun at the ready.

We did two shows a day, helicopter ready. I don't remember where we were this time. I was escorted to my quarters one night and given a glass Coke bottle of water for drinking, brushing my teeth and washing. The regular drinking water was often disease-ridden.

The room was tiny with a small bed, draped in mosquito netting.

"You'll hear footsteps all night, Miss Paige. It's your guard. Sleep well and welcome to the Ambassador Hotel."

Nothing like the GI's sense of humor.

When I got into bed—basically just a mattress with a thin cover—I found a liberal amount of sand and a few spots of body warmth. I was so tired I couldn't even worry about who, or what, had been there before me.

If I wanted an adventure, I sure got it in Vietnam. There were surprises around every corner. The lieutenant who was assigned to me asked if I'd like to see another part of Vietnam, "one you won't see in the newspapers."

It was getting dark.

"I probably shouldn't do this," I said, "but I'd love to go. Please tell me it's safe. I don't want Bob mad at me."

We drove along a beautiful, still primitive stretch of beach. At intervals there would be a little house. We stopped at one and went inside. There was a tiny bar, a few GI's drinking beer and a Vietnamese bartender.

My Lieutenant "Jim" said, "A family lives here. Dear old Dad tends bar and behind that closed door lives his family. He runs a little business on the side by prostituting his daughter."

"Oh my God, I'm sick, I can't even take that in."

As he said, "Neither could I," a GI opened that door and hurriedly left.

When we reached my quarters, I thanked Jim.

"I've seen a lot of Asian countries and sadly I remember one glaring fact. In a male-dominated culture, women are expendable."

"You're right," he said. "I wanted you to see how raw parts of this life are. The kind of thing we aren't used to."

Saigon reminded me of a small Paris. Tudor Street was the main avenue. It was a constant shock, most of it remaining within me including the pain of what I saw mixed with the mystery and fascination of where I was. Tiny, naked babies were sold in cardboard boxes on street corners.

One day, Bob brought Jerry Colonna and me to a field hospital where they bring the wounded with the worst injuries.

I saw men whose arms and legs were bloody stumps, and one man whose face was completely blown off trying to talk to me. Many of the stumps were unbandaged. You want to run. You want to cry. You want to stare. But you have to glue on this "smiley face" and hopeful demeanor.

There was a moment when Bob was clearly exhausted and said, "I can't do this anymore today. Will you and Jerry cover it?" "Of course," we answered. It had to be hard to be as upbeat as Bob Hope was expected to be all the time.

The Army could not do enough for us. You'd better not ask for anything, because you were very likely to get it.

There was the day when we were in Nha Trang having breakfast in the mess hall. I asked about the helicopters that fired the missiles. How could that be?

My question was answered when a soldier approached me and said, "Miss Paige, the general would like to meet you."

Before I knew what was happening, I was walking toward a man smoking a cigar. He was a wizened old Army general, the epitome of Robert Duvall's character in *Apocalypse Now*. He wore the familiar Vietnam beret and stuck out his hand as he said, "I hear you're interested in how we fire the helicopter missiles."

I mumbled something about "How did you know?" when he said, "Come with me."

There was a helicopter, a pilot who introduced himself and someone holding a jumpsuit and a helmet.

"We thought you'd like to fire one of these things, so you'll know how it feels."

"Are you serious?"

He was. And as I climbed in beside the pilot, someone said, "If you get sick, Miss Paige, you'll have to clean it up."

I yelled, "Don't count on it!"

The copter had dual controls. Two of everything. There was something that looked like a hand brake at my right side with a button on top. The pilot said, "When I say 'Now,' push that button, but not before."

I grasped the "brake," and suddenly we took off, leaving my stomach somewhere else. The scenery was gorgeous, very primitive, with Madame Nhu's palace tucked in the mountains. There were also some very large rocks in the water.

"See that one ahead, Janis?" the pilot pointed out. I said I did. "When you hear 'Now,' push that button."

I did as I was told, and when I fired at the rock, I felt the missile under me and saw it hit the rock. I can't describe the power of that deadly thing and the feeling that it took me with it. I can still feel that weird sensation.

We landed, and I exited to applause and laughter and my gratitude for the experience of a lifetime.

This same area was also full of sand fleas. I walked out one day to hear the reigning Miss World—Ann Sidney of the UK—get this horrified look on her face. She'd been suffering from a strange fungus between her fingers that itched like crazy, and now she was looking at me with a kind of terror.

"Janis!" she yelled, "your legs, your legs! Look at your legs!"

It turned out that something had bitten me from my ankles clear to my butt; the skin was dark red all the way down. I went to the medic and asked, "What is it?"

"I really don't know," he admitted. "Does it itch?"

"No."

"Well then, let's just leave it alone."

We finally figured out it was sand fleas that had attacked me, and I had literally hundreds of bites. Why they didn't itch, I don't know. But it took almost six months for them to disappear completely.

Over 58,000 men and women died, were wounded or found missing in the Vietnam War, and many of those who survived were left with PTSD and the hatred of an ungrateful nation. I saw men come home and get spat on and vilified. They never heard, "Thank you for your service." It was beyond shameful.

As for me, following my time there, I returned home a different person. I was shattered with my own form of PTSD. It affected me so badly and so deeply that I sat in my office for three weeks unable to function.

Finally, my husband Ray demanded, "You've been sitting here staring into space for weeks now. Snap out of it!" But for a long time, I couldn't. People just don't appreciate how atrocious this war was and how devastating for those who participated. But I do.

To all of the Vietnam veterans and those who never made it home, I say, "Thank you eternally for your service and your sacrifice."

Judy Garland

*I've always taken The Wizard of Oz very
seriously, you know. I believe in the idea of
the rainbow and I've spent my
entire life trying to get over it.*

If I'm a legend, why am I so lonely?

–Judy Garland

The first time I met Judy Garland, I was a tongue-tied and awestruck starlet on a street at MGM. I managed to sputter out, "I'm so pleased to meet you, Miss Garland."

There stood Dorothy of my lifelong love *The Wizard of Oz*. She began to talk with me when the man and woman with her interrupted, "No time for that, Judy, we'll be late."

"Nice to meet you, Janis," she said while being hurried away.

Like everyone else, I simply adored her. We had been born three months apart—she in June and I in September of 1922. Our careers took us in different directions, and in 1951 I was starring in my first Broadway show. That same year, Judy opened the long-closed but still famous Palace Theatre in New York City. Her run was for four weeks, but she stayed nineteen and broke all box office records. A massive hit! She also saved The Palace from its rumored wrecking ball finale. And at 106 years young, she's finally ready for remodeling.

Tickets were impossible to get, so I called my agent for help. The following day, he phoned to say that the tickets would be waiting for me at the box office. I picked them up to find they were Judy's house seats. When I tried to pay, I heard, "No charge, Miss Paige. Enjoy the show."

The theater was packed, electric with anticipation. I would forever remember that I had seen the greatest performer in the world. She left every tiny bit of herself on that stage and with her audience. No one could raise the goosebumps like Judy.

She had taken her bows for *Be a Clown* when she walked to the footlights and sat down, her legs folded beneath her. The lights dimmed, the spot picking up this sole, small figure, still wearing her clown outfit.

I was sitting very close to them both when her brother-in-law and conductor Jack Cathcart raised his baton to begin. She quietly stared at us, not moving. A few instruments were heard but stopped with a signal from Jack.

As he raised his baton again, Judy shook her head, saying quietly, "I can't, I can't." I was sitting in full view of this intimate moment shared by us all. I heard Jack softly whisper, "Come on Judy, you can do it, here we go, honey, here we go." He raised his baton a third time.

She seemed close to tears when suddenly that first plaintive "Somewhere (breath) over the rainbow (breath) way up high" began. "There's a land that I heard of (breath), once in a lullaby." The orchestra softly joined her. A little stronger now, Judy continued, gaining that Garland power until "If happy little bluebirds fly (breath) beyond the rainbow, why (breath), oh why (deep breath) can't I?"

As she held that pitch-perfect last note seemingly forever, the house came down in an ovation. Like the great vaudevillian she was, she had touched the hearts of each and every one of her audience members. Including me.

After her many bows and the curtain came down, I climbed the stairs at the side of the stage and entered the wings. There was Judy, her face stained with tears, still wearing the clown wardrobe and with Hugh Martin's arm around her. They were slowly pacing back and forth, still on stage in back of the curtain.

Not knowing what to do, I turned to leave when I heard, "Janis, Janis." We hugged and then I heard, "I'm sick today. I'm sorry, I wasn't very good." I glanced at Hugh, her pianist, and he answered with a small but helpless shrug.

"Didn't you hear us out there, Judy?" I asked. "We adored your performance. Thank you, too, for my wonderful seats and for sharing yourself with us."

"When will I see you again?" she asked.

"Any time you wish, sweetheart," I answered. "Now get some rest, please. Take care of yourself and I'll see you soon."

"Soon" was like our iffy showbiz plans. "Soon" would be almost seven years later after a movie for me in New York, more vaudeville and clubs, *The Pajama Game* on Broadway, my TV series, Las Vegas and the film *Silk Stockings* at Metro.

I was living in California when my friend Pete Rugolo called.

"I was with Judy today, Jan, when I mentioned your name," Pete said. "'Oh, I love her,' Judy replied. 'We're having dinner with her and Sid Friday night at Chasen's.'"

The original is now a Bristol Farms supermarket. My memories of Chasen's and the owner Dave Chasen greeting his guests stay with me. It was a much-loved restaurant of its day, and the memories remain.

Pete and I were greeted by Dave and ushered to a round table with Judy, her husband Sid Luft and another couple I'd never met.

"Sit by me, Janis, so we can get caught up," Judy said.

"We're *always* getting caught up," I laughed in reply. "I'm so glad to see you again."

Judy was nursing a glass of white wine and I ordered the same. The captain took everyone's order and Judy and I began to chat. We were telling funny stories on ourselves and having fun. The others were talking business.

Suddenly, we were interrupted by Sid's "business partner," or so he called himself. He pointed at Judy and me and announced that neither one of us knew how to make money.

"You may be stars, but you're stupid about money," he charged, with no evidence whatsoever.

Both this man and his wife were rather unlikable and uncomfortable in the ambiance of Chasen's. I had tried talking with her, but she preferred her Scotch, so I let her be.

Judy did not answer his rudeness, but I did.

"I can't speak for Judy, but I can for myself. Excuse me, but you know nothing about me or my money. You have no right to speak to either one of us as you did."

I was polite, smiling and seething at the same time. Fortunately, we were saved by shrimp cocktails and dinner. Sid remained quiet throughout our short verbal tussle.

We went back to their house where Pete, Sid and the purported business partner and wife played poker. I knew nothing about poker and couldn't care less, so Judy and I settled down in a quiet room away from the game.

I had also begun to hear rumors of Judy's erratic behavior. I'd never seen it, so I chose to ignore them.

I loved speaking with Judy. She was one of the smartest, most discerning people I'd ever met. She was also blessed with a sharp and delicious sense of humor. We were laughing and enjoying ourselves when the wife appeared at the top of a short flight of stairs.

The woman was by now unsteady on her feet. She slurred, "Judy, get me a drink!"

Who is this woman? I wondered.

Judy looked at her and quietly answered, "Get your own drink. You know where it is." I waited for a drunken explosion in reply, but through a nasty stare, she uttered something under her breath and left.

I broke the silence.

"Why do you let people speak to you like that, Judy?"

"I guess I've had a lot of practice, Janis," she finally responded.

When Pete drove me home that night, I was still fuming about Sid's business partner and his drunken wife.

"Yeah," he said, "she got so drunk we had to stop the game. Besides, Sid owes him $100,000." That's a lot of money. Closer to a million today.

The next time I heard from Judy was early in 1968. I was getting ready to replace Angela Lansbury in *Mame* on Broadway. The phone rang and it was Judy.

"Where are you, honey? I want to see you! I'm staying with Liza," she said. She was hesitant and continued, "Can I come and stay with you?"

A red flag went up and I knew I had to ask some questions. I called a friend and she gave me some very bad news. Of course, I'd heard rumors about my friend, but I too had experienced rumors and I hated them.

"You must not take this on, Jan," a friend warned me. "Liza is taking care of her and Judy is very shaky. You'd have an enormous job ahead of you. She needs so much more than any of us can give her. Please let Liza care for her. She knows her, and you don't know *this* Judy."

I thanked her and sadly hung up.

I simply did not know what to do. Judy moved to London and married again shortly before her death.

One afternoon, I turned on the news to hear that "Judy Garland died today In London. An overdose of sleeping pills is suspected." I sobbed my heart out for what was and what would never be again.

The woman whom I considered the greatest performer in the world had joined the ages.

Judy Garland
June 10, 1922 - June 22, 1969

When you have lived like I've lived, when you've loved and suffered, been madly happy and desperately sad, well, that's when you realize that you'll never be able to set it all down. Maybe you'd rather die first.

Dinner at the White House

Whether you love this country or not, America gives us the freedom to choose. I chose to love, respect and protect my right to happiness. If the road is rough, grab your courage and don't give up!

—Janis Paige

In 1966, I was sent a fascinating script based on a book by one of our stellar and prolific authors, E.L. Doctorow: his *Welcome to Hard Times*. I loved the project, but when I heard who was in the cast, I said "Yes!" without another thought.

Henry Fonda was to star with Rita Hayworth. Just hearing that combination was exciting, particularly since Miss Hayworth was going to appear after a lengthy screen absence. I'd never met either one of them and I, along with everyone else, was greatly anticipating this film. Aldo Ray, Keenan Wynn and I were their co-stars. MGM had cast with great care for this unusual story. Just reading the script was exciting.

A week before we were to begin filming, Miss Hayworth pulled out. The reason given to us was that she had "cold feet about going back to work" and a fine actress named Janice Rule replaced her.

It was not an easy shoot. The story was placed sometime in the 1800s, with the usual wagon trains, dust, heat, costumes of the times and the accompanying stress that always hovers near any film. So much anticipation disappeared with Rita's exit. She was in the superstar category and, as such, irreplaceable.

When the filming was finished, Metro asked me to travel through Oklahoma and Texas to promote the picture. Naturally, I agreed. I always loved that part of my profession that involved seeing new places, meeting new people, eating new food, hearing new opinions and whatever else comes from such an opportunity.

There were always surprises. My first one was the oil well on the grounds of the courthouse in Oklahoma City. I'd never seen so many wells in my life as I traveled through Oklahoma into the great state of Texas.

Traveling from Amarillo to San Antonio to Waco, Tyler and Austin, I saw a lot of Texas and I loved it. Texans are proud of their heritage and will tell you so before you can ask, in case there's any doubt. Pride in one's state or country had not yet become a racist thing. We could still feel our own pride in America and the humorous word-jousting about whose state is the best. At our core, we were all Americans, and it was all good fun.

When I arrived in Austin, I was presented with a Certificate of Honorary Citizenship of Texas before a joint session of their legislature. I was given the key to the city and all manner of Texas hospitality. The graciousness of those gentlemen could easily spoil you with their Texas charm—and they did.

At the time I received my Honorary Citizen's decree, I was one of only six women to be so honored. In today's politically correct world, I don't know if that speaks well for Texas or not, but I neither cared nor questioned their choice of me. I'm still proud of my Texas heritage.

When President Kennedy was assassinated in Dallas in 1963, I, along with millions of others, grieved for what might have been. I was in the Broadway show *Here's Love*. Each night, I left my grief in the wings, did the show and picked up my zombie-like aura again as we lived our lives post-Kennedy.

One day in my dressing room, I began to write a letter to President Johnson. I wished him well and poured out my feelings to him. I mailed it, never thinking that my letter, along with all the millions of others he'd receive, would even be read.

While in San Antonio, I was treated to a luncheon by the mayor and members of the City Council. They informed me that President Johnson had his home in Johnson City, not far from San Antonio. I mentioned my letter and how much I wished him well.

The beautiful St. Anthony Hotel where I was staying—and where we had lunch—had been decorated by the famous Dorothy Draper. It was exquisite. I might add that a Texas politician like the President or maybe just a Texan could charm his way through anything. I'd call it a subtle flirtation with everyone. Fascinating!

I was asked if I would visit Brooks Army Medical Center and readily agreed. However, I wasn't ready for what I saw. Napalm was now being liberally used against the enemy, but it was likewise used on many of our own soldiers burned in the attacks. Countless lives were saved by flying them directly to the skin bank at Brooks.

The officer with me asked if I would visit the burn ward. A kind and gentle nurse was with me. Bed after bed held a napalm survivor in various stages of healing.

As I went from bed to bed, I saw one very young man lying on his back, staring at the ceiling and shaking all over. The top half of his body was covered with small square patches of "skin" on top of his own raw flesh beneath. The squares did not quite meet, and this meticulous pattern covered his chest.

"He had his surgery yesterday," the nurse told me. "He's in great pain."

"Hello," I said to him, "I'm so sorry. I wish I could help you." His eyes found me and then returned to the ceiling and the pain.

When I'd finished and returned to my car, I broke down completely, crying like I'd never stop. My officer and our driver sat quietly, letting me cry it out.

"Oh my God!" I blurted. "I'm so sorry."

"Please don't worry, Miss Paige," they replied. "We know this is very hard."

When I returned home, I spotted an envelope one day that read "The White House" on the outside. I thought it was an ad from a department store in San Francisco where I had shopped many times. I rather carelessly ripped it open, only to find it was an invitation to the actual White House for a State Dinner for the Prime Minister of the United Kingdom Harold Wilson and his wife.

Ray was busy in the office when I ran in with the news.

"Well, we're not going, are we?" he asked.

"Where are you, honey?" I asked back. "There is no way we're NOT going. It's *our* White House! It's a dream come true!"

We made reservations for a hotel and ordered a limousine, and of course I had to have a new dress. We found one, had it altered and was told when I could pick it up. It wasn't finished until the day before we left.

When I tried it on, they had obviously altered it for someone else and I couldn't wear it. I was devastated and close to tears.

"What else do you have?" Ray asked.

"Well," he was told, "we just got a few of James Galanos in this morning, but they need pressing."

Ray had great taste, and when the clerk brought out what she had, he said, "Try this one, honey."

When I walked out to show Ray, he said, "That's it, sweetheart, that's it!" My entire outfit was finished that day. It looked perfect, and I felt the same way.

From meeting the President, First Lady and their daughters and going through that line of dignitaries, to the exquisite protocol of the evening, everything was practiced, comfortable and truly unforgettable.

When all of the guests were at their seats for the dinner, one heard the President's theme music. "Pomp and Circumstance" brought President Johnson and Mrs. Wilson. Our First Lady accompanied Prime Minister Wilson. Everyone stood until the President arrived at his table.

I watched President Johnson get closer and closer to our table until he stood directly across from me. Before we sat down, he gave me an undeniable wink.

It was then that I heard a voice ask, "May I seat you, Miss Paige?" When I looked to say, "Thank you," I was looking at the tall and handsome Secretary of State Dean Rusk.

A sign on the fireplace over the President's shoulder read, "God Bless This House –John Adams." Here I sat, surrounded by our past, present and future. As I walked to the ladies' room, I saw the Presidential china, past and present, in glass cases. I'd make a lousy First Lady, I thought. I'd never get any work done.

Suddenly there came a familiar voice from the other side of the restroom.

"Hi Janis, I didn't know you were here."

There she stood in her floor-length, solid beaded gown with matching beaded coat, which someone had been holding for her while she was in a stall. I wondered if there was a bead left in China.

I've never been good when I got a zinger or a knife in my back. I stayed hurt. I don't know what happened to me that night, but this time I had an answer, timed perfectly: "I don't know how you missed me. I was seated with the President."

I wasn't going to let anybody ruin my perfect night at The White House. And perfect it was.

Henry Fonda

*I must have had faith that day. When I left, I
was Henry Fonda, unemployed actor, but a man.*

—Henry Fonda

In 1966, I was cast in a most intriguing and fascinating film called *Welcome to Hard Times* from the novel by E.L. Doctorow, of *Ragtime* fame. It was a psychological western set in the late 1800s.

I loved the book and thought the cast was terrific. Needless to say, I was excited and looking forward to working with Mr. Henry Fonda, Janice Rule, Aldo Ray, Keenan Wynn and some of the finest character actors of the time.

Mr. Fonda was a total professional, lines ready and always knew what he was doing. He was also distant, quiet and seemingly unapproachable. He would sit in his folding chair with "Mr. Fonda" on the back, his long legs sprawled out in front of him, quiet, private, mysterious and surrounded by what seemed to be his own private circle of no man's land where mere humans dare not tread.

There were rumors of his remoteness. So, between those rumors and my own timid hesitations, I had formed my own interpretation of "Fondaland."

I was, however, desperate to speak with him about a subject near and dear to my heart. From what I had read, it was one important to Fonda, too. Dare I try to enter that small, tight world without being a bothersome intrusion? I simply did not know.

A few years earlier, I had read an unforgettable little book called "Death of a Man," by Lael Tucker Wertenbaker, wife of the late Charles Wertenbaker. He was the foreign editor for Time magazine, and while living in France, he was diagnosed with colon cancer.

The Wertenbakers had made a most unusual pact. When he felt he could no longer tolerate the pain, she would help him to die. It was beautifully written, poignant, sad, courageous and soul touching. It's been so many years and it still breaks my heart. She spared the reader nothing, and as such we not only read the truth, but we lived it, too.

The great playwright Garson Kanin, who wrote *Born Yesterday*, adapted the book for Broadway and re-titled it *A Gift of Time*. It starred Fonda and co-starred Olivia de Havilland. Regretfully, I did not see it, but I read an article about Mr. Fonda's special love for this play.

Unfortunately, in spite of its star and name cast, the play ran for only 91 performances. I wanted to know about Henry's experience with this marvelous property. Only 91 performances. What went wrong?

I could drive people bonkers with my insatiable curiosity, and now I pondered how I could pique Mr. Fonda's curiosity about my curiosity.

There I stood, staring at his back. Here was the opportunity of a lifetime, and there he sat. seemingly unavailable. It was a word often used to describe Henry Fonda.

I took a deep breath and thought, this is silly. What can he do but reject me, ignore me, tell me not to bother him, bug off, get lost? Before I could stop myself, I heard the words leave my mouth: "Excuse me, Mr. Fonda, could I speak with you about *A Gift of Time*?"

He looked up from under his dusty, well-worn hat and asked, "How do you know about *A Gift of Time*?"

I figured that I'd better take advantage of what might be a very short meeting, and I poured out my love and admiration for the book. I wondered if I could impose on him to share his experience in playing that heartbreaking role.

Henry's reaction was anything but distant and unapproachable. He jumped up, brought a chair for me and began to tell me about his love for this project. He became animated, open and obviously very moved by the content and the role.

Then his memories, still fresh, invoked a surprising statement.

"Olivia de Havilland ruined that beautiful play," he said. "She never understood the woman she portrayed, never, and she never understood the relationship between those two people. She helped the man she loved die, for God's sake."

The silence was palpable. He had shared an intimate moment that still hurt, and the emotional memory still seemed so raw. Not knowing how to respond or if I should, I remained silent.

"We're ready, Mr. Fonda."

The call to work broke the moment. Finally, I spoke.

"I'm so grateful that you had the opportunity to know these people and to give them life," I said.

My brief encounter had slipped into history. He thanked me for my interest and was happy to find someone who felt the way he did,

"Thank you, Janis," he said.

"Oh no, Mr. Fonda, thank *you*, thank *you*."

"Call me Hank," he said as he unfolded his lanky frame, stood and ambled that famous Fonda walk toward the set.

For a few moments, I had found him very approachable.

I always addressed him as "Mr. Fonda." Calling Henry Fonda "Hank" never came easily to me, but I did as he said, sometimes.

Keenan Wynn called him Hank. Now there was another one-of-a-kind actor. I adored working with him. Good actors don't act, they just *are*. He made me better than I was, and I didn't even have to try. Somehow, they just rub off.

When my time arrived to actually do a scene with Hank (I'm still not comfortable with that after all these years), I got the surprise of my life.

The scene called for him to bathe in a big wooden tub, still wearing that old, sweat-stained, dusty hat. I delivered my lines and he delivered his—except not to me. For a moment, I was thrown for the proverbial loop. I tried to find him and failed.

"My God!" I thought, "he's acting without me. I'm invisible! I'm not needed! Is it me?"

We finished the scene and came around for close-ups. It was the same thing! He worked solo, with only the camera as his co-star. Sometimes we're the teacher, and sometimes we're the student. I was a student that day. The trick is to know the difference.

Yet our scene worked. What happened? I was to find that out a few years later, when I worked with an actor who hadn't bothered to learn his lines.

Time is money, and after trying several rehearsals, each a struggle, we shot one scene but never did get it right. Much is expected of a professional, so in order to get the shot, I had to work over and without the lazy bum.

Suddenly, I realized that I was working the Fonda way, and it worked! It also became a necessary weapon in my artistic arsenal. If your fellow actor can't give you what you want or need, you'd better learn to give it to yourself. Thank you, Mr. Fonda. I wish I'd had the nerve to discuss the "Fonda method" with you.

Through the years, I have heard that many actors who worked with Henry Fonda experienced the same reaction as mine. If you were unaware of how he worked, you felt invisible.

I understand that the luminous Katherine Hepburn broke him of that habit when they worked together in *On Golden Pond*. I guess the magical Hepburn told him politely to knock it off. He won his only Oscar for that role.

Henry Fonda
May 16, 1905 – August 12, 1982

My Moveable Feast

*LIFE IS EITHER A DARING ADVENTURE
OR NOTHING AT ALL.*

–Helen Keller

The decade of the Sixties proved to be a kind of embarrassment of riches for both Ray and me.

Starting with meeting Ray, his tolerating me through the "adult mumps," his many kindnesses and, most of all, his great sense of humor made this the greatest time of our lives. Neither of us knew what good fortune lay ahead, including a life-changing education of a world we'd never experienced.

While Ray and his partner wrote the score for the full-length Yogi Bear film at Hanna-Barbera Studios, I was doing television, a pilot at Metro and a summer stock tour of *South Pacific* in the huge outdoor theaters in the East (including Washington, D.C.).

Unfortunately, I was introduced to an oyster called the Chincoteague. To an unaware oyster lover, this delicacy was hiding Hepatitis B from the polluted Chesapeake Bay.

A few months later, I began to rehearse for the role of Adelaide in *Guys and Dolls*. If one was fortunate enough to work for Edwin Lester and his Civic Light Opera, you had the best of everything. Playing that delicious character was just the icing on the cake.

We had an enormous hit while I continued to ignore an increasing fatigue and the mystery of just not feeling well. By the end of the first week, my doctor diagnosed me with Hepatitis B and ordered the entire company to get gamma globulin shots—"Now!"

The memory of *Adelaide's Lament*, Dan Dailey as Sky Masterson using his dancer's grace in *Luck Be a Lady*, and our cast hand-picked by Mr. Lester will always be alive in me.

Two months of bed rest was my punishment for eating polluted oysters out of season. How was I to know?

I wonder if there's a production of *Guys and Dolls* somewhere that could use a 97-year-old Adelaide. If so, give me a call. My agent died.

Back healthy again in 1962, I did the film *Please Don't Eat the Daisies* with David Niven and Doris Day; *The Caretakers* with Joan Crawford, Herbert Marshall and another stellar cast; and, finally, *Follow the Boys* starring Connie Francis, supported by a very talented cast, in Nice, France. All of this, and then my marriage to Ray in Nice in August, 1962.

Then came 1963, which brought me to Broadway and Meredith Willson's *Here's Love* while Ray was a coast-to-coaster until I left the show in May of 1964. We had a lovely, touristy journey home, stopping to pay our awed respects to not only man's ability to dream but to fulfill those dreams as well. Mt. Rushmore in South Dakota is one stunning example.

When we returned home, Ray was given the music of a song called *Dindi* and fell in love with the late, great Antonio Carlos Jobim's melodic and innovative Bossa Nova sound. They began working together and in 1966, Ray went to Brazil and I followed later.

When we signed with Chappell Music in 1967, they suggested that Ray visit a few of our representatives, beginning with Sweden, and he agreed. He wanted me with him, and of course I said, "When do we leave, honey? This is so exciting."

It was also the first vacation I'd ever had without working. I could be just a tourist for a change.

In November of 1967, I joined him in New York City. The night before we left for Sweden, Chappell gave us tickets to see Zero Mostel's closing night on Broadway in *Fiddler on the Roof*. What a glorious gift! Zero was brilliant as Tevye, but that night was also a magical display of a company leaving everything on the stage for us to remember always.

We lost count of the bows demanded by a loving and grateful audience. Ray, being Jewish, prompted some unfamiliar behavior as we watched Zero onstage. My usual questions followed as we walked back to our hotel that night.

"I'm so full of tonight, Jan," he said. "Watching Zero, I found myself back in yeshiva school with the rabbi's smelly, tobacco-stained beard in my face. I was always wrong, and one day I spat at him, left and never finished school.

"I was in the seventh grade. My love of books helped finish my education, and I went to work at a very young age in a Greek restaurant.

"I began to fool around with lyrics when I was around eleven. Around fifteen, with my partner Lou, we sold our first song to Sophie Tucker at about one o'clock in the morning. She came out of some famous speakeasy on Rush Street in Chicago. I got in front of her and began to sing.

"Sophie stopped, listened and then asked me how much the song cost. She gave me cash on the spot, took our budding effort and got in her limo. I've often wondered if staying in school would have ultimately won me an Oscar. I doubt it, and I don't question fate."

The next day, in November 1967, we flew to Stockholm and began our memorable journey to places and experiences we'd never seen and would never see again. Some were life-changing for us both.

Stockholm was an interesting mix of the very old and the new. The hotel was simple, modern and looked as if it had been decorated by Ikea. The city was very clean, with fabulous food, sophisticated citizens and beautiful women. I tagged along with Ray while he met his sub-publishers in Scandinavia.

We were treated to luncheon at the indescribably beautiful Opera House Restaurant, situated in an enormously high-ceilinged room. In its center was a long and tantalizing "groaning board" of food.

The entire experience was one of complete luxury. There was a gigantic window and—visible from anywhere one sat—a view of part of the King's Palace. You could have fooled me. I thought that's where we were.

Old Stockholm began around the 13th century. Its narrow, ancient streets and aged buildings took us back into its history. Suddenly, they looked strangely out of place when we saw a movie theater's lights and marquee advertising *The Sound of Music*. We hadn't seen it yet and I said, "Let's go in, honey, it'll have English subtitles so we'll understand it."

"I'm freezing," Ray said. "Maybe I can get warm."

Surprise! We didn't have to struggle through English titles. The Swedes had to struggle through their own Swedish ones. Yes, the film was shown in English and meant even more when we visited Salzburg and Vienna.

Ray's mother was born in a little village in Sweden called Vaxjo. We rented a car and drove through a perfectly directed, Ingmar Bergman day: gray, gloomy, cold and weirdly empty of traffic.

Sadly, no records were found.

"The church records were all burned in a fire many years ago," we were told. "We're so sorry." So were we.

We ferried from Malmo, Sweden, to Copenhagen, Denmark. An experience in itself.

Denmark

> *To me, Denmark is still a Hans Christian Andersen fairytale, with its endlessly happy ending.*
>
> —Janis Paige

If I could pick a favorite hotel anywhere in the world, the one in Copenhagen would be close. It was old, elegant, with the changing of the guard outside our balcony each day.

We adored Denmark. Its civility, its food, a fish called a plaice and its cobblestoned, no-cars-allowed, walking street. It was then called The Oestergaard. I loved its cacophony of footstep sounds and beautiful shops selling everything Danish, including the works of a designer I still cherish today.

His name was Bjorn Wiinblad. He was a prolific artist whose imaginative pottery, china, paintings and famous cases are still sought and collected today.

Their walking street also provided its citizens and visitors countless coffee shops, irresistible pastries and a view of elegant women smoking big fat cigars as they enjoyed reading, eating or just relaxing. The cigars took some getting used to, but all in all we thought Denmark to be the happiest country we'd seen.

It was December, so the famous Tivoli Gardens were unfortunately closed for the winter. However, there really is a Little Mermaid. When we visited her, she was sitting in the water a short distance away from the shore, watching the ebb and flow of life in Copenhagen.

Like the Melancholy Dane, so went the day we visited Elsinore. It was gray, cold, damp and fascinating. Did Hamlet really roam these dreary halls, reciting his lonely, frightening and rather paranoid thoughts? I chose to think so and still do.

The *pièce de résistance* was sending home two of those puffy, sleep-inducing, down-filled comforters found in our Northern European hotels. I still have them, too. No wonder they are passed down as part of family history. They are!

We left the "set" of Copenhagen and flew to Munich, Germany. From fantasy to reality. So fast, so fast.

Munich

> *At Munich, we sold the Czechs for a few months' grace, but the disgrace will last as long as history.*
>
> –F.L. Lucas

On our way to Munich from Copenhagen, my trusty Michelin Guide told me that Dachau was about ten miles outside the city. We planned to see this still-living Nazi hell on earth ahead of everything else. Munich was a torn-up mess, as if they were remaking everything. Chappell Music had made reservations at the "best hotel" with the words, "We'll pick you up tomorrow for lunch."

We were shown to an old but rather elegant hotel. On my way to check out the rest of the suite, I tripped over some unseen something on the floor and took a header. I tried to get up, but my feet kept hitting something I couldn't see.

"I think it's under the carpet, honey," I said.

Ray pulled that once-fine old Oriental rug back to where I sat on the floor and, unfortunately, I was right.

"What the hell is this?" he asked rhetorically. "At least they could put up a 'Watch Your Step' or something. Better yet, fix the damned thing."

Whatever Munich was "fixing" on the outside had not yet reached our suite. I should have gotten hazard pay.

There was a two-inch-high board in the floor that had risen from the rest. They simply put the carpet over it and left it for their guests to find it, as I had. Ray called to complain, only to hear, "I'm so sorry, Mr. Gilbert, we'll move you to a different suite."

"What about the floor?" Ray demanded.

"Munich suffered a great deal of damage from your Allied bombing raids during the war," he was told. "With the Olympics coming in less than five years, we have a lot of work to do."

Mind you, all of this was said in that well-trained, quietly untroubled manner of a good hotel desk clerk. We were moved to a safer suite.

At seven a.m., I awoke to a giant toothache. Oh my God, it hurt! All we had was aspirin until Ray could wake our Chappell office for a dentist. They gave us an address and directions, and we found our way.

The door to the dental office was in the back of the building. That's when I saw the reality of a Munich still hiding their truth. There was a broken metal stairway, with two of the steps cracked in half. The area in back of the building looked as if it still had severe bomb damage.

The office was on the second floor. I was terrified at what I thought I'd find. When I opened his door, a bigger bomb hit me. The office was immaculate, and I was greeted by a warm, English-speaking nurse. Everything was modern and comforting as the doctor seated me in that chair we all know so well. He spoke wonderful English, knew what to do to fix me up until I got home—and I knew I was safe.

I asked the dentist about Munich and the still broken backs of the city. How did he become a dentist, etc.

"I was never a Nazi, but I was a German soldier," he explained, "captured and sent to Canada until the end of the war. We were encouraged to learn a trade, and I chose dentistry. I was good at it, and my new office is the result of learning instead of fighting and killing."

I enjoyed this man, and when I got home my own dentist complimented him on his work and my luck in finding him.

Dachau

> *ALL THE DACHAUS MUST REMAIN STANDING. THE DACHAUS, THE BELSENS, THE BUCHENWALDS, THE AUSCHWITZES, ALL OF THEM. THEY MUST REMAIN STANDING BECAUSE THEY ARE A MONUMENT TO A MOMENT IN TIME WHEN SOME MEN DECIDED TO TURN THE EARTH INTO A GRAVEYARD.*
>
> —ROD SERLING

The next day was dark, cold and depressing as we made our way to Dachau. This first death camp in the diabolical Nazi scheme to eliminate millions of helpless and innocent human beings was as dark and gray as the day.

The first thing we saw was the barbed wire, high, ugly and loathsome. There was a heavy and tangible sadness, all too real.

We joined a group of three others and began to view what was left of Dachau and what they would allow us to see. The museum of pictures was the most difficult to view. They were so vividly alive and terrifying.

The picture I'll never forget was one of a young boy with arms raised, a yellow Star of David on his sleeve, staring at a helmeted Nazi soldier with a machine gun pointed at him. He had just arrived at Dachau and was so tiny and so alone, standing in front of the horror he would come to know all too well.

There were very few words exchanged that day in Dachau. So much of this man-made hell had been cleaned up, but there were still many places behind heavy, locked doors that the travel guide ignored.

There is an eternal flame burning in a shrine to the thousands buried in Dachau. We stood for a long time, both of us lost in our thoughts of what we had just experienced. Somewhere, the pictures and text of the day American forces liberated Dachau will live forever. Just open the record books. Even the insane stupidity of the Holocaust deniers could not deny the sickening truth before us all.

What made this unholy place even worse was that it was the model for all the other hells that followed, like Auschwitz, Buchenwald and the countless others scattered over Austria, Germany, Poland and the other Nazi-occupied countries.

Along with the millions of Jews annihilated were hundreds of Catholic priests tortured on the experimental tables or exterminated in the gas chambers. There were Protestants, gays and purported spies who also were imprisoned in these camps. The world will never know a complete count of the lives once born to disappear without so much as a trace.

SALZBURG

> *SALZBURG IS A MOUNTAIN TOWN WITH A RUSHING RIVER RUNNING RIGHT THROUGH THE CENTER, EVERYTHING IN THE RAIN VARIOUS SHADES OF GREEN AND BROWN.*
>
> —JONATHAN CARROLL

The next day, we drove through a serenely beautiful, snow-covered Austrian Bavaria to Salzburg, Mozart's home, and the medieval Hohensalzburg Castle. No matter how perfect the day, we still passed a sign with one word: Lodz. It was another Nazi concentration camp.

Salzburg looked like the set of an operetta. We saw Mozart's home. his piano and his life everywhere. We stayed at the Goldener Hirsch Hotel. Small, fabulous food and kind people.

Berchtesgaden and Hitler's Eagle's Nest were about a half hour away, but we found it closed for the winter. However, we did see the SS barracks built underground with tunnels leading to Hitler's home beneath the Nest. That door was locked, too.

Hitler's massive paranoia permeated everything. Simply walking down the narrow flight of stairs to the SS quarters deep below could get you shot from the guns buried in the walls.

As I remember, there were three stops before one reached the bottom. Claustrophobia finally drove me back to the surface and that clean, cold alpine air. The villagers of Berchtesgaden were silent about anything Hitler or the Third Reich, as was Salzburg.

Medieval history is fascinating. One can see centuries of change in one visit. We can see the beginning, as in the castle guarding Salzburg, which was begun in the 10th century and continued its growth until the present, still alive today. We can visit Hohensalzburg Castle and listen to a musical concert filling the air.

As in Shakespeare's *Hamlet*, when the melancholy Dane roamed Elsinore's turrets—danger lurking everywhere—writers have managed to romanticize them. In December of 1967, they were freezing. Thick stone walls, floor-to-ceiling fortresses.

First, they saved their lives, then they figured out how to survive. In Elsinore, gigantic tapestries hung on the bare walls, and the fireplaces helped against the cold. Even the massive amount of clothing worn made sense.

If I were blessed with an extra, more youthful time zone, I'd see the castles wherever I could find one. Whether in a book or in life. they constantly stretch my imagination. Please, don't wake me up!

Vienna

> *Lord, if there is a heartache*
> *Vienna cannot cure, I hope*
> *never to feel it. I came home cured*
> *of everything except Vienna.*
>
> —Scott Jameson

The Imperial Hotel in Vienna was an experience beyond anything I could even imagine.

It was built in 1863 and became one of the palatial homes of the Emperor Franz Joseph and his wife, Empress Elizabeth. It was grandeur beyond description. When you're not ready for such splendor, a good pinch or two finally brought me back to the present while still in the past.

It was beautiful from the outside, but that first step inside took one's breath away.

As we approached the desk, I heard the unmistakable voice of James Mason chatting with the desk clerk. He seemed right at home in this palace as we checked in beside him. Ray was getting a cold or something, so he didn't seem to notice or care about Mr. Mason. Besides, there were certain English actors who always seemed to live a layer above the rest of us.

A gentleman took our bags and our room key, and with his meticulous manners instructed, "Please follow me."

We began to climb a red-carpeted stairway watched over by two gigantic paintings of the Emperor on one side and the Empress on the other. They had been painted by the famous Franz Xaver Winterhalter.

The halls were expansive, as were the very tall doors that seemed to match the ceilings—but the knobs were what I adored. They were much higher than the doorknobs I'd grown up with. I loved feeling smaller than my surroundings, and the Imperial accommodated me at every turn.

Ray had only one day in Vienna before he got sick. We were both very quiet driving from Munich and the memory of Dachau. I believe his flu was a leftover from that horrific experience.

I called the front desk about a doctor, and again, they were more than helpful. Ray was even cared for by the kind and caring help. Night or day, they attended to his needs.

"Sorry, honey," he said, "you'll have to see Vienna on your own until I feel better. Go see your opera tonight. I'll be fine."

The concierge got me a ticket to Franco Zeffirelli's production of *La Bohème*. I bought an English libretto, had coffee during intermission, Vienna-style, and saw snow falling on the stage. It was beautiful. Even more beautiful was walking back to the Imperial through actual huge, soft snowflakes that made Vienna seem ethereal, as if I were walking through a Christmas card.

The next morning, however, I too had Ray's flu. I received the same care that he did. We got to know our caretakers well as they brought soup, medicine, but most of all, themselves. They were the magic cure that got us well in a hurry.

The one thing I just had to see before we left Vienna was the Lipizzaner stallions and their famous Airs Above the Ground.

Our concierge arranged seats for us for the following day. Neither of us was 100%, but it didn't matter. We were in their baroque and beautiful palace with its huge chandeliers hanging over a sand-filled ring.

When the music began and they entered in perfect synchrony, tears welled in my eyes. I gave a silent "Thank you" to the late General George Patton for saving them during WWII.

That day, the Lipizzaners performed their ancient rituals in their own palace with their stunning Austrian crystal chandeliers, of course, and why not?

As we trained to Venice, we spoke of our journey and what we'd seen. So many emotions, such depths and highs we'd never forget. I loved stopping at borders and showing our passports as we crossed from country to country with new languages, food, customs and cultures.

I miss boundaries. They educated me and gave me the opportunity to explore. Without boundaries, whether personal or on a map, we're watching people, laws, customs and cultures disrespected and ultimately changed or lost forever.

I'm so grateful that I can look back, relive and remember before the world became so homogenized that I can hardly recognize my own country.

VENICE

> *How do I describe Venice? Simply put, I can't. The greatest writers in the world have tried but Venice continues to tease us, hiding her "secrets" in plain sight.*
>
> –Janis Paige

We trained to Venice. Ray had never been there, and there was no way I was going to let him miss this treasure. As we left the train, he said, "We need a cab, honey."

"He's coming," I said.

A smiling gentleman with a sign saying "Gilbert, Daniele Hotel" introduced himself. He took our bags and suddenly we were in front of our cab on the Grand Canal. The look on Ray's face was worth the journey.

"Oh, my God," I heard him say. "Oh, my God, this is so beautiful!"

It was December, and everyone told me that Venice would be cold, rainy and unpleasant.

"Venice is beautiful anytime," I replied, "and we may not come this way again."

The Grand Canal lay before us, the lights reflected in the water as gondolas floated by and the nightlife of Venice emerged. Our water taxi let us off at the Daniele Hotel and I heard Ray say, "I don't believe this, this isn't real!"

We spent four or five days there, and the sun shone brightly without a cloud in sight. We visited Lido Isle, San Marcos Square and the Doges Palace. We fed the pigeons as they stood on my head and saw the Bridge of Sighs from a gondola ride.

"What does that mean honey, why 'Sighs'?" Ray asked.

"Because it was the last time the prisoners would ever see Venice again," I replied. "They 'sighed' their goodbye as they crossed it."

Ray always wanted to see Venice again. But once would have to be enough.

Do we choose our fate or does fate choose us? Perhaps a little of both.

ISRAEL

> *THE ONLY THING CHICKEN ABOUT ISRAEL*
> *IS THEIR SOUP.*
>
> –BOB HOPE

Our last stop before London and home was Israel, post-Six Day War. Five months earlier, we would not have been able to witness their tiny, tentative steps toward peace.

"Shalom" was the first word I heard as we boarded our flight. We had made reservations at the King David Hotel in Jerusalem, only to hear the words, "We have no more rooms, but we have you booked in another hotel."

This inconvenience allowed us to observe and be a part of the historic aftermath of the war, which took place five months prior to our arrival.

It was late and dark when we boarded a small bus carrying us to our new quarters. We drove for what seemed to be forever until we heard, "Here we are, The Judea Gardens. Please go sign in."

As we approached a flight of stairs, we passed the tail of an Egyptian fighter plane. A sad remembrance when I saw a row of what looked like Motel 6 rooms. When he opened the door, it was a far cry from the Imperial in Vienna or the other elegant hotels in which we'd stayed. This was closer to my Vaudeville days, so I almost felt at home.

There was a sliding glass door to a tiny balcony that showed absolutely nothing beyond. In the daylight, we saw camels and desert. At least it had a bathroom, bed and chair and was immaculately clean.

"Are you hungry?" a voice from heaven asked.

"Yes, we are," we said.

"I'll be right back with some food for you," the man, Ibrahim, said. It was simple but very tasty.

Ibrahim hovered around us, cleared everything and wished us a very good night.

"I'll be at your service during your stay," he said. "It will be my pleasure."

Here was a young man who lived in the Arab sector and had worked in Jerusalem most of his life.

"Is he for real, honey?" I asked while staring at the closed door. "Can we take him home when we leave?"

"Go to bed," my weary husband said. "We'll talk about it tomorrow when you're sane."

What an education we had that first day in Jerusalem. We hired a driver who spoke English, adored Israel and was an education in himself as he showed us around this ancient city.

No matter your religious beliefs or non-beliefs, this place was a part of us. When we passed Ezekiel's little stone house or walked the Ways of the Cross, my long-ago Sunday School lessons came flooding back and so did the Bible's familiar names and places. We missed nothing that time would allow.

The day we drove to Bethlehem was also quite the trip into the past. Its Byzantine Church of the Nativity was another example of how the ever-changing centuries stayed connected. In 1967, we could see into the past.

We had missed the tour when we saw a young priest coming out of the church. He asked if he could help us. We seemed to be the only visitors around.

"Could we see the inside?" Ray asked.

"You just missed the tour," the priest said, "but I'll be happy to show it to you."

When we were through, he said, "I was on my way to lunch; would you join me?" He took us outside and we settled on the ancient sunlit steps while his wife served us sandwiches and tea. He was Greek Orthodox and explained the religious divisions of this living wonder.

Two hours later, we thanked him and his wife for their hospitality and incredible kindness. The picture of that day, on the steps of the Church of the Nativity reached our core. We were just people at ease with one another, sharing simple truths.

After decades of being closed off to old Jerusalem, the Six Day War had opened the Damascus Gates and we could go inside. I began by trying a small, sweet thing sold from a huge tray held by a woman at the steps of the gate.

"What's wrong with you, Jan?" Ray asked. "Do you want to be sick here, too?"

I ate it anyway.

A few more steps and we were in a twisting, narrow-pathed city resembling a huge marketplace. There were dead chickens hanging in stalls. Every kind of unfamiliar food, clothing, etc. was sold in similar stalls. We saw many Arabs in their native attire and women with their faces covered.

Suddenly, we found ourselves lost and couldn't even ask where we were.

"We're not very smart, honey," Ray observed.

"Where do we go from here?" I asked. "Do I look scared, Pops, because I am."

We simply began walking. Suddenly, I saw some daylight from somewhere. We headed toward it to find a break in the wall, but there was no way out. We could see part of the Tower of David, but that was it.

It was then that a man dressed in a suit said, "You're not safe here."

"We're lost," Ray said. "Can you help us?"

"Follow me and I'll show you out. It's not far."

Ray and I didn't have to speak. We mentally asked the same question: Do we trust him? As we found freedom once more and thanked him profusely, he left us with a warning to be careful and disappeared.

I wanted to see Jericho, where Joshua fought the battle. Ray was not as keen about it as I, but we drove to what seemed to be an Israeli border guard. We crossed a rather small bridge and followed the road to Jericho.

Our poor little rental car would only go so fast, and the scenery was anything but scenic. It was a dry, rocky desert with several hills to match.

"It looks a little like someone forgot to live here," I said.

"I wish this car would go faster," Ray replied. "Something makes me wish we were somewhere else."

"The guard would not have let us go if it was dangerous, honey," I insisted.

Another ten minutes and then we saw what was left of a recent battle. Here was a burned-out tank, spent shells all over both sides of the road, a small bus on its side and a half-burned military vehicle of some kind.

I was looking for a souvenir when I heard Ray yell, "Get the hell in this car, NOW!" Then I heard "ba-ba-boom, ba-ba-boom" from somewhere above me and saw two men on the top throwing grenades at one another.

I woke up when Ray told me to "Move your ass, NOW!" He floored the gas pedal, but it did no good. Thank God we weren't far from the border.

When we finally reached the guard, Ray said, "They're shooting back there."

This tanned and very fit Israeli soldier simply smiled.

"They weren't shooting at you," he assured, "they were firing at the enemy."

"Do they know the difference?" Ray asked.

We had only one day left before London and home when the hotel manager asked to see us.

"We've enjoyed having you in our hotel, Mr. and Mrs. Gilbert. You've been constantly interested in Israel's past, present and future. Our desire for a lasting peace begins tonight, and we invite you to witness the first Arab/Israeli meeting in a social setting."

Of course, we said yes.

The dinner was held in an unadorned meeting room. There was a long table set for twenty people, including us. The mayors sat at the ends of the table. The Arabs sat on one side, the Israelis on the other.

There was a subtle, sometimes awkward tension when it began. There were both Arab and Israeli entertainers, genuine belly dancers, food (both

Arabic and Israeli) and a spreading warmth through the room. Both sides were speaking to one another, and we became a part of this amazing evening.

A man rose, the room came to attention and he explained the reason for this evening. He introduced his Arabic counterpart, guests and even us. Everyone was greeted with applause. Then he asked us to stand and shake the hand of the person sitting across on the other side.

Many people had tears in their eyes, including me. We then raised our glasses to "peace in our time." After expressing our gratitude for this gift to us, we excused ourselves to catch a very early flight to London.

Saying farewell to Ibrahim was the most difficult farewell of all.

"I'll never forget you," he said. "I shall miss you."

This smiling young man not only attended to our every need but added to our education as well. He was adorable!

LONDON

IT IS NOT THE WALLS THAT MAKE THE CITY, BUT THE PEOPLE WHO LIVE WITHIN THEM. THE WALLS OF LONDON MAY BE BATTERED, BUT THE SPIRIT OF THE LONDONER STANDS RESOLUTE AND UNDISMAYED.

—GEORGE VI

As we exited El Al Airlines at Heathrow Airport, there it was once more. "Shalom! Shalom! Come see us soon, again. Shalom!"

Chappell Music was a London-based company, and they made reservations at Hotel Claridge. From our ever-eventful journeys, Claridge's and London proved to be just what we needed. Its quiet elegance and staff to match helped us to finally take a deep breath and slow down—that is, except for a meeting at Chappell, we had three days before we flew home.

There were several messages for us, mine from my agent.

"Where are you, Jan?" one of them asked. "They want you to replace Angela Lansbury in *Mame*. Please call us."

Am I never going to touch down? I wondered. We made a date to meet everyone in New York before we returned to California.

Our day in London was precious. We wanted to bring home some gifts for family and friends, so we headed to Harrod's, a travel experience in itself. Back then, we could still fly with items now banned on today's airlines, so we headed for the lower floor.

Like wide-eyed kids in a candy store, we searched. Food temptations were everywhere. There was absolutely nothing one could want that could not be found at Harrod's in 1967.

We shopped and then sat at the marble counter and had lunch. Civility and the softly modulated voices of the English joined our day. We rode a double-decker bus, had tea at the Connaught Hotel and watched London go by at one of their tall, curved windows.

It was a cold, crisp December day, but a fragile winter sun shone through. There was no "foggy day in London Town" for us.

The next time I saw London was in 2005. The 2001 terrorist attack on New York City changed everyone's world forever. It left a giant scar on the hearts of Americans, but the world itself became targets and London was no exception. The great writer Alvin Toffler wrote of "future shock." I experienced just that when I again saw London.

Some two months earlier, London had suffered one of its deadly and cowardly suicide bomber attacks on the subway and also a double-decker bus. Many people had died, and when we arrived there were still boarded-up spots left unrepaired.

When we boarded a double-decker, you could no longer speak to the friendly driver. He was harried, seated behind a thick plastic wall, and you shoved your fare through a tiny slit in the bottom. You could not even get your hand through.

There was no friendly "Good day," either. There was, in fact, no talking at all. He couldn't hear me, and I couldn't hear him.

To me, London had turned that shade of gray I saw in East Berlin. It seems to be the color of the loss of freedom. It was all around us.

When we got off at Harrod's for lunch, there was an armed guard at every landing and constant questions from the polite men guarding us. My heart hurt as I missed their former smiles.

The main purpose of the trip to London was to see an ailing friend of my husband. I simply tagged along. He lived close to Windsor Castle, and of course we couldn't leave without seeing it.

We parked at the bottom toward the back of the castle and walked a curving, steep hill to the top to gasp at its monolithic size. The Queen was not in residence at the time, but all of the English ghosts certainly were. It was so massive that it dwarfed everything around it.

The Crown Jewels are housed there, but today you have to get in line and step on a slow-moving treadmill that takes you by the jewels, crowns, tiaras and rings. They are breathtaking—but no stopping for details. There are too many genuine worries about theft and terrorism today.

To a terrorist, nothing seems sacred except death.

I'm deeply grateful for history, good and bad. My educators knew the absolute importance of history for the sake of a better future. I deeply resent being robbed of the truth of history while left with the ever-growing need to sterilize it.

I saw this in London, Berlin, Munich and see it now here in America. Members of this generation called Millennials demand that they feel no pain, not even hurt feelings.

What about mine, kids?

When you bullhorn our voices of rightful protest, we are silenced by your ignorance and disrespect of the First Amendment. Shame on ye of so little faith in your own ideology. If it was inspiring you, you wouldn't need stuffed animals, puppy videos and Playdough to quiet you.

You can't erase our terrible Civil War by destroying the statues of the messengers who fought it. It's history, it happened, and you can't will it out of existence or make it disappear just because it makes you feel uncomfortable.

To the empty choices of a generation that can't and won't feel pain, here is a news flash: History is filled with pain. It's also filled with growth, victories, inventions, ideas, etc. For God's sake, leave history to those who inherited it. If you can't teach the truth, at least take a long hard look at what your lies produce: Just more lies!

"Mame"

> *Your job, sweetheart, is to put*
> *the goosebumps on my arm,*
> *not on yours.*
>
> –Ray Gilbert

After we checked into our hotel, I called my agent.

"Where were you, Jan, where did you go? We just missed you a couple of times, but you were gone again."

"It's a long, eventful story," I said, "too long for today. Tell me about *Mame*."

"We have a meeting tomorrow at the Winter Garden Theatre. They've arranged seats for you to see the performance tomorrow night."

"I can't wait, Eric," I said excitedly.

"Neither can they, Jan," he said.

I met the producers, director, writers, choreographer, costumer and stage manager. Everyone was lovely to me. What I didn't know at the time was that the great Angela Lansbury herself had recommended me to replace her in the show. Thank you, dear lady.

It isn't often one sees a perfect show, but *Mame* was one of these rarities. It simply had everything an audience could ask for, and I felt so lucky to know Angie.

I'd never replaced anyone before, so I wasn't ready for the reactions of a few of Angie's loyalists. I understood it. Loyalty was a quality that I deeply admired, but I was struggling with my own adjustments as well. After all, everything was new to me, but I was the only thing new to them.

The late, great choreographer Onna White became a lifelong friend while she was whipping me into the best shape of my life. I'd always worked out, danced and taken care of myself, but until I met Onna, I didn't know how tough getting ready could be.

She was a loving, generous drill sergeant, constantly pushing me to be ready for opening night. I've never been readier, except for those ever-present butterflies. I mean, look at whose shoes I was trying to fill.

Angela was the first one to tell me to get a lot of rest.

"This is a physically taxing show, Janis," she warned.

She was right, but it was worth every moment.

Certainly, last but not least, was the support and help I got from the producers, Jimmy Carr and John Bowab.

In-between—if there was an in-between—I had twenty-three costume changes and fittings for my new wardrobe. Between learning the dances and choreographing the twenty-three costumes, it took three people to help me. I was instructed to stand perfectly still and not get in the way.

From a complete costume change, including jewelry, came a dance. I also learned my lines, my songs, my blocking and made it through dress rehearsal. Whew!

Both Angela and the original Vera, Bea Arthur, were taller than I. When they cast my Vera, we were about the same height. Unfortunately, she pulled a muscle a few weeks after we opened and had to leave the show. Bea had left with Angela and Jane Connell (Agnes Gooch) for a limited production of *Mame* in Los Angeles.

When Bea left, the tall, elegant and wonderful Anne Francine took her place. She was, however, quite tall, and I began having a problem matching her stride. I was also intimidated by her very presence.

One night after the show, she asked rather impatiently, "Why can't you keep up with me in (the number) 'Bosom Buddies'?"

Here it was. I took a deep breath and replied, "You're taller than I am, Annie. The number was choreographed for Angela and now for you. My original Vera and I were the same height. It never occurred to me that it would be difficult."

Anne stared at me, her eyes got big and then I heard, "Oh, good Lord, Janis, that never occurred to me. I'm so sorry."

As I stood there, the rather imposing Anne seemed to disappear, replaced by a pussycat named Annie. I adored her, and we remained friends until she left us far too many years ago.

Fitting in while maintaining my own persona proved to be a quiet but huge growth spurt for me. Mame Dennis and I grew together, and she was a joy to discover each and every show.

The only problem I was still having was with a couple of my songs and the discomfort I felt. I simply could not seem to speak up for myself and ask for help or change. One night after the bows, Helen Gallagher (my Gooch) stopped by. She was very no-nonsense, exactly what I needed.

"I want to talk to you about the struggle you're having with some of the music," Helen said just that simply. "You're going to develop vocal problems. I teach singing, Jan, and I know. There is someone I want you to see. How about tomorrow? I'll meet you there."

Her honesty and generosity floored me. She was right. We met the next day at the beautiful, old Ansonia. Seeing an apartment at the Ansonia was an experience in itself, but Helen's recommendation was a truly kind, caring man filled with the assurance I so sorely needed.

"This won't take long, Janis," he said. "If you have time, we can go to work now." I did, and steadily developed not only a healthier voice but a lasting joy as well.

A few months into my run, Angela was offered a new musical called *Dear World*. Don Pippin, the conductor of *Mame*, left with Angela and I got a new one.

His name was Shep Coleman. His first words to me were the missing pieces to my performance: "What can I do for you, Janis? Do you want to change anything?"

"Oh gosh, Shep, I'd love to do 'If He Walked into My Life' a little differently."

"Tell me what you want," he replied, "and we'll do it at orchestra rehearsal. I told him what I wanted and what I worried about.

"You take care of the stage, Janis, and leave the orchestra to me."

I did, and Shep was true to his word. He gave me the freedom to grow in the role and do justice to Jerry Herman's perfect score.

When Don Pippin came back to see the show, he told me, "I loved the show, Janis, and I have to admit I felt some jealousy at how you and Shep worked together. I wished that I had been conducting."

A generous comment by a superb conductor and musician.

About six months after I left the show, John Bowab called me about a summer tour of *Mame*. I'd have my own company and play the huge tents and theaters open for the summer.

As usual, John mounted a wonderful cast to support me and we knew nothing but success. We broke a big star's record, and in Niagara Falls we followed the great Jack "Forever 39" Benny.

I was standing backstage on Jack's closing night when I saw him running around, looking for things he needed. He had his violin and bow in one hand, going through his pockets with his other, tracing and re-tracing his steps, still looking and moving toward the wings.

"Can I help, Jack?" someone asked.

"No, thanks," he said. "When Mary watches me running around like this, she says, 'Why don't you stick a broom up your ass and sweep the floor while you're at it?'"

With that, he was onstage, leaving us with a soul-satisfying belly laugh. There was the one and only Jack Benny.

Above: *In the film* Please Don't Eat the Daisies *with the great David Niven (1960).*

Below: *With Bob Hope and my husband (Don Porter) in* Bachelor in Paradise *(1961).*
Inset: *A publicity photo for* Bachelor in Paradise.

Above: *With Bob and Lana Turner, my costars in* Bachelor in Paradise. *Bob was a prince and Lana a great actress and lovely human being.*

Left: *My unforgettable wedding day with Ray (1962) as covered in the newspaper in Nice, France, where we were wed.*

Above: *With Ray Gilbert just days (hours?) before he became my husband, in my short-term apartment overlooking the sunlit Mediterranean in Nice, France. What a glorious time it was.*

Right: *From an interview shoot for* TV Guide *in the 1960s.*

Left:
At Checkpoint Charlie with Ray during our European honeymoon in 1962, in the area separating East from West Berlin in Germany. The Berlin Wall had been up for less than a year at the time.

Right:
A very energetic me performs at Camp Casey in South Korea in front of our American troops in 1962. Look at all of those guys sitting in the mud.

Above: *With Robert Stack in the feature* The Caretakers, *from 1963. It was an underappreciated film that really allowed me to stretch as a dramatic performer, portraying a patient in a mental institution.*

Right: *Craig Stevens, me, Laurence Naismith and writer Meredith Willson in the world premiere 1963 Broadway production* Here's Love. *It didn't go as well as I would have liked.*

Left:
With Craig Stevens in Here's Love.

Below:
Christmas 1963. It was a Saturday night. Former President Harry Truman and future President Richard Nixon joined the cast of Here's Love *(Laurence Naismith, Craig Stevens and me). Talk about a thrill. However, it was clear that Truman didn't much like Nixon.*

Right:
In Thailand with one of Bob Hope's shows and a group of pilots. Bob loved pilots and would do anything for them.

Below:
Performing for the soldiers at the Bien Hoa Airbase outside of Saigon, Vietnam, with the Bob Hope troupe in 1964.

Above left: *On one of the Bob Hope specials in the Sixties, Bob plays a beatnik while I struggle to keep a straight face. It got a roar from the audience.*

Above right: *With the great Henry Fonda in a scene from the 1967 western feature* Welcome to Hard Times.

Below left: *Fooling around on the set of* Welcome to Hard Times *with the magnificent Keenan Wynn. Keenan was such a generous actor.*

Below right: *With the great Red Skelton doing a skit where I struggled to keep my poker face.*

Left:
Starring as Mame in the play of the same name on Broadway.

Below:
Performing the opening number in Mame, *"It's Today."*

Section VI
The 1970s

South Africa

MY DREAM NEVER DIED. IT JUST PATIENTLY WAITED
FOR THE OPPORTUNITY TO COME TRUE.

−Janis Paige

When I was six years old, my grandfather gave my sister and me a lighted globe of the world. I've often wondered if he knew what a difference that gift made in my young life. I was simply fascinated, and my love of maps, atlases and the world began there and never left me.

As I stared at this incredible gift, my finger found the Cape of Good Hope at the bottom of the world in Africa.

"Why don't people fall off down there, Grandpa?"

He explained gravity as best he could, while I kept up my six-year-old stream of questions.

"I'm going to go there one day," I decided.

"It's a very long way, honey, I don't know how you'd make it," he replied.

"I'm going to go, Grandpa, you'll see. I'm going to go!"

I was one determined little girl.

It was one day in June, 1971 when the phone rang. It was Eric, my agent, calling from New York City.

"Hi Jan," he said, "how would you like to be in the first international company of *Applause* in South Africa?"

I fell silent.

"Jan, are you still there? Where'd you go?"

"To South Africa," I said. "I'm still here, Eric. Tell me about *Applause*."

I could hardly breathe.

"An organization called Johannesburg Opera and Dramatic Society is producing the show, and they want you to star in it. You're the only one they asked for."

"I don't have to think about it, Eric, the answer is yes! My passion for South Africa began when I was six years old, so you can understand what this offer means to me. Please don't lose this over some technicality that I can live without."

Eric assured me that he wouldn't, while adding, "But this is South Africa, I want you safe. I'm excited for you, Jan. I'll get back to you with the deal. It's difficult to get into South Africa and they're tough on visas, so I'll get busy on that, too."

As calm as I was with Eric, inside I was the opposite. There was disbelief mixed with the sheer wonder of life's surprises. I knew a little something about their politics, most of it bad, but I had also learned to be a good voyager by first keeping my mouth shut against what I neither knew nor with what I might disagree.

I was, after all, a guest in this foreign land, and until I had further education, I was not about to expound on bits and pieces gleaned from bits and pieces. Whatever the unknowns, and there were many, they could never have kept me away from what was a life-changing experience. God, fate and karma all smiled on me that day, and I was grateful enough not to ask, "Why me?"

"Oh, please, honey, come home early so that I can tell you what happened today," I said on the phone to my husband.

I wanted to call the world and yet keep everything a secret. "Don't count your chickens before they hatch" was an old saying from my childhood that tried to scratch its way into my brain at the same time I wanted to yell the news from my rooftop.

Playing the waiting game in the Seventies was just that. There were no cell phones, laptops, email, texting, etc. We waited for something we now call snail mail.

I was already making my lists when my husband came home.

"Hi, sweetheart, what's new?'

'I have a cold bottle of champagne in the fridge. Would you like some?"

Without a beat, he repeated, "Hi, sweetheart, what's new? And yes, I'd love a glass of champagne."

I brought out the bottle and two of my highly prized Baccarat flutes.

"This champagne either means something very good or something very bad," Ray observed. "Which is it?"

"I hope you'll think it's good, honey," I said. "Cheers."

I began to relate my incredible day. Ray listened intently until I finally said, "What do you think about it?"

"Well, I'll never keep you from going, honey. I know what this trip means to you. I miss you already and I'll worry about you, but this kind of chance only comes around once, so you take it."

I started to cry and said, "I worry about you being all right without me. I don't do this easily, believe me. I feel guilty and excited and scared all at once. The contract is for three months. We rehearse and open in Johannesburg for a month, then go to Cape Town for a month and finish with a month in Durban. I'll be home the end of December."

"Jody and I will be fine," Ray assured me. "I don't want you to worry about us. I love you and mazel tov! Now, I just had an idea. Would you leave a week early and do some work for me in Rio? It will save me a trip."

"Of course I will, honey," I replied. "When I hear from Eric, I'll get the travel schedule and we'll figure it out. I don't know how to thank you for always understanding and being so unselfish."

"When we married, I knew about your career. The last thing I would do is to take it away from you. Your talent is part of you. I would never interfere with that. That's not up to me."

The following days and weeks flew by as the deal was sealed and contracts were signed. There was no way I could have known what lay ahead of me. Unfortunately, I would find out too late that contracts meant nothing to Bill Trollip and JODS.

Eric wanted me paid in America in dollars and not in the South African tender called the rand. My salary would be paid in three increments: one third at the end of my first month in Johannesburg and the subsequent two-thirds to follow.

When I look back, we should have requested their rand as payment. At least I would have known that I wasn't being paid.

My leaving time was finally near. The only thing I did not have was my visa. We were in the process of getting it in Los Angeles when Eric said that Bill Trollip would have it waiting for me at the airport when I arrived. Mr. Trollip said that he could "pull strings" there and save us the trouble and time.

"I'd sure rather have it in my hand, Eric," I said warily.

"Don't worry, Jan," he said. "I've checked and double-checked, and everything seems fine. Now, have a great trip and don't worry about anything. I'm a phone call away."

"And half a world," I interrupted.

If I had any qualms about this trip, they were momentary at best, but still present. Not having my visa in my hand and the promised schedule troubled me, but we rationalized it away with, "They've been vetted and are, for all intents and purposes, reliable."

We had no reason to mistrust Mr. Trollip when he told us not to worry. South Africa and the Cape of Good Hope won out over my fears. In truth, deep inside somewhere, I never doubted that I was destined to go on this journey.

Sometime in July, I received my copy of the *Applause* script and the musical score. By the time I was ready to leave, I knew my lines, the show and all of the songs. It not only saved time but gave me a certain confidence when meeting a new cast.

It was a wonderful score and book. After all, the show was based on one of Bette Davis' most famous films, *All About Eve*.

Ray and our little Miniature Schnauzer, Jody, drove me to the airport and Varig Airlines. My eyes were red from the intermittent crying I'd done at the thought of leaving them, my home, my horses and my responsibilities.

Wherever I've gone, the unspoken need for stability always seemed to firmly and deeply plant my lower half wherever I was, while the upper half held my wings. How could I be ready to stay and ready to fly at the same time?

Ambivalence was always painful while I paid my dues with the ever-present guilt and insecurities, mixed in with the sheer joy and excitement of a new nest, albeit temporary. It's so different now, I thought.

Thanks to Ray, I can fly and be rooted too, all at the same time. He made this possible for me.

Varig Airlines would take me to Rio de Janeiro, the first leg of this very long-awaited miracle.

"You're ready for this, honey?" my husband asked. "Don't be afraid of anyone or anything."

"That's easy for you to say," I blubbered. "You're never afraid."

"Remember that I love you, and won't let anything happen to you," Ray assured me. "Now go, honey, and knock 'em dead! Call me when you get to Rio."

With that, one more hug and the doors closed against me changing my mind.

We had lived in Rio three times when Ray was writing with Antonio Carlos Jobim and our other Brazilian writers. I always seemed to forget that at a certain point in the flight, I would no longer see the Big Dipper or the familiar constellations in the Northern Hemisphere. I always flew at night, and like every other time, I looked for the Dipper—but it was gone.

My earlier visit to the Hayden Planetarium in New York City had prepared me well, and I'll never forget finding Pegasus and the Southern Cross for the first time. We were now on our way to a different part of our amazing and ever-gifting planet.

Seeing that strange new sky always made me homesick. I was too excited to sleep and, as always, when Corcovado came into view, our pilot's Brazilian pride inspired him to circle this astounding sight for us to see and remember always.

I took care of business for Ray and the writers, saw friends and seemingly, in the blink of an eye, the week was gone, and the beginning was beginning.

The South African Airlines flight was to leave Rio at eleven p.m. There had been a couple of hijackings in the world, and caution was the order of the day. The women and men were separated into different rooms and, for the first time, I was patted down.

To say it was creepy was an understatement. The no-nonsense attitude of the woman performing her duty on me was nonverbal. I spoke a pretty good Portuguese. But without a word, she took away my manicure scissors and my nail file. They were thrown into a large container nearby, gone forever.

Jets had not yet reached South Africa. The airports were still too small to handle them, so we were on the old reliable four-engine prop plane. It was to be a very long flight, so every spare inch of space was occupied.

I was reminded of my three flights with Bob Hope on his USO shows for the troops overseas. The only difference was that there was no Bob, no familiar faces and a fascinating new dialect.

The stewardess got me settled in and brought me a glass of champagne. So far, I was doing fine, watching the passengers go by and indulging in the sheer excitement of where I was and where I was going.

I was seated on the aisle, but the window seat beside me remained empty. We were fastening our seat belts when a very large man got on and proceeded to put his small bag in the overhead bin above me. He was wearing a suit that seemed much too small for a man who could only be described as muscular.

The man politely excused himself as he struggled past me and sank into his seat. No words were exchanged as I said to myself, *This poor man looks so uncomfortable.*

He was trying to straighten his jacket when he reached around to untwist it, and I saw the very large gun holstered under his arm. He quickly covered it with his coat and began to fasten his seat belt.

My heart stopped. Were we being hijacked? I looked for a stewardess, and when she reached me, I grabbed her hand, pulling her toward me so that I could whisper.

"The man sitting next to me is wearing a gun. How did he get on the plane?"

"Oh, Miss Paige, no need to worry. Since the hijackings, we have been carrying air marshals for everyone's protection. You're quite safe where you are."

I thanked her, feeling slightly foolish but relieved. Sort of.

They served us a small meal, but my seatmate never ate or slept. He never loosened his tie, either, and when I finally introduced myself, he nodded politely. Except for the few times he went to the lavatory, his quiet "Excuse me, please" were the only words he spoke to me. He was the epitome of all-business.

I don't remember how long I slept, but I woke to the sun trying to break through the tiny slit in the still-closed curtain at the window. My favorite smell of fresh coffee joined the sun—and I was up.

"Are you ready for breakfast, Miss Paige?" the stewardess asked in her sunny dialect.

"I'm starved," I said. "Give me ten minutes and I'll be ready."

When I looked in the mirror in the lavatory, I couldn't believe how rested I looked. It's magic already, I thought. As I sat back down, coffee and breakfast were accompanied by the rolling waves of excitement at finally getting closer to the Cape of Good Hope.

I wrote Ray a long letter about Rio, the man with the gun and the present time over the Atlantic Ocean. I wrote him at least three times a week, keeping up a running narrative of everything so that he could, in a way, share it with me.

Everything was done in longhand, but unlike the coded messaging of today, I wrote in detail. The stationery was the thin "air mail" paper, so that several pages would not be so costly in the postage department. Those letters still lay in my file cabinet. Ray kept them all.

The pilot's voice came through my reverie with that vocal sound I can recognize and remember today.

"If you look to the right of the aircraft," he said, "you'll see the red soil of West Africa."

There it stretched in front of me. I would come to be very familiar with the red dirt of South Africa and its red rivers as well.

People will often say that there is no difference between the South African dialect and the one spoken by the Australians. Yet I found a vast difference and have never been fooled. I'm no smarter than anyone else. I've just been blessed with an insatiable curiosity coupled with the great good fortune of having lived and worked in both places.

Lunch was finished, and I must have checked and double-checked everything I had to have ready when we landed. The Atlantic Ocean was gone when I heard the pilot's announcement, "Please fasten your seat belts, we are approaching Johannesburg and we'll be on the ground in fifteen minutes."

Tears welled as I suddenly felt so far away from everyone and everything I knew.

When the wheels touched down, I did my usual *salaam* to the pilots and crew by applauding. I learned that with my first Bob Hope tour, and

I still do it every time I fly. I learned: Always say "Thank you," ladies and gentlemen, especially when it's for your life.

It was August 21, 1971. This journey began when I was six. *I'll be all right*, I thought. *I'm older now and wiser. I'll be okay.* I repeated this as I tried to quiet those all-too-familiar butterflies.

"I made it, Grandpa!" I whispered. "I'm in South Africa, and the Cape of Good Hope is not far away. I told you I'd make it."

"Welcome to Johannesburg. It's been a pleasure to serve you," the stewardess said over the intercom. "Please check your belongings and have a lovely stay."

I had finally planted myself on South African soil, and as I reached the bottom of the stairs, I stepped aside and took three or four very deep breaths of South African air. Then I entered a rather small room with a railing all around it. Except for the deplaning passengers, everyone else was on the other side of that railing.

I stood for about ten minutes when it occurred to me to ask if someone was picking me up.

"Have you cleared customs yet, Miss Paige?" the man in the customs line asked. "Do you have your visa?"

I reiterated what I'd been told, that it would be waiting for me when I arrived.

"I'm sorry, Miss Paige, there's nothing here yet."

To say that I was uneasy is an understatement. I kept looking around, but no one came forward.

Another ten or more minutes went by and suddenly someone said, "Mr. Trollip is waiting for you. He's right over there." When I looked, I saw a man wearing very dark glasses, a dark suit and a hat. This someone had been standing in the same spot, unmoving and nonverbal, while I sweated through my introduction to South Africa, alone.

I didn't want to think too much, so I walked over to him and introduced myself.

"I know who you are, Miss Paige," he said.

But I sure don't know you, Mr. Trollip, I thought.

The words were on the tip of my tongue and I felt the most intimidating combination of fear and anger. You were there when I came into the room, and yet you let me wonder and worry with my excitement turning into fear.

Instead, I asked, "Mr. Trollip, are you aware that I have no visa? You assured my agent that it would be waiting for me upon my arrival. I've come a long way, had a long flight and would appreciate some information."

"I'm afraid it'll be another half hour before it gets here," he replied, "so we'll have to wait."

If my husband were here, you'd be on the floor, I thought, *but he's not here so be careful, Jan, you don't know the script yet.*

I sat quietly until the visa arrived and my bags and I were in the car to my hotel. If Mr. Trollip was an example of a South African citizen, no wonder the stories were so critical and unkind about his country.

It was about seven p.m. when we reached the hotel. I had a suite in what seemed to be a rather old hotel, but nice. At that point, I was too tired to care about anything except a shower, a bite to eat and sleep.

When I asked Mr. Trollip about my schedule, his answer was, "You'll have it tomorrow." When he left me in the lobby, he bade me goodnight with, "Your rehearsal starts tomorrow at ten a.m. A car will pick you up at nine-thirty."

Somehow, I knew not to protest anything at that point. "Jet lag, don't hit me now!" I begged. I called Ray, told him I had to sleep fast and then I hit the bed.

When the operator woke me at seven a.m., I was still in exactly the same position as when I went to sleep the night before. I ordered coffee and Danish, got dressed in my rehearsal clothes and, just before I closed the door, I saw my baseball cap with the American flag on the front. I shoved it on my head and off I went.

A good night's sleep and my cap that said, "Don't push me around, I'm an American and we don't like it" gave me a shot of courage.

When I met my escort to the rehearsal hall, I found him to be the opposite of Mr. Trollip. As he introduced himself, he said, "We're so thrilled to have you In South Africa and to be with you in *Applause*." Things were definitely looking up. I thanked him for his delightful welcome, and off we went.

They drive on the wrong side of the road in South Africa—or at least a different side—and as I constantly applied my imaginary brakes, I wondered how I was going to learn to drive without killing some unsuspecting citizen.

I did drive and managed to stay out of trouble, but every time I had to make a turn, my heart was in my throat. I'd always have to slow down to re-think how it's done when the cacophony of impatient horns would push me through.

The familiar first-day jitters of a new show, new players, and old tried-and-true insecurities were now finding their place alongside a new, complicated and rather mysterious country. I was feeling every inch of my responsibility to this long-awaited chapter in my life, but I needn't have worried about the company of *Applause*.

When I opened the door, I was greeted by a huge wave of warmth and a standing ovation. Tears welled in my eyes at their reception. I thanked them and proceeded to make my way to each and every one, asking their names.

To a person, I carried the same excitement I'd had at the prospect of working together. I felt completely supported and at one with the cast. Sometime, somewhere, in my many lives, I had been here before. Nothing seemed terribly unfamiliar except for driving on the wrong side of the road.

Believe me, I would have remembered that.

There was exceptional talent in the show, but I knew little about the cast. We in America were virtually unaware of the extraordinary creativity alive and well in South Africa. During my stay, I saw some marvelous performances. When I met the actors, I told them how much America was missing by not having the opportunity to share their acting gifts.

When Mr. Trollip and his black glasses arrived, he approached me with a woman he called Pat Bray. Oh, he did ask me if I had slept well, and I assured him that I had.

"Mrs. Bray will handle your press interviews, wardrobe fittings, hair and such," he said.

I turned to Mrs. Bray and again asked for a schedule.

"I like to know things ahead of time so that I can be prepared. I'm a stranger here, and a bit of history on the interviewer would also be helpful."

"I have your rehearsal schedule with me, but the press will have to wait," she said.

I thanked her and did not pursue the press statement.

As I watched them leave, I felt the same rigid, impenetrable persona that I had met on my arrival at the airport. Everyone in the show was a South African, and yet Bill Trollip and Pat Bray were the polar opposite of the warm and charming company of *Applause*.

When they left, we went to work. Our director Otto Pirchner was the first to warn me of the differences.

The first day of rehearsal is always filled with the emotions that accompany unfamiliarity. Here I was, meeting a new culture. But new culture or not, getting to know one another always came first. A sense of humor about yourself was also a great ice-breaker.

The typical South African citizen was soft-spoken, with a kind of gentility often found in the English. I made sure to know everyone's name and a little something about them. Hopefully, it helped to get us through those shaky first-day nerves.

Outside of the blocking and direction, we were way ahead of schedule on our first day. Now it was just about working together and getting comfortable. They were all hard workers, very talented and professional. One of the dearest things ever said to me came from Sheila Holliday, my pal in the show.

We had stopped for a break and I flopped down on a couch nearby. Sheila came over and sat down beside me. She took my hand and said, "I want you to know that we loved you the moment you came into the rehearsal hall, wearing your little Yankee Doodle cap with the American flag on it."

I teared up as I told her how much that meant to me.

"I was so nervous that day, and I'm a long, long way from home. I guess that cap was my security blanket. From now on, it's my Yankee Doodle, Sheila Holliday cap."

"I wish your husband was here with you," she added.

"Oh, Sheila, this is a journey I have to take alone," I insisted. "South Africa and I have been joined together since I was six years old, and this opportunity is no accident.

"Over a cup of tea, I'll tell you the saga of why I feel so deeply about this time in my life. I know I have obstacle courses ahead of me, and Ray would always try to protect me. Someday we'll make this trip together, but for now, there are lessons to learn and wisdom to gather."

I continued to Sheila, "I've already had to test my patience for what I consider unnecessary and strange behavior from Bill and Pat. I'm the only one Bill wanted for the show, but I'd never know it from their attitude."

Our break was over, and when we stood up, we silently gave each other a hug. Sometimes, that's all we need, a quiet hug. As we went back to work, I told Sheila how thrilled I was with our company,

When we finished our first day, Otto said, "I need to speak with you, Janis. Where can we go to talk?"

There it was again, that sense of urgency and not-so-subtle mystery.

"Let's go back to my hotel," I offered. "We can relax and have some privacy there."

I laughed and made some remark about feeling paranoid too early. His expression told me that I wasn't far from the truth.

When we sat down, I asked if we were being bugged. He laughed and said he didn't think so, but there were difficulties I needed to know about.

"I got here three weeks prior to your arrival," Otto said. "I wanted to work with the dancers and get what I could on its feet so that we could concentrate on the rest of the show."

"You did a wonderful job, Otto. I'm so pleased with everything."

He thanked me and proceeded to tell me of the problems he'd had in dealing with Bill and Pat Bray.

"I've tried to put my finger on it, Janis, but it's not easy."

"What is it you feel, Otto?" I asked.

"Maybe I'm dealing with a cultural thing, but they seem to make problems where there are none. They've constantly questioned me even during my rehearsal time with the dancers. I've had to stand my ground more than once when it just wasn't necessary. This may not happen to you, but I want you ready for what is so different from how we work in America."

I began to tell Otto about my airport and visa mess when I arrived.

"I thought I was going slightly crazy, Otto. Frankly, I've never met a stranger man in my life, and then I met his counterpart, Pat Bray. She finally gave me my rehearsal schedule today when my agent, Eric, had asked for it countless times.

"It was the same with my visa," I continued. "We were in the process of getting it in America when Bill Trollip called to say that he was getting it and it would be with him. Not only did he keep me waiting and wondering where he was; he didn't have my visa and I had to wait again. Until now, I was feeling pretty lonely in my impressions about Trollip and company. I hate this kind of crap, Otto, but I can hear my husband saying, 'Don't buy trouble, honey, wait until it finds you.'"

I expressed to Otto how much I loved the show and how wonderful the company was.

"Maybe this is nothing more than control by intimidation," I surmised, "and it's stupid. Trollip has tried it with both of us now, and what's the point? Our job is to get this show ready for opening night. I've been so excited about this project, and we can't let them get in the way of why we're here. We'll have to be our own support now."

So, the work began. Remember, this was 1971 in a nation with a government controlled by apartheid. There were no blacks allowed onstage or in the theater, except for the poorest of the poor black crew. They set up and moved the scenery but slept on bare cement floors.

No black people were permitted in the audience, either. When I told the stage manager that I had the same lovable, loyal and expert black woman of the theatre working with me in three of my Broadway shows and only lost her when she retired, his answer was curt and positive: "But not here, Miss Paige. Not here."

That subtle wall of fear was evident once again. The root word in Afrikaans, the language of the ruling force, was "apart." Black people could not vote, marry outside their race or own property. Barely ten years prior to my arrival, the government removed them from their homes and forced them to live in townships like Soweto, outside of Johannesburg.

No matter what color you were, speech was guarded, and any political thoughts in disagreement with the government were repressed for fear of jail or, far worse, death.

Every day, I thanked God for America's growth and constant battle to make us better as citizens and as a country. We had our Constitution and our Bill of Rights, but most of all, we had free speech. There was none of that here.

I'd been told that Bill Trollip's father was a member of the South African Parliament. As my grandmother used to say, "The fruit doesn't fall far from the tree, sweetheart." No book would have taught me what I was living through.

South Africa became a daily history lesson. I don't have the time or space to relate it here, but to be there in 1971 was more of my great good fortune because there was a sea change brewing and it was palpable.

Tony Farmer, our set designer and someone who became a friend, asked me if I knew who Athol Fugard was.

"He's a playwright from Cape Town, isn't he?" I replied.

"How would you like to see him in person?" he asked.

"Are you serious, Tony? Where? When? I'd be thrilled beyond words."

"There's a catch," he cautioned, "and I'd be unfair if I didn't warn you."

"I take it the operative word is 'warn,' yes?"

"He's written a new play called, *People Are Living Here*. He and his wife are performing it tomorrow night outside of Joberg. Believe me, it's nothing fancy. It's a small, outdoor arena in the round. Very primitive, dirt stage and wooden bleachers."

"Sounds perfect to me, Tony," I assured him with a laugh, "but why are you warning me?"

"As you know by now," he said, "whites are part of the segregation of South Africa, but this audience will be a mixed crowd. We could be arrested."

"For going to the theater?" I asked, incredulous. "Well, maybe it's time I find out what it means to be an American."

Needless to say, I, along with the mixed crowd of Fugard admirers, were not arrested. Instead, we watched two very talented actors, including his wife in bare, big-bunioned feet on that rough dirt stage, involve and move us with their creativity.

Many years later, I saw this play again in a New York theater. It had sets, a proper stage, a packed house and great reviews. Everything it so richly deserved. As I watched, I still saw that vast, star-filled African sky with the Southern Cross overhead and the excitement interspersed with the omnipresent fear.

We may have been afraid that night, but we were there and became a part of the unstoppable change coming to South Africa.

In 1971, there was no television in South Africa. That media form did not arrive there until 1976, so we passed the time by talking to one another. The human contact was remarkable, and I never missed the TV.

During the countless talks with the company, their curiosity about TV was a favorite subject. I warned them about the good and the bad. You will have work, and that's wonderful, but what we're doing now will ultimately fade and you'll be watching television at dinner instead of asking about someone's day. It will subtly creep into your lives and will one day be addictive.

"My husband hates it," I explained to them, "and said to me one day, 'I have a great idea on how to beat the Russians. Just send them six million television sets and they'll pacify themselves to death.'

"I'm treasuring this time with you," I said. "I'll take it home with me and never forget it or you. Sadly, I'm watching the end of an era in your history."

My wardrobe was very well executed and was finished without problems. My hairdresser was talented, with a marvelous sense of humor and, except for that constant façade of cold and wary behavior on the part of Trollip and Bray, we were in very good shape for opening night.

They had provided me with an exceptional company including our orchestra conductor Bob Adams and his musicians. The technical difficulties that Mr. Trollip wrote about somehow escaped us. And speaking for myself, I hadn't a hint of trouble, nor had anyone else.

One day during rehearsals, I had a later call and decided to visit the swimming pool on the roof of my hotel. I had never heard of anything like that, so I got my suit on, wore my cover-up for the elevator and made my way to the pool.

There it was, with a glorious view of Johannesburg. I was the only guest there and couldn't wait to relax for an hour or so.

There were no lounge chairs in sight, so I looked around for someone to help me. It was then that I saw a small, covered cubicle at the other end of the pool. As I walked toward this tiny house, I said "Hello" a few times on my approach.

What happened next scared the very life out of me. Suddenly, without a word, a very tall, muscular black man appeared. He was dressed in tailored black shorts, a white coat with brass buttons and a white helmet, not unlike those worn by the South African military.

What shook me to my core were the huge, round, white, red and black discs in his earlobes. The edges of the lobes held them in place as if he had been born with them. To say he was imposing was the understatement of all time.

This man was a Zulu, and without his hotel uniform, I wondered how it must have felt to see him in his native Zululand. It was a moment I'll never forget. I felt intimidated by his formidable stature and his eyes. When I found my voice, I meekly said, "Hello, is there a chair I can use?"

He answered in their lovely, vocal lilt.

"Of course, Madam, where would you like to sit?"

"Over there, please, where I can enjoy the view."

He set up the lounge chair for me, gave me a towel and returned to his little area where I had found him. He was every inch the warrior of his Zulu history. As I write this, how I wish I'd had, if only for a few moments, a cellphone with a camera. I have no picture of my proud and slightly arrogant Zulu waiting on me, a mere woman.

The day was glorious, and I was so grateful for the few hours I had to just relax. South Africa had vast skies. Everything in Africa seemed to loom larger than life itself, and the skies were no exception. The day was crystal clear with huge fluffy cloud faces floating by.

Whether it was a sunny day or a thunderstorm moving swiftly from one side of the horizon to the other, the weather was entirely unpredictable. The day could be flawless, and then suddenly you could see the black and angry clouds forming and watch the lightning shattering this example of South Africa's artwork.

The rain would fall in heavy sheets while the sun played hide-and-seek. Then, the *pièce de résistance* would appear, with the rainbows that hung in this unforgettable painting of South Africa's heavens.

As I watched a storm pass by one day, I was reminded of scenery in a play where the set has to be changed for the next act. Everything moved so swiftly, disappearing as if someone were pushing them into the wings, making way for a brand-new sky.

How do I describe the awesomeness of this extraordinary part of our world? I could scarcely believe it myself.

I'd been there at the pool for about a half hour or so when the silence was rudely broken by a woman's voice saying, "It's Pat Bray, Miss Paige. You have an interview in about forty-five minutes. I'll wait and take you there."

I opened my eyes, and there she stood. Light blue strict suit, white blouse, sensible shoes and wearing her damned attitude. I was stunned at this simple lack of manners, and while trying to keep the anger from my voice, was unsuccessful. I did not like this woman who had not seen fit to even meet me halfway.

"Mrs. Bray, my work call is one p.m. today. At the very least, you could have warned me."

I stifled a fight and a firm "Hell no, I won't go!" Instead, I reminded her that a call this morning would have kept me from the uncomfortable position I was in right then.

"I find your behavior unprofessional, Mrs. Bray. Please don't do this to me again. Now, excuse me, I'll get dressed and meet you in the lobby."

I left her sitting in my lounge chair while I caught the elevator to my suite.

"Congratulations, Mrs. Bray," I said to myself. "I'm finally angry and I resent having to handle you on top of my real responsibilities." I dressed, had my interview and went to rehearsal. I couldn't wait to tell Otto about the latest Bray treatment.

"No wonder this country's in trouble," I told him.

Tony, our set designer, was a huge part of my education about South Africa. I liked him enormously and he knew, very early on in our friendship, that I wanted to find out all that I could about his country.

One time during rehearsals, he invited me to dinner.

"I want you to see another side of Johannesburg and South Africa," he said. "We have many problems you won't hear about in your country."

He took me to a beautiful hotel that I had not seen or even knew about. The dining room was definitely a cut above where I was staying, and so was the hotel.

When we sat down and Tony had ordered us a glass of delicious South African wine, I asked him about the hotel.

"Is this considered a five-star place, Tony?"

He said it was.

"And how is my hotel rated?" I asked.

"The Quirinale is a four-star hotel," he answered. (Note: It much later became a drug-riddled brothel and closed in 2001.)

He seemed to know why I asked, but I let it go. My contract called for a five-star facility, I thought. My trust in Bill Trollip had been misplaced. *My God, what's next?* I wondered.

"Look Tony," I said, "that waiter over there looks like the man who helped me at the pool the other day."

"You are looking at one of our greatest problems, Janis. He is a Zulu. Also, he is not a waiter but a busboy. In their homeland, they are considered warriors, with enormous pride in their heritage and customs. Tribes are a male-dominated society. The male role is to dominate and produce children. The woman's role is everything else."

Tony went on, "As our cities grow and the various cultures westernize, the pull of the money draws the men to work. The problem is that the only kind of work they can get is what they consider women's work. An integrated citizenry will never be until this government is gone forever."

"Now I understand why I felt like I did when I met my first Zulu," I replied.

When I told Tony the story of my short-but-sweet day at the pool, I explained, "In other words, I should have gotten *him* the lounge chair and not the other way around. He was polite and helpful but terse, and I felt every moment of his Zulu pride and history.

"We've lived through segregation too, Tony," I told him. "We've been fighting against it since the Civil War. We made slow strides until a brave black woman named Rosa Parks finally refused to give up her bus seat to a white man. Only then did this simmering pot erupt into massive civil disobedience that changed us forever.

"I was an adult then, and I watched as white Americans turned the dogs on black and white Americans when they attempted to enforce their Constitutional rights to live equally. We won, but we still struggle. There are so many layers to the reasons that progress moves at a snail's pace sometimes, but it's ever-moving and ever-changing. I've seen it for myself."

Our fascinating and revealing conversation continued.

"Our country was born out of the sheer burden of oppression and taxation," I explained. "We got fed up, dumped all the tea in Boston Harbor and proceeded to form a nation of the people, by the people and for the people. Freedom was and is very expensive. But try to take it from us. It's our life's blood."

I treasured my short, sparse but oh-so-invaluable and educational sessions with Tony Farmer.

When that all-important dress rehearsal night arrived, we were more than ready for opening night. At least, the cast, costumers and orchestra were. As I read and re-read the clippings and reviews I'd kept all of these years, I was reminded once again of how devious one person could be. But I digress.

Our dress was scheduled to begin at six p.m. and to continue until we were finished. I opened the stage door to find the theater completely dark save for a work light on the stage.

Suddenly, from a dark backstage, in walked Ivan Berold, one of our principal cast members. When I looked behind him, I saw the company standing in the dark.

"What's going on, Ivan? Where is everybody? Where are the lights and the scenery?"

I felt a small but ticking panic begin.

Ivan proceeded to tell me that the crew had gone on strike and refused to show up. I felt sick.

"When did you find out, Ivan?"

"When I came in tonight," he replied. "None of us had been informed."

"Let me speak to the company," I said. "Good God, Ivan, we open in three days."

I told those confused souls how sorry I was and that I, too, knew nothing. I asked where Bill Trollip was. No one had seen him. That small ticking panic was fast becoming a full-blown fear. Were all our suspicions coming true?

"We have an entire production here, ready to go," I insisted. "I'm going to find Bill. He needs to make this right for everyone concerned."

I walked to the front of the stage and asked for Bill. There was no answer.

"You have an entire company of people here who deserve an answer about this situation," I said. "Please answer me, Bill, where are you?"

Another long moment of silence, then, "I'm here, Janis."

"It's dark out there, Bill. Would you let us see you, please?"

Everything seemed to be moving in slow motion when he finally raised a hand.

"Would you come down front so that I can see you, please?"

Bill slowly walked to the front-row seats, still wearing those damned round, black-on-black glasses.

"Now, on behalf of everyone standing here in the dark, what do you want us to do? We're ready to go and have been for a week. What now?"

"I'm working on it and I'll let you know," he replied curtly.

Before I could utter another word, Bill walked away toward the back of the house. *Are you married, Mr. Trollip?* I thought. I wondered if she felt as abused and battered as I did.

I stood there in a kind of mental paralysis. If I called Eric, my agent in New York, could he answer all of my questions concerning the show? There was so much that I don't know. I felt set up. Otto and I had had to deal with difficult and at times unacceptable behavior, but we never stopped working and getting the show ready for its opening.

I was still standing in that same spot when Ivan, Otto, my leading man Michael McGovern, and Otto's assistant Wendy de la Harpe approached me.

Ivan was the first to speak.

"We want you to go back to the hotel, Janis. We're going to stay here and help get this show ready. There is nothing you can do here until we can see the sets in the theater."

I stared at them all, shaking my head in disbelief.

"I've never been through anything like this in my career," I told them, "and I've never felt so helpless. We're owed an explanation beyond what we just heard."

"Please get some rest, Janis, you're going to need it," someone said.

I thanked them and told them I loved them all and when I got back to the hotel, I called Ray.

"You won't believe what happened tonight, honey, even if you had seen it for yourself," I said into the phone. I cried, ranted and poured out my heart to him. That was one expensive telephone call, but it was worth it.

Completely exhausted, I fell into a deep sleep.

No matter how ready we were, JODS postponed the show for a few days due to what was described to the papers as "technical difficulties." At least it was true. Like everything else in South Africa, postponing an opening night was another first for me. I hated the feeling I had, but the choice was not mine.

Opening night, once we got to it, held a packed house. Except for the continuing technical difficulties like the sound system constantly fading in and out, and the timing of sets not moving on cue, my wonderful company pulled it off.

The audience never knew of the countless compensations made that night by true professionals. After the horrendous week prior to the opening, all of the rehearsals and work kicked in and our second night went off without incident. We were finally in our run, and it felt good.

A few days after we opened, Bill Trollip called. He invited me to have lunch the following day at his ranch outside of Johannesburg.

"You can meet my wife and children," he offered. A host of feelings sped through me and I wondered at the reason behind his invitation. I was always uncomfortable around this man, but I thanked him and accepted his invitation.

"It's hot out there so bring your suit for a swim," he added. "I'll pick you up at eleven a.m."

I immediately called Ivan and recounted Bill's call. We'd had enough trouble in this show and I didn't want any more bad feelings, but I didn't trust him.

Ivan assured me that I had done the right thing and that I'd be all right.

"Before you leave tomorrow, however, there is something we think you should know," he said. "May we come over?"

"Of course," I said, wondering what was next. I was about to find out, and my distrust and discomfort toward one Bill Trollip was, unfortunately, justified.

We settled down and what I heard left me sickened and depressed. Their story was well documented, except that I didn't know it. The issues, it turned out, had happened before I had arrived in South Africa.

"Bill Trollip lives on a ranch outside of Johannesburg, and he raises a prize breed of cattle," I was told. "One morning, one of Bill's farmhands ran to the house, yelling about a bull on his property due to a broken fence. Bill grabbed a knife, ran down to where the bull was hogtied and castrated him where he lay.

"The bull bled to death, and the South African animal society sued him for cruelty to an animal and brought him to court. He was found guilty, fined 1,500 rand, and that was that.

"But there was no reason whatsoever for him to kill the animal. A halter over his head and a couple of hands to take him back where he belonged was all that had to be done. That, and fix the fence. The inhumane and cruel treatment—not to mention the pain and ultimate death of this innocent animal—was beyond belief to his fellow citizens."

Ivan continued. "This isn't the end, Janis. Sometime after the lawsuit, Bill traveled to Switzerland to buy a bull to breed to his existing cow. The bull cost 50,000 rand, according to Bill."

"How much is that in dollars?" I asked.

"Well, the rand is worth more than the dollar, so the price would have been in excess of fifty thousand dollars."

"Good lord," I said, "I've known horses that cost that much, but never a bull. Go on, please."

Ivan, who knew Bill well and had visited his ranch, said that Bill "brought the bull home and when the cow was ready to be covered, he and his ranch hands prepared to witness the assignation. If you see any of the ranch, Janis, you will see a large ring, fenced in much the same as any other ring.

"The cow was waiting when they sent in the bull. Bill was standing alone, and his hands were directly across the ring, opposite him. The bull entered the ring and went toward the cow. Suddenly, it spun around and ran directly toward Bill, impaling him and goring him from his throat to his groin. The bull tossed him and gored him a second time.

"When the hands pulled Bill away, he was near death. Months of operations followed while they sewed him back together."

I listened, transfixed at this horrific story.

"This is the man I'm seeing tomorrow," I replied, "and I can never let on that I know a thing. Now I believe he's capable of anything."

"Would you feel better if Maryanne and I came to pick you up when you get ready to leave?" Ivan asked.

"Yes! Yes! Yes! If you don't hear from me by three p.m., assume the worst and get there as fast as you can. And don't take 'No' for an answer."

He laughed and said, "Just call us. We're not far away."

"Thank you so much, Ivan, I feel much better. When it comes to Bill Trollip, I get a little paranoid, I guess. I don't trust him."

Bill was still wearing those black-on-black glasses that seemed to be a part of his DNA. The trip to his ranch was uneventful, and it was very interesting for me to see what South Africans called the Veldt. His house had a wide covered veranda (or porch as we would call it in

America). I don't remember much about the house, but I do about his wife and children.

He was married to a simply beautiful woman. She was quiet, very nice, but for lack of a better word, subdued, maybe even withdrawn. Perhaps she had heard negative things about me from her husband and was as uneasy as I was under whatever façades we wore.

Their children were absolutely charming, and I felt immediately comfortable with them. I had no intention of putting on my swimsuit until the kids said, "C'mon, Miss Paige, take a swim with us."

"You can do that after we have lunch," their mother said.

We spoke of everything except the show as I shared my longtime curiosity about South Africa. As usual, the creepy, uneasy feeling I always had around Bill was there through lunch, too. What was it about this man? I couldn't relax, ever.

It was time for the kids and our swim. I got my suit on and followed them outside. There were about eight steps from the veranda to the pool, and I sat down on a lounge chair with their son and daughter peppering me with questions about America and my home.

Did I have a dog? Was I married? Did I have children? They were adorable, speaking in that soft South African dialect I so enjoyed. I told them about my husband and that he had written "Zip-A-Dee-Doo-Dah," which they sang for me. I said I had two dogs and my horses, and I jumped and showed them. It was hot and they soon ran into the pool as I settled back to watch them.

It was quiet when suddenly I heard Bill's voice from the veranda above me. How long had he been there? I hadn't a clue.

"I could have gotten Ginger Rogers, you know," he said.

Nothing surprised me anymore, and I was not about to give him the satisfaction of shocking me with anything.

"Then why didn't you?"

"Because I wanted you," he replied.

Oh my God, I was so tired of these games. Why hadn't he just said what was on his mind and gotten it over with? Instead, in the same, weird, conversational tone he had used, I told him that Ginger was a friend of mine and that if she had gone through what I have with this show, she would have been on the first plane home.

I waited through the silence and then, "I raise prize cattle. I went to Switzerland and paid 50,000R for the bull I found. He's in the ring right now. Would you like to see him?"

Here it comes, I thought.

"Bill, I would love to see a steer that cost 50,000 rand."

I wrapped a towel around myself and joined him on the short, uphill walk to the ring.

The ring was large, and the fence not unlike the ones we used for horses. The wooden slats that made up the fence were stacked by three, with space in between. I remember that the top rail came to my shoulders and I could rest my arms on it. The lower railing was about a foot off the ground, so that you could rest your foot. The middle one was evenly spaced between the two.

As I approached the ring, I saw a huge animal with rather long and slightly twisted horns. He was light in color, indescribably powerful and quite handsome, if bulls are your thing. There was a similar animal about ten feet away.

"He's impressive, to say the least, Bill," I said.

Even my wariness, paranoia and mistrust of this man did not prepare me for his next piece of outrageous behavior.

We were standing about three feet from one another when he tore his shirt from under his pants and lifted it to his chin, exposing his entire chest, throat and gut.

"That bull did this to me," he said.

What I saw was beyond ugly, and my first thought was that this man is crazy. Somehow, I instinctively knew that I was supposed to react, but by now the verbal and emotional jousting had become a kind of protection for me.

The satisfaction of my shock was not going to be his today, so I stared at the mess in front of me and simply said, "It's a wonder he didn't kill you, Bill."

By now, I was beyond any personal emotion about him, but what I saw I will never forget. His prize, 50,000R bull had ripped his body to shreds. His upper half was an ugly, tortuous patchwork of oddly colored scars. Thank God he didn't drop his pants because I could see that the longest scar continued into his groin, past the belt on his trousers.

If I had been his wife and had seen what he did to me that day, I would have been long gone with at least an apology for his appalling behavior. Ice water ran through my veins as I calmly said, "Good lord, Bill, I can't believe you lived, let alone survived such an attack."

"I did almost die," he said.

My God, I thought, *his karma was waiting for him*. Out of all the bulls he must have seen, he chose this one. He may have escaped the limited South African courts, but universal justice was about to exert its power. There was no stopping this perfect storm.

As I took in this Frankensteinian display of Bill Trollip's upper half, I paid a silent homage to my husband. He would have been so proud of me while he knocked Trollip cold for insulting his wife—bull or no bull.

No wonder I felt creepy in the presence of this strange and unpredictable man. He was all of that and, as I would discover, an avenger against anyone who dared stand up to his utter duplicity.

It was getting late, and I called Ivan and Maryanne to pick me up. I thanked Mrs. Trollip, gave the kids a hug and thanked them both for their hospitality. No mention was ever made of Trollip's outrageous physical display in my presence, and no apology for his lack of control.

Shortly after *Applause* opened, Otto left for New York, his work being finished in Johannesburg. Several days later, we both discovered that Trollip had planned the last word.

This time, he chose to thrust a knife in our backs, along with our reputations.

We had no instant contact information back then as we have today, so for a certain period of time one was left ignorant and defenseless of the factual details. We continued to work, withstand and finally overcome the obstacle course that Bill had so unfairly dumped on the company of the show.

As usual, there was no apology forthcoming. Arrogance never apologizes.

On this night, Bill walked into my dressing room, demanding to speak with me. I was due onstage in fifteen minutes. I told him that his behavior was unprofessional and that he would have to wait until after the show, when I'd be happy to speak to him.

He refused to leave, and that's the first time I lost my temper throughout this whole mess.

"Get out of my dressing room now, Bill!" I fumed. "This half hour belongs to me and everyone in the theater seems to know it but you!"

I left him there as I headed for the stage. I had to leave, but he wouldn't.

My phone was ringing when I opened the door at my hotel around eleven-thirty.

"Hi, sweetheart, how's my girl tonight?" Ray asked.

"I was hoping the call was from you, honey. I sure got myself into a South African hornet's nest when I accepted this job. I adore the cast, I have wonderful and supporting friends, but oh, my God, between Bill Trollip and Pat Bray, my anger at this injustice seems to be the only thing keeping me on my feet."

"I'm sorry, sweetheart," Ray replied, "but I've got some bad news for you. Eric called me today and I told him to let me tell you."

"About what, what's going on? Nothing would surprise me now."

There was a pause and then, "Bill Trollip sent a letter to *Variety* blaming you and Otto for the complete failure of *Applause*. He said something to the effect that you weren't ready, and that Otto was not up to directing, along with some other lies."

"We're playing to packed houses!" I yelled. "Failure, my foot!"

"There's more," he said.

I felt like someone had kicked me in the gut when I said, "Tell me everything." And Ray did.

"He's posting a closing notice at the end of your first week, so you're not going to be paid."

Here we had all worked so hard to protect the production, been total professionals in the face of constant unprofessionalism and unforgivably shameful behavior from one Trollip and one Bray. To be issued the coup de gras in such a backstabbing and devious manner left me livid with rage—not only for myself but for Otto, who had pulled off a small miracle.

But the *coup de gras* of *coups de gras* came when I found out that I would not be paid. When the closing notice was posted, I chose to stay until the end of the show in Johannesburg. I worked three weeks without getting paid for the sake of the company.

The Cape of Good Hope and the Wild Coast

There is nothing like returning to a place that remains unchanged to find the ways in which you yourself have altered.
—Nelson Mandela

Somewhere between the closing night of *Applause* and my leaving for home, a trip was planned by Wendy and her husband Roland. They wanted me to fulfill my dream of seeing the Cape of Good Hope. Ray told me not to come home until I had taken my journey of a lifetime.

"You pay for everything, honey, and I'll see you in a few weeks. Thank Wendy and Roland for me, take pictures and remember, I love you."

Roland gave us his Jaguar, wished us well and Wendy and I began our unforgettable journey, still driving on the wrong side of the road.

Johannesburg was a fast-growing modern city, but it wasn't long before I was seeing a part of the Afrikaner's past with its strict and rigid way of life. Here I could still see black-clad, black-bonnetted and powerful women as butchers. Unsmiling, unfriendly and untrusting, still living and working in their fading history. An old "Voortrekker" (migrant pioneer) still stood in the square outside of Bloemfontein.

We drove through the Great Karoo to their beautiful wine country when I heard Wendy say, "Table Mountain is wearing her tablecloth for you today, Jan."

Suddenly, Cape Town lay before us, and my heart was pounding so fast I could scarcely breathe. What was it about this part of the world that fascinated me so? It's a secret kept even from me, I guess.

A description of Cape Town remains elusive. It had a meeting-of-the-world atmosphere but remained entrenched in the vestiges of its very early history. After all, it began in 1652, founded by the Dutch as a trade center.

We had only three days and wasted no time.

When I finally met the Cape, I also met acres of straw flowers filling their space in brilliant colors. In disbelief, I said, "I always thought they weren't real, Wendy. I could pick lychee nuts and kiwis, too. No farmer's market prices here, just all I could eat if I wished." This was, remember, 1971. I'm sure there is some law today stating, "If you eat, you die."

Everything was so blissfully uncrowded as we walked that long, steep road to the top and the view of the Cape.

"Do you want to take the tram?" Wendy asked.

"No, I want to walk all the way."

As we reached the top, I whispered, "I made it, Grandpa. It took me forty years, but I made it!"

But in all of my dreams of the Cape, I wasn't prepared for what I saw.

There before us were two oceans meeting with an endless line of flotsam and jetsam as the whirling tides merged the blue Atlantic with the pale blue-gray of the Indian Ocean. the Cape waves crashed against and between the gigantic rocks beneath us, and I thought about the sailors aboard their ancient sailing ships, often terrified through these stormy waters on their way to India.

Within our time constraints, Wendy served up a feast for me. We saw colonies of the little Cape penguins, wild ostrich and Cape zebras. Baboons would appear suddenly and, just as swiftly, disappear. All one has to do is to see those fangs they bare, including the little ones, to realize they are definitely not pet-able.

Cape Town was a world unto itself, from its history to its beautiful, new theatre, the arts, education and medicine. The world's first heart transplant was performed in Cape Town by the late Dr. Christiaan Barnard in December, 1967, just four years before.

As 1971 marked the last few years without television in the country, I would never see all of this beauty again. Each year would bring vast changes and the world would shrink. All too soon, the massive, nature-swallowing resorts, the cheap fares to far-off places, broken boundaries, massive migration, the disrespect and ultimate loss of cultures would be replaced by globalism—with new and ever-growing colonies of billionaires now setting the tone of the world.

All of this was overseen and overrun by social media moguls, loyal to nothing but power. All too fast, we are becoming throwaways, too, along with the planned obsolescence of the things we demand.

But I digress.

As we began our journey over the Wild Coast, now called the Garden Route, I was ill-prepared for the jolting shock and acceptance of primitive life, still touched by no civilization except their own.

We would seemingly be the only car on the road at six a.m. One morning on our way to somewhere, Wendy pulled over to the side of the road. There on the Indian Ocean was a tiny stretch of beach, untouched and peaceful in the morning sun.

"Would you like to take a swim, Jan?" she asked.

"I don't have a suit," I answered.

"C'mon, Jan, who needs suits!" she said as she stripped off her clothes. "There's no one around."

With that, off came my clothes and I was in the warm and welcoming Indian Ocean, lost in a kind of pure solitude.

As we drove through the Transkei, all we could see was South Africa's version of goldenrod. The fields were green and rolling and the bright blue sky, with its ever-nomadic clouds, completed the vista before us.

We were passing a farm fenced in white when Wendy stopped and bought two miniature pineapples. With a few deft strokes of a big knife, they were trimmed, cored and cut to eat. We sat on the fence, eating our heavenly tasting fruit and trying to sop up the juice as it ran down our chins.

We were watching a bare-breasted Transkei woman tending the field. She was wearing the traditional blanket wrap worn by the region's women.

On the porch of their little house sat her husband, dressed in his ill-fitting westernized clothing. With the onset of religious missionaries demanding no nudity, he was sadly out of place while she still wore her native clothing.

"She does all the work and he does all the sitting," Wendy observed.

As we watched the two of them, a very tall and totally naked young man ran toward us. I don't know where he came from but in one hand, he was holding a huge erection. The rest of him consisted of an enormous white-toothed grin as he frantically waved and yelled at us as he drew closer.

Sticky, pineapple juice-covered faces and hands stayed that way. We barely got in the car in time as he reached the fence. As we drove off, he was still smiling, yelling and displaying his offering.

"Is he an example of what's ahead of me?" I laughed. I didn't even have time to take a picture. Who would believe me?

As we approached Umtata, the city in the Transkei, two horses were copulating in the middle of the dirt-paved street. People just kept on walking.

"Someone is going to have a free horse in about a year," I said.

Oudtshoorn and the ostrich farm was next. This was again a solo opportunity to meet and watch Lucy the ostrich as she lovingly tended to her pile of huge eggs. Once the ostrich mates, they are monogamous. Lucy and her mate had been "married" for nineteen years.

We stood at the fence, Lucy's mate at one end of a large pasture and she at the other. We quietly watched her motherly ritual, turning each chick egg against too much of the hot African sun.

When she finished, she approached us and simply stood motionless. She was right out of Disney's *Fantasia*, feminine with huge brown-black eyes rimmed by thick black eyelashes. As she stared at me, unmoving, she let me snap a few close ups of her beautiful, expressive face.

While I stared back at her, I said, "Are you sure you're an ostrich, Lucy? I feel like we've met before." I could swear I heard her say, "We have, Janis."

"Oh Jan," Wendy laughed. "You're so funny and so much fun."

"I'm afraid Africa's making me a little goofy, Wendy. I just spoke to an ostrich and she answered me."

As we drove toward our next stop, baboons suddenly sprang from the side of the road. There were several hanging onto the radio antenna while baring those vicious fangs at us through the windows. I learned that their behavior was protecting their territory. They would be gone as fast as they appeared when the next family's territory began. Amazingly, they know not to cross those invisible boundary lines.

We were driving through Pondoland, headed for Port St. Johns, dinner, a shower and sleep. A little off schedule as usual. There was a dense jungle on one side of the road and a river on the other. I could see monkeys swinging from trees, along with brightly colored birds.

"Oh Wendy," I cried out, "can I take a quick picture of the sun setting on the river? It's so perfect."

"This can be unsafe, Jan," she warned me. "Leave your door open and move fast."

I ran back, got my pictures and began to wind the roll of shot film as I neared the car. I saw my open door, but I also saw four huge, dark bare feet.

As I looked up, I eyed two African men in loincloths, carrying spears and heart-stopping expressions. I smiled, said, "Photograph, I take photograph."

"Get in the car as fast as you can, Jan, and hang on!"

Everything in me felt too slow and too fast at the same time. I was still closing the door as we sped down the road. When I looked back, they were gone.

"Who were they, Wendy? My God, where did they come from?" I gasped.

"We must never do that again, Jan. People have been known to disappear and are never found."

As hard as I tried to keep my imagination from torturing me with pictures of what could have happened, it didn't work. I was mute until we reached Port St. Johns and our hotel.

It was almost dark as we checked into a very small, simple hotel for the night. We dumped our bags in the room and headed for the dining room. Our jungle adventure had not dimmed our appetites and we were starving.

Their dining room resembled one of the unembellished lunchrooms from my childhood. Formica-covered tables, chairs to match, paper napkins, salt and pepper in the middle. There were two or three other diners finishing their meals, and us. We ordered and ate our simple food. Nothing ever tasted better!

We were just finishing when a man approached and asked if I was an American. I said yes and introduced Wendy. He hesitated as if puzzled and asked, "May I sit down?"

"Please do," we said.

He asked how we knew one another, where we had been and where we were going. He listened and then in a worried tone, warned, "What you are doing is very dangerous. Please be careful."

Whoever named The Wild Coast was far closer to the truth than the now famous Garden Route, but it's hardly conducive to future tourism.

Our destination was the Sani Pass, where Wendy's husband Roland and his brother were waiting for us. Our lodging was lovely, quietly nestled somewhere in the Drakensberg mountain range.

Ever surrounding me was the mysterious South Africa, assuring me that I was blessed beyond words. I would never experience this again, as the primitive met the unstoppable progress.

Early the following morning, Wendy and I joined a worn and well-traveled Jeep and driver. We were headed to a tiny mountain-locked colony called Basutoland, now renamed the Kingdom of Lesotho. What I didn't know was that through my long life, I would be able to recall the terror in my body at the road ahead of us.

It had been carved out of the mountainsides by human hands. It was a narrow one-lane road with a mountain on one side and a sheer drop to the canyon floor below on the other. I counted six vehicles left where they had landed when they fell. There was no top on the Jeep, so my fear of heights was kept in check by a running silent prayer: "Please, God, don't leave me here."

Suddenly around a turn, there was a Jeep coming down. The driver backed up to a small turnabout so we could pass. You always backed up, never down. As we faced the countless hairpin turns to the top, the first thing I saw was a large sign above us. It said, "Enter in Peace" in the native language.

There was a small, simple bare room with a customs desk and a man asking for our passports. They were stamped and we entered the tiny country.

"There are no cars here, Jan," Wendy said. "They ride little horses."

Again, I had stepped back in time. When you click on information about the region today, one finds there are cars, trucks, traffic, a few tall modern buildings, everything looking like everything else. I only remember their welcoming smiles. No English needed. Just a smile in return.

What goes up must come down. I picked up my silent prayer for our safe return, hung on to the hold bar and we started down that death-defying road. We were forced to back up twice, accommodating a Jeep going up.

The worst part was seeing the wrecks below that steep mountainside. There were no railings or fences ever. Where would they have put them? I thought, as we slowly maneuvered the very edges of the Sani Pass.

Like the pilots who flew me safely all over the world, so did our silent, patient and skilled driver. Our thanks and gratitude were met by a dazzling smile and an African "Thank you."

The day was related over a lovely and, at times, "the end is near" sadness. I packed that night, ready for our trip back to Johannesburg and the reality of suing JODS and Bill Trollip.

There were heart-stopping silences, shared laughs and thrilling vistas. This experience belongs to few. I'm beyond grateful to those who cared enough to give it to me.

Even today, paved, widened in places and traveled by the tourist world, it's still considered one of the world's most dangerous roads.

The Christmas Tree

Sometimes change is subtle and sometimes it knocks you flat. The trick is to get up again and again and again and, yes, again.

—Janis Paige

In 1972, my husband's heart attack filled me with fear. Not only had I not experienced a heart attack with anyone in my family, but it scared me beyond words.

Was this my funny, talented and loving husband with a sick heart? What happened? When did it start? How long had he known?

He was not a self-talker, so if he was suspicious, I would be the last to know. Not a good plan and not fair to anyone, but a choice made all too often in similar circumstances.

According to the doctor, it was a minor one but a heart attack nonetheless. The treatment was successful, and he was released from the hospital with some strict rules for his convalescence. He adhered to them and began to look and feel better.

I picked up my life where I had left it, but something was missing. I asked the doctor many times about Ray's attitude. He was always polite and at times distant, but a part of him was gone from me. I could not understand it, and there was no one to listen or seemingly understand.

I felt guilty if I asked about myself when there was a heart attack patient who naturally came first. I felt unwanted, useless and sad but kept my mouth shut against any tension that some truth might have exacerbated.

If we could have expressed our true feelings, our silent but screaming fears about the future, our disappointments in each other and our oft unreasonable expectations of one another, perhaps he would never have asked me to go.

"The truth will set you free," we hear. Perhaps it would even have set us free from heart attacks. I've come to believe that hiding those freeing truths from ourselves and those we love keep us bound to that all-too-scary unknown. Not only will it give you a heart attack, but a variety of other ills as well—a lack of trust being one of them.

In October, my agent called with an offer to do a dinner theatre appearance in Omaha, Nebraska. I didn't want to leave, especially with Thanksgiving and Christmas ahead of us. I wanted the holidays to be special and memorable.

When I expressed my feelings, however, my husband answered with, "I want you to go. I'll be fine."

If someone had kicked me in the gut, I wouldn't have hurt as much as I did from those words. I protested, but he was adamant.

Ray had invested in a small business that he seemed to enjoy. The owner was a young woman he had met at the bank and they became partners.

"Who will take care of you?" I asked. "Who will cook for you?"

"I've spoken to Linda and she said she would help me," he replied. "I'll pay her, of course. I'll be fine."

The fight was gone from me. The first week in November, I left for Omaha, not knowing if I had a marriage or anything else left.

The theater was on the outskirts of Omaha. My hotel was a motel room with a kitchen. The stars lived there because it was within walking distance of the show.

Things were changing in my profession. Dinner theatre had become big, and even the likes of Lana Turner played it. I called Ray to give him my telephone number. He thanked me and that was that.

I threw myself into rehearsals. Business was good and so were the audiences, but a black cloud of worry hung over me and I fought my imagination from going wild.

A cold knot of apprehension never left me, and I was caught between that ever-familiar rock and a hard place. Nothing had ever hurt so much, especially the absence of any communication from my husband. No matter what was wrong, I wanted someone to please tell me.

One night, a woman who was connected with the theater invited me over for Thanksgiving dinner. They had a lovely home, a fire in the fireplace and those memorable Thanksgiving dinner smells wafting through us, along with the warmth one wants to feel at the holidays.

As nice as she was, her husband was the opposite. She had everything except his respect. His obvious control over his family left them unsure and cautious, with great gaps of silence as we suffered through the wait for those words, "Dinner is served."

"I shot these ducks myself," he crowed, "so be careful of the buckshot."

In quiet disbelief, I stared at my plate. Just like that duck, I felt helpless, shot full of buckshot and simmering with suppressed rage, Outwardly, I was a polite guest, but inside my target was this unbearable and pompous ass with Ray's passive-aggressive attitude thrown in for good measure.

My appetite completely vanished.

There was no way I was going to eat his buckshot-riddled duck. I somehow proceeded to keep a forgettable conversation going while intricately moving my food around on their expensive china, As I sipped my wine, I mixed the buckshot, the poor little duck, the yams, the green bean casserole and the gravy, until I had—to the best of my ability—camouflaged what was left on my plate.

"Too much buckshot for ya," he laughed. "They won't hurt if you swallow a few."

When you experience unbridled arrogance, it never disappoints. He's lucky he didn't end up wearing my buckshot-riddled Thanksgiving dinner.

This man, who was married to an obedient and frightened woman, was nothing more than an ugly misogynist. Would this battered woman wake up? Unfortunately, I didn't think so. The trappings of wealth and position took care of her and her children, so only time would finish this sad tale.

It would have been so easy for me to bring this insensitive and selfish jerk to his knees, but it would have caused havoc with his wife and kids. I hurt for them as I hurt for me, but I swallowed my words and kept my explosive mouth shut.

When I could politely extricate myself, I thanked my hosts profusely and left with the words, "Holiday or not, the theatre awaits, time to go to work."

I was exhausted, and my civility was hanging by a thinly worn thread along with my self-control as I drove away. I could have had Thanksgiving dinner at Thrifty's instead of dodging his lousy buckshot!

When I reached the motel and asked for messages, there were none. Not even "Happy Thanksgiving, honey. How are you doing?" It was the first time I didn't try to stop the tears. I sobbed until I stopped, knowing there were more where those came from.

Christmas approached, and the only contact with Ray was what I initiated. He was, as always, polite but cryptic.

"What's wrong, honey?" I pleaded. "I'm lonely and scared about us."

"There's nothing wrong," he said. "I'll see you when you get home."

I finally stopped fighting in this vacuum, but the sick feeling in my gut never left. I simply put myself on automatic pilot to finish the run of the show.

When I left the theater on Christmas night, it was snowing with big, soft flakes sticking to my face. Everything was quiet and new as I made my way to the motel. No matter where I was, I was always the first one outside when we had a snowfall. I loved the silent softness of the newly fallen snow and the feeling of winter coming on.

As I approached the supermarket, I stopped, as if someone had called my name. I looked around to see nothing except a wet, cold, snow-covered and sparse little Christmas tree lying on its side. It and two others were all that was left of the truckload brought in for the Christmas holiday.

I stood there looking at that sorry little tree when I suddenly turned to find a clerk.

"I want to buy that little tree over there. Do I pay you?"

"Christmas is over, lady," the clerk said. "Take it, it's yours."

"Oh please, please wait for me, I'll be right back," I said.

The market and Thrifty Drug closed at midnight. I had about twenty minutes before we turned into a pumpkin.

"Please keep this for me," I said. "I promise I'll be right back."

I ran to Thrifty's. There, I bought lights, extension cord, tinsel, red cellophane garland and the last box of little silver balls to hang on my tree. Tree toppers were gone, so I bought red satin Christmas ribbon.

Next came whatever cheese I could find, crackers, a can of ham spread and something Thrifty called champagne. I was like a crazy person, running around buying Christmas stuff when it was almost over.

I quickly paid my bill, grabbed my packages and ran back next door to pick up what was now my Christmas tree. They were locking up and I barely made it. The nice clerk loaded me up for the block and a half walk to the motel.

As I carefully dragged my tree and myself home, I felt something I had not felt for months. A heavy weight had dropped away, and I was feeling happy, deeply happy.

First, I took my packages up that slippery flight of stairs. Then I retraced my steps to get my tree. I set it inside the door and quickly cleared off the table between the twin beds. I dried the tree and carefully strung the lights on its frail little limbs.

When I finished, I immediately turned the lights on, only to be delightfully surprised that they blinked on and off. I then added a big red satin bow to its skinny little top.

"Are you feeling beautiful yet," I asked, "because you are!"

It was then one-thirty a.m. and I was starving. I laid out my cheese and crackers and ham spread and opened the Thrifty champagne with a toast to "us." I ate my Christmas dinner as I finished dressing my tree.

The next time I looked at the clock, it was three-thirty a.m., and my little tree was absolutely gorgeous in her Christmas finery. With my tree and with snow softly falling, I fell into a peaceful sleep that night. The first one in a very long time.

I finished the show on New Year's Eve. Still no message from home, but by now I didn't expect one. I packed, ready to leave the next day.

I awoke to that dreaded sadness, but I also knew I was different. I had survived the fears, the loneliness, the rejection, my imagination and those awful "what ifs." No matter what was ahead, I'd survive that, too. The victim feeling in me was gone.

I didn't know it then, but I had finally taken care of Janis, who was prepared to live and, if necessary, to fight another day.

No matter how painful it would be to face whatever the music might bring, I was stronger, wiser and determined not to allow myself to feel like a victim of anything or anyone ever again. There were lies in my life and the time for truth had arrived.

My leavin' day was overcast, cold and ready for more snow. I left my still-blinking little tree and said goodbye as I descended those icy stairs to the street below.

As the car pulled away, I don't know why but I remembered what my Guardian Angel had told me on my frightening, six-year-old, first day of school so long ago.

"I'll never leave you," she said. "I'll always be with you. Sometimes I may look different, but I promise you, it will always be me."

As we drove away, I softly whispered, "I should have known it was you when a tree called my name. Thank you, my angel. Stand by, I'll be needing you very soon.

Ray Gilbert, You Died Tonight

Oh the days dwindle down to a precious few, September, November. And these few precious days, I'll spend with you. These precious days, I'll spend with you.

—Kurt Weill & Maxwell Anderson

The seven and a half hours I waited to hear them say "We're so sorry, Mrs. Gilbert, but we lost him" were beyond devastating. They were the last words I expected to hear.

Did they say "we lost him"? What do you mean, you "lost him"? I didn't know what to do with those words or the pinpoints of thought racing through my brain. I felt weak and pressed my hands, my arms and my entire body against a wall to hold me up.

Maybe if I pressed hard enough, I reasoned, I could become a part of that wall and not fall down.

Oh my God, I thought, *I never had a chance to tell him I loved him or say goodbye. It's too late for everything now.* What was I going to do without him and his wisdom? Disbelief and reality joined the tears rolling down my cheeks as I stood motionless in front of these strangers.

After what felt like an eternity, I found my voice.

"Where is he?" I asked. "Can I see him? I have to see him!"

"We would not advise that, Mrs. Gilbert," I was told.

"You lost a wonderful man!" I cried.

The uncomfortable silence was palpable. It was finally broken when someone said that there were papers to be signed. My hands wrote my name as I fulfilled my responsibilities and, one by one, those in the room made their silent exit.

I stood alone in that sterile room. The bed was made, and everything looked as if no one had been there, but someone had—and he was my husband. He left his clothes, his robe, his slippers, his brush, his shaving brush and soap. I could smell his cologne as I carefully folded and packed what was left in his shopping bag.

There seemingly was nothing left of me, and like a robot I walked down the hall, into the elevator and out those doors to my car. I was leaving my husband in this vast place where they make people well, and sometimes they lose them.

"I'm so sorry, Pops," I whispered. "I'm so sorry to leave you here."

It was raining hard, and I wondered when it had started. I put his shopping bag with his belongings folded and tucked safely inside on the seat beside me, and I drove home.

As I made my way along the wet, dark and quiet Sunset Boulevard, I remembered the night he came home and quietly spoke the words, "Honey, I need an operation."

"What kind of operation?" I asked, trying to be calm.

"I need a bypass. I have blockage somewhere in my arteries, and they have to fix it."

He never said the words, but I knew he was scared and so was I. Both of us were too scared to admit it. Here we had a crisis, and neither one of us would let the words come.

As long as I live, I will regret that protection of one another and of ourselves. Why didn't we know that there was something far more important than our stupid fears? My mind kept tracing and retracing the past and the last three days, when we had time and each other.

Monday, March 1, 1976

We were due at the hospital at ten a.m. Ray had his favorite breakfast of corn flakes, and I asked him how he felt.

"It's a Zip-A-Dee-Doo-Dah day," he replied, "and I'm gonna get out in it! You drive, honey."

So we climbed into my little green Alfa Romeo sports car that he had gifted me, and we poked along Sunset Boulevard to the UCLA Medical Center and the end of his life.

As I let him out and went to park, he said, "Honey, I don't want you to come in with me. It's just red tape stuff—you know, paperwork and tests. I want you to take care of your horses. Go ride Adam, give him a hug for me and come back this afternoon."

"No, I don't feel right about this, Pops!" I cried. "This feels terrible. Please, let me be with you. You might need me there for something."

"Honey, please do this for me," he urged. "I'm all right."

What do I do now? Do I insist and upset him, or let him go?

"Please sweetheart, I'm all right."

I gave Ray a hug, kissed him and watched him walk away. As he went through the door, he waved once and was gone.

I'll never understand why I didn't stay with him that day. Maybe we would have talked about how frightened we both were and shared some truths with one another. Why do we pretend to be so weak, when we are really so damned strong?

All too often, we find it out too late. We create our own sadness and regrets, and we find that out too late, too.

Tuesday, March 2, 1976

Tuesday was spent in copious tests and papers to be read and signed, with people coming and going constantly. All of this was done while Ray was instructed to rest. We both had a good laugh out of that one. His sense of humor was still alive and well, even as he faced a terrifying tomorrow.

I stayed at the hospital through his dinner, and when I saw that he was getting tired, I said, "I better go, honey. There's another mouth waiting to be fed."

"Give her a big hug for me, will you?"

"The house is so empty right now," I said. "I can't tell you how much it means to have her there when I open the door. She is such a comfort, always loving and protective, and seems to know that something is different.

I can't imagine my life without my animals. Thank you for understanding and loving them too."

Shortly after I had finished *Mame* on Broadway, Ray had said, "The time has come for you to care about something other than your next job. You've always loved horses, it's time you have one."

My birthday present was a stunning, dark gray, five-year-old mare named Joy.

Show business always seemed to be a natural for me, but now, for the first time in my life, I was a rank amateur. Joy wasn't, however, and I learned a kind of courage and guts I never thought I had. I fell, got bucked off her, I even got kicked and knocked cold and ended up in the emergency room.

No matter how scared Ray was, he never asked me to give up my horses. I was forty-five and learning how to be bad before I was good. All of this was done in the presence of a bunch of ribbon-winning kids as young as nine. The generation gap kept me mute and alone in my efforts, but to stop was unthinkable. So, I didn't.

When I won my first blue ribbon, Ray turned to the stranger sitting next to him and, with great and gleeful pride, said, "That ribbon only cost me $15,000."

The future was still ahead of us when I thanked him for my new life.

"But why do I still feel guilty when I take the time for me?" I asked.

"You can stop punishing yourself now, honey," he said. "it's okay to stop and smell the roses."

I hated to leave the hospital, but it was getting late. I sat on the side of his bed and bid farewell.

"I'll see you tomorrow" was followed with a hug and a kiss.

"I love you, sweetheart," I said. "Please rest now. I'll see you tomorrow."

Tomorrow came, but Ray didn't come with it.

Wednesday, March 3, 1976

The catheterization was scheduled for three p.m. when the phone rang at eight-thirty this morning.

"Hi, honey, they're taking me down now," Ray said. "They had an opening and I can go earlier."

"No!" I screamed. "They can't! I'm not there! Please, please, Pops, don't let them do this. Please tell them to wait until I get there, or do it this afternoon. What difference does it make? This isn't right! I have to go with you to the operating room. Please don't do this, please wait, I'm leaving now!"

My protests fell on deaf ears.

"Oh, honey, I want to get this over with. It's going to take a few hours and I don't want you sitting here worrying."

"No matter where I am, I'm going to worry," I insisted. "I don't understand you, I can't--"

"Now listen to me," he interrupted, "I want you to go to your class and then be the first face that I see when I wake up. I have to go, sweetheart. I'm on the gurney now. I love you. I'll see you later."

No one can ever tell me that there isn't a cosmic connection to those we love.

I hadn't been in my class fifteen minutes when a sickening "gut clutch" told me that something was terribly wrong.

"I have to go," I said, and ran to the phone.

"Oh, Mrs. Gilbert, we've been trying to reach you. It's about your husband."

"Oh my God, what about my husband? What about my husband?" I repeated. my voice shaky and rising as the premonition became all too real.

"I'm sorry, but I'm not at liberty to discuss that with you. But you should get here as quickly as you can."

I couldn't breathe. I couldn't think. I remember driving like a maniac, parking like a maniac, running like a crazed person into the hospital, into the elevator, down the hall and into his room.

Seeing everything so empty terrified me. As I turned, I saw the nurse.

"The doctors are on their way," I was told.

"Is he alive?" I asked.

That question was greeted by four somber-faced, white-coated men entering his room.

"Is he alive?" I asked again.

"We have him on a heart-lung machine, and we ask your permission to do the bypass."

"Oh, no. Ray made me promise that I wouldn't let you hook him up to anything. 'If God wants to take me, let me go, honey,' he said. I don't understand, how bad is he? What are his chances?"

A long pause, and then, "About five percent."

"I have no choice," I said. "I'm going to break my promise to him and take your rotten odds."

It was approaching one-thirty a.m. as I drove up and parked outside my very dark house. No lights, just the whimpering sounds of our shepherd, Jennie. She was so glad to see me, as I was to see her.

I turned on some lights and everything was just as I had left it. Nothing had changed except my life.

Jennie hadn't been fed since early morning, so I fixed her food and that's when the tears started.

"Don't do this," I said to myself. "Don't fall apart now. There's all the calls to make and people to be notified, so much to do. Where do I start? What's first?"

I picked up the shopping bag holding his belongings and carefully put his brush, shaving mug and shaving brush on the counter in his bathroom. I used to kid Ray all the time about his always using a shopping bag, and he'd quip back, "Would you rather I carried a purse?"

Ray loved his shaving time because he could think and oftentimes write. I put his slippers and pajamas where he always had them, slowly put away the clothing he had worn to the hospital, and then I saw his robe.

His smell was everywhere, a combination of shaving soap, cologne—and Ray.

I stood motionless in that no man's land of nothingness for a long time. How long has it been now since they told me they lost him? Is it tomorrow already? When did I last speak to him?

Suddenly, all of the shouldn'ts, should-haves, why-didn't-I's? and I'll-tell-him-laters opened the floodgates. There I stood, tears rolling down my face. No shoulder to cry on now, no arms around me now when I'm hurting, no "Don't worry, honey" when I am so damned scared.

I put on his robe, tied the sash and began to walk the floor.

Where is he now? If I go in the bedroom, will I see him? What's first this morning? Did I eat anything? Who cares? Where do I start? I have to call ASCAP, our attorney, Ray's brother, etc. etc. etc.

When the stillness, the ghosts and the loneliness became too much, I called our housekeeper.

"Mrs. Sikora, Mr. Gilbert died!" I sobbed.

"I'll be right there," she said. She arrived, uniform and all, put her arm around me and walked me into the dawn.

Eventually, there was a shower, hot coffee, the phone, a pad for lists and the sorrow door opening and closing while I made one call after another.

"Oh, Jan, I'm so sorry!" was the theme of the day. It was sprinkled with "What can I do?" and "How can I help?" but there was nothing and nobody but me now to take care of what I knew and what I didn't know.

"So here I am, honey," I said to Ray, "alone, scared and wondering what to do about anything."

Approximately three months after Ray's death, I was invited to brunch at a friend's home. I was finding it increasingly difficult to be just one, when everyone else seemed to be in twos.

My pain was my own, and at times I simply needed to be alone with it. I disappeared into a small room overlooking the guests below. I stood there wishing I were home when a soft voice said, "I'm so sorry to hear about your husband, Miss Paige."

I turned around and replied with a "Thank you." He introduced himself as Dr. Tom Johnson.

"You won't understand this now," he said, "but his passing was his gift to you."

I answered with a shocked, "How can you say that to me?"

He continued with, "From now on, what you do with your life is up to you. It's yours now."

I live those words every day in some way. I was reborn during that horrendous night of loss—and you were right, Tom. I didn't understand your words then, but I do now.

If Ray could come back, he'd say, "I knew you had it in you all the time. Remember when I used to say, 'You're the smartest woman I ever met, but you won't take responsibility for it. I won't be here forever, you know.'"

He was right. There was a world of work still to be done. When help, caring, wisdom and love stand in front of us, we must find a way to be open and vulnerable enough to hear it, feel it, take it in and let it live and be nurtured.

Ray Gilbert
September 15, 1912 – March 3, 1976

We have to get over ourselves before we can ever find ourselves.

After Ray/Life 101

> *Where do we enroll in Life 101? Where are the classes dealing with the loss of a job, a loved one, a relationship? Unfortunately, those lessons are mostly learned through trial by fire and the school of hard knocks.*
>
> —Les Brown

Of one thing I'm sure: Life moves on in spite of grief or the intense pain of loss. Recalling that time, it's as if a giant hand shoved me through a door and slammed it shut with the words, "Grow up!"

I just hit the ground running.

After the funeral and the reception and the guests had gone, only the stillness and my dog Jennie's warmth remained. Each night, I would hug her tightly and finally drift off to sleep, only to awaken without the rituals, comfort and security of marriage.

All too soon, I realized that my very successful career had absolutely nothing to do with the reality of Ray's music profession. Through my years in vaudeville, films, television and the Broadway stage, I knew my craft well—but it mattered not.

For the first time in my life, my buffers were gone. My agents, managers, business managers, etc., could not help me now in the cold stare of this new business world. They previously had taken the blows, saving me for the creative or artistic side of my career. I had been handled by so many people that I didn't even know how to make out a deposit slip at the bank. Ray had always done that job, too.

I remember the day that I had to face the truth. I was so embarrassed at my adult stupidity, but I had to begin sometime.

When I approached the teller's window, she immediately told me how sorry she was about Mr. Gilbert. I thanked her and said, "I need your help. I'm ashamed to ask this, but I don't know how to deposit this money."

"Oh, Mrs. Gilbert, please don't worry about that," she assured. "I'll be happy to show you."

That day, I began to learn the human everyday steps taken by millions of people in so many countless ways I had yet to learn.

A year before we were married, Ray showed me his will. He had left it to me to run his music publishing business, with a share to his daughter Joanne. When I questioned his decision, his answer was, "I know you'll do the right thing."

"But how will I know the right thing, honey?" I asked. "I'd always do my best for you but--"

"That's what I mean," he interrupted. "Just do your best."

The discussion was over as he said, "Let's go eat, I'm hungry."

Sometimes you have to jump without a net and trust that you'll be okay. Two days after Ray's death, I was sitting quietly, living in yesterday and the day before yesterday, when the phone rang.

A music publisher was calling, wanting to buy Ray's music catalogues. He expressed his grief at Ray's death and then proceeded to present his "generous" offer. As uneducated as I was in the music business world, even I knew that his offer was grossly unfair.

"Thank you very much," I replied, "but your offer is premature. I don't even know what I own yet, so my answer will have to be 'No' for the near future."

Suddenly, his caring attitude went to black. The silence was deafening, followed by a different tone of voice.

"Don't tell me you're going to handle things," he snapped. "You're crazy, lady, you'll lose it all."

The conversation ended with a cold hang-up. I was stunned at the treatment.

I fielded three more calls that day concerning Ray's catalog. I hadn't had a chance to grieve, let alone think about the future, but their behavior demanded an answer (albeit temporarily).

It seemed an eternity before I answered the next offer. When I responded negatively, the ensuing silence was palpable, and I was scared.

"Well," he said, "you won't get another offer like mine."

Before I could answer, he too hung up. Good lord, is this the way conversations end in the music business?

I sat with the receiver still in my hand, remembering the not-quite-buried experience of my mother's favorite way of settling an argument: a slammed-down phone, leaving me angry, hurt, unfinished, scared, abandoned and, of course, feeling guilty.

Future therapy would teach me that the body never forgets, so the angry hang-up simply flushed up the past feelings of futility. But this was different because I was different. *I'm doing the best I can*, I thought. *Why do I still feel guilty?*

What happened that day was the beginning of the beginning. Outside of what I'd learned when Ipanema Music was formed, there was so much more I had to learn and understand.

One by one, I pulled out those files, spread them on the office floor and began to read everything concerning Ray's music. I had a legal pad and a box of Kleenex for the intermittent tears that always appeared.

Many nights, I was on that floor until two or three o'clock in the morning. As I read, I'd write the information I needed and the questions to be asked. There was no Google then, just reference books, which I used as best I could.

Through my basic Musical Education 101, I experienced emotions I didn't know I had. They ranged from rage to grief to feeling sorry for myself to intense loneliness and back again. I'd gotten my foot in the door, so to speak, and I never closed it.

When I needed a few friends, they appeared to buoy my spirits and gently push me in the right direction. The late Hannah Russell, one of Ray's oldest friends, was the first. Along with being in the music business most of her life, she knew people who could help with the importance of continuity.

Ray's longtime attorneys took over the immediate problems, and they were wonderful. But there was something else nudging me in a new direction. I had the full responsibility for someone else now, and I carefully kept my fears and doubts to myself. Trust became elusive and uncomfortable in such unfamiliar territory.

I learned to tolerate and finally accept the emotional peaks and valleys during that first year. The people I came to love the most were the friends who never told me, "It's time to snap out of it, Jan."

I very quickly learned that grief travels solo. All too soon, the words of condolence and sympathy cease as life picks up where it left off. Your sorrow very quickly belongs only to you and that hidden place where you never snap out of it.

In the mid-Sixties, when Ray began to write with Antonio Carlos Jobim and their corporation was formed, Ray had a small home office built. Writing this today sounds as if we lived in the Dark Ages, but there were no home computers then, just miles of files, neatly kept in hanging folders, labeled as to their content.

I knew how to file a copyright form, the contents of the catalogs and the lead sheets, should they be requested by anyone involved with the music business. I continued to work, and Ray was extremely busy in Brazil. A new world had opened for him, and I'd never seen him happier or more fulfilled. He was in the middle of what he loved best and it was exciting for me as well to be an asset to him in my own way.

Jobim was a young Brazilian musician who began to change music forever. His bossa nova beat and his song *The Girl from Ipanema* grabbed the world and never let go.

Before we met, Ray had enjoyed a long working relationship with the late, world-renowned Brazilian performer, Carmen Miranda. He was well prepared for this new Latin sound.

Who was I now?

I was on my own and completely unprepared for the avarice, attempted manipulations and quiet threats over what I stood to lose if I tried to handle the legacy left me by myself. I hadn't even thought of that when I answered another call.

"I'm so sorry to hear about Ray, Mrs. Gilbert."

I thanked him, and then I heard, "We publish one of his songs and it's up for renewal soon. I'll get the contract off to you today. All you have to do is sign it and mail it back."

Everything in me stopped dead cold with only my gut instinct screaming, "Be careful." I thanked him but declined the offer.

Approximately two months after Ray's death, our tax man died and left me in a terrible mess. He had been very ill, keeping it quiet while he continued to keep everything going. The first I knew of any trouble was when a man showed up at my door, flashed his credentials and then demanded a $10,000 check for back taxes.

I did not invite him in while he insisted that I owed the money. I asked him to wait outside while I called our attorney. Ed Mosk, our lawyer, hit the roof and told me that this was unheard of and to have this man call his office. The taxman did, and he got an earful from the elegant Ed.

Some months after that, instead of a former publisher renewing one of our songs, I renewed it myself and placed it in our own company, under our own control. There were other calls and a few quiet threats, but each one only strengthened my resolve to protect what Ray had worked so long and hard for.

My Sociopath

> *If, instead, you find yourself often pitying someone who consistently hurts you or other people, and who actively campaigns for your sympathy, chances are close to 100% that you are dealing with a sociopath.*
>
> —Martha Stout

About a year and a half after Ray died, I had just wrapped up a television show and was on my way home. As I came into the house, the phone was ringing. The voice on the other end said that he had my jewelry.

"You left it in the dressing room," he said.

"Oh, good Lord, thank you so much for letting me know!" I replied. "Can I meet you somewhere and pick it up?"

"I'm not far from you," he said. "Can I bring it over?"

I protested, but he insisted, and that began my first sortie with what is known as a sociopath. Big word, bigger problem.

I recognized him as the associate producer on the show I had just shot. He was tall and fairly good-looking, with a sweet, gentle demeanor and a sense of humor. I took my jewelry, thanked him for his thoughtfulness and said goodnight. He also expressed his condolences on the death of my husband. I was still so raw under the façade of coping.

The next call came with the words, "I'd love to take you to dinner. Are you available?"

"Well, I guess so," I said.

He knew wine, had very good manners, was attentive, funny and interested in my favorite subject, my horses. As I listened to him, I began to feel the warm needies subtly stir within. I felt safe and cared for. Gosh, Jan. Do ya' think?

The following days and weeks were spent relying on this person who had suddenly entered my life. He cleaned out my garage and had a sale. He was extremely organized, with a bit of pragmatism thrown in.

By now, I was definitely seeing someone. I had strong moments of guilt about Ray, but the load of grief, work and the future seemed easier somehow, and I was ready for some much-needed relief.

He took me to see his apartment in the Valley. He spoke about his mother and how worried he was about her living alone. He needed to see her in Cape Cod, he said. And then he asked, "Would you like to come with me? I'd love her to meet you."

Of course, I said a grateful "Yes," as he knew I would.

Her house was Cape Cod old. The property was breathtaking, with a large parcel of land jutting out to the ocean. She was sitting on a gold mine and adored her home, with no thought of moving. She was then seventy-six, a New Englander to her bones, educated, brave and strong. I liked her a lot.

She also saw the sun rise and set in her son. It was to be expected, I supposed. He seemed so caring, concerned and gentle.

Unfortunately, his mother and I were the perfect combination of trust and need. Our shared disease, among other problems, was a kind of emotional deaf, dumb and blindness.

Of course, he'd mentioned marriage.

"After we give the relationship some time," he said, "and you're ready. I realize it's too soon now."

There was always one tiny little spark of something that I didn't want to think about. It appeared when we made love. He was practiced, knew what to do to please, everything went off as planned—but something was missing.

Putting my finger on the missing piece wasn't easy, but it's safe to say that he wasn't present, not *there*. I felt disconnected from him, and when all satisfaction had been completed, lonely.

I had been taught very well not to question, not to know and not to ask. If I did, I might be rejected and ashamed for doubting. Don't rock the boat, Jan. Don't lose him, Jan. *Oh my God, Jan, please don't lose him!*

I should have been singing, "I'm leaving on a jet plane, don't know when I'll be back again," but all of the signs weren't visible just yet, and I breathed a sigh of relief that he was still there.

Then came the day when I arrived home to find a moving van in my driveway, with the new man in my life unloading his furniture.

"What are you doing?"

My control was fragile, and I could feel the anger, embarrassment and helplessness rising in me as I raised my voice.

"We never talked about you moving in here!" I fumed. "I've never lived with anyone in my life, and I'm not starting now!"

He broke the silence.

"I thought it was a given when we spoke of a possible marriage," he said. "My mistake, I guess. What the hell do I do now? I have no place to go."

Oh, Mister C, you master of manipulation you. Did I wake up to the con in my presence and now in my home? No, he still had some wiggle room with me, and he knew it. I hadn't seen enough, felt enough, been lonely enough and used enough. My education in sociopathy was just beginning.

After he moved in, my anger and hurt turned into a controlled hostility. Every time I looked at my husband's bathroom or his thinking room, I saw unfamiliar and unwanted furniture, books, bric-a-brac and clothing.

I was too angry to realize that my precious space was once again invaded, just as it was as a child. I was angry then too, but of course I didn't have any right to speak up for myself. I didn't dare. This man was now a victim with no place to go, and my mother's victim stance was all too painfully familiar. So was trying to fix the victim's problem.

Behind my back, my boarder was very busy. A new job occupied his days and most nights. He had convinced his mother to sell her precious house with the promise that she would live with him for the rest of her life. Even his mother did not escape his diabolical schemes.

About six weeks later, his mother called. She was stoic, but I knew something was wrong.

"Where are you?" I asked.

"Well, he picked me up at the airport with his secretary. Do you know her?"

I told her I did not.

"Where are you?" I asked once again. A hesitation, and then, "I'm in a very small apartment on a street called Sweetzer. He said that this is my new home."

I asked what had happened to her living with him and his words were, "It wouldn't work out." There was no hiding her heartbreak.

"Sweetheart," I told her, "I'm on my way. I'm not far."

What I saw when I got there was a nice, very small apartment. The stunning part was that all of her furniture had been dumped there before she arrived. He had lied big, and I was sickened at what he'd done.

Any attempt to talk about her feelings was completely off limits, so I didn't try. I saw her several times and did what I could to make her life at least comfortable. I marketed, took her shopping and fixed dinners for the two of us. I even found her a contemporary friend, but West Hollywood and Cape Cod remained a world apart and I was running out of options.

Not once did I ever hear her say one word against her son, and I found myself between the well-known rock and a hard place as I kept quiet.

Oh, she did drop one tiny bomb when she said, "He told me that they were getting married!"

"Who?"

"His girlfriend," she said, "his secretary."

I stood quietly with a dose of self-hatred and disbelief joining that final truth I'd not had the guts to face. Along with his fraudulent treatment of his mother, my freeloader had been using my home as a parking lot—with me as a twenty-four-hour unpaid attendant.

Everything in me was finally on my way out, but now I was involved, not only with his mother but with his kids. What do I do about them?

The sad answer came quickly when he made a stupid but arrogantly predictable move. His ugly game was finally exposed.

He had three girls aged eighteen, sixteen and thirteen. Of course, we'd met. After all, he'd told them we might get married. He had invited all of us to dinner to celebrate his new job. We were chatting with one another when the check came.

As we watched him search through every pocket and he finally asked, "Could I borrow your card? I left mine at home," the silence spoke volumes as I gave him my card. The bill was $150, plus tip.

"I'll give you the money when we get back," he lied. "Remind me." I was still reminding him about my money the day his ass hit the driveway and I finally stood up for myself.

Funny how that little spark of disbelief fights for its life until the truth snuffs it out.

His work was sometimes twenty-four hours a day.

"I'll stay with my friend who lives near the studio tonight," he said. "We're doing night shooting and we're behind."

I, too, was working. Between learning to run Ipanema Music Corp. and doing a lot of television, his familiar absence was acceptable, even welcome. I had a full plate and couldn't handle more, but whether I wanted it or not, more was waiting for me.

His kids had my telephone number and all of the necessary information in case of an emergency. The phone woke me, and I knew it was late.

"Jan, I'm so sorry to wake you, but I need to speak to my dad."

The voice of his eldest daughter sounded worried.

"I know it's three in the morning, but I have to talk to him, please."

"He's not here, honey, he's working tonight and staying with his friend. He said he had an early call this morning."

She said she had called the numbers that she had for two hours but couldn't find him. *I'm going to be sick*, I thought, but told her that I'd try too.

"If I'm successful, I'll have him call you," I said. "Try not to worry."

As I hung up the phone, I thought, *First me, then your mother and now your kids. You bastard!*

I got dressed, put the leash on Jennie, my German Shepherd, turned on the lights in the house, locked the door and climbed into my little Alfa Romeo. It roared to life as we made our way through the empty streets.

It was going on four a.m. when I pulled up to his friend's house. There was a carport, but no car. I drove up and down the street in case he was parked elsewhere. Everything quiet except for my crystal-clear brain. The cobwebs were gone. The lies, including the ones I told myself, were gone as well. But most of all, gone was that whore called hope.

Dawn was a misty light as I reached home. The house beckoned to me as it always had, but this time it was different. I was filled with resolution. Or was it revolution? Whatever it was felt good, but I had a lot of work ahead of me.

Coffee, I needed coffee. I love coffee, and when it was done, it never tasted better than it did as I made my lists for the day.

At seven a.m., I called a moving company. I didn't care which one.

"I need you this morning early," I said.

"Eight-thirty okay?"

"That's perfect," I said.

I then called my friends who lived in Palos Verdes.

"Can you come now?"

I filled them in briefly and they were on their way.

There was much I did not know about this man, and I had no intention of being alone with him when I moved him out. I then got boxes and proceeded to get rid of everything belonging to him. I worked as if my life depended on it. Except for his damned furniture, everything was piled in the living room, ready for the movers.

My last call was to him.

I called the numbers he'd left, but no answer. His service was the last one I called.

"Leave a message and I'll call you as soon as possible," his voice said.

I told him that his daughter had been trying to reach him all night. I had been calling as well, with no success. I reminded him that his kids were not my responsibility.

"Please call your daughter! She needs you. Now, I've called a moving company to pack up and move you out. They will be here at eight-thirty. Do you have an address for delivery? Because if you don't, I'll send it to the house on Carpenter. Please don't ask any questions or tell me more lies. Just show up and get out. And don't give me your 'Poor me' routine, I can't hear you anymore."

Sociopaths lack one fundamental characteristic: They feel no empathy for anyone other than themselves. They can lie, steal, seduce, help, advise, make love, charm, cheat and show warmth, care and kindness.

What you don't know is that *he* is his only agenda. He does not feel guilt, shame or contrition. Only he and his creature comforts matter, not yours. He knows how to manipulate until you're wrong and apologizing with, "What was it I did?"

Sadly, his mother died a few years later, away from the security and safety of her Cape Cod home.

When he moved out, he stole my three Nikon camera lenses with their leather cases. His mother had given me a plum pudding for Christmas. He stole that too, along with a bottle of Scotch I'd bought for her.

I had sent him to my dentist and my doctor. He never paid them. Of course, I never knew this until they called trying to find him. They both called and then one day, so did the IRS. No wonder he wanted his mother's house. He owed them $55,000, a lot of money in 1979 (or anytime, for that matter).

When I returned their call, I said, "Here is his phone number, his work number and his address. He owes my dentist, my doctor, me and God knows who else. We may not get paid, but I'm sure you will.

"Now, may I ask a favor? Please don't call me again."

And they didn't.

When I discovered that he had stolen my camera lenses, I was livid. It was Christmas Eve when Jennie and I drove to the address his mother had given me on Roxbury Drive in Beverly Hills.

I parked and knocked on the door of his new home. There was Christmas music playing, every light in the apartment was on and there was a festive aura as he opened the door. The look of shock and awe on his face was worth the trip.

"I'm not here to wish you a Happy Yuletide, so don't waste my time on your finely tuned charm," I told him. "I'm here to get my camera lenses. You and I have the same lenses except that I have leather cases and your cases are plastic. I realize that this offends your elitist sensibilities, but I must insist that I get back to leather and you get back to plastic."

"I don't think I have them, Jan," he lied.

"You don't have to think," I said. "Just get me my lenses. I'm not leaving without them. Maybe I'll even get a chance to meet your future wife."

The look on his face prompted me to say, "Your mother told me. Congratulations!"

He almost ran to the hall closet, opened it and had the gall to say, "Well, what do you know, I *do* have them. I'm sorry Jan."

"You can keep the plum pudding your mother gave me," I said, "and the bottle of Scotch, too. By the way, my doctor, my dentist and the IRS called. They haven't been paid. I gave them your home number, work number, service number, your friend's number and address and certainly last but not least, your new address. Or is this her new address? But that's never been very important to you, has it?

"Well, I think I've covered all your many bases," I continued, "so I'll just take my lenses in their leather cases and enjoy my ride home."

As I descended the stairs, my last sight was of a pale, no longer smugly secure man, holding a glass of warm wine. I guess he'd forgotten he had it. It was a Christmas to remember, with my life a work-in-progress instead of a work-in-retrograde.

Remember when I warned that sociopaths don't ever change? Ten years after my sociopath entered and left my life, the phone rang. Unbelievable as it seemed, there he was.

"Hi, Jan! Just wondered if you're lunch-able?"

After I picked myself up off of the floor, I started to laugh.

"Is that funny?" he asked.

"Oh God yes, it's funny," I assured him. "You're finally funny. Today, the whole world is funny. No, I'm not 'lunch-able.' You couldn't find one word that would bring us together again. If I cared, I'd be insulted that you think I'm still so stupidly gullible. Now please don't call again, ever. It makes you look so broke. I'm going to say goodbye now and hang up."

My relationship with this man knocked me flat. Everything that I thought I knew was tested, with failing grades. Through a variety of circumstances, I woke up to the fact that I was a lie, living a lie. I owe him tuition for the lessons I learned. It's expressed in gratitude. I survived.

As my life progressed, there were a few familiar and sexy possibilities who tried to enter my newly formed safety zone. They might as well have been wearing a sandwich board announcing, "Sociopath here. Speak to me at your own risk."

∽

Japan

Sometimes you have to jump without a net, trusting you'll be all right.

–Dr. Jack Rosenberg

Two years after my initial beginning struggle to educate myself, I made my first visit to one of our sub-publishers. Our music was played all over the world and it was time to introduce both myself and me to this new position I held.

The old saying "When the student is ready, the teacher will come" must be true. I don't know if I was ready, but the teachers came from everywhere. Most of those lessons were painful and ego-bruising but proved to be invaluable wake-up calls for my future.

I learned to juggle both of me—when to be Janis Paige and when to be Mrs. Gilbert. Trial and error were constants. I cried tears of frustration, fear and, yes, anger in private. I was also human and often got tired of the misogynistic practices of the business world of 1978.

The "Me Too" movement was nowhere in sight when I was a fledgling businesswoman in a man's world. Ray's attorneys were wonderful then and always, but I was still Ray's widow. Somehow, I knew that I would have to develop a new identity as my education grew and decisions would be made.

I needed my own attorney to help me in this new and unfamiliar territory in which I found myself. I found someone with years of knowledge, and he was respectful of me and my efforts.

"What do you need from me, Janis?" he asked.

"I need you to fight for me, Bill," I said, "and shove me in the right direction."

When he knew that I was reading the small print so that I could be educated in what and where I was, his words were, "I wish all my clients read the small print, Janis."

"It's a terribly depressing job, Bill. I have no idea of what some of it means, so explain it to me."

When I found out we were in a twenty-five percent tax bracket to our sub-publishers, I asked why it was so high.

"It's always been that way," he replied.

"When the contract is up for renewal, let's try to cut it to fifteen percent and see what happens."

"You'll never get it," Bill assured me.

"What do we have to lose for trying?"

I got a call one day, picked up the phone and heard, "Congratulations, you got your fifteen percent."

"Oh Bill, thank you," I replied.

"As a matter of fact," he added, "I'm asking fifteen percent on all new contracts for my clients. You've made a big difference, Jan."

During this time, Jack Lord offered me a role on *Hawaii Five-0*. I could fly to Hawaii, do the show and fly from there to Japan. You have to start sometime, I thought.

Before I could change my mind, I was on my way. Jack was simply wonderful to me, and when the show's team found out that I loved mangos, there was a sack of those delicious things waiting for me in my dressing room each morning.

Jack and I were chatting one day when I told him that I was on my way to Japan.

"Alone? You're going there alone?" he asked.

He gave me his card and wrote a name on it.

"This is my attorney in Tokyo, Janis. I'm going to tell him to expect your call if you need anything, and I mean *anything*."

My last night in Hawaii was spent with Jack and his lovely wife. I couldn't have asked for more than to be a part of the *Hawaii Five-0* cast and crew.

I'd always heard about how tough Jack was, how difficult he was to work with. but I found the exact opposite. He was highly intelligent and caring. And if tough meant protective of the giant hit that he and everyone enjoyed, then that was a huge asset. Unfortunately, toughness gets a bad rap when it's really one's determination and hard work.

I'd been in Japan twice before when I was a part of the Bob Hope Christmas shows to entertain our troops. To me, Japan was the inside of a huge hangar on a military base. This was different, however. Very different.

There was my favorite ocean once more, and here I was, flying into a new world in a new place in my life.

I guess I'd fallen asleep during the flight because I remember waking up to, "Tokyo is having an earthquake, and we'll be landing shortly. Please fasten your seat belts."

That sure woke me up!

"Not now, not now," I whispered to myself.

I'm sure my silent prayers helped the pilot set us down safely. I gave my usual round of applause, and when I deplaned, I never felt so alone.

My reservation was at the New Otani Hotel, and I needed a cab. I must have looked lost, because I was.

Then I heard an Aussie voice say, "Are you lost? May I help?"

I looked at a smiling man wearing one of those Australian hats they were famous for. I asked, "Do I look as lost as I am? I need to go to the New Otani Hotel and I don't know how to get a cab."

"Oh, you don't want a cab," he assured me. "That will cost you at least seventy-five dollars. There is a bus that everyone uses and it costs seven dollars and fifty cents."

This very nice man helped me to get my bags, got me on the bus, and off we went. When I reached my hotel, I thanked my new Aussie friend profusely and was on my own again.

I checked in, and after a very long walk to the elevator and my room on the 40th floor, I tipped the bellhop and heard him say, "*Arigato, Arigato.*"

When he left, I looked at the closed door and said to myself, Arigato *sounds like the Portuguese word* Obrigado, *meaning,* "Thank you."

I awoke feeling strangely rested and readied for my eleven a.m. pickup from Victor Music. When I began that long walk to the lobby, I saw a large glass window with a lovely garden beyond. There was a short, marble wall where one could sit or have coffee in the restaurant. I had noticed none of this the night of my arrival.

The lobby looked as if it were a mile away as I nervously began my walk toward it. There was background music playing when I heard a very familiar song.

In disbelief, I stopped, sat down and just listened. Out of the thousands and thousands of songs that could have been played at that moment, Astrud Gilberto was singing *Dindi*. Tears sprang to my eyes as I remembered the history of that beautiful Brazilian love song.

Ray knew of Antonio Carlos Jobim, and Jobim knew of Ray—but they hadn't yet met. Jobim needed to have an English lyric written and sent Ray the music.

In Brazil, *Dindi* was a term of endearment. Ray loved the melody and immediately began to write a lyric. On a beautiful, clear and sunny day, we decided to drive to Big Bear in the Southern California mountains. Of course, my little Miniature Schnauzer, Jody, was with us.

As we drove along what seemed to be the top of the world, Ray suddenly pulled off to observe a vista of the valley below. It was so clear in that year of 1964.

"I'm going to walk Jody, honey," I told him. "I'll be back soon."

I saw an envelope in his hands as he said, "Okay, see you soon."

We were gone about half an hour, and when I returned, he gave me the envelope and said, "This is for you, sweetheart."

On it, in his funny handwriting, were the lyrics to *Dindi*—complete, perfect and so moving.

"This old envelope was all I had to write on," he said, "and everything came so fast, I didn't want to lose it."

"I'll keep it forever, Pops," I assured Ray. And I have.

That day, sitting on that banquette in far-off Tokyo, I felt as if Ray had reached out to me saying, "Thank you, honey. I'm here and I love you."

Dindi was the beginning of their partnership and the formation of Ipanema Music Corp. Its growth was the reason for my journey and the ensuing bits of craziness that followed.

The head of Victor Music was waiting for me. He spoke very limited English, and I knew only one word of Japanese: *Arigato*. If there was just one word to know, at least I'd learned the best one.

As we left the hotel that day, it was very cold.

"We will walk," he said. "It's not far."

We began side by side, but this man kept increasing his pace and soon I was falling behind him, still trying to keep up a polite conversation while looking at his back. Each time I got caught up, he would go faster.

Suddenly, it occurred to me that I'd missed something, involving Japanese protocol. "Following" him meant just that. I didn't realize that he expected me to follow him six paces behind. When I slowed down, so did he, and our walk ended with me quietly and obediently in my rightful position as a female.

Oh, what I'd give to have had a chance to snap a selfie that day. I still laugh at the mental picture produced by my lesson in Japanese culture.

When I was introduced to the office staff and the man's assistant, I was relieved to hear English once more. His assistant took me to lunch and introduced me to shabu-shabu (a dish of thinly sliced meat and vegetables boiled in water). Unforgettably delicious, but you don't ask for a doggie bag.

The ritualistic service with Japanese food was unfamiliar to me, so I simply asked for help. That luncheon with a warm, friendly and intelligent young Japanese man was surprising and so informative for us both. We discussed music, politics, WWII and the booming, economic results from the loss of their military.

"You took our sovereignty away," he said. "We had to do something."

"To be fair," I replied, "Japan had a great deal to do with that loss."

He paused, smiled and said, "You are absolutely right, Janis. Talking and not shooting was by far the most productive way to face the future. At least, start there."

In the days to follow, I saw the burgeoning Japanese economy soaring. A grapefruit cost six dollars. Prices were ridiculous. American music, western dress and of course blue jeans could not be stopped as our influence rolled over the old into this new world.

I was blonde, very fit, pretty and a woman alone. I came that way to Japan from America ready to go to work. Unfortunately. I wasn't prepared for the kind of work certain Japanese men expected from me.

As I entered the elevator at my hotel one day, I joined three American businessmen busily talking shop, another American, and a Japanese man. The three Americans got off, still talking. Next, the other American found his floor and got off.

I was now alone with the Japanese man and twenty-five floors to go. I stood quietly waiting, but when the doors closed this man suddenly positioned himself right in front of me, back to the doors. He bowed and then said, "I want make love with you."

"What did you say?" I asked, incredulous. "What did you say?" I repeated in shock.

He bowed again and said, "I want make love with you." Just that easily.

Towering above the man by some six inches, I got in his face and yelled, "Who do you think you are? Get out of here!"

When the door opened to another passenger, he simply bowed again saying, "So sorry, thank you very much," and exited.

My insulted femaleness was smoking. As I waited for the 40th floor, I saw the latest Japanese rider smiling at me. When the doors opened and I could get off, I muttered, "Get over it, mister!" and ran to my room.

I have no idea why that poor man was smiling, but I wasn't taking a chance.

When my sense of humor finally returned and I had a clear picture of how I'd handled the elevator proposition, I started to laugh. I laughed even harder when I asked myself if being an American would have increased the amount of yen I would have earned in that transaction.

"I hope Ray saw this," I thought. "He'll be laughing into next year."

I witnessed the old passing the torch to the new in Japan. I saw obi-clad women, eyes down with hands tucked in their kimono sleeves, walking six paces behind their men. In the Ginza district were jeans-clad copycats of American musical groups.

At night, Tokyo was blinding due to the millions of lights everywhere. From my window on the 40th floor, the gigantic Sapporo Beer sign lit up my darkened room. The influence of western culture had invaded Tokyo, and there was no end in sight.

The Japanese were extremely devoted to strict order and pragmatism. To avoid the danger of a disease epidemic in an extremely crowded city, the citizens wore surgical masks. "Why aren't we that smart?" I wondered.

While standing on a corner in the middle of a crowd of people one day, the light changed, and I found myself helplessly swept along to the other side of the street. To get back to where I was, I simply stood in the middle of another masked mob, who kidnapped me back to where I'd been.

I soon learned to be careful and stayed away from queues, too. Their built-in cultural sense of order was evident everywhere, and it was obviously working.

When I left for home, I stopped in Hawaii for a week of business. When I hit my bed that first night, I awoke fourteen hours later with the words, "Are you all right, Miss Paige? We're sorry to frighten you, but we got worried when you slept so long."

"Thank you," I said, "I'm fine and craving coffee and a Danish."

That sleeping experience never found me again, but I felt new, refreshed and so grateful that I'd landed on my feet, ready for my next "journey of a thousand miles."

Section VII
The 1980s

Reveille

There are two mistakes one makes on the road to truth:
Not going all the way and not starting.

—Buddha

Some eight years after Ray's death, I began to be symptomatic of nothing in particular but...something. When one something would get some help, another something would take its place.

What I didn't know was that the screwed up, still unrecognized and for the most part ignored part of me was finally screaming for help. Everything I thought I knew scared the hell out of me. It's what I didn't know that was finally waking me up to what I had yet to learn. I'd barely just begun—and I was sixty-three.

I was approaching a crisis in my life, a deep, dark and scary chasm that kept me from seeing the opportunities quietly waiting to be discovered. Fortunately, Dr. Paul Geller understood, and there wasn't a pill to fix the real problem. I always relied on Paul to level with me, and this time was no exception.

Sitting across his desk from him, I said, "Well, what do you think?"

I wasn't ready for his reply.

"You're not handling stress well, Janis, and if you don't make some changes, you're going to face something terminal."

I could scarcely get the word out.

"Terminal?" I asked. "Are you talking cancer, Paul?"

"I'm talking cancer and anything else that can become terminal."

"My God, Paul, since Ray died, I've had nothing but stress," I admitted. "It's everywhere. It's even stressful trying not to be stressed. I've had to learn to live without him, make decisions about his professional life when I'm now the only one responsible for my choices.

"I'm flying by the seat of my pants all over the place, but I'm determined that his life's work be safe with me. Believe me, Paul, show business is a walk in the park compared to the music business."

I continued, "After all of these years, I'm still catching up with everything he never told me and knowing I never will. I'm deeply grateful for what I have, but I'm also feeling helpless and, at times, overwhelmed. Why, when I'm doing the best I can, do I feel so angry and guilty?"

Paul sat quietly listening to my tirade and then said, "I want you to talk to someone, Jan. You need another kind of help. No medicine is going to ease your situation. I know someone who I like and trust. Here's her telephone number. Give her a call and start to save your life."

I sat stunned, defeated and still hearing Ray's disapproving voice when years ago he had negated our getting any outside help that I felt we needed. He was a closed system when it came to therapy.

Ambivalence played the starring role in this drama as I drove home clutching the number Paul had given me. The only therapy I knew had been when I worked with Dr. Hutschnecker on his book *The Will to Live* so many years ago. He allowed my curiosity to take flight, and I was encouraged to probe and ask until I understood what Arnold had written.

"After all, Jan," he said, "this book is for you and all of the others who are in the dark about their somatic selves."

I remember the excitement each time we'd work on a chapter. Hours of questions, and at the end he'd say, "That's enough for today. We deserve some champagne and caviar. We're ready, Florita, come join us." How I loved those learning times when I felt so important and useful.

Obviously, Arnold was just the beginning, I surmised, as I drove home. You never went far enough, and as Grandma would so often say, "The chickens have come home to roost, honey." What a funny, old-fashioned saying.

I could never understand it as a child, but it's making its own countrified sense to me now.

It's the same as what Arnold wrote in 1950 when he spoke about the body/mind concept: "If you don't pay attention, I'll be heard, one way or another."

Good God, I thought, *would I rather get sick than find out my mother was wrong about me? Do I owe her the rest of my life?*

Paul hit me in the face with reality, and I knew deep down that he was right. I may be headed in the right direction as far as my post-Ray responsibilities were concerned, but I was obviously headed in the opposite direction from what was best for my welfare.

"Why can't I do both?" I whispered. *You can start by not asking questions you can't answer,* I thought. *The merry-go-round, the pretty horses and the music are gone. The circus left town, Jan. What now?*

Still ruminating, I opened the door and went to the phone. With no place to go and no escape route, I dialed the number in my hand. After I nervously introduced myself, Dr. Carole Rubenstein said, "I have some time tomorrow, Miss Paige. How is one o'clock?"

"That's fine," I said. "Thank you so much."

Whenever I'd stand in the wings waiting to go onstage, I'd get what I began to call my gut clutch. Others called it stage fright. I sure have it today, I thought, as I found my way to Dr. Rubenstein's office.

Am I performing today, too? Is pleasing the doctor the same as pleasing the audience? I don't even know the doctor. I know an audience better than I know the doctor. Hell, I know an audience better than I know myself.

I parked and walked to the door. "At least I got here by myself," I whispered.

Dr. Rubenstein proved to be exactly what I needed, but I don't think either one of us knew it at that first meeting. She listened intently, hearing me unload my feelings and fears. During the next three or four sessions, I began to be defensive, angry and difficult.

I knew she was there to help me, but I'd end up apologizing and leave, feeling defeated. She wanted me to do some breathing exercises, and the first time I tried them I burst into tears. I was angry and embarrassed at feeling so vulnerable.

"I can't do this!" I cried. "Why do I have to breathe like this?"

"These are what we call energy breaths, Janis. When you do them correctly, they relax the tightness inside and working becomes easier. Please don't worry about the tears and anger. We'll try it again next week."

I sobbed most of the way home that day. I've taken directions all of my life, why couldn't I do it now? Why did I feel so helpless? Why did breathing make me so angry and explosive? I'm sixty-three and wondering who I've been all of these years and where I was going now. I was terrified.

As I neared my home, I suddenly, for some unknown reason, remembered a simple statement that I had seen pasted on my friend Kenny Nelson's dressing room mirror in 1970. I had just witnessed a brilliant new play called *The Boys in the Band*, and I went backstage to congratulate him.

I teared up as I read, "I know I am I, because my little dog knows me." When I turned to Kenny, he said, "That goes everywhere with me, Janis. It's the last thing I see before I go onstage. It keeps me grounded and reminds me of what's real."

Why I remembered that now, I couldn't say.

There was a surprise waiting for me when I arrived for my next session with Dr. Rubenstein. When we sat down, she said, "I want to talk to you, Janis."

Uh-oh, I thought. Am I getting fired? I'm not doing so good so far. Where will I go if she gives up on me?

There it was again, that old, familiar feeling of "I'm not good enough."

"I'm going to recommend a different kind of therapist for you, Janis," she said.

Tears welled up as I thought, "I'm right. She *is* giving up on me."

I don't want to leave. I liked her so much. What if the new therapist can't help me? *I'm so lost, Carole*, I thought, *please don't send me away.*

"You need something I can't give you right now. I want you to see the therapist who trained me. I came from his group and I deeply feel that this is the right move for you."

Sadness turned into a kind of quiet terror at the thought of baring my soul to a group, a bunch of strangers. After a lifetime in show business, I always felt different from the rest of the world. The joke was on me; I wasn't.

"I'll call Dr. Rosenberg for you, Janis, and you can make an appointment to see him. Please remember, you are not alone. I only want to help you in any way I can. I hope you'll give him a chance; he's wonderful! Here's his number. Call me if you have any questions."

Before I could think too much, I called Dr. Rosenberg.

I was sixty-three and about to take my first shaky and tentative baby steps toward someone I scarcely knew: Me. It would prove to be the hardest work I've ever done, but by far the most gratifying.

One night in group, after a hard-earned, victorious moment of self-discovery, I had an epiphany.

I had probed and dissected countless scripts and song lyrics, struggling to understand and find their truth. Why, then, had I declared that same struggle to my own reality off limits?

That night, I passed the point of no return on my own personal journey. It had been a long and bumpy ride toward a life of greater clarity. I'd do it again, but this time I'd know better how to get out of my own way and stay out.

> *"Don't tell me what to do!" That phrase can be verbal or quietly hostile. The problem with "Don't tell me what to do!" is that you can't tell yourself what to do.*
>
> *-From the wisdom of Dr. Jack Rosenberg*

Therapy and Dr. Jack Rosenberg

The 11th Commandment: Lighten up.
—Dr. Jack L. Rosenberg

"What brought you here, Janis?"
"My life."
"Why now?"
"It's getting late."
"Late for what?"
"To find the missing pieces."
"What's missing?"
"Me!"

Up until now, it seems I've owned only a part of my life, with the rest of me screaming for something I don't understand. Is there anything beyond getting older and finally dying? With all I've accomplished and survived in my life, did it matter?

After my last session with Dr. Rubenstein, I quickly made an appointment to see Dr. Jack Rosenberg and his co-therapist and wife, Dr. Beverly Kitaen-Morse. I was shaky and feeling exposed but answered their questions as best I could.

Somehow, I knew that I had reached a point in my life when the emotional dam in me was breaking and I was feeling like an angry and helpless child. Like politicians, show people also hid any therapeutic help they might need. After all, I thought, "I'm a star. I can't show anything but perfection. It's my job."

They asked questions, explained group therapy and asked me how I felt at the prospect of working in this manner. I was not eager.

"Dr. Rosenberg," I said, "my life has been spent in show business. I've been private with my personal life, and just the thought of sharing it with strangers is a daunting idea. I don't think I can do it or want to do it. I'm embarrassed just thinking about it."

Dr. Rubenstein's greatest gift to me was to send me to a group. I did not go quietly, gracefully or eagerly. For three weeks, I was a silent, hostile non-participant. I hated being there.

"What I ask of new clients," Dr. Rosenberg said, "is that they give me a month, once a week. If, at the end of that month, you don't want to stay, you're free to go, no questions asked."

A month, huh? I thought. *Well, at least I have an out.* I hesitated and then, "Okay, I'll try for a month."

"As a matter of fact, we can start tonight," Jack said.

"Tonight?"

My mind slammed on the brakes. *I'm not ready for this*, I thought.

"Your group meets on Thursday night, six to eight in the evening. We're about ready to start now."

I'll never know if that was a strategy or an accident, but whatever it was changed my life. Walking into that room, however, drained me, and outside of meeting everyone, I was mute.

Lighten up? What I didn't know was that I'd have to travel in the dark before I could ever reach the light and Jack's 11th Commandment.

After introductions, a vow of confidentiality was agreed on by each group member personally. Then the rules of group were given to me.

"No discussions of who is in the group outside of the therapy session. You can discuss your own work, but never the work of someone else. If someone is working (speaking), please wait until they're finished to make comments."

So, I began what I knew would be only a month.

"You don't have to talk, Jan," Jack assured me, "but when you do, we can begin to help with whatever the problems are."

Three weeks into my one-month deal with Jack, the screwed-up and repressed part of me broke loose and one of my newly met, unsuspecting groupmates was the target.

He was working, and something he said prompted an angry, knee-jerk reaction to this undeserving victim of my rage. When I finished my stupid tirade, I burst into tears of shame and embarrassment at what I'd done.

First of all, I had impulsively interrupted this man's work, and that was not allowed. The rules of behavior in group were made very clear to me. For three weeks I'd sat mute, counting the days until I could leave. I apologized profusely at my unwarranted outburst and then I heard Jack quietly ask, "Do you want to work, Janis?"

Feeling completely exposed, I replied, "I guess I'd better, Jack. I don't know what happened."

Just the few visits with Dr. Rubenstein had shown me that there was something I was refusing to allow to surface. Good lord, I thought, I'm not a thief or a murderer. I work hard and make mistakes like everyone else until I know better. What am I hiding?

When I finally became involved in my own junk, I understood how vitally important it was to respect the group rules. Our patient response to Jack and Beverly's "Anyone want to say something about what you just experienced?" was invaluable to me.

"Your comments must always include your personal reaction to the previous work," they added.

It took me quite a while to understand the value of that time-controlled, cooling-off pause, while we listened and found a less-volatile comment on the previous work. I began to realize that my groupmates whom I joined every Thursday night were the teachers I so badly needed. Not only did they socialize me in a far different way, but they gave me a safe place to be wrong, to be right and to finally explore what I had sorely missed growing up.

No longer strangers, these people were becoming my family, and I was finally being seen and heard.

"We'll have to stop now."

My first therapy session ended with that phrase. Hearing those words left me scared, angry and feeling abandoned again. Wasn't therapy supposed to make me feel different? Not yet, Jan. There's work to do and for me, there was no way out.

I'd gone kicking and silently screaming all the way to that first night when all I could feel or understand was that everyone in the room was smarter, wiser, calmer, saner and more patient that I could ever be. Of course, they had all been where I was that night, a beginner in real life, and they were in a different grade than I.

My sister and I were taught to behave. Our good manners along with our educations were sacrosanct. No matter how devastating The Great Depression, we went to school, displayed our well-taught upbringing and never did anything to bring shame on the family.

"Children should be seen and not heard" was the mantra when we were small. We also grew up with the sad reality of my mother's unhappiness. There was never any discussion or explanation, leading to some understanding that her unhappiness was not our fault. The role of fixer began to fit me perfectly.

Therapy would show me that fixing begins with me.

Sooner or later, some unsuspecting lover, husband and now therapist was going to feel my pain. Dr. Rubenstein had sent me to a group so I could develop some family skills in dealing with my past.

One night, working on the latest man in my life, Jack said, "Janis, you keep looking 'out there' for what you want. It's not 'out there.' You never get anything from 'out there.' It all starts *in here*."

As he said those last words, Jack pointed to his gut. My gut had been screaming for years. Perhaps I was finally ready to hear and accept the truth about the real journey I was still avoiding. I only know that it all began that night.

Like life itself, the road to me was rocky and at times almost impassable. Mostly, it reminded me that I had a new and better way of taking care of my life, especially the one I spent with myself.

Decisions involving my right to speak the truth, however, still led to ambivalence and the fear of retribution. I learned long ago to travel my own road, but when it came to secrecy involving me—resulting in gossip, disloyalty and the ensuing hypocrisy—I deeply resented having to handle the pain of betrayal caused by someone's duplicitous behavior.

None of us wants to be found out, but when we are, we need to fess up and apologize. We risk losing a relationship, but the courage to admit the truth is freeing and character-building, albeit lonely.

Sadly, the truth can also run into what Jack and Beverly called a closed system. These people are so tightly zipped into their own rigidity that the ball is once again back in your court. That's when one's ethics, integrity and self-respect make the final choice foggy, and hazardous.

Many internal battles over the old stuff ensue, leading to the well-earned victories over myself and my choices. For me, therapy was the most difficult work I'd ever known, but at the same time also the most rewarding.

I continue to use what I learned in therapy every day. Mostly, it reminds me that I have a new and better way of taking care of my life, especially the one I spend with others. Decisions involving my right to speak the truth, however, still cause ambivalence and the fear of retribution.

But I'm not finished, yet, I thought. *Wasn't therapy supposed to make me feel different? Not yet, Jan. There's work to do and, for me now, there's no way out.*

The False Self

> *Courage doesn't happen when you have all of the answers. It happens when you are ready to face the questions you have been avoiding your whole life.*
>
> —Shannon L. Adler

Through years of tears and painful exploration—often discouraging, often enlightening and, more often than not, left wondering if I would ever get to the other side of me—I grew fixated on getting to know the real Janis.

One night in group, I did just that.

No trumpets sounded and there was no applause, just a quiet graduation for the years of commitment and hard-won loyalty to Janis.

I came to group therapy that night depressed, angry and feeling alone. As usual, Jack took our numbers. On a scale of one to ten, how we were doing and how we were handling everything. It was a simple barometer for us to know our own feelings and that of our groupmates.

Needless to say, both of my numbers were low and so was I. I sat there hating everyone for being well while I was still sick.

"Who wants to work? Raise your hands."

Jack put things in order as we began the journey for that night. I did not raise my hand. I sat unsmiling and dark and empty, and I couldn't bring myself to find out what I knew to be the truth.

"It's too late," I lamented. "I'm not good enough."

The old familiar chant was back. How dare I be different! How dare I have a life of my own!

"What's going on with you, Jan?" I heard Jack ask.

"There's no writing on me," I blurted out. "There's no writing on me."

Then came the tears, flowing like a river.

"I'm scared to death. I've worked so hard to have nothing. I can't find me! Why am I so depressed?"

Jack turned to Beverly, his wife and co-therapist, smiled and said, "Congratulations! The False Self is gone. After all of the hard work and dedication, the prize is the loss of the False Self. Now you can start to live a new way, make decisions a new way. You can now have your own direction. It's all up to you. You did the work, and we're proud of you!"

I also learned something else. The old stuff always lurks somewhere near, ready to pounce, ready to take you back to old pain, old lies, old problems, old needs to be fixed.

"How does it feel, Jan, to claim your own life?" Jack asked. "Decide for yourself. Say 'No' and don't feel that punishing guilt!"

After the newfound me tentatively tried me out and the world didn't fall around me, nobody was angry or disappointed. There was no silent treatment. I wondered why it had taken so long for me to feel this freedom of my soul.

My late husband used to say, "You're so damned smart, honey, but you don't want to take responsibility for the gift you have. You've gotta have street smarts to protect you from the *gonifs* out there. I worry about you."

Everything Ray ever said to me went in and stayed. It always made sense, but I wasn't ready to hear it. Well, I finally heard you, honey. I heard Jack and Beverly, and I heard my group. But there were earlier voices, earlier words that seemed to take precedence over any new thoughts or actions.

Ray used to say, "You listen, but you don't hear."

Believe me, honey, I listen and I hear now. And I finally earned my street smarts. I like who and where I am today, and I'm so far from that sixty-three-year-old woman who faced a bunch of strangers the night I entered therapy that I wonder sometimes what happened to her.

Oh, she's still here, but I take reasonably good care of her today.

The self-defending, knee-jerk reactions I used to have are gone. Life is so much easier, funnier, more gratifying, creative and just plain satisfying as a result.

Even when I forgot that I had a guardian angel, she was always there. I just kept my emotional door closed and I couldn't hear her knocking.

Before accepting the gift of therapy, I was in the same emotional quicksand that kept women like me struggling to be perfect. It's what happens when you're raised in a house of secrets with no awareness of your history. No questions were asked because we weren't allowed that freedom as children.

Did anyone in my family ever wonder or question how and what we were learning except to keep our mouths shut? No. Any mention of my father would send my mother into a deep and punishing depression. So, we kept quiet. I didn't know the first thing about being a woman or who and what embodied a man.

Thank God I lived and grew up in a simpler time, a kinder time and, in many ways, a better time. The onslaught of demands on our undeveloped psyche was minimal back then compared to today's sad no-childhood children. Our sexual awakenings were tempered by time, culture and behavior.

We had time to grow. Self-degradation was unknown to us. Today, it's somehow become sexy, with unbelievably lasting and painful consequences.

In Hollywood, if you don't have a shrink, people think you're crazy.

-Johnny Carson

Victory over Myself

IN READING THE LIVES OF GREAT MEN, I FOUND THAT THE FIRST VICTORY THEY WON WAS OVER THEMSELVES. . . . SELF-DISCIPLINE WITH ALL OF THEM CAME FIRST.

—President Harry Truman

The only real victory is the one we have over ourselves. Nothing means anything until you can feel the peaceful strength in your gut that comes from the victory over your own baggage.

Finally, a decision is made, completely from what is the truth. What do you want Jan? What is good for you and not earned because you gave away part of yourself to keep someone else victorious over your wants and needs?

Ultimately, you heard you. You saw you and you saw it through all of the shit from the past and the words of a voice not your own.

Victory, Jan!

If there is one message that I could leave for the world, it would be to never stop your own journey. It's a lonely one but it must be, so that your truth is not invalidated by someone else's opinion of you.

The work never stops. Today was a good day for growth, and tomorrow will be the same if you continue to feel deserving of your own evolution. It's not the years that matter but the result of the dedication to your betterment as a partner in this world.

Each and every day, I am a better friend, a better employer, a better patient, with a new understanding of not only myself, but of the other guy, too. Whoever said it's not the quantity of life but the quality that counts was right.

Maybe it's my very early Sunday School training, but I've always believed in a powerful something way beyond myself that loves and protects me when I can't or won't. Were you my Guardian Angel that sat on my right shoulder as I walked my six-year-old legs to school so long ago? I was scared, alone and talking my way into courage that first day. You're still here, aren't you? At least I choose to believe you are.

When I awoke today, it was December 22, 2016. If there wasn't something beyond what I've witnessed, experienced and seen during this sad and regressing world, I would have joined the muddied ones and lost myself.

THE GRAY AREA

*PART OF ME LONGS TO DO A JOB WHERE
THERE'S NO GRAY AREA.*

—JODIE FOSTER

THE GRAY AREA or no-man's land between right and wrong is now too vast, too easily yielding to the iffy part of us. We need to shrink that space until we can see the shores of right and wrong again and feel our conscience once more.

I'm talking about the pain caused by bullying, gossiping, lying, cheating, stealing, disloyalty, betrayal and hurting someone for the sake of a false feeling of power, or just the good old, garden-variety cowardice of not taking responsibility for the pain caused to another human being.

All of this and more is in that gray area where we now give ourselves permission to be dishonest, self-aggrandizing, rigid, unethical, cruel and just plain mean. We permit ourselves and others to live in that area because we can. No longer are there consequences. Shame has been erased from our vocabulary, only to be replaced by "I have my rights!"

When did our disgustingly permissive parenting endorse an equally permissive educational system? No judgments, no cheating, accept everyone, no-holds-barred and no proper punishment for the agony and suffering committed simply because we can.

Instead of a class on how to use a condom, perhaps a course in self-discipline coupled with the recognition of what it means to have a guilty conscience and the value of same is in order.

On second thought, is it even possible to find teachers who could or would teach the wisdom and worth of these subjects? They no longer teach American history, or how this exceptional country was born—so how can we assume that wisdom will supersede what is, in my opinion, a sadly destructive ideology?

Young minds don't know the difference until it's too late to save our heritage. One has to fight evil where it resides, but even the definition of it has been polluted to fit the new freedoms demanded by the "Me! Me!" crowd.

There is the evil of a Bin Laden and his ilk of generational haters. There is also the thoughtless evil of the countless Facebook sins perpetrated on unknowing others with whom they disagree, hate and envy. Some of this unwarranted malice results in the lasting and unanswerable pain of suicide.

Families have been torn apart from the unreasonable and unthinkable evil found in too many of our young people today. If we don't find some constructive and teachable answers to this dark abyss in our country, who and what will we be?

I grew up in a much different time. I am fully aware of this fact, but there are certain facets of our character that should remain immovable. These rules of life are not easy to maintain but are universal. It takes enormous inner faith in one's own ability to remain ethically intact.

We can fail—and do—but we need to embrace truth, integrity, a moral compass and the self-respect that comes with the discipline so necessary to be a trustworthy human being.

It is nearly forgotten in today's America that "We the People" also pay the bills for everything. No longer are we asked or even informed before another gigantic bill comes due. America and her so-called representatives of the people have for too long gone off the tracks of truth, trust, oaths of office and their promise to serve the good of the country instead of themselves.

I truly believe that there are good and decent men and women in government who practice ethics, knowing that without them we are lost. These people are vilified and silenced by the uncontrollable voices that can no longer tell the truth, let alone live it.

There are antibiotics for almost any disease today except one for immorality. We are the only antibiotic that can fix that one. The choice is ours. It begins with us and our wish for the true freedom that comes with responsibility for one's own behavior.

Would that we could stop getting away with it, step outside of the protection of groupthink and group actions and have the guts to clean up our own junk.

One of the things that can save us is self-discipline. We owe this training to one another, and we owe it to ourselves to realize how it feels to take responsibility and not expect someone else to do the job for us.

Australia

Kiwis, koalas, kangaroos and the Aussies.
God bless them all.

—Janis Paige

"G'dye, Miss Pyge. Welcome to 'Stralia. I'm here to drive you to your hotel."

I had just flown over that scary Pacific Ocean again, but this time jetting in the ivory-towered 747. That vast, black ocean was still below as I remembered our Christmas trips to Vietnam, Korea and Japan. We had no jets then, so we flew in a four-engine prop plane flown by angel pilots. Flying in that beloved 747 was a far cry from the Bob Hope tours.

Phasing out those magnificent planes was the beginning of the end of comfort for future passengers forever. I'm amazed that "Sardine Airlines" is not painted on the sides of their planes.

The Australians reminded me of my growing up in America with only that charming accent setting them apart from the rest of my world. For years, the land Down Under had produced some extraordinary productions.

It was common to admire and embrace the talents of their actors and actresses in films, television and even commercials. Remember *Crocodile Dundee* star Paul Hogan, tossing another "shrimp on the barbie," among his other accomplishments?

In 1988, *Mission Impossible* was filmed in Queensland, Australia, and here I was facing a new adventure on a new continent. It became a seemingly endless trip with three hours in Sydney customs and two and a half hours more to Brisbane. I simply turned off the tired button and waited for a bed, any bed, anywhere.

As we finally drove to our destination, I watched in amazement as a momma kangaroo hopped along with her baby tucked safely in her pouch. The baby was blissfully riding along, enjoying the view as I wondered where they were going.

There were other kangaroos too, strangely ignoring the traffic as I watched a creature I'd only seen in zoos and in pictures.

My driver suddenly slowed down and pulled off to the side of the road.

"There's a koala in that tree on your right," he said. "Can you see him?"

It took me a few minutes to locate the teddy bear. He was asleep and absolutely adorable.

"Don't try to cuddle that one, Miss Pyge," he warned. "Those claws are sharp and their dispositions not much better. They don't even like other koalas."

"Thanks for warning me," I said. "I'll try to resist."

What I found irresistible, though, were the Aussies themselves. They were kind, open, helpful and generous. In 1988, there was still a kind of not-caught-up-yet-to-the-rest-of-the-world aspect. I took a deep breath of Australian air, gave in to a slower pace and began to relax.

When I finished filming, I had only two days and two nights left before my scheduled flight back to America. I desperately wanted to see Sydney, and not just the inside of the airport. I needed only to ask, and the producers arranged everything for me.

The Queensland shore reminded me of some of our beaches in America. I saw little else during my working trip. Surfers and surfboards, souvenir shops and bikinis, with only the delightful Australians and their dialect setting it apart from the familiar beachy atmosphere I'd find in California, New Jersey or Hawaii.

I was rather astounded that there were studios sitting out in the middle of nowhere. It was still kind of primitive, very much so by today's standards. It was like stepping back into early America, with a familial feeling we simply don't have on the job anymore.

Arriving in Sydney, I found my hotel warm and welcoming. And after a good night's sleep, I began to fall in love with the city, its sights and its citizens.

The one memory that overwhelms the others was my first sight of Sydney's harbor. If you haven't seen it, you've missed one of the world's wonders. No picture and no description could ever do justice to the perfect blending of the old embracing the new. It's one of the few natural harbors. The opera house sat on a little island all its own. It's simply stunning.

Sydney Harbor was a bit reminiscent of San Francisco, Seattle and Boston but retained its own unique charm. I began my day with a walk over their beautiful Sydney Harbor Bridge that first morning.

As I continued my view from the bridge, I became acutely aware of the human wisdom and imagination used to protect Sydney's harbor. We've all seen and experienced the sad and unrelenting vestiges of unstoppable progress. In 1988, Sydney was much smaller and slower than it is today. It's now become a very important center for progress, but still remains respectful of its past.

After my bridge walk, I caught the ferry to that outer-space structure called the Sydney Opera House. When I looked back at where I'd been on the bridge, I saw a kind of perfection around me.

I was alone that day but never lonely. I had countless Australians ready to help me to find my way. I even had someone show me some of the magnificent theaters and halls at no charge. It's very different today, but whatever the cost, consider it a gift to your deeper senses.

When I returned to my hotel that day, I'd seen the harbor, part of Sydney, visited a couple of art galleries and had my first introduction to their Aboriginal art. I was also given a short but fascinating history of Australia's Aboriginal people.

When I returned to my hotel, I had a small, Aboriginal painting called Dreamtime wrapped and ready for my luggage and our flight back to America.

It was around six p.m. when I stopped at the hotel desk for messages. I was asked if I had seen Sydney at night.

"It's quite an experience, Miss Pyge, one you shouldn't miss," I was assured.

With so little time left, I agreed. When it got dark, a driver picked me up and Sydney at night proved to be the cherry on the cake. It was an awesomely different experience than the one I'd had during the day.

The water was like glass. No ripples to disturb the countless rainbow-colored lights reflecting from the city and its shore. Their bridge, too, was bathed in light, matched by that gorgeous Opera House looking like a gigantic bird ready to take flight.

Trying to describe the beauty of Sydney at night was an exercise in futility. It simply joined my forever memories of Chicago's Outer Drive and the view of New York City from the New Jersey side of the George Washington Bridge.

The following day, I began that long flight home to America. My hopes for another chance to see Australia never materialized due to life's change of plans. I will, however, never forget the kiwis, koalas and kangaroos. Most of all, my eternal gratitude goes out to those Aussies who live Down Under.

Don't worry about the world coming to an end today. It's already tomorrow in Australia.

-*Charles Schulz*

Soaps

> *Soap operas are like TV boot camp. You have to be able to self-direct, learn a ton of dialogue in a short amount of time, and deliver a performance in one or two takes.*
>
> —Andrea Navedo

When I was on Broadway and sleeping until nine or ten in the morning, my breakfast would be coffee, half a grapefruit, a doughnut and a soap opera. It was a habit I thoroughly enjoyed, while I wondered if I could ever do what these amazing actors did.

They seemed to be operating at a different talent level, as if they were separated from the rest of us. I'd always admired their ability to learn copious lines of dialogue each day and portray such a variety of characters, sometimes changing overnight.

Often, their role would run for years and become attached to the character that finally owned the part. That's as far as I got toward soaps until I got a call one day.

"Janis, this is John Conboy. I produce a soap called *Capitol*, and I have a marvelous part I want you to do. Would you take a meeting with me? The show has had wonderful reviews, but unfortunately we've been cancelled and have only three more months to go."

I loved John's honesty, and we met the following day.

"I've never done a soap, and from what I hear, they're very different from what I've done all my life," I admitted to him. "It's making me nervous just thinking about it. I don't want to let you down, but I confess, my intense curiosity was alive and well whenever I watched one."

John asked one of the show's leading characters if they would work in being introduced. That assurance was what I needed, and I said "Yes."

I would play a catatonic woman with no memory who finally speaks after being in a mental hospital for twenty years. Did I really think before I jumped, taking a leap of faith with no net? Time would tell.

Learning lines was never a problem, but there were too many other surprises to consider on my way to feeling even a little bit satisfied with my work. The birthing pains were just that. It was the emotional ups, downs and doubts that I took home each night that were the most difficult to handle.

Finally, I accepted the fact that the clock running the show for everyone involved was real. There was no time for retakes and deep discussions of character choices, You soon learned that "That's a take" meant "That's a take, moving on."

"But, but, but..."

"Moving on!"

My fellow cast members assured me that they all went through the same thing.

"One of these days it will all click," I was told, "and you'll wonder what you ever worried about." They were right. One day I heard and felt that click. I also realized that every part one plays, whether on TV, on Broadway, in films or in life itself, has a similar click.

"It's a take, moving on, no time for perfection, that will have to be good enough" made me work even harder.

To me, my profession has always been a great analogy for living life each day. Some days I felt that I was an utter failure, but the next day, with its inevitable changes, the strive for perfection begins again.

Ah, perfection. I don't even know what that word means anymore. I think it's similar to happiness. We have the right to pursue it, but it's always our responsibility to listen for those inevitable clicks and then move on.

The inventive, brave and supportive cast members with whom I worked helped me to love and respect the art of the soap opera. I had the great good fortune of acting runs on two more serial daytime drama hits. One was *General Hospital*, on which I received a heart transplant and saw the strict technique of the preparation for that intricate operation.

I was hooked up to everything necessary to save my character's life. We rehearsed, and when I was finally ready for the scene, they called "LUNCH!" I felt their scripts piling up on me and then silence.

A few minutes passed and then my muffled "Hey" brought their laughter. I was unhooked, had lunch, got hooked up again and the "surgeon" gave me a new heart. All of it was technically correct! Amazing!

John Conboy called again, asking me to replace the irreplaceable Dame Judith Anderson on NBC's *Santa Barbara* after she passed away.

"What did you say, John? That's impossible!" I protested.

"We want you to make this your own, Janis, and not copy Dame Judith," John assured me.

"Good," I replied, "because I couldn't copy Dame Judith if I became Dame Judith."

I still remember that first day of work after Dame Judith was gone. Louise Sorel and Nicolas Coster had worked with her for years. As I made my entrance to the scene, I tried hard not to look at Louise's face as she made her instantaneous adjustment to this new Minx Lockridge.

They were both gracefully stoic and welcoming to this new member of their family. Minx went through many changes, but I learned and thoroughly enjoyed my two years-plus on that wonderful show.

I was incredibly fortunate to work with some of the best actors I've ever known. I also made lifelong friends with people who today remain available, loving and caring. Francesca James and Louise Sorel are never far away,

I think Dame Judith Anderson achieved perfection—but I'm sure she would have disagreed with me. Perfection is achieved by anyone who cares deeply about their job. But to me, she was perfect.

Above:
Lucy the Ostrich and her egg. I befriended Lucy during my life-altering trip to South Africa in 1971, and she grew to trust me implicitly.

Left:
A bare-breasted Transkei native woman we passed during my iconic 1971 journey along the Wild Coast of South Africa.

Left:
Lucy the Ostrich, with whom I had an almost spiritual connection while visiting South Africa. She was able to look right into my soul.

Below:
Baboons in the Cape of Good Hope. They would spring up suddenly by the side of the road, baring their fangs at us as we drove past.

Above: *On the death-defying Sani Pass where I feared I'd meet my end, along the Wild Coast of South Africa. This route is exactly as treacherous and crazy as it looks, maybe more.*

Below: *I've always loved horses. This is Calazar, a great, great horse. He could jump anything. Oh, how I loved him. And oh, the guts I had.*

Above: *In Venice, Italy with armfuls of birds during my 1967 trip with Ray.*

Below: *Starring onstage in* Born Yesterday *in 1970, in the role originated by Judy Holliday (Billie Dawn) both on Broadway in 1946 and in the 1950 feature. It was written for the stage by the great Garson Kanin.*

Above: *This is me with Jellybean Joe (named for Ray's brother). He was born at 3 a.m. on the coldest day of the year in March 1973.*

Below: *Me with Adam, the greatest horse in the world. He had a big red heart on his rump.*

Above: *With the amazing Carroll O'Connor on* All in the Family *in 1976. I got hate mail for daring to kiss Archie Bunker. I'd told no one that my husband Ray had died two months prior. During rehearsal, I started to read a self-help book when Carroll saw my anxiety. So, I told him about Ray. He took both my hands in his, closed my book and said, "Open the door to life. That's the answer you'll find." What a brilliant actor and phenomenal man he was.*

Right: *Performing at the Bob Hope Theatre in Dallas, on the campus of SMU.*

Above:
In my role on the CBS soap opera Capitol *in 1987.*

Right:
On the ABC soap General Hospital *in 1989.*

Above left: *The great Dr. Jack Rosenberg, who took me on my journey into group therapy. It was the most difficult work I've ever known, yet at the same time the most rewarding.*

Above right: *Dr. Beverly Kitaen-Morse, Jack's wife and an extraordinary therapist in her own right.*

As Minx Lockridge in the NBC soap Santa Barbara *(1992).*

Section VIII
The 1990s & 2000s

Celebrating my 90th birthday with a performance in the Rrazz Room in San Francisco (September 2012). It was such a thrilling evening.

Losing My Voice:
A Lesson Finally Learned

Listen to others, but don't lose your own voice. Unfortunately, the other voices were louder than mine.

–Janis Paige

Several years ago, I wanted to perform again and started singing lessons. I still sang well, but from neglect and non-use I developed a break in my voice and was working on it.

Nothing was going fast enough, however, and one day I ran into Shirley MacLaine at the sports doctor. We exchanged "Glad to see yous" and "What's news?" and then she asked me what I was doing. I related the singing effort.

Shirley said that she'd found a miracle teacher who had fixed her break and added one octave to her voice. Through her books, she had become quite famous for her ability to talk to God along with her fierce and unshakable faith in herself.

"What can go wrong?" I thought. I got the man's number and called for an appointment.

As he opened his door, I totally ignored my gut instinct to run, and fast. There he stood in a Hanes undershirt, bare arms, chest hair and a motorcycle in the driveway.

"Don't be judgmental, Jan," I thought, as I met a man who was also not very friendly.

I was shown to a small room with a keyboard on a table. There was no piano and none of the trappings of a singing instructor. I told him that Shirley had recommended him, and he asked me to sing a few scales.

"I can fix this problem!" he announced and proceeded to demonstrate some of the worst sounding exercises I'd ever heard. They were guttural, screaming sounds, and my throat began to hurt.

"That's all part of the process," he said. "Now get the emotion out of you and let's go again."

"Right now, my voice *is* my emotion," I replied, "and you don't seem to have respect for that fact."

From my teens, I had been trained in the Bel Canto method of singing, the same Italian method used by Tony Bennett, who, in his nineties was still thrilling audiences everywhere with his amazing voice. Tony once said in an interview I heard that every day of his life he practiced his Bel Canto training. I only wish that I had been as respectful of my voice as he. I'd still experience the wonderful feeling of vocal freedom.

Unfortunately, I left this "miracle" teacher too late. After three months, my top voice was gone—and I couldn't carry a pitch, *any* pitch. I walked out of there sick to my stomach and scared to death. What now?

It was then that a teacher I knew recommended that I make an appointment at the famous Vanderbilt Voice Center at Vanderbilt University in Nashville, Tennessee to work with the famous Dr. Robert Ossoff. Singing had always been so easy for me. Now, I was terrified, and so discouraged that I was open to try anything.

At the Voice Center, I spent a week going through copious tests—including a camera placed down my throat—confirming that I had bowed vocal cords that had been badly abused. My throat, too, was tender.

When I was ushered into Dr. Ossoff's office, it was filled with framed Gold Records from the people whose voices he had saved as well as countless signed pictures.

The doctor listened as I told him of my problems, and when I mentioned the name of the teacher, I saw a look fleetingly cross his face. I asked if he knew him. He said that he had heard of him and that was that.

I was finally told to go home and not speak for three months and then return, and they would put me on some kind of a program. I would, however, have to return to the clinic several more times.

Three months? There was no way I could remain speechless for three months. I was running a business. It simply wasn't feasible.

I went home devastated and unsure of what my future held.

Once back in Los Angeles, I began a series of supervised, gentle humming and scales sessions. After a few months of very careful work, it was suggested that I go see a highly recommended doctor in Beverly Hills, Dr. Edward Kantor. This time, his camera showed a small improvement in the condition of my vocal cords. They were still bowed but a little better.

In his office at the time was a man whom Dr. Kantor introduced to me as a singing teacher. I felt so hopeless, but this man said that he could help me—and Dr. Kantor said that he was very good.

That is how I met Bruce Eckstut. I started to study with him, and it changed my life. I wanted so badly to work again, and he helped make it possible. I regret that I never worked with Dr. Ossoff, but circumstances and responsibilities took precedence. I felt fortunate to have found such a worthy replacement.

The week I began to work with Bruce was, in a word, terrible! I could not hold a pitch even on one note for a second or two. I simply would slide off to nothingness. When I tried my top voice, absolutely nothing came out.

The worst and most painful part was, I had a sense memory of how it felt to sing. And while I could hear the pitches in my head, the sound I produced was plain ugly.

There were many incomplete lessons where I would dissolve into tears and go home swearing to never go through this again. Then I'd come back and begin once more.

I had to surmount what had been done to me, or in truth what I had allowed to be done. Would I ever learn the difference? I began to slowly improve. I had come a long way and still had a long way to travel.

One day Bruce suggested that we get an accompanist and begin to work on some songs.

I didn't want anyone to hear me. But a musical genius entered my life the day Bruce introduced me to Bill Schneider. I apologized for certain notes I may hit, and he began. I was always a good musician, but Bill and Bruce introduced me to the brave new world of trusting my gut instead of trusting a sound I no longer had.

Bill's endless variety of chords would speak to me in a new way of interpreting my material. I was constantly and beautifully challenged to try, and he was always there. Along with Bruce's vocal training and their patience and encouragement while I trusted myself once more, I began again.

But the old voice was gone.

Every once in a while, I'd hear remnants of it. A sound here and there would spark it, and the production of a note would have me feeling that old love of singing again.

I do it differently now, and singing has become so precious to me in a far different way.

Without my previous vocal power, I've had to lean on the lyrics and the story and what the writer wanted me to know. I've discovered so much about singing, but I will never again be able to take off like I used to and sing anything, in any key.

I was not accustomed to feeling unpredictable in singing, but I've worked so that I don't have to know those times any longer. Shades of color began to enter my new vocal life—and it was so damned exciting!

While it's true that the old voice may be gone, I'm eternally grateful for my lesson finally learned.

When you're singing, you're using extra muscles, and it requires a lot of exercise and breathing. You can't do that if you're a sissy. If I have any fitness advice for people, I'd tell them to sing more. It's good therapy, too.

-*Willie Nelson*

A New Millennium

Even after I lost my voice, I never quit. I don't know what the word means.

-Janis Paige

"Good morning, Jan. Let's go to New York and just be tourists," announced my dear friend, the late Jimmy Gallagher.

On a coat-crisp November day in 2000, we took our first subway ride to the Twin Towers and a two-hour lunch at the hypnotic Windows on the World. We visited Trinity Church and paid our respects to Alexander Hamilton's grave. Saw the inside of the New York Public Library, topped off by a very dry martini while rotating a changing New York at night high above Times Square. We toasted our great good fortune, never dreaming that in less than a year, those same Twin Towers would be gone along with nearly 3,000 of our citizens.

With a broken heart, we still pick up the pieces.

In 2002 and 2003, there was no way I would allow my sick voice to stay that way, so I began a painful journey of mending. Finally, I owed it to myself to find a way past my voice and to test my ability to perform again. When I felt somewhat ready, I rented the Cinegrill Cabaret Lounge in Hollywood for a few hours on a Sunday, invited about 65 guests, and tried me out. I still loved it!

The year 2005 took me to London with friends, from the sanitized Tower of London to the breathtaking history of Windsor Castle, its ghosts and the Crown Jewels. The terrorist bombings that July had changed London, too. Armed guards were stationed on every floor in Harrods. The people were ever polite, but now wearing an aura of watchfulness. So sad!

In 2006, I received my first invitation to be a presenter at the Tony Awards. I finally learned how it felt to stand on that vast stage at Radio City Music Hall and be a proud member of the Broadway community I so loved and cherished.

I began a series of eye operations in 2008 to save my sight. The first was called a corneal cell graft. I was awake throughout the procedure and knew the moment my own cornea was gone. I thanked God for the old and said a blessing for the new.

The following year (2009), I was healthy enough to break in my new act at the Gardenia Restaurant & Lounge in West Hollywood. A month of Wednesdays, and then on to 2010 at the Rrazz Room in San Francisco. I was deeply grateful for the rave reviews that I struggled to earn.

Finally, 2012 brought me a return engagement at the Rrazz Room, with a packed house celebrating my 90th birthday. My best friend Nina Estes was there, along with Bruce Eckstut and Bill Schneider—still in their supportive roles—to share this incredibly special day with me during my rollercoaster ride of a life.

The years leading up to 2020 were, for the most part, about saving my sight and finishing the journal that eventually became this book. There's much more to fill in, but I have to stop sometime—so why not here? It is, after all, how I began.

Boundaries

> *Givers need to set boundaries, because takers rarely do.*
>
> —Rachel Wolchin

Boundaries! It's a wise and evolved parent who has boundaries and who teaches their child to have them.

When there is no education or knowledge of boundaries, that rightful space we all need can become invaded or build walls of self-defense. True boundaries are flexible. If we are fortunate enough to own our own and to accept our right to have them, we can control that precious space between inundation and abandonment.

I grew up with no knowledge of a personal boundary. A boundary, to me, was a line on a map separating countries or states. If someone had told me that I was entitled to a boundary, a personal space, I probably would have been wracked with guilt and fear. Whatever personal space that was rightfully mine belonged to my mother.

My mother had no boundaries, so how was she going to respect mine? I was in my sixties and deep into therapy before I began to tentatively understand boundaries.

"You mean that I have a right to privacy? To my own thoughts? To my own things? My own body? My own voice? I have a right to speak up on my own behalf?" Not on your life did I believe that.

When one is not given their own space, one begins to instinctively, primitively fight for it. Judgments and opinions are then easily formed about the kind of child you are. "She's difficult, overly sensitive, moody, withdrawn, passive, aggressive, etc. etc."

Think of the time and opportunities missed when as adults we have to go back and revisit what could have been taught in our formative years. How many times have I had the old stuff rear its never-ending don't-forget-me, I'll-never-go-away persona?

You can very easily develop knee-jerk reactions, feelings of abandonment, paranoia and a general sense of constant fragmentation. I should know; that's how I grew up. And until I entered therapy, I had never heard of a boundary.

Now, it's something that I no longer have to fight for. I've learned to respect my own boundaries and recognize that early childhood feeling of being invaded and too scared and dependent to react, except to withdraw.

Loyalty

Loyalty to the country always. Loyalty to the government when it deserves it.

—Mark Twain

A friend is someone who walks into a room when everyone else is walking out.

—Garry Moore

Loyalty is a quality I expect, but all too often am disappointed and hurt when I don't get it in return.

I don't know if the lack of loyalty is a character flaw or a self-protective shield against having to stand up and be counted, to declare oneself for another. To be unafraid to make a statement, to be disliked because of a stance taken, is to me a show of one's moral courage and at the very least an opportunity to grow.

I saw such unabashed loyalty when I was with Bob Hope on our Christmas journeys to entertain our servicemen and women. They lived the need for selflessness every moment. They were a demonstration to me of the deepest form of loyalty. Thank God for those truly great human beings. Not only did I see much, but I took away what is unforgettably embedded in my soul.

My grandfather was fiercely loyal, both to himself and others. Maybe that's why it's so important to me. When I needed his loyalty and protection, he was always there.

I had a best friend for forty-three years. We had a relationship of adventures, laughs, despair and growth. It took me thirty-five years to finally discern her seeming inability to feel or express loyalty to those who had been loyal to her.

Being a fixer until I woke up to reality, I felt enormous pain and disappointment when I could not receive what I thought was important to any relationship. It was never forthcoming.

One day, I finally acknowledged the feeling inside me, unexpressed and crying to get out to some form of truth. I asked this best friend not to call me until I could sort out what was happening because I was losing respect for her—and more importantly, for myself.

I told her that I was not punishing her, but that it was time I stopped punishing myself and paid attention to why she hurt me so many times with her refusal to look at her part in this little drama. She protested, but I remained steady and firm. She never faced the truth about her own inner work, she simply obeyed me. When we again spoke, I was different, and she was just glad to talk to me again.

She never questioned my decision, just continued being needy and relieved. We're still friends, but the six months that I dared to take for myself made me realize that the problem was mine. I too was needy and could finally stand on my own emotional feet.

A man is not an orange. You can't eat the fruit
and throw the peel away.

-Arthur Miller

WHAT PISSES ME OFF

> *STICKS AND STONES MAY BREAK MY BONES, BUT*
> *WORDS WILL NEVER HURT ME.*
> —ANONYMOUS

> *ONLY IN NIRVANA WOULD THIS APPLY.*
> —JANIS PAIGE

Now that I've reached the advanced age of 97, life is flying by so fast that I've had to realize that I am just three years away from the once-ripe old age of 100. Yay!!!!!!!

And given that I have no idea what life holds for me going forward, I am giving myself permission to finally admit what pisses me off. Mind you, what follows isn't everything that pisses me off. There are fresh new pisser-offers presenting themselves daily, such as the illegitimate impeachment crisis that we're having to endure as I write these words. But I digress.

I've experienced a lifetime in a profession I've loved. But because of my position in the public eye, I've also had to keep my personal opinions to myself no matter how much it hurt or how unfair I felt it was.

I'll never forget what Jack Warner said to me when I was initially hired at Warner Bros: "You represent the studio now, Janis, so always act like a star, speak like a star and dress like a star. If you can't afford to dress like a star for special occasions, go to the wardrobe department and they'll loan you what you need."

The irony of that simple statement escaped me until I started to write this chapter and I suddenly found it funny. I was so grateful for the $150 per week that being ungrateful, suspicious or insulted never entered my young and untried mind.

Needless to say, I visited the wardrobe department many times.

We kids raised during the Great Depression never forget what we didn't or couldn't have. Ask any one of them who is still around. They'll remember the holes in the soles of their shoes.

I'm living in the greatest, most generous country in the world. I love, respect and honor my American birthright. If you think that I'm happy with some of the decisions from the other side, I'm not. Now all of you America haters, go do something about it. I'm finally speaking up for myself!

Number one pisser-offer du jour for me is this new crop of female Congresswomen and their complete lack of respect for anything American. They certainly cash their hefty paychecks, and I doubt they'll turn down the lifetime pensions and perks offered from this purportedly "garbage" and "racist" country.

My long life in show business allowed me to hear some raw, disgusting and derogatory words and phrases, but the shock of experiencing some of these filthy epithets from under a Muslim headscarf was, at once, ugly and repulsive, yet sadly enlightening.

Frankly, I think we should thank them for finally exposing the seemingly uncontrollable, underbelly loathing of anything American, Israeli, Jewish or Caucasian. I'd say shame on Reps. Omar, Tlaib, Pressley and Cortez, but they seem to be devoid of anything resembling shame. All I can see and hear is a very unhealthy abundance of lies, supported by their tiresome, accusatory rhetoric.

Their elected job is to solve some of the dire needs of this country, not lobby for their stupid, destructive and America-killing political ideology.

My grandfather used to say, "Freedom is not free, it comes with the price of trying to hang on to it!" Consider what would happen to these women if they had used the same disgraceful language against the heads of Iran, Saudi Arabia, China or North Korea. We're all too familiar with that form of justice.

Instead, they exercised their American freedom to vilify our country, our laws and, I might remind them, mine. America is not their personal property, it belongs to us: "We the People."

My late husband was a Jew. His parents immigrated from Russia and Sweden, respectively. He was a caring and protective citizen, intolerant of any racist remarks or behavior, as am I.

I say to these Congresswomen: Before you accuse America and its citizens of running "concentration camps" and Nazism, get your lazy, ignorant selves to Dachau, Bergen-Belsen, Auschwitz or Buchenwald. As hard as they've tried to sanitize these living hells, making them tourist-ready for the curious to come, the unspeakable horrors remain.

When we saw Dachau in 1967, the gas chambers and the Dr. Mengele experiment rooms remained locked. Even then, the aura of death hung heavy in the air.

Remember, ladies, that some of my hard-earned tax dollars go to protecting you and helping to support your shameful moral cowardice. I want my money back!

My lasting life lessons were learned by trusting and being betrayed by the "drama queen" victims, liars and their lies, cons (I should know, I once married one), manipulators, gossips, and "zipped up" people with their secret skeletons. These types seem to attach themselves to anyone close to fame, yet anyone can be a target.

I left the "last but not least" at the end of my sadly long list.

Is it me or are hypocrites and their hypocrisy soaring as we search for the real truth and meaning behind their two-faced statements?

The last time I looked, I still have my First Amendment rights. Now that I've reached 97 years of age, I have the scars to prove it to finally express what pisses me off. That's also why I was inspired to write a book.

So, c'mon now. I deserve a few minutes to let off a bit of steam. After all, it's been building up for nearly a century.

By the way, is anyone going to defend any of these kinds of people who pollute the very air we breathe? I think not!

Oops, just one more, please.

Among other things, the misuse of the contracted word drives me up the nearest wall. The purpose of the contracted word was to soften the English language and make it more euphonious. I hate to disillusion you, but there is no "u" in didn't, couldn't, isn't, shouldn't, etc. These words are not pronounced "did'*unt*," "could'*unt*," "is'*unt*" or "should'*unt*."

Budding or professional actors studying their craft with the amazing Larry Moss will be stopped mid-sentence. You'll be given a concise lesson on the correct use of the contracted word. He'll firmly ask that you not do it again, followed by a polite, "Continue."

Thank you for your patient indulgence. I just could'*unt* help myself.

The Murder of the American Soul

> *A MAN DIES WHEN HE REFUSES TO STAND UP FOR THAT WHICH IS RIGHT. A MAN DIES WHEN HE REFUSES TO STAND UP FOR JUSTICE. A MAN DIES WHEN HE REFUSES TO TAKE A STAND FOR THAT WHICH IS TRUE.*
>
> —Martin Luther King Jr.

Growing up an American has been a privilege, a gift of hope, truth and freedom with the responsibility to protect, promote and preserve this unique experiment called the United States of America. The one thing I thought I'd never witness is its destruction by the very people it serves.

But that is exactly what's happening.

I am watching a race to not only destroy our precious Constitution but the Bill of Rights that guard those freedoms. We've always been a nation of laws. Respecting and protecting those gifts has kept us free up to the present.

Just look at our higher educational system. Schools that once promoted this great country have been hijacked by years of subversive professors, hiding their hypocrisy and using our precious First Amendment rights against anyone who turns away from their groupthink.

The result of this assault on our educational system has been the insidious teaching of anarchy, resulting in violent, screaming confrontations by students who feel and act like they're political geniuses.

For the most part, they are quickly able to discuss Black history, Muslim history, Middle Eastern history, Latino history and Asian history. But when it comes to American history, the verbal derision begins. When I expressed my concern over what seems to be a cultural war, I was told by someone who works for me that "America has no culture."

After I picked myself up off the floor, I asked why she made such a hurtful remark to me, an American.

"Please tell me," I said, "I want to know."

"I'm sorry, Miss Paige," she replied, "I didn't mean to hurt you, but America has too many cultures to have just one."

This comment was made so factually that I knew that it had to have been taught. Our educational system is poisoning the minds of young people who have not been taught a simple and basic loyalty to the freedoms this country provides. Everything we fought and died for in the Civil War, including the great strides we've made, have been lost.

No matter who I am, what I believe, how I feel, if I were born white then I'm the enemy and anarchy rules. The problem with anarchists is that they do a beautiful job of tearing down but there's never a plan to build something better.

All of the education in the world cannot stop their utter stupidity. Not only have we lost the right of free speech, we've also lost a few generations of young people who can no longer think for themselves. Like robots, they can be whipped into an often-terrifying frenzy, resulting in someone's death.

Masked mobs of cowards now dominate a peaceful demonstration of the right to have an opposing opinion. Black Lives Matter is now permitted to defy the laws and segregate themselves in dorms, classrooms and social gatherings, even demanding that their rooms be repainted using their war colors.

With no intention of obeying our laws, the lily-livered heads of these so-called seats of higher learning lay down in the face of the demolition of America.

Our broken system of immigration will remain shattered until our American culture is dead and buried, right down to our language. The degree of hate toward America and its citizens is stifling any positive thoughts by violence of every kind. Town hall meetings are now disrupted by mobs screaming over the speakers. Each day, we watch a well-planned murder of our First Amendment rights, and nothing is being done to arrest this fast-moving fire of deceit.

We spit on and disrespect members of our police force without a thought as to their safety and protection. I always thank each law enforcement officer I see for risking his or her life for millions like me.

We thank our Armed Forces for their service but not The Thin Blue Line standing tall against the filthy epithets and violence displayed by the masked cowards perpetrating the death of my country.

My great grandparents were immigrants from Norway. My father's family was from the Netherlands and my grandfather's parents from France. They were the proudest and most grateful Americans I've ever known. They instilled in me the value of this country and how fortunate we all were to be Americans.

Nothing or no one is perfect. Perfection is something we strive for, an unending and ongoing endeavor to better understand ourselves and our personal responsibilities. We pay rapt attention to our feelings, safe rooms, puppy videos and counselors. These are not children I speak of. I'm talking about college students ill-prepared for the hurts that life and adulthood will bring to these crybabies without a thought as to who will provide that safety.

We now serve a growing generation of immature children unable to face their future without a sickening paralysis of self-promotion and destructive decisions.

The addiction to cellphones and their seductive apps rob us of whatever abilities we might develop. Our mental and emotional need to still hear the sound of a different drummer is now drowned out by the cacophony of calls using the new buzzword "racist."

Instead of a search for inner integrity, we now search for power. The readily available signs of this new definition of success surround the greedy fast-trackers whose only aim is to be the newest millionaire or (why not?) the newest billionaire. The growing list seems uncontrollable as we watch the world's poor, uneducated, disrespected and unprotected continue to exist under the guise of their so-called bleeding-heart philanthropy.

America's generosity is stretched to the breaking point while we taxpayers foot the bill for free education, free breakfasts, free lunches and—if necessary—free dinners. All of this, while we quietly and obediently tolerate how mean and purportedly racist we are.

These screaming, filthy-mouthed anarchists drown out reasonable speech and problem-solving attitudes while they stomp on the First Amendment rights of everyone.

In my lifetime, America and her citizens have known many adversities, some shaking us to our very core. Somehow, we picked ourselves up even while deeply scarred physically, mentally and emotionally—and carried on.

I've never seen my country so fragile, leaving countless Americans feeling aimless, scared and paralyzed. We watch in total disbelief as part of the FBI is now accused of political interference in a national election. They are spending millions of our heard-earned dollars on the possibility of an arrogantly destructive misuse of their awesome power.

Only a nine by six-foot jail cell will satisfy me if this is found to be true. However, I won't hold my breath until justice is served. Money and power seem to never be called to account. Only the American public continues to be hurt by the lies and complete lack of integrity so easily promised by those in office.

I'm watching the death of the United States of America as we once knew it. Governors of states are defying federal law along with their compliant, activist judges issuing their dilatory orders. Men and women who took a solemn oath to protect and serve are steadily breaking their vows, pushing us toward the destruction of the very fiber of America.

I've never been a comparatist, but what I now witness each day is forcing me to wake up to a secret and subversive government that includes many members of Congress. Their so-called loyalty to the people who pay their outlandish salaries, perks and Cadillac health care leave me and countless others disgusted, poorer and sickened by their "I'm better than you" attitude.

I'd bet my life that not one of their precious bodies has shown up for a one o'clock doctor's appointment, only to leave a crowded and understaffed office five hours later. There is no change for us because once again, we're no longer allowed a voice on our own behalf. They represent themselves—and we pay for it.

Wake up, you poor, guilt-riddled American public. Stop listening to the groupthink. Read the Constitution and the Bill of Rights and stand up for what has always belonged to you.

I grew up in a melting pot known as America. What is happening today is an invasion of hate and avarice. We either carelessly, or with intent, left the barn door open and never bothered to fix the broken locks.

Your children and grandchildren will never know the amazing idea that became this country. Thank God that I did.

Growing up in a free country, obeying its laws and rules of behavior, respect for the rights of others and pride in something other than myself formed me into the person I am today. I like her, warts and all. I feel the same way about my country, and no one can ever change my American heart and soul.

Each time a man stands up for an ideal, or acts
to improve the lot of others, or strikes out against
injustice, he sends forth a tiny ripple of hope.

-Robert F. Kennedy

I Have Found Another Day

Ho trovato un altro giorno.
(I have found another day.)

—Francesca Rubino

THE ABOVE WERE the first words spoken by the late Francesca Rubino upon waking each new and blessed day.

The last chapter of my book was to be titled "The Final Paige." I thought that rather clever and provocative, but the writing door was stuck. I always felt a nagging little depression when I'd start, so procrastination hung around.

A few weeks ago, I was speaking to my dear friend of many years, Francesca James, when she mentioned her grandmother's daily ritual.

"Oh, that's it!" I said. "Do you mind if I use those words as the final chapter in my book?"

"I'd love that, Jan. Just give her credit for it."

And so, I am.

Giving well-deserved credit is done throughout my book. It may seem small and insignificant, but it's quietly painful and demeaning when the recipient of your efforts is too self-serving to admit your help. The bigger person would freely say, "Look what someone did for me. I'm so grateful!"

I'm choosing to use this space to express my gratitude to those who have helped me to get here.

Speaking only for myself, as I've emerged above the often dark, dense and seemingly hopeless yesterdays, I had one of those amazing epiphanies that happen when we're ready. Mine came in a familiar mass email. Something stopped me from even opening it.

"No more," I said as I deleted it.

Like opening a window to fresh air, my life began to rise. I found that my greatest teachers were those who tried to demote me. My mind, my spirit, my hope for a future and ultimately my health were being threatened by betrayals, manipulations and lies by those whom I trusted.

When I found my emotional balance once more, the most amazing people entered my life, including a far more integrated me.

My genuine thanks go to all of you crafty smart-asses for my giant growth spurt.

There are so many names and faces in my memory bank and limited time and space to list them all. They're still very much with me, however, their friendships alive and well in my heart.

First, my forever gratitude goes to my late husband Ray Gilbert. Not only for my new and expanding life, but for his constant encouragement and belief in me when all too often, I couldn't believe in myself. He instilled qualities in me that I found only after his death.

Ray was the oldest of old souls. He brought love and wisdom to my life. I still haven't forgotten a word he said to me. There was something in the quiet way he spoke that forever changed me. I heard you, honey. I heard you. And I'm still hearing you. I've also kept my promise to you: "I'm doing my best and always will."

To my dedicated, non-political and disciplined schoolteachers who helped to prepare us for the blessings of our American citizenship. Verbally or physically intimidating a teacher was severely punished by getting expelled from school permanently. The thought never occurred to us. We were taught respect.

To Wendy and her husband Roland de la Harpe, for arranging my trip to Cape Town and up The Wild Coast of South Africa. Thank you for giving me the adventure of a lifetime.

To Ceil and Joe, for the operas at the old Met, always followed by re-living them at a tiny little place called La Luna in Little Italy, New York City.

To my South African friends and the cast of *Applause*. I'm so sorry that we weren't allowed to fulfill our promise to ourselves as performers and to the audiences so deserving of our beautiful production. Your support never wavered, nor your loyalty.

To Ivan and Maryanne Berold, who gave me the gift of Kruger National Park and the animals I'd only seen in zoos. That day began very early and the first thing we saw was a pride of seventeen lions sprawled on the road after their kill. They were asleep on their backs, their fat and well-filled tummies rising and falling in the morning sun.

One female stood guard while we were privileged to watch the other performing her dance of seduction. She used all of her feminine wiles on the "king" until he swatted her away, yawned and went to sleep. Nothing primitive about that! We had to wait until they awoke, each trotting off into the jungle. As long as I live, I'll never forget that weekend in Kruger.

Thank you, Bobby (last name withheld), for fulfilling my wish to stay up all night after a performance of *The Pajama Game*. You introduced me to my first mimosa, Wall Street shuttered and dark after business hours, the barren and empty streets making us feel that we were the only people in the world. We witnessed the Battery to the bottom of Manhattan, watching the lights on the Statue of Liberty welcoming a still dark but faintly visible dawn.

Our all-nighter ended with our being the first customers in a tiny bakery at five a.m. I can still see us drinking fresh black coffee with freshly baked, still warm sourdough bread, butter and honey. A sack of fresh doughnuts to go were bought for me by a true romantic.

To Ron and Crystal Patterson who helped my computer and me to "see" and cross the finish line to my book. My grateful thanks to you both.

To Beth Laski, who never lost faith in my book or in me. It seems like we've always known one another. The day I packed my book away ready for storage was painful. I'd given up on completing it. "If the universe finds it, they can have it," I said.

An hour later, Beth called.

"There's someone I want you to meet, Jan. He's an editor for your book."

A few days later, she brought an enthusiastic man named Ray Richmond to my home. In his hand were a couple of my chapters. He promised to help me shepherd my book to completion, and he was as good as his word. You hold the results of his pledge in your hands.

I could spend the rest of my life expressing appreciation to those who have brought joy, meaning and adventure to my existence. But please allow me to conclude here with the understanding that everyone who has meant something to me—whether they are still with us or passed on—has my sincere and abiding appreciation. Because of you, I've enjoyed quite the magical ride.

Those are lines no one will ever need to read between.

CPSIA information can be obtained
at www.ICGtesting.com
Printed in the USA
LVHW100855090321
680643LV00024B/42